FANNY TROLLOPE

PARIS AND
THE PARISIANS

ALAN SUTTON · Gloucester
HIPPOCRENE BOOKS, INC. · New York

First published 1836

Copyright © in this edition 1985
Alan Sutton Publishing Limited

This edition first published in Great Britain 1985
   Alan Sutton Publishing Limited
   30 Brunswick Road
   Gloucester GL1 1JJ

British Library Cataloguing in Publication Data

Trollope, Frances
   [Paris and the Parisians in 1835]. Paris and
   the Parisians.
   1. Paris (France)—Social life and customs
   I. [Paris and the Parisians in 1835]   II. Title
   944′.36063   DC715

   ISBN 0-86299-219-2

This edition first published in the U.S.A. 1985
   Hippocrene Books, Inc.
   171 Madison Avenue
   New York, N.Y. 10016

ISBN 0-87052-209-4

Cover picture: detail from The Boulevard de Clichy
under Snow, *1876, by Norbert Goeneutte.*
The Tate Gallery, London.

Typesetting and origination by
Alan Sutton Publishing Limited.
Photoset Bembo 9/10
Printed in Great Britain
by The Guernsey Press Company Limited
Guernsey, Channel Islands.

BIOGRAPHICAL NOTE

The publication of *Domestic Manners of the Americans* in 1832 created a furore in the United States, and made Fanny Trollope a celebrity in England. The British enjoyed this 'putting down' of their ex-colonial cousins in Fanny's censorious way, and delighted in the anecdotes of the hog-keeping and naively uncouth citizens of Cincinnati and other areas within her purview. The Americans read pirated editions with great indignity, and it aroused outrage in every state. Who was this Englishwoman that called herself a lady and wrote such gross distortions about their glorious and free nation?

Frances Milton Trollope was born on 10 March 1780. She was the daughter of the Reverend William Milton and his wife, who were living at the time in the village of Stapleton, just north of Bristol. Fanny (as all that multitude of girls christened Frances in this period were called) had an elder sister, Mary; and a younger brother, Henry. Shortly after Henry's birth their mother died, at which time the family were living at Heckfield in north Hampshire, their father having been awarded the living there soon after Fanny's birth.

William Milton being the vicar, the family were automatically accepted among the local gentry, and Fanny would have had ample opportunity to mix with interesting and well educated people. Dinner parties with the local gentry seemed to be part of their normal life, and one guest at a party given by Mr. Shaw Lefevre, the Member of Parliament for the Borough of Reading was Mrs. George Mitford, who wrote the following to her daughter:

> . . . (the dinner party was joined by) Mr. Milton, his wife, and two daughters, the younger of whom, Miss Fanny Milton, is a very lively pleasant young woman. I do not mean to infer that Miss Milton may not be equally agreeable, but the other took a far greater share in the conversation, and playing casino a great part of the evening with Mr.

S. Lefevre, Mr. Monck, and your old Mumpsa, it gave me
an opportunity of seeing her in a more favourable light than
her sister.

This early interesting insight shows that from an early
period Fanny had plenty of self-confidence, a confidence that
was called upon time and again in the tribulations of her later
life. The reverend Milton's wife referred to in the extract was
Fanny's stepmother, as by this time her father had remarried.

Fanny's brother, Henry was educated at Winchester and
afterwards expressed an interest in obtaining a position in the
War Office. Through the influence of the vicar's neighbours,
and especially Mr. Lefevre, the position became available, and
Henry prepared to leave for London. Fanny saw this as an
opportunity to leave the sleepy environment of Heckfield, and
together with her sister Mary, they pressurised their father
into letting them go with Henry, to look after him, and set up
a home in London. In the spring of 1803 the three young
Miltons moved into a terraced house in Keppel Street off
Russell Square.

With letters from friends in Heckfield, Winchester and
Reading, the Miltons had no trouble in finding new acquaint-
ances in London. Henry brought young colleagues from the
War Office for small dinner and card parties, and together
with visits from country friends, and trips to the theatre,
Fanny found her new life much to her liking.

Five years sped by with their circle of friends widening all
the time. Then, in the summer of 1808, Henry brought home
a young barrister friend who was to change Fanny's life. From
the first, Thomas Anthony Trollope paid considerable attention to Fanny, not a little to her consternation, although,
because few men paid such attentions, she was extremely
flattered. She was by now twenty-eight years old and no
previous possibility of marriage had arisen. We can, perhaps,
presume from this that she was no great beauty.

They looked an ill-matched pair; he was large and slow, she
was small and quick. But even so, his attentions increased
with every visit, and he lost no opportunity in visiting Keppel
Street to see her. When he could not visit he sent notes.
Finally, in a long and ponderous letter written in November

1808, he proposed to her, detailing the particulars of his income and prospects. After further exchanges of letters, Fanny travelled home to Heckfield to discuss the possible engagement with her father, who then visited Thomas Anthony in London, to assess him and discuss his prospects – they turned out to his full satisfaction.

Thomas Anthony and Fanny were married in the spring of 1809, and moved into number 16 Keppel Street, a house that Anthony owned, only a few doors away from Fanny's previous home. They settled down to a routine of married life. Fanny had a house to furnish, staff to employ and a social life to organise. A year later, on 29 April 1810 their first son, Thomas was born. Fanny found motherhood easy and enjoyable, and Thomas was followed by Henry in 1811, Arthur in 1812, Anthony in 1815, Cecilia in 1816 and finally Emily in 1818.

It was in 1818 that Thomas Anthony's legal practice began to decline. He had an over-bearing manner that did little to gain him clients and goodwill, together with this he suffered from prolonged bouts of sick headaches that kept him in bed for a day or two at a time. With the loss of income, together with the expenditure of a growing family economies had to be made. Thomas Anthony had leased 300 acres of farmland near Harrow in 1816, with the vain idea of becoming a farmer. In view of this, they decided to sell the Keppel Street house and build a new house on their rented Harrow property.

Thomas Anthony had an uncle with a considerable estate which he was destined to inherit. With both his uncle and aunt being in their sixties, and childless, Fanny looked upon this as being a saving grace to Thomas Anthony's failure to support his family financially. In 1817 Thomas Anthony's aunt died, and both he and Fanny were suprised to hear of his uncle re-marrying soon after – but worse was to follow – for soon they heard that his uncle was the father of a son! He had an heir, and Fanny's expectations of financial security evaporated overnight.

Thomas Anthony's career slowly declined to a point where he hardly bothered going to town, and by 1824 the family finances were at a low ebb. In the spring of 1824, Arthur was sent for the holidays to Heckfield to stay with Fanny's father;

soon after a short note came to say that Arthur was ill, then, unbelievably a letter to say that he had died. Fanny and Thomas Anthony immediately journeyed to Heckfield, and not long after her return to Harrow Fanny had another message, this time to say that her father had died. This double blow took a heavy toll.

Despite the financial restraints, Thomas Anthony took Fanny away during the long vacation from his chambers in September. It was during the long vacation three years earlier that they had journeyed to Paris, and Fanny first met Frances Wright, the young Scots social reformer. When in Paris, the Trollopes usually stayed with the Garnett family; originally friends of Fanny's father, and frequent visitors to Heckfield, the Garnetts had left England for New Jersey in 1797 where they had remained until the death of Mr. Garnett in 1820. Mrs. Garnett and her three daughters had then left the United States to live in Paris.

One American that Fanny met at the Garnetts' home was Washington Irving, but whatever impression he made on Fanny is not recorded. Frances Wright, however, made a considerable and immediate impact. Fanny invited Frances to stay with her at Harrow when she was next in England, and this invitation was shortly taken up.

The 1824 long vacation did not take them as far as Paris; the Isle of Wight was the furthest point from home, but throughout the year she received news of Frances Wright and her sister Camilla who were now back in the United States.

In the spring of 1826, Fanny and Thomas Anthony became concerned with their second son, Henry's progress at school. They decided that he was now old enough to begin a career, and that a complete change might be good for him. They chose a counting house in Paris as that would also improve his French, and they journeyed with Henry to Paris to see him settled in lodgings with a clergyman. Whilst in Paris they visited the Garnetts and caught up on the latest news from Frances Wright. She and her sister Camilla had moved to the south western United States, and in a place called Tennessee had started a colony called Nashoba, with the intention of buying slaves, educating them and keeping them long enough to earn their keep, and then freeing them. Fanny was amazed at the drive and energy of Frances Wright in starting such an impossible task, and in bringing her visions to fruition.

Back at Harrow, Fanny amused herself and took away the worries of Thomas Anthony's financial affairs with amateur theatricals. It was at this period that Fanny met a young French artist – Auguste Hervieu – who was trying to make a living from giving drawing lessons. He had left France for political reasons, and Fanny took him under her wing. Often a romantic, Fanny had a knack of turning these good deeds to her benefit, for in later years it was Hervieu who illustrated many of her books.

Thomas Anthony's finances now reached desperate levels, and rent on the Harrow estate due to Lord Northwick, their landlord, fell short. In desperation the family moved into a refurbished cottage on the farm and let the large house. Shortly after this move, Fanny had a surprise visit. Frances Wright was in England, and came to look up her old friend Mrs. Trollope. She described Nashoba in enthusiastic detail, she envisioned an integrated community of blacks and whites – she even had a mulatto woman who had joined the colony to teach French – Ah, if Mrs. Trollope could only see for herself.

And why not? Why could Fanny not go to see Nashoba herself? She could also take Henry, who was not doing well in Paris. At first Frances Wright tried to dissuade Fanny, but on discovering the depth of her determination, details were settled with Thomas Anthony.

It was absurd, there would be passage and travelling expenses, and no doubt Miss Wright would want some investment in her colony. But Fanny was unshakeable. In talking over the possibilities they eventually reached an agreement where Fanny and Henry would go out to survey the siting of an emporium for selling British goods, and eventually Thomas Anthony would follow with Thomas, and a selection of goods for sale. It was finally decided that Cecilia and Emily would go with their mother, and for good measure Auguste Hervieu would accompany them also.

On 4 November 1827 the party, including Frances Wright, embarked on the sailing ship *Edward* to sail for the New World.

The party landed at New Orleans a few days after Christ-

mas, and made a lengthy trip up the Mississippi towards
Frances Wright's colony near Memphis. The steamboat made
a strong and lasting impression on Fanny; the remorseless
spitting of the Americans, their appalling table manners,
feeding with their knives, and using a pocket knife to clean
their teeth.

New to western America, Fanny became accustomed to a
local expression – 'getting along' – which she later translated
as meaning to get along with as few of the comforts of life as
possible. Eventually, after a further arduous journey across
land, they reached Nashoba. Instead of the paradise as exp-
ounded by Frances Wright they saw only desolation. She saw
a few acres raggedly cleared, with the ever-present stumps and
the ground 'a mess of rotted mud' with a few buildings of the
most primitive nature. It was not a place to stay with her
family, but she had no money. She had thought of Nashoba as
being her base, where Henry could find some occupation, and
from where she could venture forth to find the ideal location
for the Trollope Emporium. After a few weeks she managed
to borrow three hundred dollars from Frances Wright, and the
family including Auguste Hervieu moved to Cincinnati. Here
she managed to rent a small house and obtain domestic help.

The months went by, and still no news came from Thomas
Anthony despite many letters sent by Fanny via the dubious
postal system. Then, one September evening, to the surprise
of all, Thomas Anthony and their eldest son Thomas arrived
unannounced. After a period of visiting the new friends Fanny
and the family had made, together with sightseeing trips,
Thomas Anthony and Fanny looked for a spot where they
could build their bazaar, the Trollope Emporium. They
eventually found a site a little from the centre towards the
river, and after buying the land, prepared to build to a plan by
Hervieu.

Thomas Anthony returned to England to collect together
the goods for the Emporium, and Fanny enthusiastically
organised the builders. After a few months the building was
nearly complete – but no money arrived from Thomas
Anthony to pay the builders who then threw down their tools
in disgust. August Hervieu lent Fanny some money, and work
continued in a desultory fashion, but by now a nickname had

arisen for this strange building by that strange Englishwoman – 'Trollope's folly'.

Fanny then fell very ill with malaria, and for weeks was in no position to consider the bazaar or anything else. Henry and Auguste Hervieu had to stave off a delegation of angry unpaid workers, but worse was to happen. The goods from Thomas Anthony eventually arrived, but instead of high quality leather articles and other similar items, they were nothing more than cheap tawdry items. They now faced financial disaster. Thomas Anthony had sent no further remuneration, and court actions for unpaid bills forced the sale of the unfinished Emporium, and the cheap goods – although they fetched little. Worse than this humiliation, they were evicted from their house for non-payment of rent.

They were taken in by sympathetic neighbours, and Henry was despatched to England in haste to inform Thomas Anthony of what had happened, to organise the sending of the return fares, and stop him acquiring any further cheap goods.

It was at this time that Fanny first thought of writing a book. She had written small pieces since childhood, but not a full book. After shrugging off the auctioning of the Emporium, and the frantic disposal of all the goods, she had time on her hands until she heard from her husband. Auguste managed to gain commissions for painting portraits of the leading citizens, and this was so successful that at one time it appeared that they might afford their own passage home. Fanny, however, in planning her book realised that, if it were to be successful, she must see more of the country before returning to England.

Eventually when the ice began to break on the Ohio, they said their farewells, and travelling through Maryland to Baltimore, they eventually reached Washington D.C.

In Washington they met up with an old friend – one of the Garnett daughters, Anna Maria, who had married an American citizen. They were overjoyed to see each other after so many years and it was arranged that they should stay at Washington for the summer. By August 1830 it was time to move on again, and now that they had reached the eastern seaboard, communications with Thomas Anthony became easier. They visited Buffalo, Philadelphia and New York, and by the spring of 1831 she was ready to come home.

Back in England, the family finances were at a very low ebb. Thomas Anthony was constantly dodging creditors, and they had moved house again, this time to an even smaller house in Harrow. Fanny now set about trying to find a publisher for her book. The first house she tried – Whittaker & Treacher – accepted it. It was called *Domestic Manners of the Americans*, published on 19 March 1832, and was an instant success, a bestseller of the day. By the end of the first summer of publication she had received over one thousand pounds from royalties. At last the family fortunes were rallying. Her success ensured that the follow-up book, a novel *The Refugee in America*, secured an advance from Whittaker & Treacher of four hundred pounds. At the age of fifty-two she was a celebrity, and now she was the bread-winner for the family.

Altogether Fanny Trollope wrote forty-one books. Thomas Anthony died in October 1835, disappointed and frustrated at his own failure. He had started working on his own book and had a half-promise from John Murray to publish it, but on his visit to Murray all he was asked was who was Mrs. Trollope? Why did she not bring her book to him?

Fanny eventually moved to a villa in Italy where she lived with her favourite son, Thomas, and his wife Theodosia. She died on 6 October 1863 at the age of eighty-three.

Anthony, who was destined to become far better known than his mother ever was, and to last as a widely read author, was never very close to Fanny. Thomas was her favourite, Henry merited a soft spot, but Anthony, the quiet one, never got much attention. When writing his first novels whilst on Post Office duty in Ireland, he was very secretive over his writing, well aware that he was greatly over-shadowed by the writings and forceful personality of his mother.

Unlike her contemporary, Jane Austen, Fanny Trollope's popularity as an author did not survive into the twentieth century. Tastes change and move in cycles. Hopefully the recent radio broadcasts plus the publication of this edition of her first and most famous book will begin a revival of the writings of this amazing Englishwoman.

ALAN SUTTON

PARIS

AND

THE PARISIANS

VOLUME I

LETTER I

Difficulty of giving a systematic account of what is doing in France – Pleasure of revisiting Paris after long absence – What is changed; what remains the same.

Paris, 11th April 1835

My Dear Friend,

In visiting Paris it certainly was my intention to describe in print what I saw and heard there; and to do this as faithfully as possible, I proposed to continue my old habit of noting in my journal all things, great and small, in which I took an interest. But the task frightens me. I have been here but a few days, and I already find myself preaching and prosing at much greater length than I approve: I already feel that I am involved in such a mizmaze of interesting subjects, that to give anything like an orderly and well arranged digest of them, would beguile me into attempting a work greatly beyond my power to execute.

The very most I can hope to do will be but to 'skim lightly over the surface of things;' and in addressing myself to you, I shall feel less as if I were about to be guilty of the presumption of writing 'a work on France,' than if I threw my notes into a less familiar form. I will then discourse to you, as well as I may, of such things as leave the deepest impression among the thousand sights and sounds in the midst of which I am now placed. Should it be our will hereafter that these letters pass from your hands into those of the public, I trust that nobody will be so unmerciful as to expect that they shall make them acquainted with everything past, present, and to come, 'respecting the destinies of this remarkable country.'

It must indeed be a bold pen that attempts to write of 'Young France,' as it is at present the fashion to call it, with

3

anything like a reasonable degree of order and precision, while still surrounded by all the startling novelties she has to show. To reason of what she has done, what she is doing, and – more difficult still – of what she is about to do, would require a steadier head than most persons can command, while yet turning and twisting in all directions to see what this Young France looks like.

In truth, I am disposed to believe that whatever I write about it will be much in the style of the old conundrum –

> 'I saw a comet rain down hail
> I saw a cloud' &c.

And here you will remember, that though the things seen are stated in the most simple and veracious manner, much of the meaning is occult, depending altogether upon the stopping or pointing of the narrative. This stopping or pointing I must leave to you, or any other readers I may happen to have, and confine myself to the plain statement of 'I saw;' for though it is sufficiently easy to see and to hear, I feel extremely doubtful if I shall always be able to understand.

It is just seven years and seven months since I last visited the capital of the 'Great Nation.' The interval is a long one, as a portion of human life; but how short does it appear when the events that it has brought forth are contemplated! I left the white banner of France floating gaily over her palaces, and I find it torn down and trampled in the dust. The renowned lilies, for so many ages the symbol of chivalric bravery, are everywhere erased; and it should seem that the once proud shield of St. Louis is soiled, broken, and reversed for ever.

But all this was old. France is grown young again; and I am assured that, according to the present condition of human judgment, everything is exactly as it should be. Knighthood, glory, shields, banners, faith, loyalty, and the like, are gone out of fashion; and they say it is only necessary to look about me a little, to perceive how remarkably well the present race of Frenchmen can do without them; – an occupation, it is added, which I shall find much more profitable and amusing than lamenting over the mouldering records of their ancient greatness.

The good sense of this remonstrance is so evident, that I am determined henceforth to profit by it; remembering, moreover, that, as an Englishwoman, I have certainly no particular call to mourn over the fading honours of my country's rival. So in future I shall turn my eyes as much as I can from the tri-coloured flag – (those three stripes are terribly false heraldry) – and only think of amusing myself; a business never performed anywhere with so much ease as at Paris.

Since I last saw it, I have journeyed half round the globe; but nothing I have met in all my wanderings has sufficed to damp the pleasure with which I enter again this gay, bright, noisy, restless city, – this city of the living, as beyond all others it may be justly called.

And where, in truth, can anything be found that shall make its air of ceaseless jubilee seem tame? – or its thousand depôts of all that is prettiest in art, lose by comparison with any other pretty things in the wide world? Where do all the externals of happiness meet the eye so readily? – or where can the heavy spirit so easily be roused to seek and find enjoyment? Cold, worn-out, and dead indeed must the heart be that does not awaken to some throb of pleasure when Paris, after long absence, comes again in sight! For though a throne has been overturned, the Tuileries still remain; – though the main stock of a right royal tree has been torn up, and a scion sprung from one of the roots, that had run, wildly enough, to a distance, has been barricaded in, and watered, and nurtured, and fostered into power and strength of growth to supply its place, the Boulevards, with their matchless aspect of eternal holiday, are still the same. No commotion, however violent, has yet been able to cause this light but precious essence of Parisian attractiveness to evaporate; and while the very foundations of society have been shaken round them, the old elms go on, throwing their flickering shadows upon a crowd that – allowing for some vagaries of the milliner and tailor – might be taken for the very same, and no other, which has gladdened the eye and enlivened the imagination since first their green boughs beckoned all that was fairest and gayest in Paris to meet together beneath them.

Whilst this is the case, and while sundry other enchantments that may be named in their turn continue to proclaim that

Paris is Paris still, it would be silly quarrelling with something better than bread-and-butter, did we spend the time of our abode here in dreaming of what has been, instead of opening our eyes and endeavouring to be as much awake as possible to look upon all that is.

Farewell!

LETTER II

Absence of the English Embassy – Trial of the Lyons Prisoners –
Church of the Madeleine – Statue of Napoleon

It may be doubtful, perhaps, whether the present period* be
more favourable or unfavourable for the arrival of English
travellers at Paris. The sort of interregnum which has taken
place in our embassy here deprives us of the centre round
which all that is most gay among the English residents
usually revolves; but, on the other hand, the approaching trial
of the Lyons prisoners and their Parisian accomplices is
stirring up from the very bottom all the fermenting passions
of the nation. Every principle, however quietly and
unobtrusively treasured, – every feeling, however cautiously
concealed, – is now afloat; and the most careless observer
may expect to see, with little trouble, the genuine temper of
the people.

The genuine temper of the people? – Nay, but this phrase
must be mended ere it can convey to you any idea of what is
indeed likely to be made visible; for, as it stands, it might
intimate that the people were of one temper; and anything
less like the truth than this cannot easily be imagined.

The temper of the people of Paris upon the subject of this
'atrocious trial,' as all parties not connected with the government are pleased to call it, varies according to their
politics, – from rage and execration to ecstasy and delight –
from indifference to enthusiasm – from triumph to despair.

It will be impossible, my friend, to ramble up and down
Paris for eight or nine weeks, with a note-book in my hand,
without recurring again and again to a theme that meets us in
every *salon*, murmurs through the corridors of every theatre,
glares from the eyes of the republican, sneers from the lip of

* April 1835.

the doctrinaire, and in some shape or other crosses our path, let it lead in what direction it may.

This being inevitable, the monster must be permitted to protrude its horns occasionally; nor must I bear the blame should it sometimes appear to you a very tedious and tiresome monster indeed. Having announced that its appearance may be frequently expected, I will leave you for the present in the same state of expectation respecting it that we are in ourselves; and, while we are still safe from its threatened violence, indulge in a little peaceable examination of the still-life part of the picture spread out before me.

The first objects that struck me as new on re-entering Paris, or rather as changed since I last saw them, were the Column of the Place Vendôme, and the finished Church of the Madeleine. Finished indeed! Did Greece ever show any combination of stones and mortar more graceful, more majestic than this? If she did, it was in the days of her youth; for, poetical association apart, and the unquestionably great pleasure of learned investigation set aside, no ruin can possibly meet the eye with such perfect symmetry of loveliness, or so completely fill and satisfy the mind, as does this modern temple.

Why might not our National Gallery have risen as noble, as simple, as beautiful as this?

As for the other novelty – the statue of the sometime Emperor of the French, I suspect that I looked up at it with rather more approbation than became an Englishwoman. But in truth, though the name of Napoleon brings with it reminiscences which call up many hostile feelings, I can never find myself in Paris without remembering his good, rather than his terrible actions. Perhaps, too, as one gazes on this brazen monument of his victories, there may be something soothing in the recollection that the bold standard he bore never for an instant wantoned on a British breeze.

However, putting sentiment and personal feeling of every kind apart, so much that is admirable in Paris owes its origin to him, that his ambition and his usurpations are involuntarily forgotten, and the use made of his ill-gotten power almost obliterates the lawless tyranny of the power itself. The appearance of his statue, therefore, on the top of the column formed of the cannon taken by the armies of France when fighting under his command, appeared to me to be the result of an arrangement founded upon perfect propriety and good taste.

When his effigy was torn down some twenty years ago by the avenging hands of the Allies, the act was one both of moral justice and of natural feeling; and that the rightful owners of the throne he had seized should never have replaced it, can hardly be matter of surprise: but that it should now again be permitted to look down upon the fitful fortunes of the French people, has something of historic propriety in it which pleases the imagination.

This statue of Napoleon offers the only instance I remember in which that most grotesque of European habiliments, a cocked-hat, has been immortalized in marble or in bronze with good effect. The original statue, with its flowing outline of Roman drapery, was erected by a feeling of pride; but this portrait of him has the everyday familiar look that could best satisfy affection. Instead of causing the eye to turn away as it does from some faithful portraitures of modern costume with positive disgust, this *chapeau à trois cornes*, and the well-known loose *redingote*, have that air of picturesque truth in them which is sure to please the taste even where it does not touch the heart.

To the French themselves this statue is little short of an idol. Fresh votive wreaths are perpetually hung about its pedestal; and little draperies of black crape, constantly renewed, show plainly how fondly his memory is still cherished.

While Napoleon was still among them, the halo of his military glory, bright as it was, could not so dazzle the eyes of the nation, but that some portentous spots were discerned even in the very nucleus of that glory itself; but now that it shines upon them across his tomb, it is gazed at with an enthusiasm of devoted affection which mixes no memory of error with its regrets.

It would, I think, be very difficult to find a Frenchman, let his party be what it might, who would speak of Napoleon with disrespect.

I one day passed the foot of his gorgeous pedestal in company with a legitimate *sans reproche*, who, raising his eyes to the statue, said – 'Notre position, Madame Trollope, est bien dure: nous avons perdu le droit d'être fidèles, sans avoir plus celui d'être fiers.'

LETTER III

Slang – Les Jeunes Gens de Paris – La Jeune France –
Rococo – Décousu

I suppose that, among all people and at all times, a certain
portion of what we call slang will insinuate itself into familiar
colloquial intercourse, and sometimes even dare to make its
unsanctioned accents heard from the tribune and the stage. It
appears to me, I confess, that France is at present taking
considerable liberties with her mother-tongue. But this is a
subject which requires for its grave discussion a native critic,
and a learned one too. I therefore can only venture distantly
and doubtingly to allude to it, as one of the points at which it
appears to me that innovation is visibly and audibly at work.

I know it may be said that every additional word, whether
fabricated or borrowed, adds something to the riches of the
language; and no doubt it does so. But there is a polished
grace, a finished elegance in the language of France, as
registered in the writings of her Augustan age, which may
well atone for the want of greater copiousness, with which it
has been sometimes reproached. To increase its strength, by
giving it coarseness, would be like exchanging a high-mettled
racer for a dray-horse. A brewer would tell you, that you
gained in power what you lost in grace: it may be so; but
there are many, I think, even in this age of operatives and
utilitarians, who would regret the change.

This is a theme, however, as I have said before, on which I
should not feel myself justified in saying much. None should
pretend to examine, or at any rate to discuss critically, the
niceties of idiom in a language that is not native to them. But,
distinct from any such presumptuous examination, there are
words and phrases lawfully within the reach of foreign
observation, which strike me as remarkable at the present
day, either from their frequent recurrence, or for something

of unusual emphasis in the manner in which they are employed.

Les jeunes gens de Paris appears to me to be one of these. Translate it, and you find nothing but 'the young men of Paris;' which should seem to have no more imposing meaning than 'the young men of London,' or of any other metropolis. But hear it spoken at Paris – Mercy on me! it sounds like a thunderbolt. It is not only loud and blustering, however; you feel that there is something awful – nay, mystical, implied by the phrase. It appears solemnly to typify the power, the authority, the learning – ay, and the wisdom too, of the whole nation.

La Jeune France is another of these cabalistic forms of speech, by which everybody seems expected to understand something great, terrible, volcanic, and sublime. At present, I confess that both of these, pronounced as they always are with a sort of mysterious emphasis, which seems to say that 'more is meant than meets the ear,' produce rather a paralysing effect upon me. I am conscious that I do not clearly comprehend all the meaning with which they are pregnant, and yet I am afraid to ask, lest the explanation should prove either more unintelligible or more alarming than even the words themselves. I hope, however, that ere long I shall grow more intelligent or less timid; and whenever this happens, and I conceive that I fully comprehend their occult meaning, I will not fail to transmit it faithfully to you.

Besides these phrases, and some others that I may perhaps mention hereafter as difficult to understand, I have learned a word quite new to me, and which I suspect has but very recently been introduced into the French language; at least, it is not to be found in the dictionaries, and I therefore presume it to be one of those happy inventions which are permitted from time to time to enrich the power of expression. How the Academy of former days might have treated it, I know not; but it seems to me to express a great deal, and might at this time, I think, be introduced very conveniently into our own language: at any rate, it may often help me, I think, as a very useful adjective. This new-born word is '*rococo*', and appears to me to be applied by the young and innovating to everything which bears the stamp of the taste, or principles, or feeling of time past. That part of the French population to whom the epithet of *rococo* is thus applied, may be understood to contain all varieties of old-fashionism, from the gentle advocate for laced coats and diamond sword-knots, up to the high-minded venerable loyalist, who only loves his rightful king the better because he has no means left to requite his love. Such is the interpretation of *rococo* in the mouth of a doctrinaire: but if a republican speaks it, he means that it should include also every gradation of orderly obedience, even to the powers that be; and, in fact, whatever else may be considered as essentially connected either with law or gospel.

There is another adjective which appears also to recur so frequently as fully to merit, in the same manner, the distinction of being considered as fashionable. It is, however, a good old legitimate word, admirably expressive too, and at present of more than ordinary utility. This is '*décousu*'; and it seems to be the epithet now given by the sober-minded to all that smacks of the rambling nonsense of the new school of literature, and of all those fragments of opinions which hang so loosely about the minds of the young men who discourse fashionably of philosophy at Paris.

Were the whole population to be classed under two great divisions, I doubt if they could be more expressively designated than by these two appellations, the *décousu* and the *rococo*. I have already stated who it is that form the *rococo* class: the *décousu* division may be considered as embracing the whole of the ultra-romantic school of authors, be they novelists, dramatists, or poets; all shades of republicans, from the avowed eulogists of the 'spirited Robespierre' to the gentler disciples of Lamennais; most of the schoolboys, and all the *poissardes* of Paris.

LETTER IV

Théâtre Français – Mademoiselle Mars – Elmire –
Charlotte Brown – Extract from a Sermon

It was not without some expectation of having 'Guilty of rococoism' recorded against me, that I avowed, very soon after my arrival, the ardent desire I felt of turning my eyes from all that was new, that I might once again see Mars perform the part of Elmire in the 'Tartuffe'.

I was not quite without fear, too, that I was running some risk of effacing the delightful recollections of the past, by contemplating the change which seven years had made. I almost feared to let my children behold a reality that might destroy their *beau idéal* of the only perfect actress still remaining on the stage.

But 'Tartuffe' was on the bills: it might not soon appear again; and early dinner was hastily dispatched, and once more I found myself before the curtain which I had so often seen rise to Talma, Duchenois, and Mars.

I perceived with great pleasure on reaching the theatre, that the Parisians, though fickle in all else, were still faithful in their adoration of Mademoiselle Mars: for now, for perhaps the five hundredth representation of her Elmire, the barricades were as necessary, the *queue* as long and as full, as when, fifteen years ago, I was first told to remark the wonderful power of attraction possessed by an actress already greatly past the first bloom of youth and beauty. Were the Parisians as defensible in their ordinary love of change as they are in this singular proof of fidelity, it would be well. It is, however, strange witchery.

That the ear should be gratified, and the feelings awakened, by the skilful intonations of a voice the sweetest perhaps that ever blest a mortal, is quite intelligible; but that the eye should follow with such unwearied delight every look and movement of a woman, not only old – for that does sometimes happen at

13

Paris – but one known to be so from one end of Europe to the other, is certainly a singular phenomenon. Yet so it is; and could you see her, you would understand why, though not how, it is so. There is still a charm, a grace, in every movement of Mademoiselle Mars, however trifling and however slight, which instantly captivates the eye, and forbids it to wander to any other object – even though that object be young and lovely.

Why is it that none of the young heads can learn to turn like hers? Why can no arms move with the same beautiful and easy elegance? Her very fingers, even when gloved, seem to aid her expression; and the quietest and least posture-studying of actresses contrives to make the most trifling and ordinary movement assist in giving effect to her part.

I would willingly consent to be dead for a few hours, if I could meanwhile bring Molière to life, and let him see Mars play one of his best-loved characters. How delicious would be his pleasure in beholding the creature of his own fancy thus exquisitely alive before him; and of marking, moreover, the thrill that makes itself heard along the closely-packed rows of the parterre, when his wit, conveyed by this charming conductor, runs round the house like the touch of electricity! Do you think that the best smile of Louis le Grand could be worth this?

Few theatrical pieces can, I think, be calculated to give less pleasure than that of 'Charlotte Brown,' which followed the 'Tartuffe;' but as the part of Charlotte is played by Mademoiselle Mars, people will stay to see it. I repented however that I did not go, for it made me cross and angry.

Such an actress as Mars should not be asked to try a *tour de force* in order to make an abortive production effective. And what else can it be called, if her touching pathos and enchanting grace are brought before the public, to make them endure a platitude that would have been hissed into oblivion ere it had well seen light without her? It is hardly fair to expect that a performer should create as well as personate the chief character of a piece; but Mademoiselle Mars certainly does nothing less, when she contrives to excite sympathy and interest for a low-born and low-minded woman, who has managed to make a great match by telling a great falsehood.

Yet 'Charlotte Brown' is worth seeing for the sake of a certain tragic look given by this wonderful actress at the moment when her falsehood is discovered. It is no exaggeration to say, that Mrs. Siddons never produced an expression of greater power.

It is long since I have seen any theatre so crowded.

I remember many years ago hearing what I thought an excellent sermon from a venerable rector, who happened to have a curate more remarkable for the conscientious manner in which he performed his duty to the parish, and the judicious selection of his discourses, than for the excellence of his original sermons. 'It is the duty of a minister,' said the old man, 'to address the congregation which shall assemble to hear him with the most impressive and most able eloquence that it is within the compass of his power to use; and far better is it that the approved wisdom of those who have passed away be read from the pulpit, than that the weak efforts of an ungifted preacher should fall wearily and unprofitably on the ears of his congregation. The fact that his discourse is manuscript, instead of printed, will hardly console them for the difference.'

Do you not think – with all reverence be it spoken – that the same reasoning might be very usefully addressed to the managers of theatres, not in France only, but all the world over? If it cost too much to have a good new piece, would it not be better to have a good old one?

LETTER V

Exhibition of Living Artists at the Louvre – The Deluge –
Poussin and Martin – Portraits – Appearance of the company

I have been so little careful about dates and seasons, as totally to have forgotten, or rather neglected to learn, that the period of our arriving at Paris was that of the Exhibition of Living Artists at the Louvre: and it is not easy to describe the feeling produced by entering the gallery, with the expectation of seeing what I had been used to see there, and finding what was, at least, so very different.

Nevertheless, the exhibition is a very fine one, and so greatly superior to any I had heretofore seen of the modern French school, that we soon had the consolation of finding ourselves amused, and I may say delighted, notwithstanding our disappointment.

But surely there never was a device hit upon so little likely to propitiate the feelings which generate applause, as this of covering up Poussin, Rubens, Raphael, Titian, and Correggio, by hanging before them the fresh results of modern palettes. It is indeed a most un-coquettish mode of extorting attention.

There are some pictures of the Louvre Gallery in particular, with which my children are well acquainted, either by engravings or description, whose eclipse produced a very sad effect. 'The Deluge' of Poussin is one of these. Perhaps it may have been my brother's striking description of this picture which made it pre-eminently an object of interest to us. You may remember that Mr. Milton, in his elegant and curious little volume on the Fine Arts, written at Paris just before the breaking up of Napoleon's collection, says in speaking of it –
'colouring was unquestionably Poussin's least excellence; yet in this collection there is one of his pictures – the Deluge – in which the effect produced by the mere colouring is most

singular and powerful. The air is burdened and heavy with water; the earth, where it is not as yet overwhelmed, seems torn to pieces by its violence: the very light of heaven is absorbed and lost.' I give you this passage, because I remember no picture described with equal brevity, yet brought so powerfully before the imagination of the reader.

Can the place where one comes to look for this be favourable for hanging our illustrious countryman's representation of the same subject? It is doing him a most ungratifying honour; and were I Mr. Martin, or any other painter living, I would not consent to be exposed to the invidious comparisons which must inevitably ensue from such an injudicious arrangement.

How exceedingly disagreeable, for instance, must it be for the artists – who, I believe, not unfrequently indulge themselves by hovering under the incognito of apparent indifference near their favourite works – to overhear such remarks as those to which I listened yesterday in that part of the gallery where Le Sueur's St. Brunos hang! – 'Certainly, the bows on that lady's dress are of a delicate blue,' said the critic; 'and so is the drapery of le Sueur, which, for my sins, I happen to know is hid just under it. . . . Would one wish a better contrast to what it hides, than that unmeaning smile – that cold, smooth, varnished skin, – those lifeless limbs, and the whole unspeakable tameness of this thing, called *portrait d'une dame*?'

He spoke truly; yet was there but little point in what he said, for it might have referred with equal justice to many a pretty lady doomed to simper for ever in her gilded frame.

On the whole, however, portraits are much less oppressively predominating than with us; and among them are many whose size, composition, and exquisite style of finishing redeem them altogether from the odium of being *de trop* in the collection. I cannot but wish that this style of portrait-painting may find favour and imitation in England.

Lawrence is gone; and though Gérard on this side of the water, and indeed too many to rehearse on both, are left, whose portraitures of the human face are admirable; true to nature; true to art; true to expression, – true, even to the want of it; I am greatly inclined to believe that the enormous sums annually expended on these clever portraits contribute more to lower than to raise the art in popularity and in the genuine estimation of the public. The sums thus lavished may be termed patronage, certainly; but it is patronage that bribes the artist to the restraint, and often to the destruction of his genius.

Is there, in fact, any one who can honestly deny that a splendid exhibition-room, crowded with ladies and gentlemen on canvass, as large as life, is a lounge of great tediousness and inanity?

We may feel some satisfaction in recognising at a glance the eyes, nose, mouth, and chin of many of our friends and acquaintances, – nay, our most critical judgment may often acknowledge that these familiar features are registered with equal truth and skill; but this will not prevent the exhibition from being very dull. Nor is the thing much mended when each portrait, or pair of portraits, has been withdrawn from the gaudy throng, and hung up for ever and for ever before the eyes of their family and friends. The fair lady, sweetly smiling in one division of the apartment, and the well-dressed gentleman looking *distingué* in another, contribute as little at home as they did when suspended on the walls of the academy to the real pleasure and amusement of the beholder.

At the exhibition this year at the Louvre are many exquisite full-length portraits in oil, of which the canvas measures from eighteen inches to a foot in height, and from a foot to ten inches in width. The composition and style of these beautiful little pictures are often such as to detain one long before them, even though one does not recognise in them the features of an acquaintance. Their unobtrusive size must prevent their ever being disagreeably predominant in the decoration of a room; while their delicate and elaborate finish, and the richness of their highly-studied composition, will well reward attention; and even the closest examination, when directed to them, either by politeness, affection, or connoisseurship, can never be disappointed.

The Catalogue of the exhibition notices all the pictures which have been either ordered or purchased by the king or any of the royal family; and the number is so considerable as to show plainly that the most liberal and widely-extended patronage of art is a systematic object with the government.

The gold medal of the year has been courteously bestowed upon Mr. Martin for his picture of the Deluge. Had I been the judge, I should have awarded it to Stuben's Battle of Waterloo. That the faculty of imagination is one of the highest requisites for a painter is most certain; and that Mr. Martin pre-eminently possesses it, not less so. But imagination, though it can do much, cannot do all; and common sense is at least equally important in the formation of a finished artist. The painter of the great day of Waterloo has both. His imagination has enabled him to dive into the very hearts and souls of the persons he has depicted. Passion speaks in every line; and common sense has taught him, that, however powerful – nay, vehement, might be the expression he sought to produce, it must be obtained rather by the patient and faithful imitation of Nature than by a bold defiance of her.

The Assassination of the Duc de Guise, by M. Delaroche, is an admirable and highly popular work. It requires some patient perseverance to contest inch by inch the slow approach to the place where this exquisite piece of finishing is hung – but it well rewards the time and labour. One or two lovely little pictures by Franquelin made me envy those who have power to purchase, and sigh to think that they will probably go into private collections, where I shall never see them more. There are, indeed, many pictures so very good, that I think it possible the judges may have relieved themselves from the embarrassment of declaring which was best, by politely awarding the palm to the stranger.

I could indulge myself, did I not fear to weary you, by dwelling much longer upon my agreeable recollections of this extensive exhibition – containing, by the way, 2,174 pictures, – and might particularise many very admirable works. Nevertheless, I must repeat, that thus hiding the precious labours of all schools, and of all ages of painting, by the promiscuous productions of the living artists of France during the last year, is a most injudicious device for winning for them the golden opinions of those who throng from all quarters of the world to visit the Louvre.

This exhibition reaches to about three-fourths of the gallery; and where it ceases, a grim curtain, suspended across it, conceals the precious labours of the Spanish and Italian

schools, which occupy the farther end. Can anything be imagined more tantalising than this? And where is the living artist
who could stand his ground against such cruel odds?

To render the effect more striking still, this dismal curtain is
permitted so to hang as to leave a few inches between its
envious amplitude and the rich wall – suffering the mellow
browns of a well-known Murillo to meet and mock the eye.
Certainly not all the lecturers of all the academies extant could
point out a more effectual manner of showing the modern
French artist, wherein he chiefly fails: let us hope he will profit
by it.

As I am writing of Paris, it must be almost superfluous to say
that the admission to this collection is gratis.

I cannot quit the subject without adding a few words
respecting the company, or at least a part of it, whose
appearance, I thought, gave very unequivocal marks of the
march of mind and of indecorum; – for a considerable
sprinkling of very particularly greasy citizens and citizenesses
made itself felt and seen at every point where the critical crowd
was thickest. But –

'Sweetest nut hath sourest rind;'

and it were treason here, I suppose, to doubt that such a
proportion of intellect and refinement lies hid under the soiled
blouse and time-worn petticoat, as is at least equal to any that we
may hope to find enveloped in lawn, and lace, and broadcloth.

It is an incontrovertible fact, I think, that when the immortals
of Paris raised the barricades in the streets, they pulled them
down, more or less, in society. But this is an evil which those
who look beyond the present hour for their sources of joy and
sorrow need not deeply lament. Nature herself – at least such as
she shows herself, when man, forsaking the forest, agrees with
his fellows to congregate in cities – Nature herself will take care
to set this right again.

'Strength will be lord of imbecility;'

and were all men equal in the morning, they would not go to
rest till some amongst them had been thoroughly made to

Louvre.

understand that it was their lot to strew the couches of the rest. Such is the law of nature; and mere brute numerical strength will no more enable a mob to set it aside, than it will enable the ox or the elephant to send us to plough, or draw out our teeth to make their young one's toys.

For the present moment, however, some of the rubbish that the commotion of 'the Ordonnances' stirred up may still be seen floating about on the surface; and it is difficult to observe without a smile in what chiefly consists the liberty which these immortals have so valiantly bled to acquire. We may truly say of the philosophical population of Paris, that 'they are thankful for small matters;' one of the most remarkable of their newly-acquired rights being certainly the privilege of presenting themselves dirty, instead of clean, before the eyes of their magnates.

I am sure you must remember in days of yore, – that is to say, before the last revolution, – how very agreeable a part of the spectacle at the Louvre and in the Tuileries Gardens was constituted by the people, – not the ladies and gentlemen – they look pretty much the same everywhere; but by the careful coquetry of the pretty costumes, now a *cauchoise*, and now a *toque*, – the spruce neatness of the men who attended them, – nay, even by the tight and tidy trimness of the 'wee things' that in long waist, silk apron, snow-white cap, and faultless *chaussure*, trotted beside them. All these added greatly to the pleasantness and gaiety of the scene. But now, till the fresh dirt (not the fresh gloss) of the Three Days' labour be worn off, dingy jackets, uncomely *casquettes*, ragged *blouses*, and ill-favoured round-eared caps, that look as if they did duty night and day, must all be tolerated; and in this toleration appears to consist at present the principal external proof of the increased liberty of the Parisian mob.

LETTER VI

Society – Morality – False Impressions and False Reports –
Observations from a Frenchman on a recent publication

Much as I love the sights of Paris, – including as we must under this term all that is great and enduring, as well as all that is for ever changing and for ever new, – I am more earnestly bent, as you will readily believe, upon availing myself of all my opportunities for listening to the conversation within the houses, than on contemplating all the marvels that may be seen without.

Joyfully, therefore, have I welcomed the attention and kindness that have been offered me in various quarters; and I have already the satisfaction of finding myself on terms of most pleasant and familiar intercourse with a variety of very delightful people, many of them highly distinguished, and, happily for me, varying in their opinions of all things both in heaven and earth, from the loftiest elevation of the *rococo*, to the lowest profundity of the *décousu* school.

And here let me pause, to assure you, and any other of my countrymen and countrywomen whose ears I can reach, that excursions to Paris, be they undertaken with what spirit of enterprise they may, and though they may be carried through with all the unrestrained expense that English wealth can permit, yet without the power by some means or other of entering into good French society, they are nothing worth.

It is true, that there is something most exceedingly exhilarating to the spirits in the mere external novelty and cheerfulness of the objects which surround a stranger on first entering Paris. That indescribable air of gaiety which makes every sunshiny day look like a fête; the light hilarity of spirit that seems to pervade all ranks; the cheerful tone of voice, the sparkling glances of the numberless bright eyes; the gardens,

23

the flowers, the statues of Paris, – all together produce an effect very like enchantment.

But 'use lessens marvel;' and when the first delightful excitement is over, and we begin to feel weary from its very intensity, the next step is backward into rationality, low spirits, and grumbling.

From that moment the English tourist talks of nothing but wide rivers, magnificent bridges, prodigious *trottoirs*, unrivalled drains, and genuine port. It is at this stage that the traveller, in order to continue his enjoyment and bring it to perfection, should remit his examination of the exterior of noble *hôtels*, and endeavour to be admitted to the much more enduring enchantment which prevails within them.

So much has already been said and written on the grace and charm of the French language in conversation, that it is quite needless to dwell upon it. That *good things* can be said in no other idiom with equal grace, is a fact that can neither be controverted nor more firmly established than it is already. Happily, the art of expressing a clever thought in the best possible words did not die with Madame de Sévigné; nor has it yet been destroyed by revolution of any kind.

It is not only for the amusement of an hour, however, that I would recommend the assiduous cultivation of good French society to the English. Great and important improvements in our national manners have already arisen from the intercourse which long peace has permitted. Our dinner-tables are no longer disgraced by inebriety; nor are our men and women, when they form a party expressly for the purpose of enjoying each other's society, separated by the law of the land during half the period for which the social meeting has been convened.

But we have much to learn still; and the general tone of our daily associations might be yet farther improved, did the best specimens of Parisian habits and manners furnish the examples.

It is not from the large and brilliant parties which recur in every fashionable mansion, perhaps, three or four times in each season, that I think we could draw much improvement. A fine party at Lady A——'s in Grosvenor Square, is not more like a fine party at Lady B——'s in Berkeley Square, than a fine party in Paris is to one in London. There are abundance of pretty women, handsome men, satin, gauze, velvet, diamonds, chains, stars, moustaches, and imperials at both, with perhaps very little deserving the name of rational enjoyment in either.

I suspect, indeed, that we have rather the advantage on these crowded occasions, for we more frequently change the air by passing from one room to another when we eat our ices; and as the tulip-tinctured throng enjoy this respite from suffocation by detachments, they have often not only opportunity to breathe, but occasionally to converse also, for several minutes together, without danger of being dislodged from their standing-ground.

It is not, therefore, at the crowded roll-calls of all their acquaintance that I would look for anything rational or peculiar in the *salons* of Paris, but in the daily and constant intercourse of familiar companionship. This is enjoyed with a degree of pleasant ease – an absence of all pomp, pride, and circumstance, of which unhappily we have no idea. Alas! we must know by special printed announcement a month beforehand that our friend is 'at home,' – that liveried servants will be in attendance, and her mansion blazing with light, – before we can dare venture to pass an evening hour in her drawing-room. How would a London lady stare, if some half-dozen – though perhaps among the most chosen favourites of her visiting list – were to walk unbidden into her presence, in bonnets and shawls, between the hours of eight and eleven! And how strangely new would it seem, were the pleasantest and most coveted engagements of the week, formed without ceremony and kept without ostentation, to arise from a casual meeting at the beginning of it!

It is this ease, this habitual absence of ceremony and parade, this national enmity to constraint and tediousness of all kinds, which renders the tone of French manners so infinitely more agreeable than our own. And the degree in which this is the case can only be guessed at by those who, by some happy accident or other, possess a real and effective 'open sesame!' for the doors of Paris.

With all the superabundance of vanity ascribed to the French, they certainly show infinitely less of it in their

intercourse with their fellow-creatures than we do. I have seen
a countess, whose title was of a dozen fair descents, open the
external door of her apartment, and welcome the guests who
appeared at it with as much grace and elegance as if a triple
relay of tall fellows who wore her colours had handed their
names from hall to drawing room. Yet in this case there was
no want of wealth. Coachman, footman, abigail, and
doubtless all fitting etceteras, owned her as their sovereign
lady and mistress. But they happened to have been sent hither
and thither, and it never entered her imagination that her
dignity could be compromised by her appearing without
them. In short, the vanity of the French does not show itself in
little things; and it is exactly for this reason that their
enjoyment of society is stripped of so much of the anxious,
sensitive, ostentatious, self-seeking etiquette which so heavily
encumbers our own.

There are some among us, my friend, who might say of this
testimony to the charm of French society, that there was
danger in praising, and pointing out as an example to be
followed, the manners of a people whose morality is
considered as so much less strict than our own. Could I think
that, by thus approving what is agreeable, I could lessen by a
single hair's-breadth the interval which we believe exists
between us in this respect, I would turn my approval to
reproof, and my superficial praise to deep-dyed reprobation:
but to any who should express such a fear, I would reply by
assuring them that it would require a very different species of
intimacy from any to which I had the honour of being
admitted, in order to authorise, from personal observation,
any attack upon the morals of Parisian society. More
scrupulous and delicate refinement in *the tone of manners* can
neither be found nor wished for anywhere; and I do very
strongly suspect, that many of the pictures of French
depravity which have been brought home to us by our
travellers, have been made after sketches taken in scenes and
circles to which the introductions I so strongly recommend to
my countrywomen could by no possibility lead them. It is not
of such that I can be supposed to speak.

Apropos of false impressions and false reports, I may repeat
to you an anecdote which I heard yesterday evening. The little

committee in which it was related consisted of at least a dozen persons, and it appeared that I was myself the only one to whom it was new.

'It is rather more than two years ago,' said the speaker, 'that we had amongst us an English gentleman, who avowed that it was his purpose to write on France, not as other men write – superficially, respecting truths that lie obvious to ordinary eyes – but with a research that should make him acquainted with all things above, about, and underneath. He professed this intention to more than one dear friend; and more than one dear friend took the trouble of tracing him in his chase after hidden truths. Not long after his arrival among us, this gentleman became intimately acquainted with a lady more celebrated for the variety of her friendships with men of letters than for the endurance of them. This lady received the attentions of the stranger with distinguished kindness, and, among other proofs of regard, undertook to purvey for him all sorts of private anecdotes, great and little, that from the mass he might form an average estimate of the people; assuring him at the same time, that no one in Paris was more *au fait* of its secret histories than herself. 'This,' continued my informant, 'might be, and I believe was, very particularly true; and the English traveller might have been justified in giving to his countrymen and countrywomen as much insight into such mysteries as he thought good for them: but when he published the venomous slanders of this female respecting persons not only of the highest honour, but of the most unspotted reputation, he did what will blast his name as long as his charlatan book is remembered.' Such were the indignant words, and there was nothing in the tone with which they were uttered to weaken their expression.

I tell you the tale as I heard it; but I will not repeat much more that was said on the same subject, nor will I give any A . . ., B . . ., or C . . . hints as to the names so freely mentioned.

Some degree of respectability ought certainly to attach to those from whom important information is sought respecting the morals and manners of a country, when it is the intention of the inquirer that his observations and statements upon it should become authority to the whole civilized world.

The above conversation, however, was brought to a laughing conclusion by Madame C——, who, addressing her husband as he was seconding the angry eloquence I have repeated, said, 'Calmez-vous donc, mon ami: après tout, le tableau fait par M. le Voyageur des dames Anglaises n'a rien à nous faire mourir de jalousie.'

I suspect that neither you nor any other lady of England will feel disposed to contradict her.

Adieu!

LETTER VII

Alarm created by the Trial of the Lyons Prisoners – Visits from a Republican and from a Doctrinaire: reassured by the promises of safety and protection received from the latter

We have really had something very like a panic amongst us, from the rumours in circulation respecting this terrible trial, which is now rapidly approaching. Many people think that fearful scenes may be expected to take place in Paris when it begins.

The newspapers of all parties are so full of the subject, that there is little else to be found in them; and all those, of whatever colour, which are opposed to the government, describe the manner in which the proceedings are to be managed, as the most tyrannical exercise of power ever practised in modern Europe.

The legitimate royalists declare it to be illegal, inasmuch as the culprits have a right to be tried by a jury of their peers – the citizens of France; whereas it appears that this their chartered right is denied them, and that no other judge or jury is to be permitted in their case than the peers of France.

Whether this accusation will be satisfactorily answered, I know not; but there certainly does appear to be something rather plausible, at least, in the objection. Nevertheless, it is not very difficult to see that the 28th Article of the Charter may be made to answer it, which says, –

'The Chamber of Peers takes cognizance of high-treason, and of attempts against the safety of the state, *which shall be defined by law.*'

Now, though this *defining by law* appears, by what I can learn, to be an operation not yet quite completed, there seems to be something so very like high-treason in some of the offences for which these prisoners are to be tried, that the first clause of the article may do indifferently well to cover it.

The republican journals, pamphlets, and publications of all sorts, however, treat the whole business of their detention and trial as the most tremendous infringement of the newly-acquired rights of Young France; and they say – nay, they do swear, that crowned king, created peers, and placed ministers never dared to venture upon anything so tyrannical as this.

All that the unfortunate Louis Seize ever did, or suffered to be done – all that the banished Charles Dix ever threatened to do – never 'roared so loud, and thundered in the index,' as does this deed without a name about to be perpetrated by King Louis-Philippe the First.

At last, however, the horrible thing has been christened, and PROCÈS MONSTRE is its name. This is a happy device, and will save a world of words. Before it received this expressive appellation, every paragraph concerning it began by a round-about specification of the horrific business they were about to speak of; but since this lucky name has been hit upon, all prefatory eloquence is become unnecessary: *Procès Monstre!* simply *Procès Monstre!* expresses all it could say in two words; and whatever follows may safely become matter of news and narrative respecting it.

This news, and these narratives, however, still vary considerably, and leave one in a very vacillating state of mind as to what may happen next. One account states that Paris is immediately to be put under martial law, and all foreigners, except those attached to the different embassies, civilly requested to depart. Another declares all this to be a weak invention of the enemy; but hints that it is probable a pretty strong *cordon* of troops will surround the city, to keep watch day and night, lest *les jeunes gens* of the metropolis, in their mettlesome mood, should seek to wash out in the blood of their fellow-citizens the stain which the illegitimate birth of the monster has brought upon France. Others announce that a devoted body of patriots have sworn to sacrifice a hecatomb of National Guards, to atone for an abomination which many believe to originate with them.

Not a few declare that the trial will never take place; that the government, audacious as they say it is, dare do no more than hold up the effigy of the monster to frighten the people, and that a general amnesty will end the business. In truth, it would be a tedious task to record one half of the tales that are in circulation on this subject: but I do assure you, that listening to the awful note of preparation for all that is to be done at the Luxembourg is quite enough to make one nervous, and many English families have already thought it prudent to leave the city.

At one moment we were really worked into a state very nearly approaching terror by the vehement eloquence of a fiery-hot republican who paid us a visit. I ventured to lead to the terrible subject by asking him if he thought the approaching political trials likely to produce any result beyond their disagreeable influence on the convenience of the parties concerned; but I really repented my temerity when I saw the cloud which gathered on his brow as he replied:—

'Result! What do you call result, madam? Is the burning indignation of millions of Frenchmen a result? Are the execrations of the noble beings enslaved, imprisoned, tortured, trampled on by tyranny, a result? Are the groans of their wives and mothers — are the tears of their bereaved children — a result? — Yes, yes, there will be results enough! They are yet to come, but come they will; and when they do, think you that the next revolution will be one of three days? Do your countrymen think so? does Europe think so? There has been another revolution, to which it will more resemble.'

He looked rather ashamed of himself, I thought, when he had concluded his tirade, — and well he might: but there was such a hideous tone of prophecy in this, that I actually trembled as I listened to him, and, all jesting apart, thoughts of passports to be signed and conveyances to be hired were arranging themselves very seriously in my brain. But before we went out for the evening, all these gloomy meditations were most agreeably dispersed by a visit from a staid old doctrinaire, who was not only a soberer politician, but one considerably more likely to know what he was talking about than the youth who had harangued us in the morning.

Anxious to have my fears either confirmed or removed, I hastened to tell him, half in jest, half in earnest, that we were beginning to think of taking an abrupt leave of Paris. 'And why?' said he.

I stated very seriously my newly-awakened fears; at which he laughed heartily, and with an air of such unfeigned amusement, that I was cured at once.

'Whom can you have been listening to?' said he.

'I will not give up my authority.' I replied with proper diplomatic discretion; 'but I will tell you exactly what a gentleman who has been here this morning has been saying to us.' And I did so precisely as I have repeated it to you; upon which he laughed more heartily than before, and rubbing his hands as if perfectly delighted, he exclaimed, 'Delicious! And you really have been fortunate enough to fall in with one of these *enfans perdus*? I really wish you joy. But do not set off immediately: listen first to another view of the case.' I assured him that this was exactly what I wished to do, and very truly declared that he could do me no greater favour than to put me *au fait* of the real state of affairs.

'Willingly will I do so,' said he, 'and be assured I will not deceive you.' Whereupon I closed the *croisée*, that no rattling wheels might disturb us, and prepared to listen.

'My good lady,' he began with great kindness, 'soyez tranquille. There is no more danger of revolution at this time in France than there is in Russia. Louis-Philippe is adored; the laws are respected; order is universally established; and if there be a sentiment of discontent or a feeling approaching to irritation among any deserving the name of Frenchmen, it is against these miserable *vauriens*, who still cherish the wild hope of disturbing our peace and our prosperity. But fear nothing: trust me, the number of these is too small to make it worth while to count them.'

You will believe I heard this with sincere satisfaction; and I really felt very grateful, both for the information, and the friendly manner in which it was given.

'I rejoice to hear this,' said I: 'but may I, as a matter of curiosity, ask you what you think about this famous trial? How do you think it will end?'

'As all trials ought to end,' he replied: 'by bringing all such as are found guilty to punishment.'

'Heaven grant it!' said I; 'for the sake of mankind in general, and for that portion of it in particular which happen at the present moment to inhabit Paris. But do you not think that the irritation produced by these preparations at the Luxembourg is of considerable extent and violence?'

'To whatever extent this irritation may have gone,' he answered gravely, 'it is an undoubted fact, – undoubted in the quarter where most is known about the matter, – that the feeling which approves these preparations is not only of greater extent, but of infinitely deeper sincerity, than that which is opposed to it. What you have heard today is mere unmeaning bluster. The trial, I do assure you, is very popular. It is for the justification and protection of the National Guard; – and are we not all National Guards?'

'But are all the National Guards true?'

'Perhaps not. But be sure of this, that there are enough true to *égorger* without any difficulty those who are not.'

'But it is not very probable,' said I, 'that the republican feeling may be quite strong enough to produce another disturbance, though not another revolution? And the situation of strangers would probably become very embarrassing, should this eventually lead to any renewed outbreakings of public enthusiasm.'

'Not the least in the world, I do assure you: for, at any rate, all the enthusiasm, as you civilly call it, would only elicit additional proof of the stability and power of the government which we are now so happy as to enjoy. The enthusiasm would be speedily calmed, depend upon it.'

'A peaceable traveller,' said I, 'can wish for no better news; and henceforward I shall endeavour to read and to listen with a tranquil spirit, let the prisoners or their partisans say what they may.'

'You will do wisely, believe me. Rest in perfect confidence and security, and be assured that Louis-Philippe holds all the English as his right good friends. While this is the case, neither Windsor Castle nor the Tower of London itself could afford you a safer abode than Paris.'

With this seasonable and very efficient encouragement, he left me; and as I really believe him to know more about the new-born politics of 'Young France' than most people, I go on very tranquilly making engagements, with but few misgivings lest barricades should prevent my keeping them.

LETTER VIII

*Eloquence of the Pulpit – L'Abbé Coeur – Sermon at St. Roch –
Elegant Congregation – Costume of the younger Clergy*

There is one novelty, and to me a very agreeable one, which I
have remarked since my return to this volatile France; this is
the fashion and consideration which now attend the eloquence
of her preachers.

Political economists assert that the supply of every article
follows the demand for it in a degree nicely proportioned to
the wants of the population; and it is upon this principle, I
presume, that we must account for the present affluence of a
talent which some few years ago could hardly be said to exist
in France, and might perhaps have been altogether denied to
it, had not the pages both of Fenelon and his eloquent
antagonist, Bossuet, rendered such an injustice impossible.

It was, I think, about a dozen years ago that I took some
trouble to discover if any traces of this glorious eloquence
remained at Paris. I heard sermons at Notre Dame – at St.
Roch – at St. Eustache; but never was a search after talent
attended with worse success. The preachers were nought; they
had the air, too, of being vulgar and uneducated men, – which
I believe was, and indeed still is, very frequently the case. The
churches were nearly empty; and the few persons scattered up
and down their splendid aisles appeared, generally speaking,
to be of the very lowest order of old women.

How great is now the contrast! Nowhere are we so certain
of seeing a crowd of elegantly-dressed and distinguished
persons as in the principal churches of Paris. Nor is it a crowd
that mocks the eye with any tinsel pretensions to a rank they
do not possess. Inquire who it is that so meekly and devoutly
kneels on one side of you – that so sedulously turns the pages
of her prayer-book on the other, and you will be answered by
the announcement of the noblest names remaining in France.

Though the eloquence of the pulpit has always been an object of attention and interest to me in all countries, I hardly ventured on my first arrival here to inquire again if anything of the kind existed, lest I should once more be sent to listen to an inaudible mumbling preacher, and to look at the deaf and dozing old women who formed his congregation. But it has needed no inquiry to make us speedily acquainted with the fact, that the churches have become the favourite resort of the young, the beautiful, the high-born, and the instructed. Whence comes this change?

'Have you heard L'Abbé Coeur?' was a question asked me before I had been here a week, by one who would not for worlds have been accounted *rococo*. When I replied that I had not even heard of him, I saw plainly that it was decided I could know very little indeed of what was going on in Paris. 'That is really extraordinary'! but I engage you to go without delay. He is, I assure you, quite as much the fashion as Taglioni.'

As the conversation was continued on the subject of fashionable preachers, I soon found that I was indeed altogether benighted. Other celebrated names were cited: Lacordaire, Deguerry, and some others that I do not remember, were spoken of as if their fame must of necessity have reached from pole to pole, but of which, in truth, I knew no more than if the gentlemen had been private chaplains to the princes of Chili. However, I set down all their names with much docility; and the more I listened, the more I rejoiced that the Passion-week and Easter, those most Catholic seasons for preaching, were before us, being fully determined to profit by this opportunity of hearing in perfection what was so perfectly new to me as popular preaching in Paris.

I have lost little time in putting this resolution into effect. The church of St. Roch is, I believe, the most fashionable in Paris; it was there, too, that we were sure of hearing this celebrated Abbé Coeur; and both these reasons together decided that it was at St. Roch our sermon-seeking should begin: I therefore immediately set about discovering the day and hour on which he would make his appearance in the pulpit.

When inquiring these particulars in the church, we were informed, that if we intended to procure chairs, it would be necessary to come at least one good hour before the high mass which preceded the sermon should begin. This was rather alarming intelligence to a party of heretics who had an immense deal of business on their hands; but I was steadfast in my purpose, and, with a small detachment of my family, submitted to the preliminary penance of sitting the long silent hour in front of the pulpit of St. Roch. The precaution was, however, perfectly necessary, for the crowd was really tremendous; but, to console us, it was of the most elegant description; and, after all, the hour scarcely appeared much too long for the business of reviewing the vast multitude of graceful personages, waving plumes, and blooming flowers, that ceased not during every moment of the time to collect themselves closer and closer still about us.

Nothing certainly could be more beautiful than this collection of bonnets, unless it were the collection of eyes under them. The proportion of ladies to gentlemen was on the whole, we thought, not less than twelve to one.

'Je désirerais savoir,' said a young man near me, addressing an extremely pretty woman who sat beside him – 'Je désirerais savoir si par hasard M. l'Abbé Coeur est jeune.'

The lady answered not, but frowned most indignantly.

A few minutes afterwards, his doubts upon this point, if he really had any, were removed. A man far from ill-looking, and farther still from being old, mounted the tribune, and some thousands of bright eyes were riveted upon him. The silent and profound attention which hung on every word he uttered, unbroken as it was by a single idle sound, or even glance, showed plainly that his influence upon the splendid and numerous congregation that surrounded him must be very great, or the power of his eloquence very strong: and it was an influence and a power that, though 'of another parish,' I could well conceive must be generally felt, *for he was in earnest*. His voice, though weak and somewhat wirey, was distinct, and his enunciation clear: I did not lose a word.

His manner was simple and affectionate; his language strong, yet not intemperate; but he decidedly appealed more to the hearts of his hearers than to their understandings; and it was their hearts that answered him, for many of them wept plenteously.

A great number of priests were present at this sermon, who were all dressed in their full clerical habits, and sat in places reserved for them immediately in front of the pulpit: they were consequently very near us, and we had abundant opportunity to remark the traces of that *march of mind* which is doing so many wondrous works upon earth.

Instead of the tonsure which we have been used to see, certainly with some feeling of reverence – for it was often shorn into the very centre of crisped locks, while their raven black or shining chestnut still spoke of youth that scrupled not to sacrifice its comeliness to a feeling of religious devotion; – instead of this, we now saw unshaven crowns, and more than one pair of flourishing *favoris*, nourished, trained, and trimmed evidently with the nicest care, though a stiff three-cornered cowl in every instance hung behind the rich and waving honours of the youthful head.

The effect of this strange mixture is very singular. But notwithstanding this bold abandonment of priestly costume among the junior clergy, there were in the long double row of anointed heads which faced the pulpit some exceedingly fine studies for an artist; and wherever the offending Adam was subdued by years, nothing could be in better keeping than the countenances, and the sacred garb of those to whom they belonged. Similar causes will, I suppose, at all times produce similar effects; and it is therefore that among the twenty priests at St. Roch in 1835, I seemed to recognise the originals of many a holy head with which the painters of Italy, Spain, and Flanders have made me familiar.

The contrast furnished by the deep-set eyes, and the fine severe expression of some of these consecrated brows, to the light, airy elegance of the pretty women around them, was sufficiently striking; and, together with the mellow light of the shaded windows and the lofty spaciousness of the noble church, formed a spectacle highly picturesque and impressive.

After the sermon was over, and while the gaily-habited congregation fluttered away through the different doors like so many butterflies hastening to meet returning sunshine, we amused ourselves by wandering round the church. It is magnificently large for a parish church; but excepting in some of the little chapels, we found not much to admire.

That very unrighteous old churchman, the Abbé Dubois, has a fine monument there, restored from Les Petits Augustins; and a sort of marble medallion, bearing the head of the immortal Corneille – immortal despite M. Victor Hugo – is also restored, and placed against one of the heavy columns of, I think, the centre aisle. But we paused longest in a little chapel behind the altar – not the middle one, with its well-managed glory of crimson light, though that is very beautiful; but in the one to the right of it, which contains a sculptured Calvary. It is, I believe, only one of *les stations*, of which twelve are to be found in different parts of the church; but it has a charm – seen as we saw it, with a strong effect of accidental light, bringing forward the delicate figure of the adoring Magdalene, and leaving the Saviour in the dark shadow and repose of death – that sets at defiance all the connoisseurship of art, and taking from you all faculty to judge, leaves only the power to feel. Under these circumstances, whether quite delusive or not I hardly know, this group appeared to us one of exceeding beauty.

The high altar of St. Roch, and the extremity of the carpeted space enclosed round it, is most lavishly, beautifully, and fragrantly adorned with flowers of the choicest kind, all flourishing in the fullest bloom in boxes and vases. It is the only instance I remember in which the perfume of this most fair and holy decoration actually pervaded the church. They certainly offer the sweetest incense that can be found to breathe its grateful life and spirit out on any altar; and were it not for the graceful swinging of the censers, which very particularly pleases my eye, I would recommend to the Roman Catholic church henceforth an economy of their precious gums, and advise them to offer the incense of flowers in their stead.

Before we left the church, about a hundred and fifty boys and girls, from ten to fourteen years of age, assembled to be catechised by a young priest, who received them behind the Lady Chapel. His manner was familiar, caressing and kind, and his waving hair fell about his ears like the picture of a young St. John.

LETTER IX

Literature of the Revolutionary School –
Its low estimation in France

Among many proofs of attentive kindness which I have received from my Paris friends, their care to furnish me with a variety of modern publications is not the least agreeable.

One fancies everywhere, that it is easy, by the help of a circulating library, to know tolerably well what is going on at Paris: but this is a mighty fond delusion; though sometimes, perhaps, our state may be the more gracious from our ignorance.

One gentleman, to whom I owe much gratitude for the active good-nature with which he seems willing to assist me in all my researches, has given me much curious information respecting the present state of literature and literary men in France.

In this department of human greatness, at least, those of the party which has lost power and place have a most decided pre-eminence. Would it be a pun to say that there is poetical justice in this?

The active, busy, bustling politicians of the hour have succeeded in thrusting everything else out of place, and themselves into it. One dynasty has been overthrown, and another established; old laws have been abrogated, and hundreds of new ones framed; hereditary nobles have been disinherited, and little men made great; – but amidst this plentitude of destructiveness, they have not yet contrived to make any one of the puny literary reputations of the day weigh down the renown of those who have never lent their voices to the cause of treason, regicide, rebellion, or obscenity. The literary reputations both of Châteaubriand and Lamartine stand higher, beyond all comparison, than those of any other living French authors: yet the first, with all his

39

genius, has often suffered his imagination to run riot, and the last has only given to the public the leisure of his literary life. But both of them are men of honour and principle, as well as men of genius; and it comforts one's human nature to see that these qualities will keep themselves aloft, despite whatever squally winds may blow, or blustering floods assail them. That both Châteaubriand and Lamartine belong rather to the imaginative than to the *positif* class, cannot be denied; but they are renowned throughout the world, and France is proud of them.

The most curious literary speculations, however, suggested by the present state of letters in this country, are not respecting authors such as these: they speak for themselves, and all the world knows them and their position. The circumstance decidedly the most worthy of remark in the literature of France at the present time, is the effect which the last revolution appears to have produced. With the exception of history, to which both Thiers and Mignet have added something that may live, notwithstanding their very defective philosophy, no single work has appeared since the revolution of 1830 which has obtained a substantial, elevated, and generally acknowledged reputation for any author unknown before that period: not even among all the unbridled ebullitions of imagination, though restrained neither by decorum, principle, nor taste, – not even here (excepting from one female* pen, which might become, were it the pleasure of the hand that wields it, the first now extant in the world of fiction,) has anything appeared likely to survive its author; nor is there any writer who during the same period has raised himself to that station in society, by means of his literary productions, which is so universally accorded to all who have acquired high literary celebrity in any country.

The name of M. Guizot was too well known before the revolution for these observations to have any reference to him; and however much he may have distinguished himself since July 1830, his reputation was made before. There are, however, little writers in prodigious abundance; and though as perfectly sure of the truth of what I have here stated as that I

* G. Sand.

am alive to write it, I should expect a terrible riot about my ears, could such words be heard by the swarm of tiny geniuses that settle in clusters, some on the newspapers, some on the theatres, and some on the busy little printing-press of the tale-tellers – could they catch me, I am sure I should be stung to death.

How well I can fancy the clamour! . . . 'Infamous libeller!' cries one; 'have not I achieved a reputation? Do I not receive yearly some hundreds of francs for my sublime familiarity with sin and misery? and are not my works read by 'Young France' with ecstasy? Is not this fame?' 'And I,' says another, – 'is it of such as I and my contemporary fellow-labourers in the vast field of new-ploughed speculation that you speak?' 'What call you reputation, woman?' says a third: 'do not the theatres overflow when I send murder, lust, and incest on the stage, to witch the world with wondrous wickedness?' 'And, I too,' groans another, – 'am I not famous? Are not my delicious tales of unschooled nature in the hands of every free-born youth and tender maid in this our regenerated Athens? Is not this fame, infamous slanderer?'

Were I obliged to answer all this, I could only say, 'Arrangez-vous, canaille! If you call this fame, take it, try it, make the most of it, and see where you will be some dozen years hence.'

Notwithstanding this extraordinary lack of great ability, however, there never, I believe, was any period in which the printing-presses of France worked so hard as at present. The revolution of 1830 seems to have set all the minor spirits in motion. There is scarcely a boy so insignificant, or a workman so unlearned, as to doubt his having the power and the right to instruct the world. 'Every breathing soul in Paris took a part in this glorious struggle,' says the recording newspaper; – 'Yes, all!' echoes the smutched mechanic, snorting and snuffing the air with the intoxicating consciousness of imputed power; – 'Yes!' answer the galopins one and all, 'it is we, it is we!' And then, like the restless witches on the barren heath that their breath has blasted, the great reformers rouse themselves again, and looking from the mischief they have done to the still worse that remains behind, they mutter prophetically, 'We'll do – we'll do – we'll do!'

To me, I confess, it is perfectly astonishing that any one can be found to class the writers of this restless *clique* as 'the literary men of France.' Yet it has been done; and it is not till the effects of the popular commotion which brought them into existence has fully subsided, that the actual state of French literature can be fairly ascertained.

Béranger was not the production of that whirlwind: but, in truth, let him sing what or when he will, the fire of genuine poetic inspiration must perforce flash across the thickest mist that false principles can raise around him. He is but a meteor perhaps, but a very bright one, and must shine, though his path lie amongst unwholesome exhalations and most dangerous pitfalls. But he cannot in any way be quoted as one of the new-born race whose claim to genuine fame I have presumed to doubt.

That flashes of talent, sparkles of wit, and bursts of florid eloquence are occasionally heard, seen, and felt even from these, is, however, certain: it could hardly be otherwise. But they blaze, and go out. The oil which feeds the lamp of revolutionary genius is foul, and such noxious vapours rise with the flame as must needs check its brightness.

Do not, however, believe me guilty of such presumption as to give you my own unsupported judgment as to the position which this 'new school' (as the *décousu* folks always call themselves) hold in the public esteem. Such a judgment could be little worth if unsupported; but my opinion on this subject is, on the contrary, the result of careful inquiry among those who are most competent to give information respecting it.

When the names of such as are best known among this class of authors are mentioned in society, let the politics of the circle be what they may, they are constantly spoken of as a Pariah caste that must be kept apart.

'Do you know —— ——?' has been a question I have repeatedly asked respecting a person whose name is cited in England as the most esteemed French writer of the age, – and so cited, moreover, to prove the low standard of French taste and principle.

'No, madam,' has been invariably the cold reply.

'Or ——?'

'No. He is not in society.'

'Or ——?'

'Oh no! His works live an hour (too long!) and are forgotten.'

Should I therefore, my friend, return from France with an higher idea of its good taste and morality than I had when I entered it, think not that my own standard of what is right has been lowered, but only that I have had the pleasure of finding it differed much less than I expected from that of our agreeable and hardly-judged neighbours on this side the water. But I shall probably recur to this subject again; and so, for the present, farewell!

LETTER X

Lonchamps – The 'Three Hours' Agony' at St. Roch –
Sermons on the Gospel of Good-Friday – Prospects of
the Catholics – O'Connell

I dare say you may know, my friend, though I did not, that
the Wednesday, Thursday, and Friday of Passion-week are
yearly set apart by the Parisians for a splendid promenade in
carriages, on horseback, and on foot, to a part of the Bois de
Boulogne called Lonchamps. What the origin could be of so
gay and brilliant an assemblage of people and equipages,
evidently coming together to be stared at and to stare, on days
so generally devoted to religious exercises, rather puzzled me;
but I have obtained a most satisfactory explanation, which, in
the hope of your ignorance, I will communicate. The custom
itself, it seems, is a sort of religious exercise; or, at any rate, it
was so at the time of its institution.

When the *beau monde* of Paris first adopted the practice of
repairing to Lonchamps during these days of penitence and
prayer, a convent stood there, whose nuns were celebrated for
performing the solemn services appointed for the season with
peculiar piety and effect. They sustained this reputation for
many years; and for many years all who could find admittance
within their church thronged to hear their sweet voices.

This convent was destroyed at *the* revolution (*par excellence*),
but the horses and carriages of Paris still continue to move for
evermore in the same direction when the last three days of
Lent arrive.

The cavalcade assembled on this occasion forms an
extremely pretty spectacle, rivalling a spring Sunday in Hyde
Park as to the number and elegance of the equipages, and
greatly exceeding it in the beauty and extent of the magnificent road on which they show themselves. Though the
attending this congregation of wealth, rank, and fashion is still

called 'going to Lonchamps,' the evolutions of the company, whether in carriages, on horseback, or on foot, are at present almost wholly confined to the noble avenue which leads from the entrance to the Champs Elysées up to the Barrière de l'Etoile.

From about three till six, the whole of this ample space is crowded; and I really had no idea that so many handsome, well-appointed equipages could be found collected together anywhere out of London. The royal family had several handsome carriages on the ground: that of the Duke of Orleans was particularly remarkable for the beauty of the horses, and the general elegance of the 'turn-out.'

The ministers of state, and all the foreign legations, did honour to the occasion; most of them having very complete equipages, chasseurs of various plumage, and many with a set of four beautiful horses really well harnessed. Many private individuals, also, had carriages which were handsome enough, together with their elegant lading, greatly to increase the general brilliancy of the scene.

The only individual, however, except the Duke of Orleans, who had two carriages on the ground, two feathered chasseurs, and twice two pair of richly-harnessed steeds, was a certain Mr. T——, an American merchant, whose vast wealth, and still more vast expenditure, is creating considerable consternation among his sober-minded countrymen in Paris. We were told that the exuberance of this gentleman's transatlantic taste was such, and such the vivacity of his inventive fancy, that during the three days of the Lonchamps promenade he appeared on the ground each day with different liveries; having, as it should seem, no particular family reasons for preferring any one set of colours to another.

The ground was sprinkled, and certainly greatly adorned, by many very elegant-looking Englishmen on horseback; the pretty caprioles, sleek skins, and well-managed capers of that prettiest of creatures, a high-bred English saddle-horse, being as usual among the most attractive parts of the show. Nor was there any deficiency of Frenchmen, with very handsome *montures*, to complete the spectacle; while the ample space under the trees on either side was crowded with thousands of smart pedestrians; the whole scene being one vast moving mass of pomp and pleasure.

Nevertheless, the weather on the first of the three days was very far from favourable: the wind was so bitterly cold that I countermanded the carriage I had ordered, and instead of going to Lonchamps, we actually sat shivering over the fire at home; indeed, before three o'clock, the ground was perfectly covered with snow. The next day promised something better, and we ventured to emerge: but the spectacle was really vexatious; many of the carriages being open, and the shivering ladies attired in all the light and floating drapery of spring costume. For it is at Lonchamps that all the fashions of the coming season are exhibited; and no one can tell, however fashion-wise they be, what bonnet, scarf or shawl, or even what prevailing colour, is to be worn in Paris throughout the year, till this decisive promenade be over. Accordingly the milliners had done their duty, and, in fact, had far outstripped the spring. But it was sad to see the beautiful bunches of lilac, and the graceful, flexible laburnums – each a wonder of art – twisted and tortured, bending and breaking, before the wind. It really seemed as if the lazy Spring, vexed at the pretty mimicry of blossoms she had herself failed to bring, sent this inclement blast on purpose to blight them. Everything went wrong. The tender tinted ribbons were soon dabbled in a driving sleet; while feathers, instead of wantoning, as it was intended they should do, on the breeze, had to fight a furious battle with the gale.

It was not therefore till the following day – the last of the three appointed – that Lonchamps really showed the brilliant assemblage of carriages, horsemen, and pedestrians that I have described to you. Upon this last day, however, though it was still cold for the season – (England would have been ashamed of such a 17th of April) – the sun did come forth, and smiled in such a sort as greatly to comfort the pious pilgrims.

We remained, like all the rest of Paris, driving up and down in the midst of the pretty crowd till six, when they gradually began to draw off, and all the world went home to dinner.

The early part of this day, which was Good-Friday, had been very differently passed. The same beautiful and solemn music which formerly drew all Paris to the Convent in the

Bois de Boulogne is now performed in several of the churches. We were recommended to hear the choir of St. Roch; and it was certainly the most impressive service at which I was ever present.

There is much wisdom in thus giving to music an important part in the public ceremonies of religion. Nothing commands and enchains the attention with equal power: the ear may be deaf to eloquence, and the thoughts may often grovel earthward, despite all the efforts of the preacher to lead them up to heaven; but few will find it possible to escape from the effect of music; and when it is of such a character as that performed in the Roman Catholic church on Good-Friday, it can hardly be that the most volatile and indifferent listener should depart unmoved.

This service was advertised as 'The Three Hours' Agony.' The crowd assembled to listen to it was immense. It is impossible to speak too highly of the composition of the music; it is conceived in the very highest tone of sublimity; and the deeply effective manner of its performance recalled to me an anecdote I have heard of some young organist, who, having accompanied an anthem in a manner which appeared greatly superior to that of the usual performer, was asked if he had not made some alteration in the composition. 'No,' he replied, 'I have not; but I always read the words when I play.'

So, I should think, did those who performed the services at St. Roch on Good-Friday; and nothing can be imagined more touching and effective than the manner in which the whole of these striking ceremonies were performed and arranged there.

The awful gospel of the day furnished a theme for the impassioned eloquence of several successive preachers; one or two of whom were wonderfully powerful in their manner of recounting the dreadful narrative. They were all quite young men; but they went through the whole of the appalling history with such deep solemnity, such strength of imagery and vehemence of eloquence, as to produce prodigious effect.

At intervals, while the exhausted preachers reposed, the organ, with many stringed instruments, and a choir of exquisite voices, performed the same gospel, in a manner that made one's whole soul thrill and quiver within one. The suffering – the submission – the plaintive yet sublime 'It is

finished!' and the convulsive burst of indignant nature that
followed, showing itself in thunder, hail, and earthquake,
were all brought before the mind with most miraculous
power. I have been told since, that the services at Notre Dame
on that day were finer still; but I really find some difficulty in
believing that this is possible.

During these last and most solemn days of Lent, I have been
endeavouring by every means in my power to discover how
much fasting, of any kind, was going on. If they fast at all, it is
certainly performed in most strict obedience to the very letter
of the gospel: for, assuredly, they 'appear not unto men to
fast,' Everything goes on as gaily as if it were the season of the
carnival. The *restaurans* reek with the savoury vapour of a
hundred dishes; the theatres are opened, and as full as the
churches; invitations cease not; and I can in no direction
perceive the slightest symptom of being among a Roman
Catholic population during a season of penitence.

And yet, contradictory as the statement must appear, I am
deeply convinced that the clergy of the church of Rome feel
more hope of recovered power fluttering at their hearts now,
than they have done at any time during the last half-century.
Nor can I think they are far wrong in this. The share which the
Roman Catholic priests of this our day are said to have had in
the Belgian revolution, and the part, more remarkable still,
which the same race are now performing in the opening scenes
of the fearful struggle which threatens England, has given a
new impulse to the ambition of Rome and of her children.
One may read it in the portly bearing of her youthful priests, –
one may read it in the deep-set meditative eye of those who are
older. It is legible in their brand-new vestments of gold and
silver tissue; it is legible in the costly decorations of their
renovated altars; and deep, deep, deep is the policy which
teaches them to recover with a gentle hand that which they
have lost by a grasping one. How well can I fancy that, in their
secret synods, the favourite text is, 'No man putteth a piece of
new cloth unto an old garment; for that which is put in to fill it
up, taketh from the garment, and the rent is made worse.'
Were they a whit less cautious, they must fail at once; but they
tickle their converts before they think of convincing them. It is
for this that the pulpits are given to young and eloquent men,

who win the eye and ear of their congregations long before they find out to what point they wish to lead them. But while the young men preach, the old men are not idle: there are rumours of new convents, new monasteries, new orders, new miracles, and of new converts, in all directions. This wily, worldly, tranquil-seeming, but most ambitious sect, having in many quarters joined themselves to the cause of democracy, sit quietly by, looking for the result of their work, and watching, like a tiger that seems to doze, for the moment when they may avenge themselves for the long fast from power, during which they have been gnawing their heartstrings.

But they now hail the morning of another day. I would that all English ears could hear, as mine have done, the prattle that prophesies the downfall of our national church as a thing certain as rain after long drought! I would that English ears could hear, as mine have done, the name of O'Connell uttered as that of a new apostle, and his bold bearding of those who yet raise their voices in defence of the faith their fathers gave them, triumphantly quoted in proof of the growing influence both of himself and his popish creed, – which are in truth one and inseparable! But forgive me! – all this has little to do with my subject, and it is moreover a theme I had much better not meddle with. I cannot touch it lightly, for my heart is heavy when I turn to it: I cannot treat it powerfully, for, alas! I have no strength but to lament.

> 'Hé! que puis-je au milieu de ce peuple abattu?
> Benjamin est sans force, et Juda sans vertu.'

LETTER XI

Trial Chamber at the Luxembourg – Institute –
M. Mignet – Concert Musard

As a great and especial favour, we have been taken to see the
new chamber that has been erected at the Luxembourg for the
trial of the political prisoners. The appearance of the exterior is
very handsome, and though built wholly of wood, it
corresponds perfectly, to all outward seeming, with the old
palace. The rich and massive style of architecture is imitated to
perfection: the heavy balustrades, the gigantic bas-reliefs, are
still vast, solid, and magnificent; and when it is stated that the
whole thing has been completed in the space of two months,
one is tempted to believe that Alladdin has turned doctrinaire,
and rubbed his lamp most diligently in the service of the state.

The trial-chamber is a noble room; but from the great
number of prisoners, and greater still of witnesses expected to
be examined, the space left for the public is but small.
Prudence, perhaps, may have had as much to do with this as
necessity; nor can we much wonder if the peers of France
should desire to have as little to do with the Paris mob upon
this occasion as possible.

I remarked that considerable space was left for passages,
ante-rooms, surroundings, and outposts of all sorts; – an
excellent arrangement, the wisdom of which cannot be questioned, as the attendance of a large armed force must be
indispensable. In fact, I believe it ever has been and ever will
be found, that troops furnish the only means of keeping a
remarkably free people in order.

It was, however, very comforting and satisfactory to hear
the manner in which the distinguished and agreeable
individual who had procured us the pleasure of seeing this
building discoursed of the business which was to be carried on
there.

There is a quiet steadiness and confidence in their own strength among these doctrinaires, that seems to promise well for the lasting tranquillity of the country; nor does it impeach either their wisdom or sincerity, if many among them adhere heart and hand to the government, though they might have better liked a white than a tri-coloured banner to wave over the palace of its head. Whatever the standers-by may wish or feel about future struggles and future changes, I think it is certain that no Frenchman who desires the prosperity of his country can at the present moment wish for anything but a continuance of the tranquillity she actually enjoys.

If, indeed, democracy were gaining ground, – if the frightful political fallacies, among which the very young and the very ignorant are so apt to bewilder themselves, were in any degree to be traced in the policy pursued by the existing government, – then would the question be wholly changed, and every honest man in full possession of his senses would feel himself called upon to stay the plague with all his power and might. But the very reverse of all this is evidently the case; and it may be doubted if any sovereign in Europe has less taste for license and misrule than King Louis-Philippe. Be very sure that it is not to him that the radicals of any land must look for patronage, encouragement, or support: they will not find it.

After quitting the Luxembourg, we went to the *bureau* of the secretary at the Institute, to request tickets for an annual sitting of the five Academies, which took place yesterday. They were very obligingly accorded – (O that our institutions, our academies, our lectures, were thus liberally arranged!) – and yesterday we passed two very agreeable hours in the place to which they admitted us.

I wish that the Polytechnic School, when they took a fancy for changing the ancient *régimes* of France, had included the uniform of the Institute in their proscriptions. The improvement would have been less doubtful than it is respecting some other of their innovations: for what can be said in defence of a set of learned academicians, varying in age from light and slender thirty to massive and protuberant fourscore, wearing one and all a fancy blue dress-coat 'embroidered o'er with leaves of myrtle'? It is really a proof that very good things were said and done at this sitting, when

I declare that my astonishment at the Corydon-like costume was forgotten within the first half-hour.

We first witnessed the distribution of the prizes, and then heard one or two members speak, or rather read their compositions. But the great fête of the occasion was hearing a discourse pronounced by M. Mignet. This gentleman is too celebrated not to have excited in us a very earnest wish to hear him; and never was expectation more agreeably gratified. Combined with the advantages of a remarkably fine face and person, M. Mignet has a tone of voice and play of countenance sufficient of themselves to secure the success of an orator. But on this occasion he did not trust to these: his discourse was every way admirable; subject, sentiment, composition, and delivery, all excellent.

He had chosen for his theme the history of Martin Luther's appearance before the Diet at Worms; and the manner in which he treated it surprised as much as it delighted me. Not a single trait of that powerful, steadfast, unbending character, which restored light to our religion and freedom to the mind of man, escaped him: it was a mental portrait, painted with the boldness of outline, breadth of light, and vigour of colouring, which mark the hand of a consummate master.

But was it a Roman Catholic who pronounced this discourse? – Were they Roman Catholics who filled every corner of the theatre, and listened to him with attention so unbroken, and admiration so undisguised? I know not. But for myself, I can truly declare, that my Protestant and reformed feelings were never more gratified than by listening to this eloquent history of the proudest moment of our great apostle's life, pronounced in the centre of Cardinal Mazarin's palace. The concluding words of the discourse were as follows:

'Sommé pendant quatre ans de se soumettre, Luther, pendant quatre ans, dit non. Il avait dit non au légat; il avait dit non au pape; il dit non à l'empéreur. Dans ce non héroïque et fécond se trouvait la liberté du monde.'

Another discourse was announced to conclude the sitting of the day. But when M. Mignet retired, no one appeared to take his place; and after waiting for a few minutes, the numerous and very fashionable-looking crowd dispersed themselves.

I recollected the anecdote told of the first representation of the 'Partie de Chasse de Henri Quatre,' when the overture of Mehul produced such an effect, that the audience would not permit anything else to be performed after it. The piece, therefore, was *remise*, – and so was the harangue of the academician who was to have followed M. Mignet.

You will confess, I think, that we are not idle, when I tell you that, after all this, we went in the evening to *Le Concert Musard*. This is one of the pastimes to which we have hitherto had no parallel in London. At half-past seven o'clock, you lounge into a fine, large, well-lighted room, which is rapidly filled with company: a full and good orchestra give you during a couple of hours some of the best and most popular music of the season; and then you lounge out again, in time to dress for a party, or eat ices at Tortoni's, or soberly to go home for a domestic tea-drinking and early rest. For this concert you pay a franc; and the humble price, together with the style of toilet (every lady wearing a bonnet and shawl), might lead the uninitiated to suppose that it was a recreation prepared for the *beau monde* of the Faubourg; but the long line of private carriages that occupies the street at the conclusion of it, shows that, simple and unpretending as is its style, this concert has attractions for the best company in Paris.

The easy *entrée* to it reminded me of the theatres of Germany. I remarked many ladies coming in, two or three together, unattended by any gentleman. Between the acts, the company promenaded round the room, parties met and joined, and altogether it appeared to us a very agreeable mode of gratifying that French necessity of amusing one's self out of one's own house, which seems contagious in the very air of Paris.

LETTER XII

Easter-Sunday at Notre Dame – Archbishop – View of Paris –
Victor Hugo – Hôtel Dieu – Mr. Jefferson

It was long ago decided in a committee of the whole house, that on Easter-Sunday we should attend high mass at Notre Dame. I shall not soon forget the spectacle that greeted us on entering. Ten thousand persons, it was said, were on that day assembled in the church; and its dimensions are so vast, that I have no doubt the statement was correct, for it was crowded from floor to roof. The effect of the circular gallery, that at mid-height encompasses the centre aisle, following as it does the graceful sweep of the chapel behind the altar, and filled row after row with gaily-dressed company up, as it seemed, almost to the groining of the roof, was beautiful. The chairs on this occasion were paid for in proportion to the advantageousness of the position in which they stood, and by disbursing an extra franc or two we obtained very good places. The mass was performed with great splendour. The dresses of the archbishop and his train were magnificent; and when this splendid, princely-looking personage, together with his court of dignitaries and priests, paraded the Host round the church and up the crowded aisle spite of the close-wedged throng, they looked like a stream of liquid gold, that by its own weight made way through every obstacle. The archbishop is a mild and amiable-looking man, and ceased not to scatter blessings from his lips and sprinkle safety from his fingers'-ends upon the admiring people, as slowly and gracefully he passed among them.

The latter years of this prelate's life have been signalized by some remarkable changes. He has seen the glories and the penitences of his church alike the favourite occupation of his king; – he has seen that king and his highest nobles walking in holy procession through the streets of Paris; – he has seen that same king banished from his throne and his country, a proscribed and melancholy exile, while the pomp and parade of his cherished faith were forbidden to offend the people's eyes by any longer pouring forth its gorgeous superstitions into the streets; – he has seen his own consecrated palace razed to its foundation, and its very elements scattered to the winds; – and now, this self-same prelate sees himself again well received at the court whence Charles Dix was banished; and, stranger still, perhaps, he sees his startled flock once more assembling round him, quietly and silently, but steadily and in earnest; while he who, within five short years was trembling for his life, now lifts his head again, and not only in safety, but, with all his former power and pride of place, is permitted to

'Chanter les *oremus*, faire des processions,
Et répandre à grands flots les bénédictions.'

It is true, indeed, that there are no longer any Roman Catholic processions to be seen in the streets of Paris; but if we look within the churches, we find that the splendour concentrated there, has lost nothing of its impressive sumptuousness by thus changing the scene of its display.

The service of this day, as far as the music was concerned, was in my opinion infinitely less impressive than that of Good-Friday at St. Roch. This doubtless arose in a great degree from the style of composition; but I suspect, moreover, that my imagination was put out of humour by seeing about fifty fiddlers, with every appearance of being (what they actually were) the orchestra of the opera, performing from a space enclosed for them at the entrance of the choir. The singing men and boys were also stationed in the same unwonted and unecclesiastical place, and though some of those hired for the occasion had very fine Italian voices, they had all the air of singing without 'reading the words;' and, on the whole, my ear and my fancy were disappointed.

Victor Hugo's description of old Paris as seen from the towers of Notre Dame sent us labouring to their summit. The state of the atmosphere was very favourable, and I was delighted to find that the introduction of coal, rapid as its progress has lately been, has not yet tinged the bright clear air sufficiently to prevent this splendid panorama from being distinctly seen to its remotest edge. That impenetrable mass of dun, dull smoke, that we look down upon whenever a mischievous imp of curiosity lures us to the top of any dome, tower, or obelisk in London, can hardly fail of making one remember every weary step which led to the profitless elevation; but one must be tired indeed to remember fatigue while looking down upon the bright, warm, moving miniature spread out below the towers of Notre Dame.

What an intricate world of roofs it is! – and how mystically incomprehensible are the ins and outs, the bridges and the islands, of the idle Seine! A raft, caught sight of at intervals, bearing wood or wine; a floating wash-house, with its line of bending naïads, looking like a child's toy with figures all of a row; and here and there a floating-bath, – are all this river shows of its power to aid and assist the magnificent capital which has so strangely chosen to stretch herself along its banks. When one thinks of the forest of masts which we see covering whole miles of extent in London, it seems utterly unintelligible how that which is found needful for the necessities of one great city should appear so perfectly unnecessary for another.

Victor Hugo's picture of the scene he has fancied beneath the towers of Notre Dame in the days of his Esmeralda is sketched with amazing spirit; though probably Paris was no more like the pretty panorama he makes of it than Timbuctoo. I heartily wish, however, that he would confine himself to the representation of still-life, and let his characters be all of innocent bricks and mortar: for even though they do look shadowy and somewhat doubtful in the distance, they have infinitely more nature and truth than can be found among all his horrible imaginings concerning his fellow-creatures.

His descripton of the old church itself, too, is delicious: for though it has little of architectural reality or strict graphic fidelity about it, there is such a powerful air of truth in every word he says respecting it, that one looks out and about upon the rugged stones, and studies every angle, buttress, and parapet, and the lively interest of old acquaintance.

I should like to have a legend, as fond and lingering in its descriptions, attached to some of our glorious and mysterious old Gothic cathedrals at home. This sort of reading gives a pleasure in which imagination and reality are very happily blended; and I can fancy nothing more agreeable than following an able romancer up and down, through and amongst, in and out, the gloomy, shadowy, fanciful, unintelligible intricacies of such a structure. How well might Winchester, for instance, with its solemn crypts, its sturdy Saxon strength, its quaintly-coffined relics of royal bones, its Gothic shrines, its monumental splendour, and its stately magnitude, furnish forth the material for some such spirit-stirring record!

Having spent an hour of first-rate interest and gratification in wandering inside and outside of this very magnificent church, we crossed the Place, or *Parvis*, of Notre Dame, to see the celebrated hospital of the Hôtel Dieu. It is very particularly large, clean, airy, and well-ordered in every way; and I never saw sick people look less miserable than some scores of men and women did, tucked snugly up in their neat little beds, and most of them with a friend or relative at their side to console or amuse them.

The access to the wards of this building is as free as that into a public bazaar; but there is one caution used in the admission of company which, before I understood it, puzzled me greatly. There are three doors at the top of the fine flight of steps which leads to the building. The centre one is used only as an exit; at the other two are placed guards, one a male, the other a female. Through these side-doors all who enter must pass – the men on one side, the women on the other; and all must submit to be pretty strictly examined, to see that they are conveying nothing either to eat or drink that might be injurious to the invalids.

The covered bridge which opens from the back part of the Hôtel Dieu, connecting *l'Isle de la Cité* with the left bank of the Seine, with its light glass roof, and safe shelter from wind, dust, or annoyance of any kind, forms a delightful promenade for the convalescent.

The evening of this day we spent at a *soirée*, where we met, among many other pleasant persons, a very sensible and gentlemanlike American. I had the pleasure of a long conversation with him, during which he said many things extremely worth listening to. This gentleman has held many distinguished diplomatic situations, appears to have acquired a great deal of general information, and moreover to have given much attention to the institutions and character of his own country.

He told me that Jefferson had been the friend of his early life; that he knew his sentiments and opinions on all subjects intimately well, and much better than those who were acquainted with them no otherwise than by his published writings. He assured me most positively that Jefferson was NOT a democrat in principle, but believed it expedient to promulgate the doctrine, as the only one which could excite the general feeling of the people, and make them hang together till they should have acquired strength sufficient to be reckoned as one among the nations. He said, that Jefferson's ulterior hope for America was, that she should, after having acquired this strength, give birth to men distinguished both by talent and fortune; that when this happened, an enlightened and powerful aristocracy might be hoped for, without which HE KNEW that no country could be really great or powerful.

As I am assured that the word of this gentleman may be depended on, these observations – or rather, I should say, statements – respecting Jefferson appear to me worth noting.

LETTER XIII

'Le Monomane'

As a distinguished specimen of fashionable horror, I went last night to the Porte St. Martin to see 'The Monomane,' a drama in five acts, from the pen of a M. Duveyrier. I hardly know whether to give you a sketch of this monstrous outrage against common sense or not; but I think I will do so, because I flatter myself that no one will be silly enough to translate it into English, or import it in any shape into England; and, therefore, if I do not tell you something about it, you may chance to die without knowing to what prodigious lengths a search after absurdity may carry men.

But first let me mention, as not the least extraordinary part of the phenomenon, that the theatre was crowded from floor to roof, and that Shakespeare was never listened to with attention more profound. However, it does not follow that approval or admiration of any kind was either the cause or the effect of this silent contemplation of the scene: no one could be more devoted to the business of the hour than myself, but most surely this was not the result of approbation.

If I am not very clear respecting the plot, you must excuse me, from my want of habitual expertness in such an analysis; but the main features and characters cannot escape me.

An exceedingly amiable and highly intellectual gentleman is the hero of this piece; a part personated by a M. Lockroi with a degree of ability deserving a worthier employment. This amiable man holds at Colmar the office of *procureur du roi*; and, from the habit of witnessing trials, acquires so vehement a passion for the shedding of blood on the scaffold, that it amounts to a mania. To illustrate this singular trait of character, M. Balthazar develops his secret feelings in an opening speech to an intimate friend. In this speech, which really contains some very good lines, he dilates with much

59

enthusiasm on the immense importance which he conceives to attach to the strict and impartial administration of criminal justice. No man could deliver himself more judgelike and wisely; but how or why such very rational and sober opinions should lead to an unbounded passion for blood, is very difficult to understand.

The next scene, however, shows the *procureur du roi* hugging himself with a kind of mysterious rapture at the idea of an approaching execution, and receiving with a very wild and mad-like sort of agony some attempts to prove the culprit innocent. The execution takes place; and after it is over, the innocence of the unfortunate victim is fully proved.

The amiable and excellent *procureur du roi* is greatly moved at this; but his repentant agony is soon walked off by a few well-trod melodramatic turns up and down the stage; and he goes on again, seizing with ecstasy upon every opportunity of bringing the guilty to justice.

What the object of the author can possibly be in making out that a man is mad solely because he wishes to do his duty, I cannot even guess. It is difficult to imagine an honest-minded magistrate uttering more commonplace, uncontrovertible truths upon the painful duties of his station, than does this unfortunate gentleman.

M. Victor Hugo, speaking of himself in one of his prefaces, says, 'Il (Victor Hugo) continuera donc fermement; et chaque fois qu'il croira nécessaire de faire bien voir à tous, dans ses moindres détails, une idée utile, une idée sociale, une idée humaine, il posera le théâtre déssus comme un verre grossissant.'*

It strikes me that M. Duveyrier, the ingenious author of the Monomane, must work upon the same principle, and that in this piece he thinks he has put a magnifying-glass upon 'une idée sociale.'

But I must return to my analysis of this drama of five mortal acts. – After the execution, the real perpetrator of the murder for which the unfortunate victim of legal enthusiasm has

---

* *Translation* – He will continue then firmly; and every time that he shall think it necessary to make visible to all, in its least details, a useful idea, a social idea, a humane idea, he will place upon it the theatre, as a magnifying-glass.

innocently suffered appears on the scene. He is brought sick or wounded into the house of a physician, with whom the *procureur du roi* and his wife are on a visit. Balthazar sees the murderer conveyed to bed in a chamber that opens from that of his friend the doctor. He then goes to bed himself with his wife, and appears to have fallen asleep without delay, for we presently see him in this state come forth from his chamber upon a gallery, from whence a flight of stairs descends upon the stage. We see him walk down these stairs, – take some instrument out of a case belonging to the doctor, – enter the apartment where the murderer has been lodged, – return, – replace the instrument, – wash his bloody hands and wipe them upon a hand-towel, – then reascend the staircase and enter his lady's room at the top of it; all of which is performed in the silence of profound sleep.

The attention which hung upon the whole of this long silent scene was such, that one might have supposed the lives of the audience depended upon their not waking this murderous sleeper by any sound; and the applause which followed the mute performance, when once the awful *procureur du roi* was again safely lodged in his chamber, was deafening.

The following morning it is discovered that the sick stranger has been murdered; and instantly the *procureur du roi*, with his usual ardour in discovering the guilty, sets most ably to work upon the investigation of every circumstance which may throw light upon this horrible transaction. Everything, particularly the case of instruments, of which one is bloody, and the hand-towel found in his room, stained with the same accusing dye – all tends to prove that the poor innocent physician is the murderer: he is accordingly taken up, tried, and condemned.

This unfortunate young doctor has an uncle, of the same learned profession, who is addicted to the science of animal magnetism. This gentleman having some suspicion that Balthazar is himself the guilty person, imagines a very cunning device by which he may be made to betray himself if guilty. He determines to practise his magnetism upon him in full court while he is engaged in the duties of his high office, and flatters himself that he shall be able to throw him into a sleep or trance, in which state he may *par hasard* let out something of the truth.

This admirable contrivance answers perfectly. The attorney-general does fall into a most profound sleep the moment the old doctor begins his magnetising manoeuvres, and in this state not only relates aloud every circumstance of the murder, but, to give this confession more sure effect, he writes it out fairly, and sets his name to it, being profoundly asleep the whole time.

And here it is impossible to avoid remarking on the extreme ill fortune which attends the sleeping hours of this amiable attorney-general. At one time he takes a nap, and kills a man without knowing anything of the matter; and then, in a subsequent state of oblivion, he confesses it, still without knowing anything of the matter.

As soon as the unfortunate gentleman has finished the business for which he was put to sleep, he is awakened, and the paper is shown to him. He scruples not immediately to own his handwriting, which, sleeping or waking, it seems, was the same; but testifies the greatest horror and aston- ishment at the information the document contains, which was quite as unexpected to himself as to the rest of the company.

His high office, however, we must presume exempts him from all responsibility; for the only result of the discovery is an earnest recommendation from his friends, particularly the old and young doctors, that he should travel for the purpose of recovering his spirits.

There is a little episode, by the way, from which we learn, that once, in one of his alarming slumbers, this amiable but unfortunate man gave symptoms of wishing to murder his wife and child; in consequence of which, it is proposed by the doctors that this tour for the restoration of his spirits should be made without them. To this separation Balthazar strongly objects, and tells his beautiful wife, with much tenderness, that he shall find it very dull without her.

To this the lady, though naturally rather afraid of him, answers with great sweetness, that in that case she shall be extremely happy to go with him; adding tenderly, that she would willingly die to prove her devotion.

Nothing could be so unfortunate as this expression. At the bare mention of his hobby-horse, *death*, his malady revives, and he instantly manifests a strong inclination to murder her, – and this time without even the ceremony of going to sleep.

Big with the darling thought, his eyes rolling, his cheek pale, his bristling hair on end, and the awful genius of Melodrame swelling in every vein, Balthazar seats himself on the sofa beside his trembling wife, and taking the comb out of her (Mademoiselle Noblet's) beautiful hair, appears about to strangle her in the rope of jet that he pulls out to its utmost length, and twists, and twists, and twists, till one really feels a cold shiver from head to foot. But at length, at the very moment when matters seem drawing to a close, the lady throws herself lovingly on his bosom, and his purpose changes, or at least for a moment seems to change, and he relaxes his hold.

At this critical juncture the two doctors enter. Balthazar looks at them wildly, then at his wife, then at the doctors again, and finally tells them all that he must beg leave to retire for a few moments. He passes through the group, who look at him in mournful silence; but as he approaches the door, he utters the word 'poison,' then enters, and locks and bolts it after him.

Upon this the lady screams, and the two doctors fly for a crow-bar. The door is burst open, and the *procureur du roi* comes forward, wide awake, but having swallowed the poison he had mentioned.

This being 'the last scene of all that ends this strange eventful history,' the curtain falls upon the enthusiastic attorney-general as he expires in the arms of his wife and friends.

We are always so apt, when we see anything remarkably absurd abroad, to flatter ourselves with the belief that nothing like it exists at home, that I am almost afraid to draw a parallel between this inconceivable trash, and the very worst and vilest piece that ever was permitted to keep possession of the stage in England, lest some one better informed on the subject than myself should quote some British enormity unknown to me, and so prove my patriotic theory false.

Nevertheless, I cannot quit the subject without saying, that as far as my knowledge and belief go, English people never did sit by hundreds and listen patiently to such stuff as this.

There is no very atrocious vice, no terrific wickedness in the piece, as far as I could understand its recondite philosophy; but its silliness surely possesses the silliness of a little child. The grimaces, the dumb show, the newly-invented passions, and the series of impossible events, which drag through these five longsome acts, seem to show a species of anomaly in the human mind that composed the piece, to which I imagine no parallel can be found on record.

Is this the result of the march of mind? – is it the fruit of that universal diffusion of knowledge which we are told is at work throughout the world, but most busily in France? . . . I shall never understand the mystery, let me meditate upon it as long as I will. No! never shall I understand how a French audience, lively, witty, acute, and prone to seize upon whatever is ridiculous, can thus sit night after night with profound gravity, and the highest apparent satisfaction, to witness the incredible absurdity of such a piece as 'Le Monomane.'

There is one way, and one way only, in which the success of this drama can be accounted for intelligibly. May it not be, that 'LES JEUNES GENS,' wanton in their power, have determined in merry mood to mystify their fellow-citizens by passing a favourable judgment upon this tedious performance? And may they not now be enjoying the success of their plot in ecstasies of private laughter, at seeing how meekly the dutiful Parisians go nightly to the Porte St. Martin, and sit in obedient admiration of what it has pleased their youthful tyrants to denominate 'a fine drama'?

But I must leave off guessing; for, as the wise man saith, 'the finding out of parables is a wearisome labour of the mind.'

Some critic, speaking of the new school of French drama-tists, says that 'they have heaved the ground under the feet of Racine and Corneille.' If this indeed be so, the best thing that the lovers of tragedy can do is to sit at home and wait patiently till the earth settles itself again from the shock of so deplorable an earthquake. That it will settle itself again, I have neither doubt nor fear. Nonsense has nothing of immortality in its nature; and when the storm which has scattered all this frothy scum upon us shall have fairly blown over and passed away, then I suspect that Corneille and Racine will still find solid standing-ground on the soil of France; – nay, should they by chance find also that their old niches in the temple of her great men remain vacant, it is likely enough that they may be again invited to take possession of them; and they may keep it too perhaps for a few more hundred years, with very little danger that any greater than they should arrive to take their places.

LETTER XIV

The Gardens of the Tuileries – Legitimatist – Republican – Doctrinaire – Children – Dress of the Ladies – Of the Gentlemen – Black Hair – Unrestricted Admission – Anecdote

Is there anything in the world that can be fairly said to resemble the Gardens of the Tuileries? I should think not. It is a whole made up of so many strongly-marked and peculiar features, that it is not probable any other place should be found like it. To my fancy, it seems one of the most delightful scenes in the world; and I never enter there, though it is long since the enchantment of novelty made any part of the charm, without a fresh feeling of enjoyment.

The *locale* itself, independent of the moving throng which for ever seems to dwell within it, is greatly to my taste: I love all the detail of its embellishment, and I dearly love the bright and happy aspect of the whole. But on this subject I know there are various opinions: many talk with distaste of the straight lines, the clipped trees, the formal flower-beds, the ugly roofs, – nay, some will even abuse the venerable orange-trees themselves, because they grow in square boxes, and do not wave their boughs in the breeze like so many ragged willow-trees.

But I agree not with any one of these objections; and should think it as reasonable, and in as good taste, to quarrel with Westminster Abbey because it did not look like a Grecian temple, as to find fault with the Gardens of the Tuileries because they are arranged like French pleasure-grounds, and not like an English park. For my own part, I profess that I would not, if I had the power, change even in the least degree a single feature in this pleasant spot: enter it at what hour or at what point I will, it ever seems to receive me with smiles and gladness.

We seldom suffer a day to pass without refreshing our spirits by sitting for a while amidst its shade and its flowers. From the part of the town where we are now dwelling, the gate oppossite the Place Vendôme is our nearest entrance; and perhaps from no point does the lively beauty of the whole scene show itself better than from beneath the green roof of the terrace-walk, to which this gate admits us.

To the right, the dark mass of unshorn trees, now rich with the flowers of the horse-chestnut, and growing as boldly and as loftily as the most English-hearted gardener could desire, leads the eye through a very delicious 'continuity of shade' to the magnificent gate that opens upon the Place Louis-Quinze. To the left is the widely-spreading façade of the Tuileries Palace, the ungraceful elevation of the pavilion roofs, well nigh forgotten, and quite atoned for by the beauty of the gardens at their feet. Then, just where the shade of the high trees ceases, and the bright blaze of sunshine begins, what multitudes of sweet flowers are seen blushing in its beams! An universal lilac bloom seems at this season to spread itself over the whole space; and every breeze that passes by, comes to us laden with perfume. My daily walk is almost always the same, – I love it so well that I do not like to change it. Following the shady terrace by which we enter to the point where it sinks down to the level of the magnificent esplanade in front of the palace, we turn to the right, and endure the splendid brightness till we reach the noble walk leading from the gateway of the centre pavilion, through flowers, statues, orange-trees, and chestnut-groves, as far as the eye can reach, till it reposes at last upon the lofty arch of the Barrière de l'Etoile.

This *coup-d'oeil* is so beautiful, that I constantly feel renewed pleasure when I look upon it. I do indeed confess myself to be one of those 'who in trim gardens take their pleasure.' I love the studied elegance, the carefully-selected grace of every object permitted to meet the pampered eye in such a spot as this. I love these fondly-nurtured princely exotics, the old orange-trees, ranged in their long stately rows; and better still do I love the marble groups, that stand so nobly, sometimes against the bright blue sky, and sometimes half concealed in the dark setting of the trees. Everything seems to speak of taste, luxury, and elegance.

Having indulged in a lingering walk from the palace to the point at which the sunshine ceases and the shade begins, a new species of interest and amusement awaits us. Thousands of chairs scattered just within the shelter of this inviting covert are occupied by an interminable variety of pretty groups.

I wonder how many months of constant attendance there, it would take before I should grow weary of studying the whole and every separate part of this bright picture? It is really matchless in beauty as a spectacle, and unequalled in interest as a national study. All Paris may in turn be seen and examined there; and nowhere is it so easy to distinguish specimens of the various and strongly-marked divisions of the people.

This morning we took possession of half a dozen chairs under the trees which front the beautiful group of Petus and Aria. It was the hour when all the newspapers are in the greatest requisition; and we had the satisfaction of watching the studies of three individuals, each of whom might have sat as a model for an artist who wished to give an idea of their several peculiarities. We saw, in short, beyond the possibility of doubt, a royalist, a doctrinaire, and a republican, during the half hour we remained there, all soothing their feelings by indulging in two sous' worth of politics, each in his own line.

A stiff but gentleman-like old man first came, and having taken a journal from the little octagon stand – which journal we felt quite sure was either 'La France' or 'La Quotidienne' – he established himself at no great distance from us. Why it was that we all felt so certain of his being a legitimatist I can hardly tell you, but not one of the party had the least doubt about it. There was a quiet, half-proud, half-melancholy air of keeping himself apart; an aristocratical cast of features; a pale care-worn complexion; and a style of dress which no vulgar man ever wore, but which no rich one would be likely to wear today. This is all I can record of him: but there was something pervading his whole person too essentially loyal to be misunderstood, yet too delicate in its tone to be coarsely painted. Such as it was, however, we felt it quite enough to make the matter sure; and if I could find out that old gentleman to be either doctrinaire or republican, I never would look on a human countenance again in order to discover what was passing within.

The next who approached us we were equally sure was a republican: but here the discovery did little honour to our discernment; for these gentry choose to leave no doubt upon the subject of their *clique*, but contrive that every article contributing to the appearance of the outward man shall become a symbol and a sign, a token and a stigma, of the madness that possesses them. He too held a paper in his hand, and without venturing to approach too nearly to so alarming a personage, we scrupled not to assure each other that the journal he was so assiduously perusing was 'Le Réformateur.'

Just as we had decided what manner of man it was who was stalking so majestically past us, a comfortable-looking citizen approached in the uniform of the National Guard, who sat himself down to his daily allowance of politics with the air of a person expecting to be well pleased with what he finds, but nevertheless too well contented with himself and all things about him to care overmuch about it. Every line of this man's jocund face, every curve of his portly figure, spoke contentment and well-being. He was probably one of that very new race in France, a tradesman making a rapid fortune. Was it possible to doubt that the paper in his hand was 'Le Journal des Débats?' was it possible to believe that this man was other than a prosperous doctrinaire?

Thus, on the neutral ground furnished by these delightful gardens, hostile spirits meet with impunity, and, though they mingle not, enjoy in common the delicious privileges of cool shade, fresh air, and the idle luxury of an *al fresco* newspaper, in the midst of a crowded and party-split city, with as much certainty of being unchallenged and uninterrupted as if each were wandering alone in a princely domain of his own.

Such, too, as are not over splenetic may find a very lively variety of study in watching the ways of the little dandies and dandiesses who, at some hours of the day, swarm like so many humming-birds amidst the shade and sunshine of the Tuileries. Either these little French personages are marvellously well-behaved, or there is some superintending care which prevents screaming; for I certainly never saw so many young things assembled together who indulged so

Morning at the Tuileries.

rarely in that salutary exercise of the lungs which makes one so often tremble at the approach of

'Soft infancy, that nothing can, but cry.'

The costumes of these pretty creatures contribute not a little to the amusement; it is often so whimsical as to give them the appearance of miniature maskers. I have seen little fellows beating a hoop in the full uniform of a National Guard; others waddling under the mimicry of kilted Highlanders; and small ladies without number in every possible variety of unbabylike apparel.

The entertainment to be derived from sitting in the Tuileries Gardens and studying costume is, however, by no means confined to the junior part of the company. In no country have I ever seen anything approaching in grotesque habiliments to some of the figures daily and hourly met lounging about these walks. But such vagaries are confined wholly to the male part of the population; it is very rare to see a woman outrageously dressed in any way; and if you do, the chances are five hundred to one that she is not a Frenchwoman. An air of quiet elegant neatness is, I think, the most striking characteristic of the walking costume of the French ladies. All the little minor finishings of the female toilet appear to be more sedulously cared for than the weightier matters of the pelisse and gown. Every lady you meet is *bien chaussée, bien gantée*. Her ribbons, if they do not match her dress, are sure to accord with it; and for all the delicate garniture that comes under the care of the laundress, it should seem that Paris alone, of all the earth, knows how to iron.

The whimsical caprices of male attire, on the contrary, defy anything like general remark; unless, indeed, it be that the air of Paris appears to have the quality of turning all the *imperials, favoris*, and *moustaches* which dwell within its walls to jetty blackness. At a little distance, the young men have really the air of having their faces tied up with black ribbon as a cure for the mumps; and, handsome as this dark *chevelure* is generally allowed to be, the heavy uniformity of it at present very considerably lessens its striking effect. When every man has his face half covered with black hair, it ceases to be a very valuable distinction. Perhaps, too, the frequent advertisements of compositions infallible in their power of turning the hair to any colour except 'what pleases God,' may tend to make one look with suspicious eyes at these once fascinating southern decorations; but, at present, I take it to be an undoubted fact, that a clean, close-shaven, northern-looking gentleman is valued at a high premium in every *salon* in Paris.

It is not to be denied that the 'glorious and immortal days' have done some injury to the general appearance of the Tuileries Gardens. Before this period, no one was permitted to enter them dressed in a *blouse*, or jacket, or *casquette*; and no one, either male or female, might carry bundles or baskets through these pretty regions, sacred to relaxation and holiday enjoyment. But liberty and unseemly sordiness of attire being somehow or other jumbled together in the minds of the sovereign mob, – not sovereign either – the mob is only vice-regal in Paris as yet; – but the mob, however, such as it is, has obtained, as a mark of peculiar respect and favour to themselves, a new law or regulation, by which it is enacted that these royal precincts may become like unto Noah's ark, and that both clean and unclean beasts may enter here.

Could one wish for a better specimen of the sort of advantage to be gained by removing the restraint of authority in order to pamper the popular taste for what they are pleased to call freedom? Not one of the persons who enter the gardens now, were restricted from entering them before; only it was required that they should be decently clad; – that is to say, in such garments as they were accustomed to wear on Sunday or any other holiday; the only occasions, one should imagine, on which the working classes could wish to profit by permission to promenade in a public garden: but the obligation to appear clean in the garden of the king's palace was an infringement on their liberty, so that formality is dispensed with; and they have now obtained the distinguished and ennobling privilege of being as dirty and ill-dressed as they like.

The power formerly intrusted to the sentinel, wherever there was one stationed, of refusing the *entrée* to all persons not properly dressed, gave occasion once to a saucy outbreaking of French wit in one of the National Guard, which was amusing enough. This civic guardian was stationed at the gates of a certain *Mairie* on some public occasion, with the usual injunction not to permit any person '*mal-mise*' to enter. An *incroyable* presented himself, not dressed in the fashion, but immoderately beyond it. The sentinel looked at him, and lowered his piece across the entrance, pronouncing in a voice of authority –

'You cannot enter.'

'Not enter?' exclaimed the astonished beau, looking down at the exquisite result of his laborious toilet; 'not enter? – forbid me to enter, sir? – impossible! What is it you mean? Let me pass, I say!'

The imperturbable sentinel stood like a rock before the entrance: 'My orders are precise,' he said, 'and I may not infringe them.'

'Precise? Your orders precise to refuse me?'

'Oui, monsieur, précis, de refuser qui que ce soit que je trouve mal-mis.'

LETTER XV

My last letter was of the Tuileries Gardens; a theme which furnished me so many subjects of admiration, that I think, if only for the sake of variety, I will let the smelfungus vein prevail today. Such, then, being my humour, – or my ill-humour, if you will, – I shall indulge it by telling you what I think of the street-police of Paris.

I will not tell you that it is bad, for that, I doubt not, many others may have done before me; but I will tell you that I consider it as something wonderful, mysterious, incomprehensible, and perfectly astonishing.

In a city where everything intended to meet the eye is converted into graceful ornament; where the shops and coffee-houses have the air of fairy palaces, and the markets show fountains wherein the daintiest naïads might delight to bathe; – in such a city as this, where the women look too delicate to belong wholly to earth, and the men too watchful and observant to suffer the winds of heaven to visit them too roughly; – in such a city as this, you are shocked and disgusted at every step you take, or at every gyration that the wheels of your chariot can make, by sights and smells that may not be described.

Every day brings my astonishment on this subject to a higher pitch than the one which preceded it; for every day brings with it fresh conviction that a very considerable portion of the enjoyment of life is altogether destroyed in Paris by the neglect or omission of such a degree of municipal interference as might secure the most elegant people in the world from the loathsome disgust occasioned by the perpetual outrage of common decency in their streets.

74

On this branch of the subject it is impossible to say more; but there are other points on which the neglect of street-police is as plainly, though less disgustingly, apparent; and some of these I will enumerate for your information, as they may be described without impropriety; but when they are looked at in conjunction with the passion for graceful decoration, so decidedly a characteristic of the French people, they offer to our observation an incongruity so violent, as to puzzle in no ordinary degree whoever may wish to explain it.

You cannot at this season pass through any street in Paris, however pre-eminently fashionable from its situation, or however distinguished by the elegance of those who frequent it, without being frequently obliged to turn aside, that you may not run against two or more women covered with dust, and probably with vermin, who are busily employed in pulling their flock mattresses to pieces in the street. There they stand or sit, caring for nobody, but combing, turning, and shaking the wool upon all comers and goers; and, finally, occupying the space round which many thousand passengers are obliged to make what is always an inconvenient, and sometimes a very dirty *détour*, by poking the material, cleared from the filth, which has passed into the throats of the gentlemen and ladies of Paris, back again into its checked repository.

I have within this half-hour passed from the Italian Boulevard by the Opera-house, in the front of which this obscene and loathsome operation was being performed by a solitary old crone, who will doubtless occupy the place she has chosen during the whole day, and carry away her bed just in time to permit the Duke of Orleans to step from his carriage into the Opera without tumbling over it, but certainly not in time to prevent his having a great chance of receiving as he passes some portion of the various animate and inanimate superfluities which for so many hours she has been scattering to the air.

A few days ago I saw a well-dressed gentleman receive a severe contusion on the head, and the most overwhelming destruction to the neatness of his attire, in consequence of a fall occasioned by his foot getting entangled in the apparatus of a street-walking tinker, who had his charcoal fire, bellows, melting-pot, and all other things necessary for carrying on the tinning trade in a small way, spread forth on the pavement of the Rue de Provence.

When the accident happened, many persons were passing, all of whom seemed to take a very obliging degree of interest in the misfortune of the fallen gentleman; but not a syllable either of remonstrance or remark was uttered concerning the invasion of the highway by the tinker; nor did that wandering individual himself appear to think any apology called for, or any change in the arrangement of his various chattels necessary.

Whenever a house is to be built or repaired in London, the first thing done is to surround the premises with a high paling, that shall prevent any of the operations that are going on within it from annoying in any way the public in the street. The next thing is to arrange a footpath round this paling, carefully protected by posts and rails, so that this unavoidable invasion of the ordinary footpath may be productive of as little inconvenience as possible.

Were you to pass a spot in Paris under similar circumstances, you would fancy that some tremendous accident – a fire, perhaps, or the falling in of a roof – had occasioned a degeee of difficulty and confusion to the passengers which it was impossible to suppose could be suffered to remain an hour unremedied: but it is, on the contrary, permitted to continue, to the torment and danger of daily thousands, for months together, without the slightest notice or objection on the part of the municipal authorities. If a cart be loading or unloading in the street, it is permitted to take and keep a position the most inconvenient, in utter disregard of any danger or delay which it may and must occasion to the carriages and foot-passengers who have to travel round it.

Nuisances and abominations of all sorts are without scruple committed to the street at any hour of the day or night, to await the morning visit of the scavenger to remove them: and happy indeed is it for the humble pedestrian if his eye and nose alone suffer from these ejectments; happy, indeed, if he comes not in contact with them, as they make their unceremonious exit from window or door. 'Quel bonheur!' is the exclamation if he escapes; but a look, wholly in sorrow and nowise in anger, is the only helpless resource should he be splashed from head to foot.

On the subject of that monstrous barbarism, a gutter in the middle of the streets expressly formed for the reception of filth, which is still permitted to deform the greater portion of this beautiful city, I can only say, that the patient endurance of it by men and women of the year one thousand eight hundred and thirty-five is a mystery difficult to understand.

It really appears to me, that almost the only thing in the world which other men do, but which Frenchmen cannot, is the making of sewers and drains. After an hour or two of very violent rain last week, that part of the Place Louis-Quinze which is near the entrance to the Champs Elysées remained covered with water. The Board of Works having waited for a day or two to see what would happen, and finding that the muddy lake did not disappear, commanded the assistance of twenty-six able-bodied labourers, who set about digging just such a channel as little boys amuse themselves by making beside a pond. By this well-imagined engineering exploit, the stagnant water was at length conducted to the nearest gutter; the pickaxes were shouldered, and an open muddy channel left to adorn this magnificent area, which, were a little finishing bestowed upon it, would probably be the finest point that any city in the world could boast.

Perhaps it will hardly be fair to set it amongst my complaints against the streets of Paris, that they have not yet adopted our last and most luxurious improvement. I cannot but observe, however, that having passed some weeks here, I feel that the Macadamised streets of London ought to become the subject of a metropolitan jubilee among us. The exceeding noise of Paris, proceeding either from the uneven structure of the pavement, or from the defective construction of wheels and springs, is so violent and incessant as to appear like the effect of one great continuous cause, – a sort of demon torment, which it must require great length of use to enable one to endure without suffering. Were a cure for this sought in the Macadamising of the streets, an additional advantage, by the bye, would be obtained, from the difficulties it would throw in the way of the future heroes of a barricade.

There is another defect, however, and one much more easily remedied, which may fairly, I think, come under the head of defective street-police. This is the profound darkness of every part of the city in which there are not shops illuminated by the owners of them with gas. This is done so brilliantly on the Boulevards by the *cafés* and *restaurans*, that the dim old-fashioned lamp suspended at long intervals across the *pavé* is forgotten. But no sooner is this region of light and gaiety left, than you seem to plunge into outer darkness; and there is not a little country town in England which is not incomparably better lighted than any street in Paris which depends for its illumination upon the public regulations of the city.

As it is evident that gas-pipes must be actually laid in all directions in order to supply the individuals who employ it in their houses, I could in no way understand why these most dismal *réverbères*, with their dingy oil, were to be made use of in preference to the beautiful light which almost outblazes that of the sun; but I am told that some unexpired contract between Paris and her lamplighters is the cause of this. Were the convenience of the public as sedulously studied in France as in England, not all the claims of all the lamplighters in the world, let it cost what it might to content them, would keep her citizens groping in darkness when it was so very easy to give them light.

But not to dwell ungratefully upon the grievances which certainly disfigure this city of delight, I will not multiply instances; yet I am sure I may assert, without fear of contradiction or reproach, that such a street-police as that of London would be one of the greatest civic blessings that King Philippe could possibly bestow upon his '*belle ville de Paris*'.

LETTER XVI

Preparations for the Fête du Roi – Arrival of Troops – Champs Elysées – Concert in the Garden of the Tuileries – Silence of the People – Fireworks

May 2, 1835

For several days past we have been watching the preparations for the King's fête, which though not quite equal to those in the days of the Emperor, when all the fountains in Paris ran wine, were on a large and splendid scale, and if more sober, were perhaps not less princely. Temporary theatres, ballrooms, and orchestras in the Champs Elysées – magnificent fireworks on the Pont Louis-Seize – preparations for a full concert immediately in front of the Tuileries Palace, and arrangement of lamps for general illuminations, but especially in the Gardens, were the chief of these; but none of them struck us so much as the daily-increasing number of troops. National Guards and soldiers of the line divided the streets between them; and as a grand review was naturally to make a part of the day's pageantry, there would have been nothing to remark in this, were it not that the various parties into which the country is divided perpetually leads people to suppose that King Philippe finds it necessary to act on the defensive.

Numberless are the hints, as you may imagine, on this theme that have been thrown out on the present occasion; and it is confidently asserted in some quarters, that the reviewing of large bodies of troops is likely to become a very fashionable and frequent, if not a very popular, amusement here. If, indeed, a show of force be necessary to ensure the tranquillity of this strife-worn land, the government certainly do right in displaying it; but if this be not the case, there is some imprudence in it, for the effect much resembles that of

> 'A rich armour, worn in heat of day,
> That scalds with safety.'

Yesterday, then, being marked in the calendar as sacred to St. Jacques and St. Philippe, was kept as the fête of the present King of the French. The weather was brilliant, and everything looked gay, particularly around the courtly region of the Tuileries, Champs Elysées, and all parts near or between them.

Being assured by a philosophical looker-on upon all such assemblings of the people as are likely to show forth indications of their temper, that the humours of the Champs Elysées would display more of this than I could hope to find elsewhere, I was about to order a carriage to convey us there; but my friend stopped me.

'You may as well remain at home,' said he; 'from a carriage you will see nothing but a mob: but if you will walk amongst them, you may perhaps find out whether they are thinking of anything or nothing.'

'Anything? – or nothing?' I repeated. 'Does that *anything* mean a revolution? Tell me truly, is there any chance of a riot?'

Instead of answering, he turned to a gentleman of our party who was just returned from the review of the troops by the king.

'Did you not say you had seen the review?' he demanded.

'Yes; I am just come from it.'

'And what do you think of the troops?'

'They are very fine troops, – remarkably fine men, both the National Guards and the troops of the line.'

'And in sufficient force, are they not, to keep Paris quiet if she should feel disposed to be frolicsome?'

'Certainly – I should think so.'

It was therefore determined, leaving the younger part of the females behind us however in case of the worst, that we should repair to the Champs Elysées.

No one who has not seen a public fête celebrated at Paris can form an idea of the scene which the whole of this extensive area presents: it makes me giddy even to remember it. Imagine a hundred swings throwing their laughing cargoes high into the air; a hundred winged ships flying in endless whirl, and bearing for their crews a *tête-à-tête* pair of holiday sweethearts: imagine a hundred horses, each with two prancing hoofs high poised in air, coursing each other in a circle, with nostrils of flame; a hundred mountebanks, chattering and gibbering their inconceivable jargon, some habited as generals, some as Turks, – some offering their nostrums in the impressive habit of an Armenian Jew, and others rolling head-over-heels upon a stage, and presenting a dose with the grin of Grimaldi. We stopped more than once in our progress to watch the ways of one of these animals when it had succeeded in fascinating its prey: the poor victim was cajoled and coaxed into believing that none of woman born could ever taste of evil more, if he would but trust to the one only true, sure, and certain specific.

At all sides of us, as we advanced, we were skirted by long lines of booths, decked with gaudy merchandise, rings, clasps, brooches, buckles, most tempting to behold, and all to be had for five sous each. It is pretty enough to watch the eager glances and the smirking smiles of the damsels, with the yielding, tender looks of the fond boys who hover round these magazines of female trumpery. Alas! it is perhaps but the beginning of sorrow!

In the largest open space afforded by these Elysian fields were erected two theatres, the interval between them holding, it was said, twenty thousand spectators. While one of these performed a piece, pantomimic I believe, the other enjoyed a *relâche* and reposed itself: but the instant the curtain of one fell, that of the other rose, and the ocean of heads which filled the space between them turned, and undulated like the waves of the sea, ebbing and flowing, backwards and forwards, as the moon-struck folly attracted them.

Four ample *al fresco* enclosures prepared for dancing, each furnished with a very respectable orchestra, occupied the extreme corners of this space; and notwithstanding the crowd, the heat, the sunshine, and the din, this exercise, which was carried on immediately under them, did not, I was told, cease for a single instant during the whole of that long summer-day. When one set of fiddlers were tired out, another succeeded. The activity, gaiety, and universal good-humour of this enormous mob were uniform and uninterrupted from morning to night.

These people really deserve fêtes; they enjoy them so heartily, yet so peaceably.

Such were the great and most striking features of the jubilee; but we hardly advanced a single step through the throng which did not exhibit to us some minor trait of national and charteristic revelry. I was delighted to observe, however, throughout the whole of my expedition, that according to our friend's definition, *'nobody was thinking of anything.'*

But what pleased me incomparably more than all the rest was the temperate style of the popular refreshments. The young men and the old, the time-worn matron and the dainty damsel, all alike slaked their thirst with iced lemonade, which was furnished in incredible quantities by numberless ambulant cisterns, at the price of one sous the glass. Happily this light-hearted, fête-loving population have no gin-palaces to revel in.

But hunger was to be satisfied as well as thirst; and here the *friand* taste of the people displayed itself by dozens of little chafing-dishes lodged at intervals under the trees, each with its presiding old woman, who, holding a frying-pan, for ever redolent of onions, over the coals, screamed in shrill accents the praises of her *saucisses* and her *foie*. This was the only part of the business that was really disagreeable: the odour from these *al fresco* kitchens was not, I confess, very pleasant; but everything else pleased me exceedingly. It was the first time I ever saw a real mob in full jubilee; and I did not believe it possible I could have been so much amused, and so not at all frightened. Even before one of these terribly odoriferant kitchens, I could not help pausing for a moment as I passed, to admire the polite style in which an old woman who had taken early possession of the shade of a tree for her *restaurant* defended the station from the wheelbarrow of a merchant of gingerbread who approached it.

'Pardon, monsieur! . . . Ne venez pas, je vous prie, déranger mon établissement.'

The two grotesque old figures, together with their fittings up, made this dignified address delightful; and as it was answered by a bow, and the respectful drawing back of the wheelbarrow, I cannot but give it the preference over the more energetic language which a similar circumstance would be likely to produce at Bartholomew Fair.

Altogether we were infinitely amused by this excursion; but I think I never was more completely fatigued in my life. Nevertheless, I contrived to repose myself sufficiently to join a large party to the Tuileries Gardens in the evening, where we were assured that *two hundred thousand persons* were collected. The crowd was indeed very great, and the party soon found it impossible to keep together; but about three hours afterwards we had the satisfaction of assembling in safety at the same pleasant mansion from which we set out.

The attraction which during the early part of the evening chiefly drew together the crowd was the orchestra in front of the palace. A large military band was stationed there, and continued playing, while the thousands and tens of thousands of lamps were being lighted all over the gardens.

During this time, the king, queen, and royal family appeared on the balcony. And here the only fault which I had perceived in this pretty fête throughout the day showed itself so strongly as to produce a very disagreeable effect. From first to last, it seemed that the cause of the jubilee was forgotten; not a sound of any kind greeted the appearance of the royal party. That so gay and demonstrative a people, assembled in such numbers, and on such an occasion, should remain with uplifted heads, gazing on the sovereign, without a sound being uttered by any single voice, appeared perfectly astonishing. However, if there were no bravoes, there was decidedly no hissing.

The scene itself was one of enchanting gaiety. Before us rose the illuminated pavilions of the Tuileries: the bright lights darting through the oleanders and myrtles on the balcony, showed to advantage the royal party stationed there. On every side were trees, statues, flowers, brought out to view by unnumbered lamps rising in brilliant pyramids among them, while the inspiring sounds of martial music resounded in the midst. The *jets d'eau*, catching the artificial light, sprang high into the air like arrows of fire, then turned into spray, and descended again in light showers, seeming to shed delicious coolness on the crowd; and behind them, far as the eye could reach, stretched the suburban forest, sparkling with festoons of lamps, that seemed drawn out, 'fine by degrees and beautifully less,' up to the Barrière de l'Etoile. The scene itself was indeed lovely; and if, instead of the heavy silence with which it was regarded, a loud heartfelt cheering had greeted the *jour de fête* of a long-loved king, it would have been perfect.

The fireworks, too, were superb; and though all the theatres in Paris were opened gratis to the public, and, as we afterwards heard, completely filled, the multitudes that thronged to look at them seemed enough to people a dozen cities. But it is so much the habit of this people, old and young, rich and poor, to live out of doors, that a slight temptation 'bye common' is sufficient to draw forth every human being who is able to stand alone: and indeed, of those who are not, thousands are deposited in chairs, and other thousands in the arms of mothers and nurses.

The Pont Louis-Seize was the point from which all the fireworks were let off. No spot could have been better chosen: the terraces of the Tuileries looked down upon it; and the whole length of the quays, on both sides of the river, as far as the *Cité*, looked up to it, and the persons stationed on them must have seen clearly the many-coloured fires that blazed there.

One of the prettiest popular contrivances for creating a shout when fireworks are exhibited here, is to have rockets, sending up tri-coloured balls, blue, white, and red, in rapid succession, looking, as I heard a young republican say, 'like winged messengers, from their loved banner up to heaven.' I could not help remarking, that if the messengers repeated faithfully all that the tri-coloured banner had done, they would have strange tales to tell.

The *bouquet*, or last grand display that finished the exhibition, was very fanciful and very splendid: but what struck me as the prettiest part of the whole show, was the Chamber of Deputies, the architecture of which was marked by lines of light; and the magnificent flight of steps leading to it having each one its unbroken fencing of fire, was perhaps intended as a mystical type of the ordeal to be passed in a popular election before this temple of wisdom could be entered.

How very delightful was the abounding tea of that hot lamp-lit night! . . . And how very thankful was I this morning, at one o'clock, to feel that the *fête du roi* was peaceably over, and I ready to fall soundly to sleep in my bed!

LETTER XVII

Political chances – Visit from a Republican – His high spirits at the prospects before him – His advice to me respecting my name – Removal of the Prisoners from Ste. Pélagie – Review – Garde de Paris – The National Guard

We are so accustomed, in these our luckless days, to hear of *émeutes* and rumours of *émeutes*, here, there, and everywhere, that we certainly grow nerve-hardened, and if not quite callous, at least we are almost reckless of the threat. But in this city the business of getting up riots on the one hand, and putting them down on the other, is carried on in so easy and familiar a manner, that we daily look for an account of something of the kind as regularly as for our breakfast bread; and I begin already to lose in a great degree my fear of disagreeable results, in the interest with which I watch what is going on.

The living in the midst of all these different parties, and listening first to one and then to another of them, is to a foreigner much like the amusement derived by an idle spectator from walking round a card-table, looking into all the hands, and then watching the manner in which each one plays his game.

It has so often happened here, as we all know, that when the game has appeared over, and the winner in possession of the stake he played for, they have on a sudden shuffled the cards and begun again, that people seem always looking out for new chances, new bets, new losses, and new confusion. I can assure you, that it is a game of considerable movement and animation which is going on at Paris just now. The political trials are to commence on Tuesday next, and the republicans are as busy as a nest of wasps when conscious that their stronghold is attacked. They have not only been upon the alert, but hitherto in great spirits at the prospect before them.

85

The same individual whose alarming communications on this subject I mentioned to you soon after we came here, called on me again a few days ago. I never saw a man more altered in the interval of a few weeks: when I first saw him here, he was sullen, gloomy, and miserable-looking in the extreme; but at his last visit he appeared gay, frolicsome, and happy. He was not disposed, however, to talk much on politics; and I am persuaded he came with a fixed determination not to indulge our curiosity by saying a word on the subject. But 'out of the fulness of the heart the mouth speaketh;' and this gentleman did not depart without giving us some little intimation of what was passing in his.

Observe, that I do no treason in repeating to you whatever this young man said in my hearing; for he assured me the first time I ever saw him that he knew me to be 'une absolutiste enragée;' but that, so far from fearing to speak freely before me, there was nothing that would give him so much pleasure as believing that I should publish every word he uttered on the subject of politics. I told him in return, that if I did so, it should be without mentioning his name; for that I should be truly sorry to hear that he had been consigned to Ste. Pélagie as a rebel on my evidence. So we understand each other perfectly.

On the morning in question, he began talking gaily and gallantly concerning the pleasures of Paris, and expressed his hope that we were taking care to profit by the present interval of public tranquillity.

'Is this interval of calm likely to be followed by a storm?' said one of the party.

'Mais . . . que sais-je? . . . The weather is so fine now, you know . . . and the opera? en vérité, c'est superbe! . . . Have you seen it yet?'

'Seen what?'

'Eh! mais, 'La Juive'! . . . à présent il n'y a que cela au monde . . . You read the journals?'

'Yes; Galignani's at least.'

'Ah! ah!' said he, laughing; 'c'est assez pour vous autres.'

'Is there any interesting news today in any of the papers?'

'Intéressante? . . . mais, oui . . . assez . . . Cependant . . .'

And then again he rattled on about plays, balls, concerts, and I know not what.

'I wish you would tell me,' said I, interrupting him, 'whether you think, that in case any popular movement should occur, the English would be molested, or in any way annoyed.'

'Non, madame – je ne le crois pas – surtout les femmes. Cependant, si j'étais vous, Madame Trollope, je me donnerai pour le moment le nom d'O'Connell.'

'And that, you think, would be accepted as a passport through any scene of treason and rebellion?' said I.

He laughed again, and said that was not exactly what he meant; but that O'Connell was a name revered in France as well as at Rome, and might very likely belong one day or other to a pope, if his generous wishes for an Irish republic were too dear to his heart to permit him ever to accept the title of king.

'An Irish republic? . . . perhaps that is just what is wanted,' said I. But not wishing to enter into any discussion on the niceties of speech, I waived the compliments he began to pay me on this liberal sentiment, and again asked him if he thought anything was going on amongst the friends of the prisoners that might impede the course of justice.

Though not aware of the quibble with which I had replied to him, he answered me by another, saying with energy –

'No! . . . never! . . . They will never do anything to impede the course of justice.'

'Will they do anything to assist it?' said I.

He sprang from his chair, gave a bound across the room, as if to hide his glee by looking out of the window, and when he showed his face again, said with much solemnity – 'They will do their duty.'

The conversation continued for some time longer, wavering between politics and dissipation; and though we could not obtain from him anything approaching to information respecting what might be going on among his hot-headed party, yet it seemed clear that he at least hoped for something that would lead to important results.

The riddle was explained a very few hours after he left us. The political prisoners, most of whom were lodged in the prison of Ste. Pélagie, have been removed to the Luxembourg; and it was confidently hoped and expected by the republicans that enough malcontents would be found among the citizens of Paris to get up a very satisfactory *émeute* on the occasion. But never was hope more abortive: not the slightest public sensation appears to have been excited by this removal; and I am assured that the whole republican party are so bitterly disappointed at this, that the most sanguine among them have ceased for the present to anticipate the triumph of their cause. I suspect, therefore, that it will be some time before we shall receive another visit from our riot-loving friend.

Meanwhile preparations are going on in a very orderly and judicious style at the Luxembourg. The trial-chamber and all things connected with it are completed; tents have been pitched in the gardens for the accommodation of the soldiers, and guards stationed in such a manner in all directions as to ensure a reasonable chance of tranquillity to the peaceable.

We have attended a review of very fine troops in the Place du Carrousel, composed of National Guards, troops of the line, and that most superb-looking body of municipal troops called *La Garde de Paris*. These latter, it seems, have performed in Paris since the revolution of 1830 the duties of that portion of the police formerly called *gendarmerie*; but the name having fallen into disrepute in the capital – (*les jeunes gens, par exemple,* could not bear it) – the title of *Garde de Paris* has been accorded to them instead, and it is now only in the provinces that *gendarmes* are to be found. But let them be called by what name they may, I never saw any corps of more superb appearance. Men and horses, accoutrements and discipline, all seem perfect. It is amusing to observe how slight a thread will sometimes suffice to lead captive the most unruly spirits.

'What is there in a name?'

Yet I have heard it asserted with triumphant crowings by some of the revolutionary set, that, thanks to their valour! the odious system was completely changed – that *gendarmes* and *mouchards* no longer existed in Paris – that citizens would never again be tormented by their hateful *surveillance* – and, in short, that Frenchmen were redeemed from thraldom now and for evermore; so now they have *La Garde de Paris*, just to take care of them: and if ever a set of men were capable of performing effectually the duties committed to their charge, I think it must be this well-drilled stalworth corps.

The appearance of a large body of the National Guard too, when brought together, as at a review, in full military style, is very imposing. The eye at once sees that they are not ordinary troops. All the appointments are in excellent order; and the very material of which their uniform is made, being so much less common than usual, helps to produce this effect. Not to mention that the uniform itself, of dark blue, with the delicately white pantaloons, is peculiarly handsome on parade; much more so, I think, though perhaps less calculated for a battle-field, than the red lower garments by which the troops of the French line are at present distinguished.

The king looks well on horseback – so do his sons. The whole staff, indeed, was gay and gallant-looking, and in style as decidedly aristocratic as any prince need desire. Shouts of '*Vive le Roi!*' ran cheerily and lustily along the lines; and if these may be trusted as indications of the feelings of the soldiery towards King Philippe, he may, I think, feel quite indifferent as to whatever other vows may be uttered concerning him in the distance.

But in this city of contradictions one can never sit down safely to ruminate upon any one inference or conclusion whatever; for five minutes afterwards you are assured by somebody or other that you are quite wrong, utterly mistaken, and that the exact contrary of what you suppose is the real fact. Thus, on mentioning in the evening the cordial reception given by the soldiers to the king in the morning, I received for answer – 'Je le crois bien, madame; les officiers leur commandent de le faire.'

We remained a good while on the ground, and saw as much as the confinement of a carriage would permit. Like all reviews of well-dressed, well-appointed troops, it was a gay and pretty spectacle; and notwithstanding the caustic reprimand for my faith in empty sounds which I have just repeated to you, I am still of opinion that King Philippe had every reason to be contented with his troops, and with the manner in which he was received by them.

Every hour that one remains at Paris increases, I think, one's conviction of the enormous power and importance of the

National Guard. Our volunteer corps, in the season of threat-
enings and danger, gave us unquestionably an immense
accession of strength; and had the threatener dared to come,
neither his legions nor his eagles, his veterans nor his victories,
would have saved him from utter destruction. He knew this,
and he came not: he knew that the little island was bristling
from her centre to her shore with arms raised to strike, by the
impulse of the heart and soul, and not by conscription; he
knew this, and wisely came not.

Our volunteers were armed men – armed in a cause that
warmed their blood; and it is sufficient to establish their
importance, that History must record the simple fact, that
Napoleon looked at them and turned away. But, great as was
the power of this critical show of volunteer strength among
us, as a permanent force it was trifling when compared to the
present National Guard of France. Not only are their numbers
greater – Paris alone has eighty thousand of them, – but their
discipline is perfect, and their practical habits of being on duty
keep them in such daily activity, that a tocsin sounded within
their hearing would suffice to turn out within an hour nearly
the whole of this force, not only completely armed, equipped,
and in all respects fit for service – not only each one with his
quarters and rations provided, but each one knowing and
feeling the importance of the duty he is upon as intimately as
the general himself; and each one, in addition to all other
feelings and motives which make armed men strong, warmed
with the consciousness that it is his own stronghold, his own
property, his own castle, as well as his own life, that he is
defending.

This force will save France from devouring her own vitals,
if anything can do it.

Among all the novelties produced by the evergrowing
experience of men, and of which so many have ripened in
these latter days, I doubt if any can be named more rationally
calculated to fulfil the purpose for which it is intended than
this organization of a force formed of the industrious and the
orderly part of a community to keep in check the idle and
disorderly, – and that, without taxing the state, compromising
their professional usefulness, or sacrificing their personal
independence, more than every man in his senses would be

'Pro Patriat'.

willing to do for the purpose of keeping watch and ward over all that he loves and values on earth.

The more the power of such a force as this increases, the farther must the country where it exists be from all danger of revolution. Such men are, and must be, conservatives in the strongest sense of the word; and though it may certainly be possible for some who may be rebel to the cause of order to get enrolled among them, the danger of the enterprise will unquestionably prevent its frequent recurrence. The wolf might as safely mount guard in the midst of armed shepherds and their dogs, as demagogues and agitators place themselves in the ranks of the National Guard of Paris.

LETTER XVIII

First Day of the Trials – Much blustering, but no riot –
All alarm subsided – Proposal for inviting Lord B——m
to plead at the Trial – Society – Charm of idle conversation –
The Whisperer of good stories

6th May 1835

The monster is hatched at last! The trials began yesterday, and we are all rejoicing exceedingly at having found ourselves alive in our beds this morning. What will betide us and it, as its scales or its plumes push forth and gather strength from day to day, I know not; but 'sufficient for the day is the evil thereof;' and I do assure you in very sober earnest, that when Galignani's paper arrived this morning, the party round the breakfast-table was greatly comforted by finding that nothing more alarming than a few republican demands on the part of the prisoners, and a few monarchical refusals on the part of the court, took place.

This interchange of hostilities commenced by some of the accused refusing to answer when their names were called; – then followed a demand for free admission to the chamber, during the trials, for the mothers, wives, and all other females belonging to the respective families of the prisoners; – and next, a somewhat blustering demand for counsel of their own choosing; the body of legal advocates, who, by general rule and common usage, are always charged with the defence of prisoners, not containing, as it should seem, orators sufficiently of their own *clique* to content them.

This was of course stoutly refused by the court, after retiring, however, for a couple of hours to deliberate upon it – a ceremony I should hardly have supposed necessary. The company of the ladies, too, was declined; and as, upon a moderate computation, their numerical force could not have amounted to less than five hundred, this want of gallantry in the Peers of France must be forgiven in favour of their discretion.

The gentleman, however, who was appointed, as he said, by the rest, to request the pleasure of their society, declared loudly that the demand for it should be daily renewed. This reminds one of the story of the man who punished his wife for infidelity by making her sit to hear the story of her misdeeds rehearsed every day of her life, and pretty plainly indicates that it is the plan of the accused to torment their judges as much as they conveniently can.

One of the prisoners named the celebrated Abbé de Lamennais, author of 'Les Paroles d'un Croyant,' as his advocate. The *procureur-général* remarked, that it was for the interest of the defence that the rule for permitting lawyers only to plead should be adhered to.

Next came a demand from one of the accused, in the name of all the rest, that permission for free and unrestrained intercourse between the prisoners of Lyons, Paris, and Marseilles should be allowed. This was answered only by the announcement that 'the court was adjourned;' an intimation which produced an awful clamour; and as the peers quitted the court, they were assailed with vehement cries of 'We protest! . . . we protest! . . . We will make no defence! . . . We protest! . . . we protest!' And so ended the business of the day.

I believe that the government, and all those who are sufficiently connected with it to know anything of the real state of the case, were perfectly aware that no public movement was likely to take place at this stage of the business. Every one seems to know that the restless spirits, the desperate adventurers engaged in the extensive plot now under investigation, consider their trial as the best occasion possible for a political *coup de théâtre*, and that nothing would have disturbed their performance more than a riot before the curtain rose.

Everything like panic seems now to have subsided, even among those who are farthest from the centre of action; and all the effects of this mighty affair apparently visible at present are to be seen on the faces of the republicans, who, according to their wont, strut about wherever they are most likely to be looked at, and take care that each one of their countenances shall be

'Like to a book where men may read strange matters.'

I thank Heaven, nevertheless, that this first day is so well over. I had heard so over-much about it, that it became a sort of nightmare to me, from which I now feel happily relieved. It is quite clear, that if the out-of-door agitators should think proper to make any attempts to produce disturbance, the government feels quite equal to the task of making them quiet again, and of insuring that peaceable security to the country for which she has so long languished in vain.

The military force employed at the Luxembourg is, however, by no means large. One battalion of the first legion of National Guards was in the court of the palace, and about four hundred troops of the line occupied the garden. But though no show of force is unnecessarily displayed, every one has the comfort of knowing that there is enough within reach should any necessity arise for employing it.

I was told the other day, that when Lord B——m was in Paris, he was so kind as to visit M. Armand Carrel in prison; and that, on the strength of this proof of sympathy and affection, it has been suggested to the prisoners at the Luxembourg, that they should despatch a deputation of their friends to wait upon his lordship, requesting the aid of his eloquence in pleading their cause against the tyrants who so unjustifiably hold them in durance.

The proposal, it seems, was very generally approved; but nevertheless, it was at last negatived on the representation of a person who had once heard his lordship argue in the French language. This is the more to be regretted by the friends of these suffering victims, since their choice of defenders is to be restricted to members of the bar: and this restriction, narrow-minded and severe as it is, would not exclude his lordship; a legal advocate being beyond all question a legal advocate all the world over.

It was not till we had sent out in one or two directions to ascertain if all things were quiet, that we ventured to keep an engagement which we had made for last night to pass the *soirée* at Madame de L——'s. I should have been sorry to have lost it; for the business of the morning appeared to have awakened the spirits and set everybody talking. There are few things I like better than listening to a full, free flow of Paris talk; particularly when, as in this instance, the party is small and in a lively mood.

It appears as if there were nothing like caution or reserve here in any direction. Among those whom I have had the satisfaction of occasionally meeting are some who figure amongst the most important personages of the day; but their conversation is as gaily unrestrained as if they had nothing to do but to amuse themselves. These, indeed, are not likely to commit themselves; but I have known others less secure, who have appeared to permit every thought that occurred to them to meet the ear of whoever chose to listen. In short, whatever restraint the police, which by its nature is very phoenix-like, may endeavour to put upon the periodical press, its influence certainly does not as yet reach the lips, which open with equal freedom for the expression of faith, scepticism, loyalty, treason, philosophy, and wit.

In an intercourse so transient as mine is likely to be with most of the acquaintance I have formed here, – an intercourse consisting chiefly, as to the manner of it, of evening visits through a series of *salons*, – amusement is naturally more sought than information: and were it otherwise, I should, with some few exceptions, have reaped disappointment instead of pleasure; for it is evident that the same feeling which leads the majority of persons you meet in society here, to speak freely, prevents them from saying anything seriously. So that, after talking for an hour or two upon subjects which one should think very gravely important, a light word, a light laugh, ends the colloquy, and very often leaves me in doubt as to the real sentiments of those to whom I have been listening.

But if not always successful in obtaining information, I never fail in finding amusement. Rarely, even for a moment, does conversation languish; and a string of lively nothings, or a startling succession of seemingly bold, but really unmeaning speculations, often make me imagine that a vast deal of talent has been displayed; yet, when memory sets to work upon it, little remains worth recording. Nevertheless, there is talent, and of a very charming kind too, in this manner of uttering trifles so that they may be mistaken for wit.

I know some few in our own dear land who have also this happy gift; and, as a matter of grace and mere exterior endowment, I question if it be not fairly worth all the rest. But I believe we have it in about the same proportion that we have good actors of genteel comedy, compared to the number which they can boast of the same class here. With us this easy, natural style of mimicking real life is a rare talent, though sometimes possessed in great perfection; but with them it seems more or less the birthright of all.

So it is with the gift of that bright colloquial faculty which bestows such indescribable grace upon the airy nothings uttered in French drawing-rooms. To listen to it, is very like quaffing the sparkling, frothy beverage native to their sunny hills; – French talk is very like champagne. The exhilaration it produces is instantaneous: the spirits mount, and something like wit is often struck out even from dull natures by merely coming in contact with what is so brilliant.

I could almost venture to assert that the effect of this delightful inspiration might be perceived by any one who had gained admission to French society even if they did not understand the language. Let an observing eye, well accustomed to read the expression so legibly, though so transiently written in the countenances of persons in conversation, – let such a one only see, if he cannot hear, the effect produced by the hits and flashes of French eloquence. Allow me another simile, and I will tell you that it is like applying electricity to a bunch of feathers tied together and attached to the conductor by a thread: first one, then another starts, flies off, mounts, and drops again, as the bright spark passes lightly, gracefully, capriciously, yet still all making part of one circle.

Of course, I am not speaking now of large parties; these, as I think I have said before, are wonderfully alike in all lands, and nothing approaching to conversation can possibly take place at any of them. It is only where the circle is restricted to a few that this sort of effect can be produced; and then, the impulse once given by a piquant word, seemingly uttered at random, every one present receives a share of it, and contributes in return all the lively thoughts to which it has given birth.

But there was one gentleman of our party yesterday evening who had a most provoking trick of attracting one's attention as if on purpose to disappoint it. He was not quite like Molière's Timante, of whom Célimène says,

> 'Et jusques au bonjour, il dit tout à l'oreille;'

but in the midst of pleasant talk, in which all were interested, he said aloud –

'*Par exemple!* I heard the very best thing possible today about the King. Will you hear it, Madame B——?'

This question being addressed to a decided doctrinaire, the answer was of course a reproachful shake of the head; but as it was accompanied by half a smile, and as the lady bent her fair neck towards the speaker, she, and she only, was made acquainted with 'the best of all possible things,' conveyed in a whisper.

At another time he addressed himself to the lady of the house; but as he spoke across the circle, he not only fixed her attention, but that of every one else.

'Madame!' said he coaxingly, 'will you let me tell you a little word of treason?'

'Comment? – de la trahison? . . . Apropos de quoi, s'il vous plaît? . . . Mais c'est égal – contez toujours.'

On receiving this answer, the whisperer of good stories got up from the depth of his armchair – an enterprise of some difficulty, for he was neither rapid nor light in his movements, – and deliberately walking round the chairs of all the party, he placed himself behind Madame de L——, and whispered in her ear what made her colour and shake her head again; but she laughed too, telling him that she hated timid politics, and had no taste for any *trahisons* which were not '*hautement prononcées.*'

This hint sent him back to his place; but it was taken very good-humouredly, for, instead of whispering any more, he uttered aloud sundry odds and ends of gossip, but all so well dressed up in lively wording, that they sounded very like good stories.

LETTER XIX

Victor Hugo – Racine

I have again been listening to some curious details respecting the present state of literature in France. I think I have before stated to you, that I have uniformly heard the whole of the *décousu* school of authors spoken of with unmitigated contempt, – and that not only by the venerable advocates for the *bon vieux temps*, but also, and equally, by the distinguished men of the present day – distinguished both by position and ability.

Respecting Victor Hugo, the only one of the tribe to which I allude who has been sufficiently read in England to justify his being classed by us as a person of general celebrity, the feeling is more remarkable still. I have never mentioned him or his works to any person of good moral feeling and cultivated mind, who did not appear to shrink from according him even the degree of reputation that those who are received as authority among our own critics have been disposed to allow him. I might say, that of him France seems to be ashamed.

Again and again it has happened to me, when I have asked the opinions of individuals as to the merit of his different plays, that I have been answered thus:–

'I assure you I know nothing about it: I never saw it played.'

'Have you read it?'

'No; I have not. I cannot read the works of Victor Hugo.'

One gentleman, who has heard me more than once persist in my inquiries respecting the reputation enjoyed by Victor Hugo at Paris as a man of genius and a successful dramatic writer, told me, that he saw that, in common with the generality of foreigners, particularly the English, I looked upon Victor Hugo and his productions as a sort of type or specimen of the literature of France at the present hour. 'But permit me to assure you,' he added gravely and earnestly, 'that no idea was ever more entirely and altogether erroneous. He is the head of a sect – the high-priest of a congregation who have abolished every law, moral and intellectual, by which the efforts of the human mind have hitherto been regulated. He has attained this pre-eminence, and I trust that no other will arise to dispute it with him. But Victor Hugo is NOT a popular French writer.'

Such a judgment as this, or the like of it, I have heard passed upon him and his works nine times out of ten that I have mentioned him; and I consider this as a proof of right feeling and sound taste, which is extremely honourable, and certainly more than we have lately given our neighbours credit for. It pleased me the more perhaps because I did not expect it. There is so much meretricious glitter in the works of Victor Hugo, – nay, so much real brightness now and then, – that I expected to find at least the younger and less reflective part of the population warm in their admiration of him.

His clinging fondness for scenes of vice and horror, and his utter contempt for all that time has stamped as good in taste or feeling, might, I thought, arise from the unsettled spirit of the times; and if so, he could not fail of receiving the need of sympathy and praise from those who had themselves set that spirit at work.

But it is not so. The wild vigour of some of his descriptions is acknowledged; but that is all of praise that I ever heard bestowed upon Victor Hugo's theatrical productions in his native land.

The startling, bold, and stirring incidents of his disgusting dramas must and will excite a certain degree of attention when seen for the first time, and it is evidently in the interest of managers to bring forward whatever is most likely to produce this effect; but the doing so cannot be quoted as a proof of the systematic degradation of the theatre. It is moreover a fact, which the play-bills themselves are alone sufficient to attest, that after Victor Hugo's plays have had their first run, they are never brought forward again: not one of them has yet become what we call a stock-play.

This fact, which was first stated to me by a person perfectly *au fait* of the subject, has been subsequently confirmed by many others; and it speaks more plainly than any recorded criticism could do, what the public judgment of these pieces really is.

The romance of 'Notre Dame de Paris' is ever cited as Victor Hugo's best work, excepting some early lyrical pieces of which we know nothing. But even this, though there are passages of extraordinary descriptive power in it, is always alluded to with much more of contempt than admiration; and I have heard it ridiculed in circles, whose praise was fame, with a light pleasantry more likely to prove an antidote to its mischief than all the reprobation that sober criticism could pour out upon it.

But may not this champion of vice – this chronicler of sin, shame, and misery – quote Scripture and say, 'A prophet is not without honour, save in his own country'? For I have seen a criticism in an English paper (The Examiner) which says, '*The* Notre Dame *of Victor Hugo must take rank with the best romances by the author of* Waverley . . . *It transcends them in vigour, animation, and familiarity with the age.*'

In reply to the last point here mentioned, in which our countryman has given the superiority to Victor Hugo over Sir Walter Scott, a very strong testimony against its correctness has reached me since I have been in Paris. An able lawyer, and most accomplished gentleman and scholar, who holds a distinguished station in the Cour Royale, took us to see the Palais de Justice. Having shown us the chamber where criminal trials are carried on, he observed, that this was the room described by Victor Hugo in his romance; adding, – 'He was, however, mistaken here, as in most places *where he affects a knowledge of the times of which he writes.* In the reign of Louis the Eleventh, no criminal trials ever took place within the walls of this building; and all the ceremonies as described by him resemble much more a trial of yesterday than of the age at which he dates his tale.'

The vulgar old adage, that 'there is no accounting for taste,' must, I suppose, teach us to submit patiently to the hearing of any judgments and opinions which it is the will and pleasure of man to pronounce; but it does seem strange that any can be found who, after bringing Sir Walter Scott and Victor Hugo into comparison, should give the palm of superiority to the author of 'Notre Dame de Paris.'

Were the faults of this school of authors only of a literary kind, few persons, I believe, would take the trouble to criticise them, and their nonsense would die a natural death as soon as it was made to encounter the light of day: but such productions as Victor Hugo's are calculated to do great injury to human nature. They would teach us to believe that all our gentlest and best affections can only lead to crime and infamy. There is not, I truly believe, a single pure, innocent, and holy thought to be found throughout his writings: Sin is the muse he invokes – he would

> 'Take off the rose
> From the fair forehead of an innocent love,
> And set a blister there;'

Horror is his handmaid; and 'thousands of liveried *monsters* lackey him,' to furnish the portraits with which it is the occupation of his life to disgust the world.

Can there, think you, be a stronger proof of a diseased intellect among the *décousu* part of the world, than that they not only admire this man's hideous extravagances, but that they actually believe him to be . . . at least they say so . . . a second Shakespeare! . . . A Shakespeare!

To chastise as he deserves an author who may be said to defy mankind by the libels he has put forth on the whole race, requires a stouter and a keener weapon than any a woman can wield; but when they prate of Shakespeare, I feel that it is our turn to speak. How much of gratitude and love does every woman owe to him! He, who has entered deeper into her heart than ever mortal did before or since his day, how has he painted her? – As Portia, Juliet, Constance, Hermione; – as Cordelia, Volumnia, Isabella, Desdemona, Imogene!

Then turn and see for what we have to thank our modern painter. Who are his heroines? – Lucrèce Borgia, Marion de Lorme, Blanche, Maguelonne, with I know not how many more of the same stamp; besides his novel heroine, whom Mr. Henry Lytton Bulwer calls 'the most delicate female ever drawn by the pen of romance' – The Esmeralda! . . . whose sole accomplishments are dancing and singing in the streets, and who . . . delicate creature! . . . being caught up by a horseman in a midnight brawl, throws her arms round his neck, swears he is very handsome, and thenceforward shows the delicate tenderness of her nature, by pertinaciously doting upon him, without any other return or encouragement whatever than an insulting caress bestowed upon her one night when he was drunk . . . 'delicate female!'

But this is all too bad to dwell upon. It is, however, in my estimation a positive duty, when mentioning the works of Victor Hugo, to record a protest against their tone and tendency; and it is also a duty to correct, as far as one can, the erroneous impression existing in England respecting his reputation in France.

Whenever his name is mentioned in England, his success is cited as a proof of the depraved state, moral and intellectual, of the French people. And such it would be, were his success and reputation such as his partisans represent them to be. But, in point of fact, the manner in which he is judged by his own countrymen is the strongest possible evidence that neither a powerful fancy, a commanding diction, nor an imagination teeming with images of intense passion, can suffice to ensure an author any exalted reputation in France at the present day if he outrages good feeling and good taste.

Should any doubt the correctness of this statement, I can only refer them to the source from whence I derived the information on which it is founded, – I can only refer them to France herself. There is one fact, however, which may be ascertained without crossing the Channel; – namely, that when one of their reviews found occasion to introduce an article upon the modern drama, the editors acquitted themselves of the task by translating the whole of the able article upon that subject which appeared about a year and a half ago in the Quarterly, acknowledging to what source they were indebted for it.

Were the name and the labours of Victor Hugo confined to his own country, it would now be high time that I should release you from him; but it is an English critic who has said, that he has heaved the ground from under the feet of Racine; and you must indulge me for a few minutes, while I endeavour to bring the two parties together before you. In doing this, I will be generous; for I will introduce M. Hugo in 'Le Roi s'amuse,' which, from the circumstance (the happiest, I was assured, that ever befell the author) of its being withdrawn by authority from the Théâtre Français, has become infinitely more celebrated than any other he has written.

It may be remarked by the way, that a few more such acts of decent watchfulness over the morals and manners of the people may redeem the country from the stigma it now bears of being the most licentious in its theatre and its press in the world.

The first glorious moment of being forbidden at the Français appears almost to have turned the lucky author's brain. His preface to 'Le Roi s'amuse,' among many other symptoms of insanity has the following:–

'Le premier mouvement de l'auteur fut de douter . . . L'acte était arbitraire au point d'être incroyable . . . L'auteur ne pouvait croire à tant d'insolence et de folie . . . Le ministre avait en effet, de son droit divin de ministre, intimé l'ordre . . . Le ministre lui avait pris sa pièce, lui avait pris son droit, lui avait pris sa chose. Il ne restait plus qu'à le mettre, lui poëte, à la Bastille. . . . Est-ce qu'il y a eu en effet quelque chose qu'on a appelé la révolution de Juillet? . . . Que peut être le motif d'une pareille mesure? . . . Il parait que nos faiseurs de censure se prétendent scandalisés dans leur morale par "Le Roi s'amuse;" le nom seul du poëte inculpé aurait dû êetre une suffisante réfutation (!!!) . . . Cette piéce a révolté la pudeur des gendarmes; la brigade Léotaud y était, et l'a trouvé obscène; le bureau des moeurs s'est voilé la face; M. Vidocq a rougi . . . Holà, mes maîtres! Silence sur ce point! . . . Depuis quand n'est-il plus permis à un roi de courtiser sur la scène une servante d'auberge? . . . Mener un roi dans un mauvais lieu, cela ne serait pas même nouveau non plus . . . L'auteur veut l'art chaste, et non l'art prude . . . Il est profondement triste de voir comment se termine la révolution de Juillet . . .'

Then follows a *précis* of the extravagant and hateful plot, in which the heroine is, as usual 'une fille séduite et perdue;' and he sums it up thus pompously:– 'Au fond d'un des ouvrages de l'auteur il y a la fatalité – au fond de celui-ci il y a la providence.'

I wish much that some one would collect and publish in a separate volume all M. Victor Hugo's prefaces; I would purchase it instantly, and it would be a fund of almost inexhaustible amusement. He assumes a tone in them which, all things considered, is perhaps unequalled in the history of literature. In another part of the one from which I have given the above extracts, he says –

'Vraiment, le pouvoir qui s'attaque à nous n'aura pas gagné

grand' chose à ce que nous, hommes d'art, nous quittions notre tâche consciencieuse, tranquille, sincère, profonde; notre tâche sainte. . . .' What on earth, if it be not insanity, could have put it into Mr. Hugo's head that the manufacturing of his obscene dramas was 'une tâche sainte'?

The principal characters in 'Le Rois' amuse' are François Premier; Triboulet, his pander and buffoon; Blanche, the daughter of Triboulet, 'la fille séduite,' and heroine of the piece; and Maguelonne, another Esmeralda.

The interest lies in the contrast between Triboulet pander and Triboulet père. He is himself the most corrupt and infamous of men; and because he is humpbacked, makes it both his pastime and his business to lead the king his master into every species of debauchery: but he shuts up his daughter to preserve her purity; and the poet has put forth all his strength in describing the worship which Triboulet père pays to the virtue which he passes his life as Triboulet pander in destroying.

Of course, the king falls in love with Blanche, and she with him; and Triboulet pander is made to assist in carrying her off in the dark, under the belief that she was the wife of a nobleman to whom also his majesty the king was making love.

When Triboulet père and pander finds out what he has done, he falls into a terrible agony: and here again is a *tour de force*, to show how pathetically such a father can address such a daughter.

He resolves to murder the king, and informs his daughter, who is passionately attached to her royal seducer, of his intention. She objects, but is at length brought to consent by being made to peep through a hole in the wall, and seeing his majesty King Francis engaged in making love to Maguelonne. This part of the plot is brought out shortly and pithily.

BLANCHE (*peeping through the hole in the wall*)

Et cette femme! . . . est-elle affrontée! . . . oh! . . .

TRIBOULET

Tais-toi;

Pas de pleurs. Laisse-moi te venger!

BLANCHE

Hélas! – Faites –

Tout ce que vous voudrez.

TRIBOULET

Merci!

This *merci*, observe, is not said ironically, but gravely and gratefully. Having arranged this part of the business, he gives his daughter instructions as to what she is to do with herself, in the following sublime verses:–

TRIBOULET

Ecoute. Va chez moi, prends-y des habits d'homme,
Un cheval, de l'argent, n'importe quelle somme;
Et pars, sans t'arrêter un instant en chemin,
Poir Evreux, où j'irai te joindre après-demain.
– Tu sais ce coffre auprès du portrait de ta mère;
L'habit est là, – je l'ai d'avance exprès fait faire.

Having dismissed his daughter, he settles with a gipsy-man named Saltabadil, who is the brother of Maguelonne, all the details of the murder, which is to be performed in their house, a small cabaret at which the foul weather and the fair Maguelonne induce the royal rake to pass the night. Triboulet leaves them an old sack in which they are to pack up the body, and promises to return at midnight, that he may himself see it thrown into the Seine.

Blanche meanwhile departs; but feeling some compunctious visitings about the proposed murder of her lover, returns, and again applying her ear to the hole in the wall, finds that his majesty is gone to bed in the garret, and that the brother and sister are consulting about his death. Maguelonne, a very 'delicate female,' objects too; she admires his beauty, and proposes that his life shall be spared if any stranger happens to arrive whose body may serve to fill the sack. Blanche, in a fit of heroic tenderness, determines to be that stranger; exclaiming,

'Eh bien! . . . mourons pour lui!'

But before she knocks at the door, she kneels down to say her prayers, particularly for forgiveness to all her enemies. Here are the verses, making part of those which have overthrown Racine:–

BLANCHE

Oh! Dieu, vers qui je vais,
Je pardonne à tous ceux qui m'ont été mauvais:
Mon père et vous, mon Dieu! pardonnez-leurs de même
Au roi François Premier, que je plains et que j'aime.

She knocks, the dooor opens, she is stabbed and consigned to the sack. Her father arrives immediately after as by appointment, receives the sack, and prepares to drag it towards the river, handling it with revengeful ecstasy, and exclaiming –

Maintenant, monde, regarde-moi:
Ceci, e'est un buffon; et ceci, e'est un roi.

At this triumphant moment he hears the voice of the king, singing as he walks away from the dwelling of Maguelonne.

TRIBOULET

Mais qui donc ma'-t-il mis à sa place, le traître!

He cuts open the sack; and a flash of lightning very melo-dramatically enables him to recognise his daughter, who revives, to die in his arms.

This is beyond doubt what may be called 'a tragic situation;' and I confess it does seem very hard-hearted to laugh at it: but the *pas* that divides the sublime from the ridiculous is not distinctly seen, and there is something vulgar and ludicrous, both in the position and language of the parties, which quite destroys the pathetic effect.

It must be remembered that she is dressed in the 'habit d'homme' of which her father says so poetically –

Je l'ai d'avance exprès fait faire.

Observe, too, that she is still in the sack; the stage directions being, 'Le bas du corps, qui est resté vêtu, est caché dans le sac.'

BLANCHE

Où suis-je?

TRIBOULET

Blanche! que t'a-t-on fait? Quel mystère infernal!
Je crains en te touchant de te faire du mal.
. . . Ah! la cloche du bac est là sur la muraille:
Ma pauvre enfant, peux-tu m'attendre un peu, que j'aille
Chercher de l'eau. . . .

A surgeon arrives, and having examined her wound says,

Elle est morte.
Elle a dans le flanc gauche une plaie assez forte:
Le sang a dû causer la mort en l'etouffant.

TRIBOULET

J'ai tué mon enfant! j'ai tué mon enfant!
(*Il tombe sur le pavé.*)

FIN

All this is very shocking; but it is not tragedy, – and it is not poetry. Yet it is what we are told has heaved the earth from under Racine!

After such a sentence as this, it must be, I know, *rococo* to name him; but yet I would say, in his own words,

D'adorateurs zélés à peine un petit nombre
Ose des premiers temps nous retracer quelque ombre;
Le reste . . .
Se fait initier à ces honteux mystères,
Et blasphème le nom qu'ont invoqué leurs pères.

As I profess myself of the *petit nombre*, you must let me recall to your memory some of the fragments of that noble edifice which Racine raised over him, and which, as they say, has now perished under the mighty power of Victor Hugo. It will not be lost time to do this; for look where you will among the splendid material of this uprooted temple, and you will find no morsel that is not precious; nothing that is not designed, chiseled, and finished by the hand of a master.

Racine has not produced dramas from ordinary life; it was not his object to do so, nor is it the end he has attained. It is the tragedy of heroes and demi-gods that he has given us, and not of cut-purses, buffoons, and street-walkers.

If the language of Racine be poetry, that of M. Hugo is not; and wherever the one is admired, the other must of necessity be valueless. It would be endless to attempt giving citations to prove the grace, the dignity, the majestic flow of Racine's verse; but let your eye run over 'Iphigénie,' for instance, – there also the loss of a daughter forms the tragic interest, – and compare such verses as those I have quoted above with any that you can find in Racine.

Hear the royal mother, for example, describe the scene that awaits her:

> Un prêtre environné d'une foule cruelle
> Portera su ma fille une main criminelle,
> Déchirera son sein, et d'un oeil curieux
> Dans son coeur palpitant consultera les dieux;
> – Et moi – qui l'amenai triomphante, adorée,
> Je m'en retournerai, seule, et désespérée.

Surely this is of a better fabric than –

> Tu sais ce coffre auprès du portrait de ta mère;
> L'habit est là, – je l'ai d'avance exprès fait faire.

I have little doubt but that the inspired author, when this noble phrase, 'exprès fait faire,' suggested itself, felt ready to exclaim, in the words of Philaminte and Bélise –

> Ah! que cet 'exprès fait' est d'un goût admirable!
> C'est à mon sentiment un endroit impayable;
> J'entends là-dessous un million de mots. –
> – Il est vrai qu'il dit plus de choses qu'il n'est gros.

But to take the matter seriously, let us examine a little the ground upon which this school of dramatic writers found their claim to superiority over their classic predecessors. Is it not that they declare themselves to be more true to nature? And how do they support this claim? Were you to read through every play that M. Hugo has written – (and may you long be preserved from so great annoyance!) – I doubt if you would find a single personage with whom you could sympathise, or a single sentiment or opinion that you would feel true to the nature within you.

It would be much less difficult, I conceive, so strongly to excite the imagination by the majestic eloquence of Racine's verses as to make you conscious of fellow-feeling with his sublime personages, than to debase your very heart and soul so thoroughly as to enable you to fancy that you have anything in common with the corrupt creations of Victor Hugo.

But even were it otherwise – were the scenes imagined by this new Shakespeare more like the real villany of human nature than those of the noble writer he is said to have set aside, I should still deny that this furnished any good reason for bringing such scenes upon the stage. Why should we make a pastime of looking upon vulgar vice? Why should the lowest passions of our nature be for ever brought out in parade before us?

'It is not and it cannot be for good.'

The same reasoning might lead to us to turn from the cultured garden, its marble terraces, its velvet lawns, its flowers and fruits of every clime, that we might take our pleasure in a bog – and for all consolation be told, when we slip and flounder about in its loathsome slime, that is is more natural.

I have written you a most unmerciful letter, and it is quite time that I should quit the theme, for I get angry – angry that I have no power to express in words all I feel on this subject. Would that for one short hour or so I had the pen which wrote the 'Dunciad!' – I would use it – heartily – and then take my leave by saying,

'Rentre dans le néant, dont je t'ai fait sortir.'

LETTER XX

Versailles – St. Cloud

The Château de Versailles, that marvellous *chef-d'oeuvre* of the splendid taste and unbounded extravagance of Louis le Grand, is shut up, and has been so for the last eighteen months. This is a great disappointment to such of our party as have never seen its interminable chambers and their gorgeous decorations. The reason assigned for this unwonted exclusion of the public, is, that the whole of this enormous pile is filled with workmen; not, however, for the purpose of restoring it as a palace for the king, but of preparing it as a sort of universal museum for the nation. The buildings are in fact too extensive for a palace; and splendid as it is, I can easily believe no king of modern days would wish to inhabit it. I have sometimes wondered that Napoleon did not take a fancy to its vastness; but, I believe, he had no great taste in the upholstering line, and preferred converting his millions into the sinews of war, to the possession of all the carving and gilding in the world.

If this projected museum, however, should be *monté* with science, judgment and taste, and on the usual scale of French magnificence, it will be turning the costly whim of *le Grand Monarque* to excellent account.

The works which are going on there, were mentioned at a party the other evening, when some one stated that it was the intention of the King to convert one portion of the building into a gallery of national history, that should contain pictures of all the victories which France had ever won.

The remark made in reply amused me much, it was so very French. – 'Ma foi! . . . Mais cette galerie-là doit être bien longue – et assez ennuyeuse pour les étrangers.'

Though the château was closed to us, we did not therefore give up our purposed expedition to Versailles: every object there is interesting, not only from its splendour, but from the

111

recollections it revives of scenes with whose history we are all familiar. Not only the horrors of the last century, but all the regal glories of the preceding one, are so well known to everybody, that there must have been a prodigious deal of gossip handed down to us from France, or we never could feel so much better acquainted with events which have passed at Versailles than with any scenes that have occurred at an equal distance of time at Windsor.

But so it is; and the English go there not merely as strangers visiting a palace in a foreign land, but as pilgrims to the shrine of the princes and poets who have left their memory there, and with whose names and histories they are as familiar as if they belonged to us.

The day we passed among the royal spectres that never fail to haunt one at this palace of recollections, was a mixture of sunshine and showers, and our meditations seemed to partake of the vicissitude.

It is said that the great Louis reared this stupendous dwelling in which to pass the gilded hours of his idleness, because from St. Germain's he could see the plain of St. Denis, over which his funeral array was to pass, and the spire that marked the spot where his too precious dust was to be laid. Happy was it for him that the scutcheoned sepulchre of St. Denis was the most distant and most gloomy point to which his prophetic glance could reach! Could the great king have looked a little farther, and dreamed of the scenes which were destined to follow this dreaded passage to his royal tomb, how would he have blessed the fate which permitted him to pass into it so peacefully!

It is quite wonderful to see how much of the elaborate decoration and fine finishing of this sumptuous place remains uninjured after being visited by the most ferocious mob that ever collected together. Had they been less intent on the savage object of their mission, it is probable that they would have sated their insane rage in destroying the palace itself, and the costly decorations of its singular gardens. Though far inferior in all ways either to the gardens of the Elector of Hesse Cassel at Wilhelmshöhe, or to those of the Grand Duke of Baden at Schwetzingen, those of Versailles are still highly interesting from many causes, and have so much of majesty and pomp about them, that one cannot look upon them without feeling that only the kings of the earth could ever have had a master's right to take their pleasure therein.

Before we entered upon the orderly confusion of groves, statues, temples, and water-works through which it is necessary to be led, we made our grey-headed guide lead us round and about every part of the building while we listened to his string of interesting old stories about Louis Seize, and Marie Antoinette, and Monsieur, and le Comte d'Artois (for he seemed to have forgotten that they had borne any other titles than those he remembered in his youth), all of whom seemed to retain exactly the same place in his imagination that they had occupied some fifty years ago, when he was assistant to the keeper of the *orangerie*. He boasted, with a vanity as fresh as if it had been newly born, of the honours of that near approach to royalty which he had formerly enjoyed; recounted how the Queen called one of the orange-trees her own, because she fancied its blossoms sweeter than all the rest; and how from such a broad-leafed double-blossoming myrtle he had daily gathered a *bouquet* for her majesty, which was laid upon her toilet exactly at two o'clock. This old man knew every orange-tree, its birth and history, as well as a shepherd knows his flock. The venerable father of the band dates his existence from the reign of François Premier, and truly he enjoys a green old age. The one surnamed Louis le Grand, who was twin brother, as he said, to that mighty monarch, looks like a youth beside it – and you are told that it has not yet attained its full growth.

Oh! could those orange-trees but speak! could they recount to us the scenes they have witnessed; could they describe to us all the beauties over whom they have shed their fragrant flowers – all the heroes, statesmen, poets, and princes who have stepped in courtly paces beneath their shade; what a world of witty wickedness, of solemn warning, and of sad reflection, we should have!

But though the orange-trees were mute, our old man talked enough for them all. He was a faithful servant to the old *régime*: and indeed it should seem that there is something in the air of Versailles favourable alike to orange-trees and loyalty; for never did I hear, while wandering amidst their aristocratic perfume, one word that was not of sound orthodox legitimate loyalty to the race for whose service they have for so many hundred years lived and bloomed. And still they blossom on, unscathed by revolution, unblighted though an usurper called them his; – happier in this than many of those who were once privileged to parade their dignity beneath their royal shade. The old servitors still move among these venenerable vegetable grandees with the ceremonious air of courtiers, offering obsequious service, if not to the king himself, at least to his cousin-germans; and I am persuaded there is not one of these old serving-men, who wander about Versailles like ghosts revisiting the scenes of former happiness, who would not more humbly pull off his hat to François Premier or Louis le Grand in the greenhouse, than to any monarch of a younger race.

Napoleon has left less trace of himself and his giant power at Versailles than anywhere else; and the naîads and hamadryads still lift their sculptured heads with such an eternity of stately grace, as makes one feel the evanescent nature of the interlude that was played among them during the empire. It is of the old race of Bourbon that the whole region is redolent. 'There,' said our old guide, 'is the range of chambers that was occupied by the Queen . . . those were the King's apartments . . . there were the royal children . . . there Monsieur . . . and there the Comte d'Artois.'

Then we were led round to the fatal balcony which overhangs the entrance. It was there that the fallen Marie Antoinette stood, her young son in her arms, and the doomed King her husband beside her, when she looked down upon the demons drunk with blood, who sought her life. I had heard all this hateful, but o'er-true history, more than once before on the same spòt, and shortening the frightful detail, I hastened to leave it, though I believe the good old man would willingly have spent hours in dwelling upon it.

The day had been named as one on which the great waters were to play. But, little as Nature has to do with this pretty exhibition, she interfered on this occasion to prevent it. There was no water. The dry winter would, they told us, probably render it impossible to play them during the whole summer.

Here was another disappointment; but we bore it heroically, and after examining and much admiring the numberless allegories which people the grounds, and to the creation of which, a poet must have been as necessary as a sculptor, we adjourned to the Trianons, there to meditate on all the ceaseless vicissitudes of female influence from Maintenon to Josephine. It is but a sad review, but it may serve well to reconcile the majority of womankind to the tranquil dreaminess of obscurity.

The next thing to be done was dining – and most wretchedly done it was: but we found something to laugh at, nevertheless; for when the wine brought to us was found too bad to drink, and we ordered better, no less than four bottles were presented to us in succession, each one increasing in price, but being precisely of the same quality. When we charged the black-eyed daughter of the house with the fact, she said with perfect good-humour, but nowise denying it, that she was very sorry they had no better. When the bill was brought, the same damsel civilly hoped that we should not think ten sous (half-a-franc) too much to pay for having opened so many bottles. Now, as three of them were firmly corked, and carefully sealed besides, we paid our ten sous without any complaining.

The looking at a fête at St. Cloud made part of the business of the day; but in order to get there, we were obliged to mount into one of those indescribable vehicles by which the gay *bourgeoisie* of Paris are conveyed from palace to palace, and from *guinguette* to *guinguette*. We had dismissed our comfortable *citadine*, being assured that we should have no difficulty in finding another. In this, however, we were disappointed, the proportion of company appearing greatly to exceed that of the carriages which were to convey them, and we considered ourselves fortunate in securing places in an equipage which we should have scorned indignantly when we quitted Paris in the morning.

The whimsical gaiety of the crowd, all hurrying one way, was very amusing; all anxious to reach St. Cloud before the promised half-hour's display of water-works were over; all testifying, by look, gesture, voice, and words, that light effervescence of animal spirits so essentially characteristic of the country, and all forming a moving panorama so gay and bright as almost to make one giddy by looking at it.

Some among the capricious variety of vehicles were drawn by five or six horses. These were in truth nothing but gaily-painted waggons, hung on rude springs, with a flat awning over them. In several I counted twenty persons; but there were some few among them in which one or perhaps two seats were still vacant – and then the rapturous glee of the party was excited to the utmost by the efforts of the driver, as gay as themselves, to obtain customers to fill the vacancies.

Every individual overtaken on the road was invited by the most clamorous outcries to occupy the vacant seats. 'St. Cloud! St. Cloud! St. Cloud!' shouted by the driver and re-echoed by all his company, rang in the startled ears of all they passed; and if a traveller soberly journeying in the contrary direction was met, the invitation was uttered with tenfold vehemence, accompanied by shouts of laughter; which, far from offending the party who provoked it, was invariably answered with equal frolic and fun. But when upon one occasion a carriage posting almost at full gallop towards Versailles was encountered, the ecstasy of mirth with which it was greeted exceeds description. 'St. Cloud! St. Cloud! – Tournez donc, messieurs – tournez à St. Cloud!' The shouts and vociferations were enough to frighten all the horses in the world excepting French ones; and they must be so thoroughly broken to the endurance of din, that there is little danger of their starting at it. I could have almost fancied that upon this occasion they took part in it; for they took their ropes and their tassels, snorted and tossed, very much as if they enjoyed the fun.

After all, we, and many hundred others, arrived too late for the show, the supply of water failing even before the promised half-hour had elapsed. The gardens, however, were extremely full, and all the world looked as gay and as well-pleased as if nothing had gone wrong.

I wonder if these people ever grow old, – that is, old as we do, sitting in the chimney-corner, and dreaming no more of fêtes than of playing at blind-man's-buff. I have certainly seen here, as elsewhere, men, and women too, grey-headed, and wrinkled enough to be as solemn as the most venerable judge upon the bench; but I never saw any that did not seem ready to hop, skip, jump, waltz, and make love.

LETTER XXI

History of the Vicomte de B—— – His opinions – State of France – Expediency

I have had a curious conversation this morning with an old gentleman whom I believed to be a thorough legitimate, but who turns out, as you will see, something else – I hardly know what to call it – *doctrinaire* I suppose it must be, yet it is not quite that either.

But before I give you his opinions, let me present himself. M. le Vicomte de B—— is a person that I am very sure you would be happy to know anywhere. His residence is not in Paris, but at a château that he describes as the most profound retirement imaginable; yet it is not more than thirty leagues from Paris. He is a widower, and his only child is a daughter, who has been some years married.

The history of this gentleman, given as he gave it himself, was deeply interesting. It was told with much feeling, some wit, and no prolixity. Were I, however, to attempt to repeat it to you in the same manner, it would become long and tedious, and in every way as unlike as possible to what it was as it came fresh from the living fountain.

In brief, then, I will tell you that he was the younger son of an old and noble house, and, for seven years, page to Louis Seize. He must have been strikingly handsome; and young as he was at the time of the first revolution, he seems already to have found the court a very agreeable residence. He had held a commission in the army about two years, when his father, and his only brother, his elder by ten years, were obliged to leave the country, to save their lives.

The family was not a wealthy one, and great sacrifices were necessary to enable them to live in England. What remained became eventually the property of our friend, both father and brother having died in exile. With this remnant of fortune he married, not very prudently; and having lost his wife and disposed of his daughter in marriage, he is now living in his large dilapidated château, with one female servant, and an old man as major-domo, valet, and cook, who served with him in La Vendée, and who, by his description, must be a perfect Corporal Trim.

I would give a good deal to be able to accept the invitation I have received to pay him a visit at his castle. I think I should find just such a ménage as that which Scott so beautifully describes in one of his prefaces. But the wish is vain, such an excursion being quite impossible; so I must do without the castle, and content myself with the long morning visits that its agreeable owner is so kind as to make us.

I have seen him frequently, and listened with great interest to his little history; but it was only this morning that the conversation took a speculative turn. I was quite persuaded, but certainly from my own preconceived notions only, and not from anything I have heard him say, that M. de B—— was a devoted legitimate. An old noble – page to Louis Seize – a royalist soldier in La Vendée, – how could I think otherwise? Yet he talked to me as . . . you shall hear.

Our conversation began by his asking me if I was conscious of much material change in Paris since I last visited it.

I replied, that I certainly saw some, but perhaps suspected more.

'I dare say you do,' said he; 'it is what your nation is very apt to do: but take my advice, – believe what you see, and nothing else.'

'But what one can see in the course of a month or two is so little, and I hear so much.'

'That is true; but do you not find that what you hear from one person is often contradicted by another?'

'Constantly,' I replied.

'Then what can you do at last but judge by what you see?'

'Why, it appears to me that the better plan would be to listen to all parties, and let my balancing belief incline to the testimony that has most weight.'

'Then be careful that this weight be not false. There are some who will tell you that the national feeling which for so many centuries has kept France together as a powerful and predominating people is loosened, melted, and gone; – that though there are Frenchmen left, there is no longer a French people.'

'To any who told me so,' I replied, 'I would say, that the division they complained of, arose not so much from any change in the French character, as from the false position in which many were unhappily placed at the present moment. Men's hearts are divided because they are diversely drawn aside from a common centre.'

'And you would say truly,' said he; 'but others will tell you, that regenerated France will soon dictate laws to the whole earth; that her flag will become the flag of all people – her government their government; and that their tottering monarchies will soon crumble into dust, to become part and parcel of her glorious republic.'

'And to these I should say, that they appeared to be in a very heavy slumber, and that the sooner they could wake out of it and shake off their feverish dreams, the better it would be for them.'

'But what would your inference be as to the state of the country from such reports as these?'

'I should think that, as usual, truth lay between. I should neither believe that France was so united as to constitute a single-minded giant, nor so divided as to have become a mass of unconnected atoms, or a race of pigmies.'

'You know,' he continued, 'that the fashionable phrase for describing our condition at present is, that we are in a *state of transition,* – from butterflies to grubs, or from grubs to butterflies, I know not which; but to me it seems that the transition is over, – and it is high time that it should be so. The country has known neither rest nor peace for nearly half a century; and powerful as she has been and still is, she must at least fall a prey to whoever may think it worth their while to despoil her, unless she stops short while it is yet time, and strengthens herself by a little seasonable repose.'

'But how is this repose to be obtained?' said I. 'Some of you wish to have one king, some another, and some to have no king at all. This is not a condition in which a country is very likely to find repose.'

'Not if each faction be of equal power, or sufficiently so to persevere in struggling for the mastery. Our only hope lies in the belief that there is no such equality. Let him who has seized the helm keep it: if he be an able helmsman, he will keep us in smooth water; – and it is no longer time for us to ask how he got his commission; let us be thankful that he happens to be of the same lineage as those to whose charge we have for so many ages committed the safety of our bark.'

I believe my countenance expressed my astonishment; for the old gentleman smiled and said,

'Do I frighten you with my revolutionary principles?'

'Indeed, you surprise me a little,' I replied: 'I should have thought that the rights of a legitimate monarch would have been in your opinion indefeasible.'

'Where is the law, my good lady, that may control necessity? . . . I speak not my own feelings, or of those of the few who were born like myself in another era. Very terrible convulsions have passed over France, and perhaps threaten the rest of Europe. I have for many years stood apart and watched the storm; and I am quite sure, and find much comfort in the assurance, that the crimes and passions of men cannot change the nature of things. They may produce much misery, they may disturb and confuse the peaceful current of events; but man still remains as he was, and will seek his safety and his good, where he had ever found them – under the shelter of power.'

'There, indeed, I quite agree with you. But surely the more lawful and right the power is, the more likely it must be to remain tranquil and undisputed in its influence.'

'France has no longer the choice,' said he, interrupting me abruptly. 'I speak but as a looker-on; my political race is ended; I have more than once sworn allegiance to the elder branch of the house of Bourbon, and certainly nothing would tempt me to hold office or take oath under any other. But do you think it would be the duty of a Frenchman who has three grandsons native to the soil of France, – do you really think it the duty of such a one to invoke civil war upon the land of his fathers, and remembering only his king, to forget his country? I will not tell you, that if I could wake tomorrow morning and find a fifth Henry peacefully seated on the throne of his fathers, I might not rejoice; particularly if I were sure that he would be as likely to keep the naughty boys of Paris in order as I think his cousin Philippe is. Were there profit in wishing, I would wish for France a government so strong as should effectually prevent her from destroying herself; and that government should have at its head a king whose right to reign had come to him, not by force of arms, but by the will of God in lawful succession. But when we mortals have a wish, we may be thankful if the half of it be granted; – and, in truth, I think that I have the first and better half of mine to rejoice in. There is a stout and sturdy strength in the government of King Philippe, which gives good hope that France may recover under its protection from her sins and her sorrows, and again become the glory of her children.'

So saying, M. de B—— rose to leave me, and putting out his hand in the English fashion, added, 'I am afraid you do not like me so well as you did . . . I am no longer a true and loyal knight in your estimation . . . but something, perhaps, very like a rebel and a traitor? . . . It is not so?'

I hardly knew how to answer him. He certainly had lost a good deal of that poetical elevation of character with which I had invested him; yet there was a mixture of honesty and honour in his frankness that I could not help esteeming. I thanked him very sincerely for the openness with which he had spoken, but confessed that I had not quite made up my mind to think that expediency was the right rule for human actions. It certainly was not the noblest, and therefore I was willing to believe that it was not the best.

'I must go,' said he, looking at his watch, 'for it is my hour of dining, or I think I could dispute with you a little upon your word *expediency*. Whatever is really expedient for us to do – that is, whatever is best for us in the situation in which we are actually placed, is really right. Adieu! – I shall present myself again ere long; and if you admit me, I shall be thankful.'

So saying, he departed, – leaving us all, I believe, a little less in alt about him than before, but certainly with no inclination to shut our doors against him.

LETTER XXII

*Père Lachaise – Mourning in public – Defacing the Tomb of
Abelard and Eloïsa – Baron Munchausen –
Russian Monument – Statue of Manuel*

Often as I have visited the enclosure of Père Lachaise, it was
with feelings of renewed curiosity and interest that I yesterday
accompanied thither those of my party who had not yet seen
it. I was well pleased to wander once more through the
cypress alleys, now grown into fine gloomy funereal shades,
and once more to feel that wavering sort of emotion which I
always experience there; – one moment being tempted to
smile at the fantastic manner in which affection has been
manifested, – and the next, moved to tears by some touch of
tenderness, that makes itself felt even amidst the vast
collection of childish superstitions with which the place
abounds. This mournful garden is altogether a very solemn
and impressive spectacle. What a world of mortality does one
take in at one glance! It will set one thinking a little, however
fresh from the busy idleness of Paris, – of Paris, that antidote
to all serious thought, that especial paradise for the wor-
shippers of SANS SOUCI.

A profusion of spring flowers are at this season hourly
shedding their blossoms over every little cherished enclosure.
There is beauty, freshness, fragrance on the surface . . . It is a
fearful contrast!

I do not remember any spot, either in church or churchyard,
where the unequal dignity of the memorials raised above the
dust which lies so very equally beneath them all is shown in a
manner to strike the heart so forcibly as it does at Père
Lachaise. Here, a shovelful of weeds have hardly room to
grow; and there rises a costly pile, shadowing its lowly
neighbour. On this side the narrow path, sorrow is wrapped
round and hid from notice by the very poverty that renders it

more bitter; while, on the other, wealth, rank, and pride heap decorations over the worthless clay, striving vainly to conceal its nothingness. It is an epitome of the world they have left: remove the marble and disturb the turf, human nature will be found to wear the same aspect under both.

Many groups in deep mourning were wandering among the tombs; so many indeed, that when we turned aside from one, with the reverence one always feels disposed to pay to sorrow, we were sure to encounter another. This manner of lamenting in public seems so strange to us! How would it be for a shy English mother, who sobs inwardly and hides the aching sorrow in her heart's core, – how would she bear to bargain at the public gate for a pretty garland, then enter amidst an idle throng, with the toy hanging on her finger, and, before the eyes of all who choose to look, suspend it over the grave of her lost child? An Englishwoman surely must lose her reason either before or after such an act; – if it were not the effect of madness, it would be the cause of it. Yet such is the effect of habit, or rather of the different tone of manners and of mind here, than one may daily and hourly see parents, most devoted to their children during their lives, and most heart-broken when divided from them by death, perform with streaming eyes these public lamentations.

It is nevertheless impossible, let the manner of it differ from our own as much as it may, to look at the freshly-trimmed flowers, the garlands, and all the pretty tokens of tender care which meet the eye in every part of this wide-spread mass of mortal nothingness, without feeling that real love and real sorrow have been at work.

One small enclosure attracted my attention as at once the most *bizarre* and the most touching of all. It held the little grassy tomb of a young child, planted round with choice flowers; and at its head rose a semicircular recess, containing, together with a crucifix and other religious emblems, several common playthings, which had doubtless been the latest joy of the lost darling. His age was stated to have been three years, and he was mourned as the first and only child after twelve years of marriage.

Below this melancholy statement was inscribed –

'Passans! priez pour sa malheureuse mère!'

Might we not say, that

> Thought and affliction, passion, death itself,
> They turn to favour and to prettiness?

It would, I believe, be more just, as well as more generous, instead of accusing the whole nation of being the victims of affectation instead of sorrow under every affliction that death can cause, to believe that they feel quite as sincerely as ourselves; though they have certainly a very different way of showing it.

I wish they, whoever they are, who had the command of such matters, would have let the curious tomb of Abelard and Eloïsa remain in decent tranquillity in its original position. Nothing can assimilate worse than do its Gothic form and decorations with every object around it. The paltry plaster tablet too, that has been stuck upon it for the purpose of recording the history of the tomb rather than of those who lie buried in it, is in villanously bad taste; and we can only hope that the elements will complete the work they have begun, and then this barbarous defacing will crumble away before our grandchildren shall know anything about it.

The thickly-planted trees and shrubs have grown so rapidly, as in many places to make it difficult to pass through them; and the ground appears to be extremely crowded nearly over its whole extent. A few neighbouring acres have been lately added to it; but their bleak, naked, and unornamented surface forbids the eye as yet to recognise this space as part of the enclosure. One pale solitary tomb is placed within it, at the very verge of the dark cypress line that marks the original boundary; and it looks like a sheeted ghost hovering about between night and morning.

One very noble monument has been added since I last visited the garden: it is dedicated to the memory of a noble Russian lady, whose long unspellable name I forget. It is of white or greyish marble, and of magnificent proportions, – lofty and elegant, yet massive and entirely simple. Altogether, it appeared to me to be as perfect in taste as any specimen of monumental architecture that I have ever seen, though it had not the last best grace of sculpture to adorn it. There is no effigy – no statue – scarcely an ornament of any kind, but it seems constructed with a view to unite equally the appearance of imposing masjesty and enduring strength. This splendid mausoleum stands towards the top of the garden, and forms a predominating and very beautiful object from various parts of it.

Among the hundreds of names which one reads in passing, – I hardly know why, for they certainly convey but small interest to the mind, – we met with that of the *Baron Munchausen*. It was a small and unpretending-looking stone, but bore a host of blazing titles, by which it appears that this Baron, whom I, and all my generation, I believe, have ever looked upon as an imaginary personage, was in fact something or other very important to somebody or other who was very powerful. Why his noble name has been made such use of among us, I cannot imagine.

In the course of our wanderings we came upon this singular inscription:–

'Ci-gît Caroline,' – (I think the name is Caroline), – 'fille de Mademoiselle Mars.'

Is it not wonderful what a difference twenty-one miles of salt-water can make in the ways and manners of people?

There are not many statues in the cemetery, and none of sufficient merit to add much to its embellishment; but there is one recently placed there, and standing loftily predominant above every surrounding object, which is strongly indicative of the period of its erection, and of the temper of the people to whom it seems to address itself. This is a colossal figure of Manuel. The countenance is vulgar, and the expression of the features violent and exaggerated: it might stand as the portrait of a bold factious rebel for ever.

LETTER XXIII

Remarkable People – Distinguished People –
Metaphysical Lady

Last night we passed our *soirée* at the house of a lady who had been introduced to me with this recommendation:– 'You will be certain of meeting at Madame de V——'s many REMARKABLE PEOPLE.'

This is, I think, exactly the sort of introduction which would in any city give the most piquant interest to a new acquaintance; but it does so particularly at Paris; for this attractive capital draws its collection of remarkable people from a greater variety of nations, classes, and creeds, than any other.

Nevertheless, this term 'remarkable people' must not be taken too confidently to mean individuals so distinguished that all men would desire to gaze upon them; the phrase varying in its value and its meaning according to the feelings, faculties, and station of the speaker.

Everybody has got his or her own 'remarkable people' to introduce to you; and I have begun to find out, among the houses that are open to me, what species of 'remarkable people' I am likely to meet at each.

When Madame A—— whispers to me as I enter her drawing-room – 'Ah! vous voilà! c'est bon; j'aurais été bien fâchée si vous m'aviez manquée; il y a ici, ce soir, une personne bien remarquable, qu'il faut absolument vous présenter,' – I am quite sure that I shall see some one who has been a marshal, or a duke, or a general, or a physician, or an actor, or an artist, to Napoleon.

But if it were Madame B—— who said the same thing, I should be equally certain that it must be a comfortable-looking doctrinaire, who was, had been, or was about to be in place, and who had made his voice heard on the winning side.

126

Madame C——, on the contrary, would not deign to bestow such an epithet on any one whose views and occupations were so earthward. It could only be some philosopher, pale with the labour of reconciling paradoxes or discovering a new element.

My charming, quiet, graceful, gentle Madame D—— could use it only when speaking of an ex-chancellor, or chamberlain, or friend, or faithful servant of the exiled dynasty.

As for the tall dark-browed Madame E——, with her thin lips and sinister smile, though she professes to hold a *salon* where talent of every party is welcome, she never cares much, I am very sure, for any remarkableness that is not connected with the great and immortal mischief of some revolution. She is not quite old enough to have had anything to do with the first; but I have no doubt that she was very busy during the last, and I am positive that she will never know peace by night or day till another can be got up. If her hopes fail on this point, she will die of atrophy; for nothing affords her nourishment but what is mixed up with rebellion against constituted authority.

I know that she dislikes me; and I suspect I owe the honour of being admitted to appear in her presence solely to her determination that I should hear everything that she thinks it would be disagreeable for me to listen to. I believe she fancies that I do not like to meet Americans; but she is as much mistaken in this as in most other of her speculations.

I really never saw or heard of any fanaticism equal to that, with which this lady worships destruction. That whatever is, is wrong, is the rule by which her judgment is guided in all things. It is enough for her that a law on any point is established, to render the thing legalised detestable; and were the republic about which she raves, and of which she knows as much as her lap-dog, to be established throughout France tomorrow, I am quite persuaded that we should have her embroidering a regal robe for the most legitimate king she could find, before next Monday.

Madame F——'s *remarkables* are almost all of them for-eigners of the philosophic revolutionary class; any gentry that are not particularly well off at home, and who would rather prefer being remarkable and remarked a few hundred miles from their own country than in it.

Madame G——'s are chiefly musical personages. 'Croyez-moi, madame,' she says, 'il n'y a que lui pour toucher le piano . . . Vous n'avez pas encore entendu Mademoiselle Z—— . . . Quelle voix superbe! . . . Elle fera, j'en suis sûre, une fortune immense à Londres.'

Madame H——'s acquaintance are not so 'remarkable' for anything peculiar in each or any of them, as for being in all things exactly opposed to each other. She likes to have her parties described as 'Les soirées antithestiques de Madame H——,' and has a peculiar sort of pleasure in seeing people sitting side by side on her hearth-rug, who would be very likely to salute each other with a pistol-shot were they to meet elsewhere. It is rather a singular device for arranging a sociable party; but her *soirées* are very delightful *soirées*, for all that.

Madame J——'s friends are not 'remarkable'; they are 'distinguished'. It is quite extraordinary what a number of distinguished individuals I have met at her house.

But I must not go through the whole alphabet, lest I should tire you. So let me return to the point from whence I set out, and take you with me to Madame de V——'s *soirée*. A large party is almost always a sort of lottery, and your good or bad fortune depends on the accidental vicinity of pleasant or unpleasant neighbours.

I cannot consider myself to have gained a prize last night; and Fortune, if she means to make things even, must place me tonight next the most agreeable person in Paris. I really think that should the same evil chance that beset me yesterday pursue me for a week, I should leave the country to escape from it. I will describe to you the manner of my torment as well as I can, but must fail, I think, to give you an adequate idea of it.

A lady I had never seen before walked across the room to me last night soon after I entered it, and making prisoner of Madame de V—— in the way, was presented to me in due form. I was placed on a sofa by an old gentleman with whom we have formed a great friendship, and for whose conversation I have a particular liking: he had just seated himself beside me, when my new acquaintance dislodged him by saying, as she attempted to squeeze herself in between us, 'Pardon, monsieur; ne vous dérangez pas! . . . mais si madame voulait bien me permettre' . . . and before she could finish her speech, my old acquaintance was far away and my new one close beside me.

She began the conversation by some very obliging assurances of her wish to make my acquaintance. 'I want to discuss with you,' said she. I bowed, but trembled inwardly, for I do not like discussions, especially with 'remarkable' ladies. 'Yes,' she continued, 'I want to discuss with you many topics of vital interest to us all – topics on which I believe we now think differently, but on which I feel quite sure that we should agree, would you but listen to me.'

I smiled and bowed, and muttered something civil, and looked as much pleased as I possibly could, – and recollected, too, how large Paris was, and how easy it would be to turn my back upon conviction, if I found that I could not face it agreeably. But, to say truth, there was something in the eye and manner of my new friend that rather alarmed me. She is rather pretty, nevertheless; but her bright eyes are never still for an instant, and she is one of those who aid the power of speech by that of touch, to which she has incessant recourse. Had she been a man, she would have seized all her friends by the button: but as it is, she can only lay her fingers with emphasis upon your arm, or grasp a handful of your sleeve, when she sees reason to fear that your attention wanders.

'You are a legitimatist! . . . quel dommage! Ah! you smile. But did you know the incalculable injury done to the intellect by putting chains upon it! . . . My studies, observe, are confined almost wholly to one subject, – the philosophy of the human mind. Metaphysics have been the great object of my life from a very early age.' (I should think she was now about seven or eight-and-twenty.) 'Yet sometimes I have the weakness to turn aside from this noble pursuit to look upon the troubled current of human affairs that is rolling past me. I do not pretend to enter deeply into politics – I have no time for it; but I see enough to make me shrink from despotism and legitimacy. Believe me, it cramps the mind; and be assured that a constant succession of political changes keeps the faculties of a nation on the *qui vive*, and, abstractedly considered as a mental operation, must be incalculably more beneficial than the half-dormant state which takes place after any long continuance in one position, let it be what it may.'

She uttered all this with such wonderful rapidity, that it would have been quite impossible for me to have made any observation upon it as she went along, if I had been ever so much inclined to do so. But I soon found that this was not expected of me.

  ''Twas hers to speak, and mine to hear;'

and I made up my mind to listen as patiently as I could till I should find a convenient opportunity for changing my place.

At different times, and in different climes, I have heretofore listened to a good deal of nonsense, certainly; but I assure you I never did nor ever can expect again to hear such a profusion of wild absurdity as this lady uttered. Yet I am told that she has in many circles the reputation of being a woman of genius. It would be but a vain attempt did I endeavour to go on remembering and translating all she said; but some of her speeches really deserve recording.

After she had run her tilt against authority, she broke off, exclaiming –

'Mais, après tout, – what does it signify? . . . When you have once devoted yourself to the study of the soul, all these little distinctions do appear so trifling! . . . I have given myself wholly to the study of the soul; and my life passes in a series of experiments, which, if I do not wear myself out here,' putting her hand to her forehead, 'will, I think, eventually lead me to something important.'

As she paused for a moment, I thought I ought to say something, and therefore asked her of what nature were the experiments of which she spoke. To which she replied –

'Principally in comparative anatomy. None but an experimentalist could ever imagine what extraordinary results arise from this best and surest mode of investigation. A mouse, for instance . . . Ah, madame! would you believe it possible that the formation of a mouse could throw light upon the theory of the noblest feeling that warms the heart of man – even upon valour? It is true, I assure you: such are the triumphs of science. By watching the pulsations of that *chétif* animal,' she continued, eagerly laying hold of my wrist, 'we have obtained an immense insight into the most interesting phenomena of the passion of fear.'

At this moment my old gentleman came back to me, but evidently without any expectation of being able to resume his seat. It was only, I believe, to see how I got on with my metaphysical neighbour. There was an infinite deal of humour in the glance he gave me as he said, 'Eh bien, Madame Trollope, est-ce que Madame —— vous a donné l'ambition de la suivre dans ses sublimes études?'

'I fear it would prove beyond my strength,' I replied. Upon which Madame —— started off anew in praise of *her* science – 'the only science worthy the name; the science . . .'

Here my old friend stole off again, covered by an approaching tray of ices; and I soon after did the same; for I had been busily engaged all day, and I was weary, – so weary that I dreaded dropping to sleep at the very instant that Madame —— was exerting herself to awaken me to a higher state of intelligence.

I have not, however, told you one tenth part of the marvellous absurdities she poured forth; yet I suspect I have told you enough. I have never before met anything so pre-eminently ridiculous as this: but upon my saying so to my old friend as I passed him near the door, he assured me that he knew another lady, whose mania was education, and whose doctrines and manner of explaining them were decidedly more absurd than Madame ——'s philosophy of the soul.

'Be not alarmed, however; I shall not bestow her upon you, for I intend most carefully to keep out of her way. Do you know of any English ladies thus devoted to the study of the soul?' . . . I am sincerely happy to say that I do not.

LETTER XXIV

Expedition to the Luxembourg – No admittance for Females –
Portraits of 'Henri' – Republican Costume – Quai Voltaire –
Mural Inscriptions – Ancedote of Marshal Lobau – Arrest

Ever since the trials at the Luxembourg commenced, we have
intended to make an excursion thither, in order to look at the
encampment in the garden, at the military array around the
palace, and, in short, to see all that is visible for female eyes in
the general aspect of the place, so interesting at the present
moment from the important business going on there.

I have done all that could be done to obtain admission to the
Chamber during their sittings, and have not been without
friends who very kindly interested themselves to render my
efforts successful – but in vain; no ladies have been permitted
to enter. Whether the feminine regrets have been lessened or
increased by the daily accounts that are published of the
outrageous conduct of the prisoners, I will not venture to say.
C'est égal; get in we cannot, whether we wish it or not. It is
said, indeed, that in one of the tribunes set apart for the public,
a small white hand has been seen to caress some jet-black curls
upon the head of a boy; and it was said, too, that the boy called
himself George S——d: but I have heard of no other instance
of any one not furnished with that important symbol of
prerogative, *une barbe au menton*, who has ventured within the
proscribed limits.

Our humble-minded project of looking at the walls which
enclose the blustering rebels and their patient judges has been
at length happily accomplished, and not without affording us
considerable amusement.

In addition to our usual party, we had the pleasure of being
accompanied by two agreeable Frenchmen, who promised to
explain whatever signs and symbols might meet our eyes but
mock our comprehension. As the morning was delightful, we

agreed to walk to the place of our destination, and repose ourselves as much as the tossings of a *fiacre* would permit on the way home.

That our route lay through the Tuileries Gardens was one reason for this arrangement; and, as usual, we indulged ourselves for a delightful half-hour by sitting under the trees.

Whenever six or eight persons wish to converse together – not in *tête-à-tête*, but in a general confabulation, I would recommend exactly the place we occupied for the purpose, with the chairs of the party drawn together, not spread into a circle, but collected in a group, so that every one can hear, and every one can be heard.

Our conversation was upon the subject of various prints which we had seen exposed upon the Boulevards as we passed; and though our two Frenchmen were excellent friends, it was very evident that they did not hold the same opinions in politics; – so we had some very pleasant sparring.

We have been constantly in the habit of remarking a variety of portraits of a pretty, elegant-looking youth, sometimes totally without lettters – and yet they were not proofs, excepting of an antique loyalty, – sometimes with the single word 'Henri!' – sometimes with a sprig of the pretty weed we call 'Forget-me-not,' – and sometimes with the name of 'Le Duc de Bordeaux.' As we passed one of the cases this morning which stand out before a large shop on the Boulevards, I remarked a new one: it was a pretty lithographic print, and being very like an original miniature which had been kindly shown me during a visit I paid in the Faubourg St. Germain, I stopped to buy it, and writing my name on the envelope, ordered it to be sent home.

M. P——, the gentleman who was walking beside me when I stopped, confirmed my opinion that it was a likeness, by his personal knowledge of the original; and it was not difficult to perceive, though he spoke but little on the subject, that an affectionate feeling for 'THE CAUSE' and its young hero was at his heart.

M. de L——, the other gentleman who had joined our party, was walking behind us, and came up as I was making my purchase. He smiled. 'I see what you are about,' said he: 'if you and P—— continue to walk together, I am sure you will plot some terrible treason before you get to the Lux-embourg.'

When we were seated in the Tuileries Gardens, M. de L——renewed his attack upon me for what he called my seditious conduct in having encouraged the vender of a prohibited article, and declared that he thought he should but do his duty if he left M. P—— and myself in safe custody among the other rebellious characters at the Luxembourg.

'My sedition,' replied M. P——, 'is but speculative. The best among us now can only sigh that things are not quite as they should be, and be thankful that they are not quite as bad as they might be.'

'I rejoice to find that you allow so much, mon cher,' replied his friend. 'Yes, I think it might be worse; par exemple, if such gentry as those yonder were to have their way with us.'

He looked towards three youths who were stalking up the walk before us with the air of being deeply intent on some business of dire import. They looked like walking caricatures – and in truth they were nothing else.

They were republicans. Similar figures are constantly seen strutting upon the Boulevards, or sauntering, like those before us, in the Tuileries, or hovering in sinister groups about the Bois de Boulogne, each one believing himself to bear the brow of a Brutus and the heart of a Cato. But see them where or when you will, they take good care to be unmistakable; there is not a child of ten years old in Paris who cannot tell a republican when he sees him. In several print-shops I have seen a key to their mystical toilet which may enable the ignorant to read them right. A hat, whose crown if raised for a few inches more would be conical, is highest in importance, as in place; and the shade of Cromwell may perhaps glory in seeing how many desperate wrongheads still mimic his beaver. Then come the long and matted locks, that hang in heavy ominous dirtiness beneath it. The throat is bare, at least from linen; but a plentiful and very disgusting profusion of hair supplies its place. The waistcoat, like the hat, bears an immortal name – 'GILET À LA ROBESPIERRE' being its awful designation; and and the extent of its wide-spreading lapels is held to be a criterion of the expansive principles of the wearer. *Au reste*, a general air of grim and savage blackguardism is all that is necessary to make up the outward man of a republican of Paris in 1835.

But, oh! the grimaces by which I have seen human face distorted by persons wearing this masquerading attire! Some roll their eyes and knit their brows as if they would bully the whole universe; others fix their dark glances on the ground in fearful meditation; while other some there be who, while gloomily leaning against a statue or a tree, throw such terrific meaning into their looks as might naturally be interpreted into the language of the witches in Macbeth –

> 'We must, we will – we must, we will
> Have much more blood, – and become worse,
> And become worse' . . . &c. &c.

The three young men who had just passed us were exactly of this stamp. Our legitimate friend looked after them and laughed heartily.

'C'est à nous autres, mon cher,' said de L——, 'to enjoy that sight. You and yours would have but small reason to laugh at such as these, if it were not the business of us and ours to take care that they should do you no harm. You may thank the eighty thousand National Guards of Paris for the pleasure of quizzing with such a complacent feeling of security these very ferocious-looking persons.'

'For that I thank them heartily,' replied M. P——; 'only I think the business would have been quite as well done if those who performed it had the right to do so.'

'Bah! Have you not tried, and found you could make nothing of it?'

'I think not, my friend,' replied the legitimatist: 'we were doing very well, and exerting ourselves to keep the unruly spirits in order, when you stepped in, and promised all the naughty boys in Paris a holiday if they would but make you master. They did make you master – they have had their holiday, and now . . .'

'And now . . .' said I, 'what will come next?'

Both the gentlemen answered me at once.

'Riots,' said the legitimatist.

'Good order,' said the doctrinaire.

We proceeded in our walk, and having crossed the Pont Royal, kept along the Quai Voltaire, to avoid the Rue du Bac; as we all agreed that, notwithstanding Madame de Staël spoke so lovingly of it at a distance, it was far from agreeable when near.

Were it not for a sort of English horror of standing before shop-windows, the walking along that Quai Voltaire might occupy an entire morning. From the first wide-spread display of 'remarkable people' for five sous apiece – and there are heads among them which even in their rude lithography would repay some study – from this five-sous gallery of fame to the entrance of the Rue de Seine, it is an almost uninterrupted show; – books, old and new – rich, rare, and worthless; engravings that may be classed likewise, – *articles d'occasion* of all sorts, – but, far above all the rest, the most glorious museums of old carving and gilding, of monstrous chairs, stupendous candlesticks, grotesque timepieces, and ornaments without a name, that can be found in the world. It is here that the wealthy fancier of the massive splendour of Louis Quinze comes with a full purse, and it is hence that beyond all hope he departs with a light one. The present royal family of France, it is said, profess a taste for this princely but ponderous style of decoration; and royal carriages are often seen to stop at the door of *magasins* so heterogeneous in their contents as to admit all titles excepting only that of '*magasin de nouveautés*,' but having at the first glance very greatly the air of a pawnbroker's shop.

During this lounge along the Quai Voltaire, I saw for the first time some marvellously uncomely portraits, with the names of each inscribed below, and a running title for all, classing them *en masse* as '*Les Prévenus d'Avril.*' If these be faithful portraits, the originals are to be greatly pitied; for they seem by nature predestined to the evil work they have been about. Every one of them looks

> 'Worthy to be a rebel, for to that
> The multiplying villanies of nature
> Do swarm upon him.'

It should seem that the materials for rebellion were in Shakespeare's days much of the same kind as they are in ours. If these be portraits, the originals need have no fear of the caricaturist before their eyes – their 'villanies of nature' could hardly be exaggerated; and I should think that H.B. himself would try his pencil upon them in vain.

On the subject which the examination of these *prévenus d'Avril* naturally led to, our two French friends seemed to be almost entirely of the same opinion; the legitimatist confessing that 'any king was better than none,' and the doctrinaire declaring that he would rather the country should have gone without the last revolution, glorious and immortal as it was, than that it should be exposed to another, especially such a one as MM. les Prévenus were about to prepare for them.

Being arrived at *le quartier Latin*, we amused ourselves by speculating upon the propensity manifested by very young men, who were still subjected to restraint, for the overthrow and destruction of everything that denotes authority or threatens discipline. Thus the walls in this neighbourhood abounded with inscriptions to that effect; *'A bas Philippe!'* – *'Les Pairs sont des assassins!'* – *'Vive la République!'* and the like. Pears of every size and form, with scratches signifying eyes, nose, and mouth, were to be seen in all directions: which being interpreted, denotes the contempt of the juvenile students for the reigning monarch. A more troublesome evidence of this distaste for authority was displayed a few days ago by four or five hundred of these disorderly young men, who assembling themselves together, followed with hootings and shoutings M. Royer Collard, a professor lately appointed by the government to the medical school, from the college to his home in the Rue de Provence.

Upon all such occasions, this government, or any other, would do well to follow the hint given them by an admirable manoeuvre of General Lobau's, the commander-in-chief of the National Guard. I believe the anecdote is very generally known; but, in the hope that you may not have heard it, I will indulge myself by telling you the story, which amused me infinitely; and it is better that I should run the risk of your hearing it twice, than of your not hearing it at all.

A party of *les jeunes gens de Paris*, who were exerting themselves to get up a little republican *émeute*, had assembled in considerable numbers in the Place Vendôme. The drums beat – the commandant was summoned and appeared. The young malcontents closed their ranks, handled their pocket-knives and walking-sticks, and prepared to stand firm. The general was seen to dismiss an aide-de-camp, and a few anxious moments followed, when something looking fearfully like a military engine appeared advancing from the Rue de la Paix. Was it cannon? . . . A crowd of high-capped engineers surrounded it, as with military order and address it wheeled about and approached the spot where the rioters had formed their thickest phalanx. The word of command was given, and in an instant the whole host were drenched to their skins with water.

Many who saw this memorable rout, in which the laughing *pompiers* followed with their leather pipes the scampering heroes, declare that no military manoeuvre ever produced so rapid an evacuation of troops. There is something in the tone and temper of this proceeding of the National Guard which appears to me strikingly indicative of the easy, quiet, contemptuous spirit in which these powerful guardians of the existing government contemplate its republican enemies.

Having reached the Luxembourg and obtained admission to the gardens, we again rested ourselves, that we might look about at our ease upon a scene that was not only quite novel, but certainly very singular to those who were accustomed to the ordinary aspect of the place.

In the midst of lilacs and roses an encampment of small white tents showed their warlike fronts. Arms, drums, and all sorts of military accoutrements were visible among them; while loitering troops, some smoking, some reading, some sleeping, completed the unwonted appearance of the scene.

It would have been impossible, I believe, in all France to have fixed ourselves on a spot where our two French friends would have found so many incitements to unity of opinion and feeling as this. Our conversation, therefore, was not only very amicable, but ran some risk of being dull from the mere want of contradiction; for to a hearty conscientious condemnation of the proceedings which led to this trial of the *prévenus d'Avril* there was an unanimous sentence passed *nem. con.* throughout the whole party.

M. de L—— gave us some anecdotes of one or two of the persons best known among the prisoners; but upon being questioned respecting the others, he burst out indignantly in the words of Corneille –

– 'Le reste ne vaut pas l'honneur d'être nommé:
Un tas d'hommes perdus de dettes et de crimes,
Que pressent de nos loix les ordres légitimes,
Et qui désespérant de les plus éviter,
Si tout n'est renversé, ne sauraient subsister.'

'Ben trovato!' exclaimed P——; 'you could not have described them better – but . . .'

This 'but' would very probably have led to observations that might have put our *belle harmonie* out of tune, or at least have produced the renewal of our peaceable sparring, had not a little bustle among the trees at a short distance behind us cut short our session.

It seems that ever since the trials began, the chief duty of the gendarmes – (I beg pardon, I should say, of *la Garde de Paris*) – has been to prevent any assembling together of the people in knots for conversation and gossipings in the courts and gardens of the Luxembourg. No sooner are two or three persons observed standing together, than a policeman approaches, and with a tone of command pronounces, 'Circulez, messieurs! – circulez, s'il vous plaît.' The reason for this precaution is, that nightly at the Porte St. Martin a few score of *jeunes gens* assemble to make a very idle and unmeaning noise, the echo of which regularly runs from street to street till the reiterated report amounts to the announcement of an *émeute*. We are all now so used to these harmless little *émeutes* at the Porte St. Martin, that we mind them no more than General Lobau himself: nevertheless, it is deemed proper, trumpery as the cause may be, to prevent anything like a gathering together of the mob in the vicinity of the Luxembourg, lest the same hundred-tongued lady who constantly magnifies the hootings of a few idle mechanics into an *émeute* should spread a report throughout France that the Luxembourg was besieged by the people. The noise which had disturbed us was occasioned by the gathering together of

'Ce soir à la Porte St. Martin!'
'J'y serai'.

about a dozen persons; but a policeman was in the midst of the group, and we heard rumours of an *arrestation*. In less than five minutes, however, everything was quiet again: but we marked two figures so picturesque in their republicanism, that we resumed our seats while a sketch was made from them, and amused ourselves the while in fancying what the ominous words could be that were so cautiously exchanged between them. M. de L—— said that there could be no doubt that they ran thus:

> 'Ce soir, à la Porte St. Martin!'
> *Answer.* – J'y serai.'

LETTER XXV

Chapelle Expiatoire – Devotees seen there –
Tri-coloured flag out of place there –
Flower Market of the Madeleine – Petites Maîtresses

Of all the edifices finished in Paris since my last visit, there is
not one which altogether pleases me better than the little
'Chapelle Expiatoire' erected in memory of Louis the
Sixteenth, and his beautiful but ill-starred queen.

This monument was planned and in part executed by Louis
the Eighteenth, and finished by Charles the Tenth. It stands
upon the spot where many butchered victims of the tyrant
mob were thrown in 1793. The story of the royal bodies
having been destroyed by quicklime is said to have been
fabricated and circulated for the purpose of preventing any
search after them, which might, it was thought, have
produced a dangerous reaction of feeling among the whim-
governed populace.

These bodies, and several, others, which were placed in
coffins, and inscribed with the names of the murdered
occupants, lay buried together for many years after the revolution in a large *chantier*, or wood-yard, at no great distance from
the place of execution.

That this spot had been excavated for the purpose of
receiving these sad relics, is a fact well known, and it was never
lost sight of from the terrible period at which the ground was
so employed; but the unseemly vault continued undisturbed
till after the restoration, when the bodies of the royal victims
were sought and found. Their bones were then conveyed to
the long-hallowed shrine of St. Denis; but the spot where the
mangled remains were first thrown was consecrated, and is
now become the site of this beautiful little Chapelle Expiatoire.

The enclosure in which this building stands is of
considerable extent, reaching from the Rue de l'Arcade to the

Rue d'Anjou. This space is lined with closely-planted rows of cypress-trees on every side, which are protected by a massive railing, neatly painted. The building itself and all its accompaniments are in excellent taste; simple, graceful, and solemn.

The interior is a small Greek cross, each extremity of which is finished by a semicircle surmounted by a semi-dome. The space beneath the central dome is occupied by chairs and benches covered with crimson velvet, for the use of the faithful – in every sense – who come to attend the mass which is daily performed there.

As long as the daughter of the murdered monarch continued to reside in Paris, no morning ever passed without her coming to offer up her prayers at this expiatory shrine.

One of the four curved extremities is occupied by the altar; that opposite to it, by the entrance; and those on either side, by two well-composed and impressive groups in white marble – that to the right of the altar representing Marie Antoinette bending beside a cross supported by an angel, – and that to the left, the felon-murdered monarch whose wretched and most unmerited destiny she shared. On the pedestal of the king's statue is inscribed his will; on that of the queen, her farewell letter to the Princess Elizabeth.

Nothing can exceed the chaste delicacy of the few ornaments admitted into the chapel. They consist only, I think, of golden candlesticks, placed in niches in the white marble walls. The effect of the whole is beautiful and impressive.

I often go there; yet I can hardly understand what the charm can be in the little building itself, or in the quiet mass performed there without music, which can so attract me. It is at no great distance from our apartments in the Rue de Provence, and a walk thither just occupies the time before breakfast. I once went there on a Sunday morning with some of my family; but then it was full – indeed so crowded, that it was impossible to see across the building, or feel the beauty of its elegant simplicity. The pale figures of the royal dead, the foully murdered, were no longer the principal objects; and though I have no doubt that all present were right loyal spirits, with whose feelings I am well enough disposed to sympathise, yet I could not read each saddened brow, and attach a romance to it, as I never fail to do during my week-day visits.

There are two ladies, for example, whom I constantly see there, ever in the same place, and ever in the same attitude. The elder of these I feel perfectly sure must have passed her youth near Marie Antoinette, for it is at the foot of her statue that she kneels – or I might almost say that she prostrates herself, for she throws her arms forward on a cushion that is placed before her, and suffers her aged head to fall upon them, in a manner that speaks more sorrow than I can describe. The young girl who always accompanies and kneels beside her may, I think, be her grand-daughter. They have each of them '*Gentlewoman born*' written on every feature, in characters not to be mistaken. The old lady is very pale, and the young one looks as if she were not passing a youth of gaiety and enjoyment.

There is a grey-headed old man, too, who is equally constant in his attendance at this melancholy chapel. He might sit as a model for a portrait of *le bon vieux temps*; but he has a stern though sad expression of countenance, which seems to be exactly a masculine modification of what is passing at the heart and in the memory of the old lady at the opposite side of the chapel. These are figures which send the thoughts back for fifty years; and seen in the act of assisting at a mass for the souls of Louis Seize and his queen, produce a powerful effect on the imagination.

I have ventured to describe this melancholy spot, and what I have seen there, the more particularly because, easy as it is of access, you might go to Paris a dozen times without seeing it, as in fact hundreds of English travellers do. One reason for this is, that it is not opened to the public gaze as a show, but can only be entered during the hour of prayer, which is inconveniently early in the day.

As this sad and sacred edifice cannot justly be considered as a public building, the elevation of the tri-coloured flag upon it every fête-day might, I think, have been spared.

Another, and a very different novelty, is the new flower-market that is now kept under the walls and columns of the majestic church of La Madeleine. This beautiful collection of flowers appears to me to produce from its situation a very singular effect: the relative attributes of art and nature are reversed; – for here, art seems sublime, vast, and enduring; while nature is small, fragile, and perishing.

It has sometimes happened to me, after looking at a work of art which raised my admiration to enthusiasm, that I have next sought some marvellous combination of mountain and valley, rock and river, forest and cataract, and felt as I gazed on them something like shame at remembering how nearly I had suffered the work of man to produce an equal ecstasy. But here, when I raised my eyes from the little flimsy crowd of many-coloured blossoms to the simple, solemn pomp of that long arcade, with its spotless purity of tint and its enduring majesty of graceful strength, I felt half inclined to scorn myself and those around me for being so very much occupied by the roses, pinks, and mignonette spread out before it.

Laying aside, however, all philosophical reflections on its locality, this new flower-market is a delightful acquisition to the Parisian *petite maîtresse*. It was a long expedition to visit the *marché aux fleurs* on the distant quay near Notre Dame; and though its beauty and its fragrance might well repay an hour or two stolen from the pillow, the sweet decorations it offered to the boudoir must have been oftener selected by the *maître d'hôtel* or the *femme de chambre* than by the fair lady herself. But now, three times in the week we may have the pleasure of seeing numbers of graceful females in that piquant species of dishabille, which, uniting an equal portion of careful coquetry and saucy indifference, gives to the morning attire of a pretty, elegant, Frenchwoman, an air so indescribably attractive.

Followed by a neat *soubrette*, such figures may now be often seen in the flower-market of the Madeleine before the brightness of the morning has faded either from their eyes, or the blossoms they so love to gaze upon. The most ordinary linen gown, made in the form of a wrapper – the hair *en papillote* – the plain straw-bonnet drawn forward over the eyes, and the vast shawl enveloping the whole figure, might suffice to make many an *élégante* pace up and down the fragrant alley incognita, did not the observant eye remark that a veil of rich lace secured the simple bonnet under the chin – that the shawl was of cashmere – and that the little hand, when ungloved to enjoy the touch of a myrtle or an orange blossom, was as white as either.

LETTER XXVI

Delicacy in France and in England –
Causes of the difference between them

There is nothing perhaps which marks the national variety of manners between the French and the English more distinctly than the different estimate they form of what is delicate or indelicate, modest or immodest, decent or indecent: nor does it appear to me that all the intimacy of intercourse which for the last twenty years has subsisted between the two nations has greatly lessened this difference.

Nevertheless, I believe that it is more superficial than many suppose it to be; and that it arises rather from contingent circumstances, than from any original and native difference in the capability of refinement in the two nations.

Among the most obvious of these varieties of manner, is the astounding freedom with which many things are alluded to here in good society, the slightest reference to which is in our country banished from even the most homely class. It seems that the opinion of Martine is by no means peculiar to herself, and that it is pretty generally thought that

'Quand on se fait entendre, on parle toujours bien.'

In other ways, too, it is impossible not to allow that there exists in France a very perceptible want of refinement as compared to England. No Englishman, I believe, has ever returned from a visit to Paris without adding his testimony to this fact; and notwithstanding the Gallomania so prevalent amongst us, all acknowledge that, however striking may be the elegance and grace of the higher classes, there is still a national want of that uniform delicacy so highly valued by all ranks, above the very lowest, with us. Sights are seen and inconveniences endured with philosophy, which would go nigh to rob us of our wits in July, and lead us to hang ourselves in November.

To a fact so well known, and so little agreeable in the detail of its examination, it would be worse than useless to draw your attention, were it not that there is something curious in tracing the manner in which different circumstances, seemingly unconnected, do in reality hang together and form a whole.

The time certainly has been, when it was the fashion in England, as it is now in France, to call things, as some one coarsely expresses it, *by their right names*; very grave proof of which might be found even in sermons – and from thence downwards through treatises, essays, poems, romances, and plays.

We were indeed to form our ideas of the tone of conversation in England a century ago from the familiar colloquy found in the comedies then written and acted, we must acknowledge that we were at that time at a greater distance from the refinement we now boast, than our French neighbours are at present.

I do not here refer to licentiousness of morals, or the coarse avowal of it; but to a species of indelicacy which might perhaps have been quite compatible with virtue, as the absence of it is unhappily no security against vice.

The remedy of this has proceeded, if I mistake not, from causes much more connected with the luxurious wealth of England, than with the severity of her virtue. You will say, perhaps, that I have started off to an immense distance from the point whence I set out; but I think not – for both in France and England I find abundant reason to believe that I am right in tracing this remarkable difference between the two countries, less to natural disposition or character, than to the accidental facilities for improvement possessed by the one people, and not by the other.

It would be very easy to ascertain, by reference to the various literary records I have named, that the improvements in English delicacy has been gradual, and in very just proportion to the increase of her wealth, and the fastidious keeping out of sight of everything that can in any way annoy the senses.

When we cease to hear, see, and smell things which are disagreeable, it is natural that we should cease to speak of them; and it is, I believe, quite certain that the English take more pains than any other people in the world that the senses – those conductors of sensation from the body to the soul – shall convey to the spirit as little disagreeable intelligence of what befalls the case in which it dwells, as possible. The whole continent of Europe, with the exception of some portion of Holland perhaps, (which shows a brotherly affinity to us in many things,) might be cited for its inferiority to England in this respect. I remember being much amused last year, when landing at Calais, at the answer made by an old traveller to a novice who was making his first voyage.

'What a dreadful smell!' said the uninitiated stranger, enveloping his nose in his pocket-handkerchief.

'It is the smell of the continent, sir,' replied the man of experience. And so it was.

There are parts of this subject which it is quite impossible to dwell upon, and which unhappily require no pen to point them out to notice. These, if it were possible, I would willingly leave more in the dark than I find them. But there are other circumstances, all arising from the comparative poverty of the people, which tend to produce, with a most obvious dependency of thing on thing, that deficiency of refinement of which I am speaking.

Let any one examine the interior construction of a Paris dwelling of the middle class, and compare it to a house prepared for occupants of the same rank in London. It so happens that everything appertaining to decoration is to be had à bon marché at Paris, and we therefore find every article of the ornamental kind almost in profusion. Mirrors, silk hangings, or-molu in all forms; china vases, alabaster lamps, and timepieces, in which the onward step that never returns is marked with a grace and prettiness that conceals the solemnity of its pace, – all these are in abundance; and the tenth part of what would be considered necessary to dress up a common lodging in Paris, would set the London fine lady in this respect upon an enviable elevation above her neighbours.

But having admired their number and elegant arrangement, pass on and enter the ordinary bedrooms – nay, enter the kitchen too, or you will not be able to judge how great the difference is between the two residences.

In London, up to the second floor, and often to the third, water is forced, which furnishes an almost unlimited supply of that luxurious article, to be obtained with no greater trouble to the servants than would be required to draw it from a tea-urn. In one kitchen of every house, generally in two, and often in three, the same accommodation is found; and when, in opposition to this, it is remembered that very nearly every family in Paris receives this precious gift of nature doled out by two buckets at a time, laboriously brought to them by porters, clambering in *sabots*, often up the same stairs which lead to their drawing-rooms, it can hardly be supposed that the use of it is as liberal and unrestrained as with us.

Against this may be placed fairly enough the cheapness and facility of the access to the public baths. But though personal ablutions may thus be very satisfactorily performed by those who do not rigorously require that every personal comfort should be found at home, yet still the want of water, or any restraint upon the freedom with which it is used, is a vital impediment to that perfection of neatness, in every part of the establishment, which we consider as so necessary to our comfort.

Much as I admire the church of the Madeleine, I conceive that the city of Paris would have been infinitely more benefited, had the sums expended upon it been used for the purpose of constructing pipes for the conveyance of water to private dwellings, than by all the splendour received from the beauty of this imposing structure.

But great and manifold as are the evils entailed by the scarcity of water in the bedrooms and kitchens of Paris, there is another deficiency greater still, and infinitely worse in its effects. The want of drains and sewers is the great defect of all the cities in France; and a tremendous defect it is. That people who from their first breath of life have been obliged to accustom their senses and submit without a struggle to the sufferings this evil entails upon them, – that people so circumstanced should have less refinement in their thoughts and words than ourselves, I hold to be natural and inevitable. Thus, you see, I have come round like a preacher to his text, and have explained, as I think, very satisfactorily, what I mean by saying that the indelicacy which so often offends us in France does not arise from any natural coarseness of mind, but is the unavoidable result of circumstances, which may, and doubtless will change, as the wealth of the country and its familiarity with the manners of England increases.

This withdrawing from the perception of the senses everything that can annoy them, – this lulling of the spirit by the absence of whatever might awaken it to a sensation of pain, – is probably the last point to which the ingenuity of man can reach in its efforts to embellish existence.

The search after pleasure and amusement certainly betokens less refinement than this sedulous care to avoid annoyance; and it may be, that as we have gone farthest of all modern nations in this tender care of ourselves, so may we be the first to fall from our delicate elevation into that receptacle of things past and gone which has engulfed old Greece and Rome. Is it thus that the Reform Bill, and all the other horrible Bills in its train, are to be interpreted?

As to that other species of refinement which belongs altogether to the intellect, and which, if less obvious to a passing glance, is more deep and permanent in its dye than anything which relates to manners only, it is less easy either to think or to speak with confidence. France and England both have so long a list of mighty names that may be quoted on either side to prove their claim to rank high as literary contributors to refinement, that the struggle as to which ranks highest can only be fairly settled by both parties agreeing that each country has a fair right to prefer what they have produced themselves. But, alas! at the present moment, neither can have great cause to boast. What is good, is overpowered and stifled by what is bad. The uncontrolled press of both countries has thrown so much abominable trash upon literature during the last few years, that at present it might be difficult to say whether general reading would be most dangerous to the young and the pure in England or in France.

That the Hugo school has brought more nonsense with its mischief, is, I think, clear: but it is not impossible that this may act as an antidote to its own poison. It is a sort of humbug assumption of talent which will pass out of fashion as quickly as Morrison's pills. We have nothing quite so silly as this; but much I fear that, as it concerns our welfare as a nation, we have what is more deeply dangerous.

As to what is moral and what is not so, plain as at first sight the question seems to be, there is much that is puzzling in it. In looking over a volume of 'Adèle et Théodore' the other day, – a work written expressly '*sur l'éducation*', and by an author that we must presume meant honestly and spoke sincerely, – I found this passage:–

'Je ne connais que trois romans véritablement moraux; – Clarisse, le plus beau de tous; Grandison, et Pamela. Ma fille les lira en Anglais lorsque'elle aura dix-huit ans.'

The venerable Grandison, though by no means *sans tache*, I will let pass: but that any mother should talk of letting her daughter of 'dix-huit ans' read the others, is a mystery difficult to comprehend, especially in a country where the young girls are reared, fostered, and sheltered from every species of harm, with the most incessant and sedulous watchfulness. I presume that Madame de Genlis conceived that, as the object and moral purpose of these works were good, the revolting coarseness with which some of their most powerful passages are written could not lead to evil. But this is a bold and dangerous judgment to pass when the question relates to the studies of a young girl.

I think we may see symptoms of the feeling which would produce such a judgment in the tone of biting satire with which Molière attacks those who wished to banish what might 'faire insulte à la pudeur des femmes.' Spoken as he makes Philaminte speak it, we cannot fail to laugh at the notion: yet ridicule on the same subject would hardly be accepted, even from Sheridan, as jesting matter with us.

'Mais le plus beau projet de notre académie,
Une entreprise noble, et dont je suis ravie,
Un dessein plein de gloire, et qui sera vanté
Chez tous les beaux-esprits de la postérité,
C'est le retranchement de ces syllabes sales
Qui dans les plus beaux mots produisent des scandales;
Ces jouets éternels des sots de tous les temps,

Ces fades lieux communs de nos méchans plaisans;
Ces sources d'un amas d'équivoques infâmes
Dont on vient faire insulte à la pudeur des femmes.'

Such an academy might be a very comical institution,
certainly; but the duties it would have to perform would not
suffer a professor's place to become a sinecure in France.

LETTER XXVII

*Objections to quoting the names of private individuals –
Impossibility of avoiding Politics –* Parceque *and* Quoique *–
Soirée Antithestique*

It would be a pleasure to me to give you the names of many
persons with whom I have become acquainted in Paris, and I
should like to describe exactly the *salons* in which I met them;
but a whole host of proprieties forbid this. Where individuals
are so well known to fame as to render the echoing of their
names a matter of ordinary recurrence, I can of course feel no
scruple in repeating the echo – one reverberation more can do
no harm: but I will never be the first to name any one, either
for praise or for blame, beyond the sanctuary of their own
circle.

I must therefore restrict myself to giving you the best
general idea I can of the tone and style of what I have seen and
heard; and if I avail myself of the conversations I have listened
to, it shall be in such a manner as to avoid the slightest
approach to personal allusion.

This necessary restraint, however, is not submitted to
without regret: it must rob much of what I would wish to
repeat of the value of authority; and when I consider how
greatly at variance my impressions are on many points to
some which have been publicly proclaimed by others, I feel
that I deserve some praise for suppressing names which would
stamp my statements with a value that neither my
unsupported assertions, nor those of any other traveller, can
be supposed to bear. Those who best know what I lose by this
will give me credit for it; and I shall be sufficiently rewarded
for my forbearance if it afford them a proof that I am not
unworthy the flattering kindness I have received.

We all declare ourselves sick of politics, and a woman's
letters, at least, ought if possible to be free from this wearily

pervading subject: but the describing a human being, and omitting to mention the heart and the brain, would not leave the analysis more defective, than painting the Parisians at this moment without permitting their politics to appear in the picture.

The very air they breathe is impregnated with politics. Were all words expressive of party distinctions to be banished from their language – were the curse of Babel to fall upon them, and no man be able to discourse with his neighbour, – still political feeling would find itself an organ whereby to express its workings. One man would wear a pointed hat, another a flat one; one woman would be girt with a tri-coloured sash, and another with a white one. Some exquisites would be closely buttoned to the chin, while the lapels of others would open wide in all the expansive freedom of republican unrestraint. One set would be seen adorning Napoleon's pillar with trophies; another, prostrate before the altar of the elder Bourbon's monumental chapel; a third, marshalling themselves under the bloody banner of Robespierre to the tune of 'Dansons la Carmagnole;' whilst a fourth, by far the most numerous, would be brushing their national uniforms, attending to their prosperous shops, and giving a nod of good-fellowship every time his majesty the king passes by.

Some friends of mine entered a shop the other day to order some article of furniture. While they remained there, a royal carriage passed, and one of the party said –

'It is the queen, I believe?'

'Yes, sir,' replied the *ébéniste*, 'it is the lady that it pleases us to call the queen. We may certainly call her so if we like it, for we made her ourselves; and if we find it does not answer, we shall make another. – May I send you home this table, sir? . . .'

When politics are thus lightly mixed up with all things, how can the subject be wholly avoided without destroying the power of describing anything as we find it?

Such being the case, I cannot promise that all allusion to the subject shall be banished from my letters; but it shall be made as little predominant as possible. Could I indeed succeed in transferring the light tone in which these weighty matters are generally discussed to the account I wish to give you of them, I need not much fear that I should weary you.

Whether it be essentially in the nature of the people, or only a transitory feature of the times, I know not; but nothing strikes me so forcibly as the airy, gay indifference with which subjects are discussed on which hang the destinies of the world. The most acute – nay, often the most profound remarks are uttered in a tone of badinage; and the probabilities of future events, vital to the interests of France, and indeed of Europe, are calculated with as idle an air, and with infinitely more *sang froid*, than the chances at a game of *rouge et noir*.

Yet, behind this I suspect that there is a good deal of sturdy determination in all parties, and it will be long ere France can be considered as one whole and united people. Were the country divided into two, instead of into three factions, it is probable that the question of which was to prevail would be soon brought to an issue; but as it is, they stand much like the uncles and nieces in the Critic, each keeping the other two in check.

Meanwhile this temporary division of strength is unquestionably very favourable to the present government; in addition to which, they derive much security from the averseness which all feel, excepting the naughty boys and hungry desperadoes, to the disturbance of their present tranquillity. It is evident that those who do not belong, to the triumphant majority are disposed for the most part to wait a more favourable opportunity of hostilely and openly declaring themselves; and it is probable that they will wait long. They know well, and are daily reminded of it, that all the power and all the strength that possession can give are vested in the existing dynasty; and though much deeply-rooted feeling exists that is inimical to it, yet so many of all parties are firmly united to prevent farther anarchy and revolution, that the throne of Louis-Philippe perhaps rests on as solid a foundation as that of any monarch in Europe: the fear of renewed tumult acts like the key-stone of an arch, keeping firm, sound, and in good condition, what would certainly fall to pieces without it.

In addition to this wholesome fear of pulling their own dwellings about their ears, there is also another fear that aids greatly in producing the same result. Many of the riotous youths who so essentially assisted in creating the confusion which ended in uncrowning one king and crowning another, are, as far as I can understand, quite as well disposed to make a row now as they were then: but they know that if they do, they will most incontestably be whipped for it; and therefore, though they pout a little in private, they are, generally speaking, very orderly in public. Every one, not personally interested in the possible result of another uproar, must rejoice at this improvement in discipline. The boys of France must now submit to give way before her men; and as long as this lasts, something like peace and prosperity may be hoped for.

Yet it cannot be denied, I think, that among these prudent men – these doctrinaires who now hold the high places, there are many who, 'with high thoughts, such as Lycurgus loved,' still dream of a commonwealth; or that there are others who have not yet weaned their waking thoughts from meditations on faith, right, and loyalty. But nevertheless, all unite in thinking that they had better 'let things be,' than risk making them worse.

Nothing is more common than to hear a conversation end by a cordial and unanimous avowal of this prudent and sagacious sentiment, which began by an examination of general principles, and the frank acknowledgment of opinions which would certainly lead to a very different conclusion.

It is amusing enough to remark how these advocates for expediency contrive each of them to find reasons why things had better remain as they are, while all these reasons are strongly tinted by their various opinions.

'Charles Dix,' says a legitimate in principle, but a *juste-milieu* man in practice, – 'Charles Dix has abdicated the throne, which otherwise must unquestionably be his by indefeasible right. His heir-apparent has followed the example. The country was in no state to be governed by a child; and what then was left for us, but to take a king from the same race which so for many ages has possessed the throne of France. *Louis-Philippe est roi,* PARCEQU'*il est Bourbon.*'

'Pardonnez-moi,' replies another, who, if he could manage it without disturbing the tranquillity about him, would take care to have it understood that nothing more legitimate than an elective monarchy could be ever permitted in France, – 'Pardonnez-moi, mon ami; *Louis-Philippe est roi,* QUOIQU'*il est Bourbon.*'

These two parties of the *Parceques* and the *Quoiques,* in fact, form the great bulwarks of King Philippe's throne; for they both consist of experienced, practical, substantial citizens, who having felt the horrors of anarchy, willingly keep their particular opinions in abeyance rather than hazard a recurrence of it. They, in truth, form between them the genuine *juste-milieu* on which the present government is balanced.

That there is more of the practical wisdom of expediency than of the dignity of unbending principle in this party, can hardly be denied. They are 'wiser in their generation than the children of light;' but it is difficult, 'seeing what we have seen, seeing what we see,' to express any heavy sentence of reprobation upon a line of conduct which ensures, for the time at least, the lives and prosperity of millions. They tell me that my friend the Vicomte has sapped my legitimate principles; but I deny the charge, though I cannot deliberately wish that confusion should take the place of order, or that the desolation of a civil war should come to deface the aspect of prosperity that it is so delightful to contemplate.

This discrepancy between what is right and what is convenient – this wavering of principle and of action, is the inevitable consequence of repeated political convulsions. When the times become out of joint, the human mind can with difficulty remain firm and steadfast. The inconceivable variety of wild and ever-changing speculations which have long overborne the voice of established belief and received authority in this country, has brought the principles of the people into a state greatly resembling that of a wheel radiated with every colour of the rainbow, but which by rapid movement is left apparently without any colour at all.

Our last *soirée* was at the house of a lady who takes much interest in showing me 'le Paris d'aujourd'hui,' as she calls it. 'Chère dame!' she exclaimed as I entered, 'I have collected *une société délicieuse* for you this evening.'

She had met me in the ante-room, and, taking my arm within hers, led me into the *salon.* It was already filled with company, the majority of which were gentlemen. Having found room for us on a sofa, and seated herself next to me, she said –

'I will present whomsoever you choose to know; but before I bring anybody up, I must explain who they all are.'

I expressed my gratitude, and she began:– 'That tall gentleman is a great republican, and one of the most respectable
that we have left of the *clique*. The party is very nearly worn
out among the *gens comme il faut*. His father, however, is of the
same party, and still more violent, I believe, than himself.
Heaven knows what they would be at! . . . But they are both
deputies, and if they died tomorrow, would have, either father
or son, a very considerable mob to follow them to Père
Lachaise; not to mention the absolute necessity which I am
sure there would be to have troops out: c'est toujours quelque
chose, n'est-ce pas? I know that you hate them all – and, to say
truth, so do I too; – mais, chère amie! qu'est-ce que cela fait? I
thought you would like to see them: they really begin to get
very scarce in *salons*.'

I assured her that she was quite right, and that nothing in the
whole Jardin des Plantes could amuse me better.

'Ah ca!' she rejoined, laughing; 'voilà ce que c'est d'être
raisonnable. Mais regardez ce beau garçon leaning against the
chimneypiece. He is one of *les fidèles sans tache*. Is he not
handsome? I have him at all my parties; and even the
ministers' ladies declare that he is perfectly charming.'

'And that little odd-looking man in black,' said I, 'who is
he? . . . What a contrast!'

'N'est-ce pas? Do they not group well together? That is just
the sort of thing I like – it amuses everybody: besides, I assure
you, he is a very remarkable person, – in short, it is M——,
the celebrated atheist. He writes for the ——. But the Institute
won't have him: however, he is excessively talked of – and
that is everything. . . . Then I have two peers, both of them
highly distinguished. There is M. de ——, who, you know, is
King Philippe's right hand; and the gentleman sitting down
just behind him is the dear old Duc de ——, who lived ages in
exile with Louis Dix-huit . . . That person almost at your
elbow, talking to the lady in blue is the Comte de P——, a
most exemplary Catholic, who always followed Charles Dix
in all religious processions. He was half distracted, poor man!
at the last revolution; but they say he is going to dine with
King Philippe next week: I long to ask him if it is true, but I
am afraid, for fear he should be obliged to answer 'Yes;' – that
would be so embarrassing! . . . Oh, by the way, that is a peer

that you are looking at now; – he has refused to sit on the trial. . . . Now, have I not done *l'impossible* for you?'

I thanked her gratefully, and as I knew I could not please her better than by showing the interest I took in her menagerie, I inquired the name of a lady who was talking with a good deal of vehemence at the opposite side of the room.

'Oh! that's a person that I always call my '*dame de l'Empire.*'Her husband was one of Napoleon's creations; and Josephine used to amuse herself without ceasing by making her talk – her language and accent are *impayables!*'

'And that pretty woman in the corner?'

'Ah! . . . she is charming! . . . It is Madame V——, daughter of the celebrated Vicomte de ——, so devoted, you know, to the royal cause. But she is lately married to one of the present ministers – quite a love-match; which is an innovation, by the way, more hard to pardon in France than the introduction of a new dynasty. Mais c'est égal – they are all very good friends again . . . Now, tell me whom I shall introduce to you?'

I selected the heroine of the love-match; who was not only one of the prettiest creatures I ever saw, but so lively, intelligent, and agreeable, that I have seldom passed a pleas- anter hour than that which followed the introduction. The whole of this heterogeneous party seemed to mix together with the greatest harmony; the only cold glance I saw given being from the gentleman designated as 'King Philippe's right hand, ' towards the tall republican deputy of whose funeral my friend had predicted such honours. The *dame de l'Empire* was indulging in a lively flirtation with one of the peers *sans tache*; and I saw the fingers of the exemplary Catholic, who was going to dine with King Philippe, in the *tabatière* of the celebrated atheist. I then remembered that this was one of the *soirées antithestiques* so much in fashion.

LETTER XXVIII

New Publications – M. de Lamartine's 'Souvenirs, Impressions,
Pensées, et Paysages' – Tocqueville and Beaumont –
New American regulation – M. Scribe – Madame Tastu –
Reception of different Writers in society

Though among the new publications sent to me for perusal I
have found much to fatigue and disgust me, as must indeed
be inevitable for any one accustomed for some scores of years
to nourish the heart and head with the literature of the *bon
vieux tempts,*' – which means, in modern phrase, everything
musty, rusty, rococo, and forgotten, – I have yet found some
volumes which have delighted me greatly.

M. de Lamartine's 'Souvenirs, Impressions, Pensées, et
Paysages' in the East, is a work which appears to me to stand
solitary and alone in the world of letters. There is certainly
nothing like it, and very little that can equal it, in my
estimation, either as a collection of written landscapes, or as a
memorial of poetical feeling, just sentiment, and refined taste.

His descriptions may perhaps have been, in some rare
instances, equalled in mere graphic power by others; but who
has painted anything which can excite an interest so
profound, or an elevation of the fancy so lofty and so
delightful?

Alas! that the scenes he paints should be so utterly beyond
one's reach! How little, how paltry, how full of the vulgar
interests of this 'working-day world,' do all the other
countries of the earth appear after reading this book, when
compared to Judea! But there are few who could visit it as
Lamartine has done, – there are very few capable of feeling as
he felt – and none, I think, of describing as he describes. His
words live and glow upon the paper; he pours forth sunshine
and orient light upon us, – we hear the gale whispering
among the palm-trees, see Jordan's rapid stream rushing

between its flowery banks, and feel that the scene to which he has transported us is holy ground.

The exalted tone of his religious feelings, and the poetic fervour with which he expresses them, might almost lead one to believe that he was inspired by the sacred air he breathed. It seems as if he had found the harps which were hung up of old upon the trees, and tuned them anew to sing of the land of David; he has 'beheld the beauty of the Lord, and inquired in his temple,' and the result is exactly what it should be.

The manner in which this most poetic of travellers, while standing on the ruins of Tyre, speaks of the desolation and despair that appear settling upon the earth in these latter days, is impressive beyond anything I know of modern date.

Had France produced no other redeeming volumes than these, there is enough within them to overpower and extinguish the national literary disgrace with which it has been reproached so loudly; and it is a comfort to remember that this work is as sure to live, as the literary labours of the diabolic school are to perish. It is perhaps good for us to read trash occasionally, that we may learn to value at their worth such thoughts as we find here; and while there are any left on earth who can so think, so feel, and so write, our case is not utterly hopeless.

Great, indeed, is the debt that we owe to an author like this, who, seizing upon the imagination with power unlimited, leads it only into scenes that purify and exalt the spirit. It is a temendous power, that of taking us how and where he will, which is possessed by such an author as this. When it is used for evil, it resembles fearfully the action of a fiend, tempting, dragging, beckoning, cajoling to destruction: but when it is for good, it is like an angel's hand leading us to heaven.

I intended to have spoken to you of many other works which have pleased me; but I really at this moment experience the strangest sort of embarrassment imaginable in referring to them. Many agreeable new books are lying about before me; but while my head is so full of Lamartine and the Holy Land, everything seems to produce on me the effect of platitude and littleness.

I must, however, conquer this so far as to tell you that you ought to read both Tocqueville and Beaumont on the United

States. By the way, I am assured that the Americans declare themselves determined to change their line of conduct altogether respecting the national manner of receiving European sketches of themselves. This new law is to embrace three clauses. The first will enforce the total exclusion, from henceforth and for evermore, of all European strangers from their American homes; the second will recommend that all citizens shall abstain from reading anything, in any language written, or about to be written, concerning them and their affairs; and the third, in case the other two should fail, seems to take the form of a vow, protesting that they never will storm, rave, scold, or care about anything that anybody can say of them more. If this passes during the presidentship of General Jackson, it will immortalize his reign more than paying off the national debt.

Having thus, somehow or other, slipped from the Holy Land to the United States of America, I feel sufficiently subdued in spirit to speak of lesser things than Lamartine's 'Pilgrimage.'

On one point, indeed, a sense of justice urges me, when on the subject of modern productions, to warn you against the error of supposing that all the new theatrical pieces, which come forth here as rapidly and as brilliantly as the blossoms of the gum cistus, and which fade almost as soon, are of the nature and tendency of those I have mentioned as belonging to the Victor Hugo school. On the contrary, I have seen many, and read more, of these little comedies and vaudevilles, which are not only free from every imputation of mischief, but absolutely perfect in their kind.

The person whose name is celebrated far above all others for this species of composition, is M. Scribe; and were it not that his extraordinary facility enables him to pour forth these pretty trifles in such abundance as already to have assured him a very large fortune, which offers an excellent excuse in these *positif* times for him, I should say that he would have done better had he written less.

He has shown on several occasions, as in 'L'Ambitieux,' 'Bertrand et Raton,' &c. that he can succeed in that most difficult of tasks, good legitimate comedy, as well as in the lighter labour of striking off a sparkling vaudeville. It is certain, indeed, that, spite of all we say, and say in some respects so justly, respecting the corrupted taste of France at the present era, there never was a time when her stage could boast a greater affluence of delightful little pieces than at present.

I really am afraid to enter more at large upon this theme, from a literal *embarras de richesses.* If I begin to name these pretty, lively trifles, I shall run into a list much too long for your patience: for though Scribe is all the favourite as well as the most fertile source of these delightful novelties, there are one or two others who follow him at some little distance, and who amongst them produce such a sum total of new pieces in the year as would make an English manager tremble to think of; – but here the chief cost of bringing them out is drawn, not from the theatrical treasury, but from the ever-fresh wit and spirit of the performers.

Such an author as Scribe is a national museum of invention – a never-failing source of new enjoyment to his lively countrymen, and he has probably tasted the pleasures of a bright and lasting reputation as fully as any author living. We are already indebted to him for many charming importations; and, thanks to the Yates talent, we begin to be not unworthy of receiving such. If we cannot have Shakespeare, Racine, and Molière got up for us quite 'in the grand style of former years,' these bright, light, biting, playful, graceful little pieces are by far the best substitutes for them, while we wait with all the patience we can for a new growth of players, who shall give honour due to the next tragedy Miss Mitford may bestow upon us.

Another proof that it is not necessary to be vicious in order to be in vogue at Paris, and that purity is no impediment to success, is the popularity of Madame Tastu's poetry. She writes as a woman ought to write – with grace, feeling, delicacy, and piety.

Her literary efforts, however, are not confined to the 'flowery path of poesy;' though it is impossible not to perceive that she lingers in it with delight, and that when she leaves it, she does so from no truant inclination to wander elsewhere, but from some better impulse. Her work entitled 'Education Maternelle' would prove a most valuable acquisition to English mothers desirous themselves of giving early lessons in French to their children. The pronunciation and accentuation are marked in a manner greatly to facilitate the task, especially to a foreigner, whose greatest difficulty, when attempting to teach the language without the aid of a native master, is exactly what these initiatory lessons are so well calculated to obviate.

It is no small source of consolation and of hope, at a period when a sort of universal epidemic frenzy appears to have seized upon the minds of men, leading them to advocate as good that which all experience shows to be evil, and to give specimens of dirty delirium that might be collected in an hospital, by way of exalted works of imagination, – it is full of hope and consolation to find that, however rumour may clamour forth tidings of these sad ravings whenever they appear, fame still rests only with such as really deserve it.

Let a first-rate collector of literary lions at Paris make it known that M. de Lamartine would appear at her *soirée*, and the permission to enter there would be sought so eagerly, that before eleven o'clock there would not be standing-room in her apartments, though they might be as spacious as any the 'belle ville' can show. But let it be announced that the authors of any of the obscene masques and mummings which have disgraced the theatres of France would present themselves, and depend upon it they would find space sufficient to enact the part of Triboulet at the moment when he exclaims in soliloquy,

'Que je suis grand ici!'

LETTER XXIX

Sunday is a delightful day in Paris – more so than in any place I ever visited, excepting Francfort. The enjoyment is so universal, and yet so domestic; were I to form my idea of the national character from the scenes passing before my eyes on that day, instead of from books and newspapers, I should say that the most remarkable features in it, were conjugal and parental affection.

It is rare to see either a man or a woman, of an age to be wedded and parents, without their being accompanied by their partner and their offspring. The cup of light wine is drunk between them; the scene that is sought for amusement by the one is also enjoyed by the other; and whether it be little or whether it be much that can be expended on this day of jubilee, the man and wife share it equally.

I have entered many churches during the hours of the morning masses, in many different parts of the town, and, as I have before stated, I have uniformly found them extremely crowded; and though I have never remarked any instances of that sort of penitential devotion so constantly seen in the churches of Belgium when the painfully extended arms remind one of the Hindoo solemnities, the appearance of earnest and devout attention to what is going on is universal.

It is not till after the grand mass is over that the population pours itself out over every part of the town, not so much to seek as to meet amusement. And they are sure to find it; for not ten steps can be taken in any direction without encountering something that shall furnish food for enjoyment of some kind or other.

There is no sight in the world that I love better than a numerous populace during their hours of idleness and glee. When they assemble themselves together for purposes of legislation, I confess I do not greatly love or admire them; but when they are enjoying themselves, particularly when women and children share in the enjoyment, they furnish a delightful spectacle – and nowhere can it be seen to greater advantage than in Paris. The nature of the people – the nature of the climate – the very form and arrangement of the city, are all especially favourable to the display of it. It is in the open air, under the blue vault of heaven, before the eyes of thousands, that they love to bask and disport themselves. The bright, clear atmosphere seems made on purpose for them; and whoever laid out the boulevards, the quays, the gardens of Paris, surely remembered, as they did so, how necessary space was for the assembling together of her social citizens.

The young men of the Polytechnic School make a prominent feature in a Paris Sunday; for it is only on the *jours de fête* that they are permitted to range at liberty through the town: but all occasions of this kind cause the streets and public walks to swarm with young Napoleons.

It is quite extraordinary to see how the result of a strong principle or sentiment may show itself externally on a large body of individuals, making those alike, whom nature has made as dissimilar as possible. There is not one of these Polytechnic lads, the eldest of whom could hardly have seen the light of day before Napoleon had left the soil of France for ever, – there is hardly one of them who does not more or less remind one of the well-known figure and air of the Emperor. Be they tall, be they short, be they fat, be they thin, it is the same, – there is some approach (evidently the result of having studied their worshipped model closely in paintings, engravings, bronzes, marbles, and Sèvres china,) to that look and bearing which, till the most popular tyrant that ever lived had made it as well known as sunshine to the eyes of France, was as little resembling to the ordinary appearance and carriage of her citizens as possible.

The tailor can certainly do much towards making the exterior of one individual look like the exterior of another; but he cannot do all that we see in the mien of a Polytechnic scholar that serves to recall the extraordinary man whose name, after years of exile and of death, is decidedly the most stirring that can be pronounced in France. Busy, important, and most full of human interest has been the period since his downfall; yet his memory is as fresh among them as if he had marched into the Tuileries triumphant from one of his hundred victories but yesterday.

O, if the sovereign people could but understand as well as read! . . . And O that some Christian spirit could be found who would interpret to them, in such accents as they would listen to, the life and adventures of Napoleon the Great! What a deal of wisdom they might gain by it! Where could be found a lesson so striking as this to a people who are weary of being governed, and desire, one and all, to govern themselves? With precisely the same weariness, with precisely the same desire, did this active, intelligent, and powerful people throw off, some forty years ago, the yoke of their laws and the authority of their king. Then were they free as the sand of the desert – not one individual atom of the mighty mass but might have risen in the hurricane of that tempest as high as the unbridled wind of his ambition could carry him; and what followed? Why, they grew sick to death of the giddy whirl, where each man knocked aside his neighbour, and there was none to say 'Forbear!' Then did they cling, like sinking souls in the act of drowning, to the first bold man who dared to replace the yoke upon their necks; they clung to him through years of war that mowed down their ranks as a scythe mows down the ripe corn, and yet they murmured not. For years they suffered their young sons to be torn from their sides while they still hung to them with all the first fondness of youth, and yet they murmured not; – for years they lived uncheered by the wealth that commerce brings, uncheered by any richer return of labour than the scanty morsel that sustained their life of toil, and yet they murmured not: for they had once more a prince upon the throne – they had once more laws, firmly administered, which kept them from the dreadful horrors of anarchy; and they clung to their tyrant prince, and his strict and stern enactments, with a devotion of gratitude and affection which speaks plainly enough their lasting thankfulness to the courage which was put forth in their hour of need to relieve them from the dreadful burden of self-government.

This gratitude and affection endures still – nothing will ever efface it; for his military tyranny is passed away, and the benefits which his colossal power enabled him to bestow upon them remain, and must remain as long as France endures. The only means by which another sovereign may rival Napoleon in popularity, is by rivalling him in power. Were some of the feverish blood which still keeps France in agitation to be drawn from her cities to reinforce her military array, and were a hundred thousand of the sons of France marched off to restore to Italy her natural position in Europe, power, glory, and popularity would sustain the throne, and tranquillity be restored to the people. Without some such discipline, poor young France may very probably die of a plethora. If she has not this, she must have a government as absolute as that of Russia to keep her from mischief: and that she will have one or the other before long, I have not the least doubt in the world; for there are many very clever personages at and near the seat of power who will not be slow to see or to do what is needful.

Meanwhile this fine body of young men are, as I understand, receiving an education calculated to make them most efficient officers, whenever they are called upon to serve. Unfortunately for the reputation of the Polytechnic School, their names were brought more forward than was creditable to those who had the charge of them, during the riots of 1830. But the government which the men of France accepted from the hands of the boys really appears to be wiser and better than they had any right to expect from authority so strangely constituted. The new government very properly uses the strength given it, for the purpose of preventing the repetition of the excesses to which it owes its origin; and these fine lads are now said to be in a state of very respectable discipline, and to furnish no contemptible bulwark to the throne.

It is otherwise, however, as I hear, with most of the bodies of young men collected together in Paris for the purpose of education. The silly cant of republicanism has got among them; and till this is mended, continued little riotous outbreakings of a naughty-boy spirit must be expected.

One of the happiest circumstances in the situation of poor struggling England at present is, that her boys are not republican. On the contrary, the rising spirit among us is decidedly conservative. All our great schools are tory to the heart's core. The young English have been roused, awakened, startled at the peril which threatens the land of their fathers! The *penny king* who has invaded us has produced on them the effect usual on all invasions; and rather than see him and his popish court succeed in conquering England, they would rush from their forms and their cloisters to repel him, shouting, 'Alone we'll do it, BOYS!' – and they would do it, too, even if they had no fathers to help them.

But I have forgotten my Sunday holiday, while talking about the gayest and happiest of those it brings forth to decorate the town. Many a proud and happy mother may on these occasions be seen leaning on the arm of a son that she is very conscious looks like an emperor; and many a pretty creature, whom her familiarity, as well as her features, proclaims to be a sister, shows in her laughing eyes that the day which gives her smart young brother freedom is indeed a *jour de fête* for her.

You will be weary of the Tuileries Gardens; but I cannot keep out of them, particularly when talking of a Paris Sunday, of whose prettiest groups they are the rendezvous: the whole day's history may be read in them. As soon as the gates are open, figures both male and female, in dishabille more convenient than elegant, may be seen walking across them in every direction towards the *sortie* which leads towards the quay, and thence onwards to *Les Bains Vigier*. Next come the after-breakfast groups: and these are beautiful. Elegant young mothers in half-toilet accompany their *bonnes*, and the pretty creatures committed to their care, to watch for an hour the happy gambols which the presence of the 'chère maman' renders seven times more gay than ordinary.

I have watched such, repeatedly, with extreme amusement; often attempting to read, but never able to pursue the

Tuileries' Gardens, on Sunday.

occupation for three-quarters of a minute together, till they at last abandon it altogether, and sit with the useless volume upon their knee, complacently answering all the baby questions that may be proposed to them, while watching with the smiling satisfaction of well-pleased maternity every attitude, every movement, and every grimace of the darling miniatures in which they see themselves, and perhaps one dearer still.

From about ten till one o'clock the gardens swarm with children and their attendants: and pretty enough they are, and amusing too, with their fanciful dresses and their baby wilfulness. Then comes the hour of early dinners: the nurses and the children retreat; and were it possible that any hour of the day could find a public walk in Paris unoccupied, it would be this.

The next change shows the gradual influx of best bonnets, – pink, white, green, blue. Feathers float onwards, and fresh flowers are seen around: gay barouches rush down the Rues Castiglione and Rivoli; cabs swing round every corner, all to deposit their gay freight within the gardens. By degrees, double, treble rows of chairs are occupied on either side of every walk, while the whole space between is one vast moving mass of pleasant idleness.

This lasts till five; and then, as the elegant crowd withdraws, another, less graceful perhaps, but more animated, takes its place. Caps succeed to bonnets; and unchecked laughter, loud with youth and glee, replaces the whispered gallantry, the silent smile, and all the well-bred ways of giving and receiving thoughts with as little disturbance to the circumambient air as possible.

From this hour to nightfall the multitude goes on increasing; and did one not know that every theatre, every ginguette, every boulevard, every café in Paris were at the same time crammed almost to suffocation, one might be tempted to believe that the whole population had assembled there to recreate themselves before the windows of the king.

Among the higher ranks the Sunday evening at Paris is precisely the same as that of any other day. There are the same number of *soirées* going on, and no more; the same number of dinner-parties, – just as much card-playing, just as much dancing, just as much music, and just as much going to the opera; but the other theatres are generally left to the *endimanchés*.

You must not, however, imagine that no religious exercises are attended to among the rich and noble because I have said nothing especially about them on this point. On the contrary, I have great reason to believe that it is not alone the attractive eloquence of the popular preachers which draws such multitudes of wealthy and high-born females into the fashionable churches of Paris; but that they go to pray as well as to listen. Nevertheless, as to the general state of religion amongst the educated classes in Paris, it is quite as difficult to obtain information as it is to learn with anything like tolerable accuracy the average state of their politics. It is not that there is the least reserve or apparent hanging back when either subject is discussed; on the contrary, all seem kindly eager to answer every question, and impart to you all the information it is possible to wish for: but the variety of statements is inconceivable; and as I have repeatedly listened to very strong and positive assertions respecting the opinions of the majority, from those in whose sincerity I have perfect confidence, but which have been flatly contradicted by others equally deserving of credit, I am led to suppose that in effect the public mind is still wavering on both subjects. There is, in fact, but one point upon which I truly and entirely believe that an overwhelming majority exists, – and this is in the aversion felt for any farther trial of a republican form of government.

The party who advocate the cause of democracy do indeed make the most noise – it is ever their wont to do so. Neither the Chamber of Deputies nor the Chamber of Peers can assemble nightly at a given spot to scream 'Vive le Roi!' nor are the quiet citizens, who most earnestly wish to support the existing government, at all more likely to leave their busy shops for this purpose than the members of the two Chambers are to quit their *hôtels*; – so that any attempt to judge the political feelings of the people by the outcries heard in the streets must of necessity lead to error. Yet it is of such judgments, both at home and abroad, that we hear the most.

As to the real private feelings on the subject of religion which exist among the educated portion of the people, it is still more difficult to form an opinion, for on this subject the strongest indications are often declared to prove nothing. If churches filled to overflowing be proof of national piety, then are the people pious: and farther than this, no looker-on such as myself should, I think, attempt to go.

LETTER XXX

Madame Récamier – Her Morning Parties – Gérard's Picture of Corinne – Miniature of Madame de Staël – M. de Châteaubriand – Conversation on the degree in which the French Language is understood by 'Foreigners' – The necessity of speaking French

Of all the ladies with whom I have become acquainted in Paris, the one who appears to me to be the most perfect specimen of an elegant Frenchwoman is Madame Récamier, – the same Madame Récamier that, I will not say how many years ago, I remember to have seen in London, the admired of all eyes; and, wonderful to say, she is so still. Formerly I knew her only from seeing her in public, where she was pointed out to me as the most beautiful woman in Europe; but now that I have the pleasure of her acquaintance, I can well understand, though you who know her only by the reputation of her early beauty may not, how and why it is that fascinations generally so evanescent are with her so lasting. She is, in truth, the very model of all grace. In person, manner, movement, dress, voice, and language, she seems universally allowed to be quite perfect; and I really cannot imagine a better mode of giving a last finish to a young lady's study of the graces, than by affording her an opportunity of observing every movement and gesture of Madame Récamier.

She is certainly a monopolist of talents and attractions which would suffice, if divided in ordinary proportions, to furnish forth a host of charming women. I never met with a Frenchman who did not allow, that though his countrywomen were charming from *agrémens* which seem peculiarly their own, they have fewer faultless beauties among them than may be found in England; but yet, as they say, 'Quand une Française se mêle d'être jolie, elle est furieusement jolie.' This *mot* is as true in point of fact as piquant in

174

expression; – a beautiful Frenchwoman is, perhaps, the most beautiful woman in the world.

The perfect loveliness of Madame Récamier has made her 'a thing to wonder at:' and now that she has passed the age when beauty is at its height, she is perhaps to be wondered at still more; for I really doubt if she ever excited more admiration than she does at present. She is followed, sought, looked at, listened to, and, moreover, beloved and esteemed, by a very large circle of the first society in Paris, among whom are numbered some of the most illustrious literary names in France.

That her circle, as well as herself, is delightful, is so generally acknowledged, that by adding my voice to the universal judgment, I perhaps show as much vanity, as gratitude for the privilege of being admitted within it: but no one, I believe, so favoured could, when speaking of the society of Paris, omit so striking a feature of it as the *salon* of Madame Récamier. She contrives to make even the still-life around her partake of the charm for which she is herself so remarkable, and there is a fine and finished elegance in everything about her that is irresistibly attractive: I have often entered drawing-rooms almost capable of containing her whole suite of apartments, and found them infinitely less striking in their magnificence than her beautiful little *salon* in the Abbaye-aux-Bois.

The rich draperies of white silk, the delicate blue tint that mixes with them throughout the apartment, – the mirrors, the flowers, – all together give an air to the room that makes it accord marvellously well with its fair inhabitant. One might fancy that Madame Récamier herself was for ever *vouée au blanc*, for no drapery falls around her that is not of snowy whiteness – and indeed the mixture of almost any colour would seem like profanation to the exquisite delicacy of her appearance.

Madame Récamier admits morning visits from a limited number of persons, whose names are given to the servant attending in the ante-room, every day from four till six. It was here I had the pleasure of being introduced to M. de Châteaubriand, and had afterwards the gratification of repeatedly meeting him; a gratification that I shall assuredly never forget, and for which I would have willingly sacrificed one-half of the fine things which reward the trouble of a journey to Paris.

The circle thus received is never a large one, and the conversation is always general. The first day that I and my daughters were there, we found, I think, but two ladies, and about half a dozen gentlemen, of whom M. de Châteaubriand was one. A magnificent picture by Gérard, boldly and sublimely conceived, and executed in his very best manner, occupies one side of the elegant little *salon*. The subject is Corinne, in a moment of poetical excitement, a lyre in her hand, and a laurel crown upon her head. Were it not for the modern costume of those around her, the figure must be mistaken for that of Sappho: and never was that impassioned being, the martyred saint of youthful lovers, portrayed with more sublimity, more high poetic feeling, or more exquisite feminine grace.

The contemplation of this *chef-d'oeuvre* naturally led the conversation to Madame de Staël. Her intimacy with Madame Récamier is as well known as the biting reply of the former to an unfortunate man, who having contrived to place himself between them, exclaimed, – 'Me voilà entre l'esprit et la beauté!'

To which bright sally he received for answer – 'Sans posséder ni l'un ni l'autre.'

My knowledge of this intimacy induced me to take advantage of the occasion, and I ventured to ask Madame Récamier if Madame de Staël had in truth intended to draw her own character in that of Corinne.

'Assuredly . . .' was the reply. 'The soul of Madame de Staël is fully developed in her portrait of that of Corinne.' Then turning to the picture, she added, 'Those eyes are the eyes of Madame de Staël.'

She put a miniature into my hand, representing her friend in all the bloom of youth, at an age indeed when she could not have been known to Madame Récamier. The eyes had certainly the same dark beauty, the same inspired expression, as those given to Corinne by Gérard. But the artist had too much taste or two little courage to venture upon any farther resemblance; the thick lips and short fat chin of the real sibyl being changed into all that is loveliest in female beauty on the canvass.

The apparent age of the face represented in the miniature points out its date with tolerable certainty; and it gives no very favourable idea of the taste of the period; for the shock head of crisped Brutus curls is placed on arms and bust as free from drapery, though better clothed in plumpness, than those of the Medicean Venus.

As we looked first at one picture, then at the other, and conversed on both, I was struck with the fine forehead and eyes, delightful voice, and peculiarly graceful turn of expression, of a gentleman who sat opposite to me, and who joined in this conversation.

I remarked to Madame Récamier that few romances had ever had the honour of being illustrated by such a picture as this of Gérard, and that, from many circumstances, her pleasure in possessing it must be very great.

'It is indeed,' she replied: 'nor is it my only treasure of the kind – I am so fortunate as to possess Girodet's original drawing from Atala, the engraving from which you must often have seen. Let me show you the original.'

We followed her to the dining-room, where this very interesting drawing is placed. 'You do not know M. d Châteaubriand?' said she.

I replied that I had not that pleasure.

'It is he who was sitting opposite to you in the *salon*.'

I begged that she would introduce him to me; and upon our returning to the drawing-room she did so. The conversation was resumed, and most agreeably – every one bore a part in it. Lamartine, Casimir Delavigne, Dumas, Victor Hugo, and some others, passed under a light but clever and acute review. Our Byron, Scott, &c. followed; and it was evident that they had been read and understood. I asked M. de Châteaubriand if he had known Lord Byron: he replied, 'Non;' adding, 'Je l'avais précédé dans la vie, et malheureusement il m'a précédé au tombeau.'

The degree in which any country is capable of fully appreciating the literature of another was canvassed, and M. de Châteaubriand declared himself decidedly of opinion that such appreciation was always and necessarily very imperfect.

Much that he said on the subject appeared incontrovertibly true, especially as respecting the slight and delicate shadows of expression of which the subtle grace so constantly seems to escape at the first attempt to convert it into another idiom. Nevertheless, I suspect that the majority of English readers – I mean the English readers of French – are more *au fait* of the original literature of France than M. de Châteaubriand supposes.

The habit, so widely extended amongst us, of reading this language almost from infancy, gives us a greater familiarity with their idiom than he is aware of. He doubted if we could relish Molière, and named Lafontaine as one beyond the reach of extra-Gallican criticism or enjoyment.

I cannot agree to this, though I am not surprised that such an idea should exist. Every English person that comes to Paris is absolutely obliged to speak French, almost whether they can or can not. If they shrink from doing so, they can have no hope of either speaking or being spoken to at all. This is alone sufficient to account very satisfactorily, I think, for any doubt which may prevail as to the national proficiency in the language. No Frenchman that is at all in the habit of meeting the English in society but must have his ears and his memory full of false concords, false tenses, and false accents; and can we wonder that he should set it down as a certain fact, that they who thus speak cannot be said to understand the language they so mangle? Yet, plausible as the inference is, I doubt if it be altogether just. Which of the most accomplished Hellenists of either country would be found capable of sustaining a familiar conversation in Greek? The case is precisely the same; for I have known very many whose power of tasting the beauty of French writing amounted to the most critical acuteness, who would have probably been unintelligible had they attempted to converse in the language for five minutes together; whereas many others, who have perhaps had a French valet or waiting-maid, may possess a passably good accent and great facility of imitative expression in conversation, who yet would be puzzled how to construe with critical accuracy the easiest passage in Rousseau.

A very considerable proportion of the educated French read English, and often appear to enter very ably into the spirit of our authors; but there is not one in fifty of these who will pronounce a single word of the language in conversation. Though they endure with a polite gravity, perfectly imperturbable, the very drollest blunders of which language is capable, they cannot endure to run the risk of making blunders in return. Everything connected with the externals of good society is held as sacred by the members of it; and if they shrink from offending *la bienséance* by laughing at the mistakes of others, they avoid, with at least an equal degree of caution, the unpardonable offence of committing any themselves.

I do not believe that it would be possible for a French person to enter into conversation merely for the pleasure of conversing, and not from the pressure of absolute necessity, unless he were certain, or at last believed himself to be so, that he should express himself with propriety and elegance. The idea of uttering the brightest or the noblest thought that ever entered a human head, in an idiom ridiculously broken, would, I am sure, be accompanied with a feeling of repugnance sufficient to tame the most animated and silence the most loquacious Frenchman in existence.

It therefore falls wholly upon the English, in this happy period of constant and intimate intercourse between the nations, to submit to the surrender of their vanity, to gratify their love for conversation; blundering on in conscious defiance of grammar and accent, rather than lose the exceeding pleasure of listening in return to the polished phrase, the graceful period, the epigrammatic turn, which make so essential a part of genuine high-bred French conversation.

But the doubts expressed by M. de Châteaubriand as to the possibility of the last and best grace of French writing being fully appreciated by foreigners, was not confined wholly to the English, – the Germans appeared to share it with us; and one who has been recently proclaimed as the first of living German critics was quoted as having confounded in his style, names found among the immortals of the French Pantheon, with those of such as live and die; *Monsieur* Fontaine, and *Monsieur* Bruyère, being expressions actually extant in his writings.

More than once, during subsequent visits to Madame Récamier, I led her to speak of her lost and illustrious friend. I have never been more interested than while listening to all which this charming woman said of Madame de Staël: every word she uttered seemed a mixture of pain and pleasure, of enthusiasm and regret. It is melancholy to think how utterly impossible it is that she should ever find another to replace her. She seems to feel this, and to have surrounded herself by everything that can contribute to keep the recollection of what is for ever gone, fresh in her memory. The original of the posthumous portrait of Madame de Staël by Gérard, made so familiar to all the world by engravings – nay, even by Sèvres vases and tea-cups, hangs in her bedroom. The miniature I have mentioned is always near her; and the inspired figure of her Corinne, in which it is evident that Madame Récamier traces a resemblance to her friend beyond that of features only, appears to be an object almost of veneration as well as love.

It is delightful to approach thus to a being that I have always been accustomed to contemplate as something in the clouds. Admirable and amiable as my charming new acquaintance is in a hundred ways, her past intimacy and ever-enduring affection for Madame de Staël have given her a still higher interest in my eyes.

LETTER XXXI

*Exhibition of Sèvres China at the Louvre – Gobelins
and Beauvais Tapestry – Legitimatist Father and
Doctrinaire Son – Copies from the Medicean Gallery*

We are just returned from an exhibition at the Louvre; and a
very splendid exhibition it is – though, alas! but a poor
consolation for the hidden treasures of the picture-gallery.
Several magnificent rooms are now open for the display of
works in tapestry and Sèvres porcelain; and however much we
might have preferred seeing something else there, it is impossible to deny that these rooms contain many objects as
wonderful perhaps in their way as any that the higher branches
of art ever produced.

The copy of Titian's portrait of his mistress, on porcelain,
and still more perhaps that of Raphaël's 'Virgin and St. John
watching the sleep of the infant Jesus,' (the *Parce somnum
rumpere*), are, I think, the most remarkable; both being of the
same size as the originals, and performed with a perfection of
colouring that is almost inconceivable.

That the fragile clay of which porcelain is fabricated should
so lend itself to the skill of the workman, – or rather, that the
workman's skill should so triumph over the million chances
which exist against bringing unbroken out of the fire a smooth
and level *plaque* of such extent, – is indeed most wonderful.
Still more so is the skill which has enabled the artist to
prophesy, as he painted with his greys and his greens, that the
tints which flowed from his pencil of one colour, should
assume, from the nicely-regulated action of an element the
most difficult to govern, hues and shades so exquisitely
imitative of his great original.

But having acknowledged this, I have nothing more to say
in praise of a *tour de force* which, in my opinion, can only be
attempted by the sacrifice of common sense. The *chefs-d'oeuvre*

of a Titian or a Raphaël are treasures of which we may lawfully covet an imitation; but why should it be attempted in a manner the most difficult, the most laborious, the most likely to fail, and the most liable to destruction when completed? – not to mention that, after all, there is in the most perfect copy on porcelain a something – I am mistress of no words to define it – which does not satisfy the mind.

As far as regards my own feelings indeed, I could go farther, and say that the effect produced is to a certain degree positively disagreeable, – not quite unlike that occasioned by examining needlework performed without fingers, or watch-papers exquisitely cut out by feet instead of hands. The admiration demanded is less for the thing itself, than for the very defective means employed to produce it. Were there indeed none other, the inventor would deserve a statue, and the artist, like Trisotin, should take the air 'en carrosse doré:' but as it is, I would rather see a good copy on canvass than on china.

Far different, however, is the effect produced by this beautiful and ingenious branch of art when displayed in the embellishment of cups and plates, vases and tea-trays. I never saw anything more gracefully appropriate to the last high finish of domestic elegance than all the articles of this description exhibited this year at the Louvre. It is impossible to admire or to praise them too much; or to deny that, wonderfully as similar manufactories have improved in England within the last thirty years, we have still nothing equal to the finer specimens of the Sèvres porcelain.

These rooms were, like every other place in Paris where human beings know that they shall meet each other, extremely full of company; and I have certainly never seen such ecstasy of admiration produced by any objects exhibited to the public eye, as was elicited by some of the articles displayed on this occasion: they are indeed most beautiful; the form, the material, the workmanship, all perfect.

The Sèvres manufactory must, I think, have some individuals attached to it who have made the theory of colour an especial study. It is worth while to walk round the vast table, or rather platform, raised in the middle of the apartment, for the purpose of examining the different sets, with a view only to observe the effect produced on the eye by the arrangement of colours in each.

The finest specimens, after the wonderful copies from pictures which I have already mentioned, are small breakfast-sets – for a *tête-à-tête*, I believe, – enclosed in large cases lined either with white satin or white velvet. These cases are all open for inspection, but with a stout brass bar around, to protect them from the peril of too near an approach. The lid is so formed as exactly to receive the tray; while the articles to be placed upon it, when in use, are arranged each in its own delicate recess, with such an attention to composition and general effect as to show all and everything to the greatest possible advantage.

Some of these exquisite specimens are decorated with flowers, some with landscapes, and others with figures, or miniatures of heads, either superlative in beauty or distinguished by fame. These beautiful decorations, admirable as they all are in design and execution, struck me less than the perfect taste with which the reigning colour which pervades each set, either as background, lining, or border, is made to harmonize with the ornaments upon it.

It is a positive pleasure, independent of the amusement which may be derived from a closer examination, to cast the eye over the general effect produced by the consummate taste and skill thus displayed. Those curious affinities and anti-pathies among colours, which I have seen made the subject of many pretty experimental lectures, must, I am sure, have been studied and acted upon by the *colour-master* of each depart-ment; and the result is to my feelings productive of a pleasure, from the contemplation of the effect produced, as distinct from the examination of the design, or of any other circumstance connected with the art, as the gratification produced by the smell of an orange-blossom or a rose: it is a pleasure which has no connexion with the intellect, but arises solely from its agreeable effect on the sense.

The eye seems to be unconsciously soothed and gratified, and lingers upon the rich, the soft, or the brilliant hues, with a satisfaction that positively amounts to enjoyment.

Whoever may be occupied by the 'delightful task' of fitting up a sumptuous drawing-room, will do well to take a tour round a room filled with sets of Sèvres porcelain. The important question of 'What colours shall we mix?' would receive an answer there, with the delightful certainty that no solecism in taste could possibly be committed by obeying it.

The Gobelins and Beauvais work for chairs, screens, cushions, and various other articles, makes a great display this year. It is very beautiful, both in design and execution; and at the present moment, when the stately magnificence of the age of Louis Quinze is so much in vogue – in compliment, it is said, to the taste of the Duc d'Orléans, – this costly manufacture is likely again to flourish.

Never can a large and lofty chamber present an appearance of more princely magnificence than when thus decorated; and the manner in which this elaborate style of ancient embellishment is now adopted to modern use, is equally ingenious and elegant.

Some political economists talk of the national advantage of decreasing labour by machinery, while others advocate every fashion which demands the work of hands. I will not attempt to decide on which side wisdom lies; but, in our present imperfect condition, everything that brings an innocent and profitable occupation to women appears to me desirable.

The needles of France are assuredly the most skilful in the world; and set to work as they are upon designs that rival those of the Vatican in elegance, they produce a perfection of embroidery that sets all competition at defiance.

In pursuing my way along the rail which encloses the specimens exhibited – a progress which was necessarily very slow from the pressure of the crowd, – I followed close behind a tall, elegant, aristocratic-looking gentleman, who was accompanied by his son – decidedly his son, – the boy 'fathered himself'; I never saw a stronger likeness. Their conversation, which I overheard by no act of impertinent listening, but because I could not possibly avoid it, amused me much. I am seldom thrown into such close contact with strangers without making a fancy-sketch of who and what they are; but upon this occasion I was thrown out, – it was like reading a novel, the *dénouement* of which is so well concealed as to evade guessing. The boy and his father were not of one mind; their observations were made in the spirit of different parties: the father, I suspect, was a royalist, – the son, I am sure, was a young doctrinaire. The crowd hung long upon the spot where a magnificent collection of embroidery for the seats and backs of a set of chairs was displayed. 'They are for the Duke of Orleans,' said the father.

'Yes, yes,' said the boy; 'They are fit for him – they are princely.'

'They are fit for a king!' said the father with a sigh.

The lad paused for a moment, and then said, *avec intention*, as the stage directions express it, 'Mais lui aussi, il est fils de St. Louis; n'est-ce pas?' The father answered not, and the crowd moved on.

All I could make of this was, that the boy's instructor, whether male or female, was a faithful disciple of the 'PARCEQU'*il est Bourbon*' school; and whatever leaven of wavering faith may be mixed up with this doctrine, it forms perhaps the best defence to be found for attachment to the reigning dynasty amongst those who are too young to enter fully into the expediency part of the question.

In the last of the suite of rooms opened for this exhibition, are displayed splendid pieces of tapestry from subjects taken from Rubens' Medicean Gallery.

That the achievement of these enormous combinations of stitches must have been a labour of extreme difficulty, there can be no doubt; but notwithstanding my admiration for French needles, I am tempted to add, in the words of our uncompromising moralist, 'Would it had been impossible!'

LETTER XXXII

Eglise Apostolique Française – Its doctrine –
L'Abbé Auzou – His Sermon on 'les Plaisirs Populaires'

Among the multitude of friendly injunctions to see this, and to hear that, which have produced me so much agreeable occupation, I have more than once been very earnestly recommended to visit the 'Eglise Apostolique Française' on the Boulevard St. Denis, for the purpose of hearing l'Abbé Auzou, and still more, that I might have an opportunity of observing the peculiarities of this mode of worship, or rather of doctrine; for, in fact, the ceremonies at the altar differ but little as far as I can perceive, from those of the Church of Rome, excepting that the evident poverty of the establishment precludes the splendour which usually attends the performance of its offices. I have no very satisfactory data by which to judge of the degree of estimation in which this new sect is held: by some I have heard them spoken of as apostles, and by others as a Paria caste unworthy of any notice.

Before hearing M. L'Abbé Auzou, or attending the service at his church, I wished to read some of the publications which explain their tenets, and accordingly called at the little bureau behind their chapel on the Boulevard St. Denis, where we were told these publications could be found. Having purchased several pamphlets containing catechism, hymns, sermons, and so forth, we entered into conversation with the young man who presided in this obscure and dark closet, dignified by the name of 'Secrétariat de l'Eglise Apostolique Française.'

He told us that he was assistant minister of the chapel, and we found him extremely conversible and communicative.

The chief differences between this new church and those which have preceded it in the reform of the Roman Catholic religion, appears to consist in the preservation of the external

186

forms of worship, which other reformers have rejected, and also of several dogmas, purely doctrinal, and wholly unconnected with those principles of church power and church discipline, the abuse of which was the immediate cause of all protestant reform.

They acknowledge the real presence. I find in the *Catéchisme* these questions and answers:

'Jésus-Christ est-il sous le pain, ou bien sous le vin? – Il est sous les deux éspèces à la fois.

'Et quand l'hostie est partagée? – Jésus-Christ est tout entier en chaque partie.

'Que faut-il faire pendant le jour où l'on a communié – Assister aux offices, et ensuite se réjouir de son bonheur avec ses parens et ses amis.'

Their clergy are permitted to marry. They deny that any power of absolution rests with the priest, allowing him only that of intercession by prayer for the forgiveness of the penitent. Auricular confession is not enjoined, but recommended as useful to children. They profess entire toleration to every variety of Christian belief; but as the 'Eglise Française' refuses to acknowledge dependence upon any *secte étrangère*, – by which phrase I conceive the Church of Rome to be meant, – they also declare, 'd'après l'Evangile, que la religion ne doit jamais intervenir dans les gouvernemens temporels.'

They recognise the seven sacraments, only modifying that of penitence, as above mentioned. They deny the eternity of punishment, but I find no mention of purgatory. They do not enjoin fasting. I find in the *Catéchisme* the following explanation of their doctrine on this head, which appears to be extremely reasonable.

'L'Eglise Française n'impose donc pas le jeûne et l'abstinence? – Non; l'Eglise Apostolique Française s'en rapporte pour le jeûne aux fidèles eux-mêmes, et ne reconnaît en aucune façon le précepte de l'abstinence; mais, plus prudente dans ses principes, elle substitue à un jeûne de quelques jours une sobriété continuelle, et remplace une abstinence périodique par une tempérance de chaque jour, de chaque année, de toute la vie.'

In all this there appears little in doctrine, excepting the admission of the divine presence in the elements of the eucharist, that differs greatly from most other reformed churches: nevertheless, the ceremonies are entirely similar to those of the Roman Catholic religion.

But whatever there may be either of good or of evil in this mixture, its effect must, I think, prove absolutely nugatory on society, from the entire absence of any church government or discipline whatever. That this is in fact the case, is thus plainly stated in the preface to their published Catechism:–

'L'Eglise Apostolique Française ne reconnaît aucune hiérarchie; elle repousse en conséquence l'autorité de tout pouvoir spirituel étranger, et de tout autre pouvoir qui en dépend ou qui s'y soumet. Elle ne reconnaît d'autre autorité spirituelle que celle qu'exercerait la réunion de ses fidèles; réunion qui, suivant les principes des apôtres, constitue seule ce que de leur temps on appelait EGLISE.

'Elle n'est point salariée par l'état. L'administration de ses secours spirituels est gratuite. Elle n'a de tarif, ni pour les baptêmes, ni pour les mariages, ni enfin pour les inhumations. Elle vit de peu, et s'en remet à la générosité, ou plutôt à la volonté, des fidèles.

'Ne reconnaissant pas d'hiérarchie, elle ne reconnaît pas non plus de division de territoire, soit en arrondissement, soit en paroisse: elle accueille donc tous les Chrétiens qui se présentent à elle pour mander à ses prêtres l'accomplissement des fonctions de ministres de Jésus-Christ.'

The *décousu* principles of the day can hardly be carried farther than this. A rope of sand is the only fitting emblem for a congregation so constituted; and, like a rope of sand, it must of necessity fall asunder, for there is no principle of union to prevent it.

After I had finished my studies on the subject, I heard a sermon preached in the church, – not, however, by M. l'Abbé Auzou, who was ill, but by the same person with whom we had conversed at the *Secrétariat*. His sermon was a strong exposition of the abuses practised by the clergy of the Church of Rome, – a theme certainly more fertile than new.

In reading some of the most celebrated discourses of the Abbé Auzou, I was the most struck with one entitled – 'Discours sur les Plaisirs Populaires, les Bals, et les Spectacles.'

The text is from St. Matthew, – 'Come unto me all ye that labour and are heavy laden, and I will give you rest . . . for my yoke is easy, and my burden is light.'

In this singular discourse, among some things that are reasonable, and more that are plausible, it is impossible to avoid seeing a spirit of lawless uncontrol, which seems to breathe more of revolution than of piety.

I am no advocate for a Judaical observance of the Sabbath, nor am I ignorant of the fearful abuses which have arisen from man's daring to arrogate to himself a power vested in God alone, – the power of forgiving the sins of man. The undue authority assumed by the sovereign pontiff of Rome is likewise sufficiently evident, as are many other abuses justly reprobated in the sermons of the Abbé Auzou. Nevertheless, education, observation, and I might say experience, have taught me that religion requires and demands that care, protection, and government which are so absolutely essential to the well-being of every community of human beings who would unite together for one general object. To talk of a self-governing church, is just as absurd as to talk of a self-governing ship, or a self-governing family.

It should seem, by the reprobation expressed against the severity of the Roman Catholic clergy in these sermons, as well as from anecdotes which I have occasionally heard in society, that the Church of Rome and the Church of Calvin are alike hostile to every kind of dissipation, and that at the present moment they have many points of discipline in common – at least as respects the injunctions laid upon their congregations respecting their private conduct.

M. l'Abbé Auzou says, in speaking of revolutionary reforms, –

'Rien n'est changé dans le sacerdoce; et l'on peut dire aussi des prêtres toujours romains, qu'ils n'ont rien oublié, qu'ils n'ont rien appris. Cependant, sous le règne de Napoléon leur orgueil a fléchi devant le grand intérêt de leur réinstallation . . . Aussi, au retour de leur roi légitime, cet orgueil comprimé s'est-il relevé dans toute sa hauteur. Rome a placé son trône à côté de celui d'un roi, un peu philosophe, a-t-on dit, mais perclus et impotent. Et enfin, lorsque son successeur, d'abord accueilli par le peuple, est tombé entre les mains des prêtres, ceux-ci, profitant de son âge et de sa faiblesse, ont exploité les erreurs d'une jeunesse fougueuse, qui cependant lui avaient valu le surnom de Chevalier Français. Alors nous avons vu ce roi sacrifier sa popularité à leurs exigences; appeler toute la nation à l'expiation de ses fautes personnelles, à son repentir, à sa pénitence; et la forcer à renier, pour ainsi dire, trente ans de gloire et de liberté. . . . Un roi que le remords poursuit, dévore, et qui ne reconnaît d'autre recours que dans le prêtre qui l'a soumis à sa loi par la menace et la terreur de l'enfer; ce roi, sous le coup d'une absolution conditionnelle et toujours suspendue, abdique, sans le savoir, en faveur de son confesseur . . .

'Roi! tu languis dans l'exil, et tes fautes sont punies jusque dans les dernières générations!

'Les prêtres, les prêtres romains se sont cependant soumis à un nouveau prince, à qui la souveraineté nationale a remis le sceptre; ils prient enfin pour lui . . . et l'on sait avec quelle sincérité.

'Mais, peuple, comme leur joug s'appesantit sur toi! . . . Dans leur fureur mal-déguisée ils le disent . . . La maison du Seigneur est déserte, et tu te rues avec fureur vers les plaisirs, les fêtes, les bals et les spectacles! Anathême donc contre les plaisirs, les fêtes et les bals! Anathême contre les spectacles!

'Ne sont-ce point là, mes frères, les paroles qui tombent chaque jour menaçantes de la chaire de l'Eglise Romaine? . . .

'Combien notre langage sera différent! Le Dieu des Juifs est bien notre Dieu; mais sa colère a été désarmée par le sacrifice que son fils lui a offert pour notre rédemption.

'Pourquoi ce sang répandu sur la croix pour nos péchés si la satisfaction de nos besoins physiques, si nos fonctions intellectuelles, si l'entraînement des passions qui constituent notre être peuvent à chaque instant nous faire tomber dans le péché et nous précipiter dans l'abîme?

'Aussi nous vous disons dans notre chaire apostolique, – Exécutez les commandemens de Dieu, adorez et glorifiez notre Père qui est aux cieux, pratiquez la morale de l'Evangile, aimez votre prochain comme vous-mêmes, et vous aurez accompli la loi de Jésus-Christ . . . et nous ajoutons, – Vous êtes membre de la société pour laquelle vous avez été créés, et cette société vous impose des devoirs; en échange elle vous procure des jouissances et des plaisirs: remplissez vos devoirs et livrez-vous ensuite sans crainte aux jouissances et aux plaisirs qu'elle vous présente. Votre participation à ces mêmes plaisirs, à ces mêmes jouissances, est encore une partie de vos devoirs, et vous aurez accompli encore une fois la loi de Jésus-Christ.'

This doctrine may assuredly entitle the Eglise Apostolique Française to the appellation of a NEW CHURCH.

M. l'Abbé Auzou goes on yet farther in the same strain:–

'Anathême! . . . Arme vieille, rouillée, émoussée, et que vous cherchez en vain à retremper dans le fiel de la colère et de la vengeance! . . . Anathême aux plaisirs! Et quoi! parceque Dieu a dit à notre premier père, Vous mangerez votre pain à la sueur de votre visage, l'homme serait condamné à rester toujours courbé sous le joug du travail? N'aura-t-il à éspérer aucun adoucissement à ses peines? . . .

'Non, sans doute . . . vous dira le clergé romain, puisque Dieu a consacré le septième jour au repos?

'Et quel est ce repos?

'Sera-ce celui, qu'en vous servant due bras du séculier, vous avez tenté de lui imposer par une ordonnance préscrivant de fermer tous les établissemens qui décorent notre cité, nos cafés, nos restaurans, pour ne tolérer que l'ouverture des officines du pharmacien? – ordonnance dont une caricature spirituelle a fait si prompte justice.'

The following picture of a fanatical Sunday takes me back at once to America. There, however, its worst effect was to steep the senses in the unnecessary oblivion of a few more hours of sleep; but in Paris I should really expect that such restraint, were it indeed possible to impose it, would literally drive the sensitive and mobile population to madness.

'Et quel est donc ce repos?

'Sera-ce l'immobilité des corps; l'abandon de toutes nos facultés; l'oisiveté; l'ennui, compagnon inséparable de l'oisiveté; la prière; la méditation, – la méditation plus pénible pour la plupart des hommes que le travail des mains; et, enfin, vos sermons intolérans et, qui pis est peut-être, si ennuyeux?

'Ah! imposer à l'homme un pareil repos ne serait que suspendre son travail pour lui faire porter, comme à St. Simon de Cyrène, la croix de Jésus-Christ jusqu'au sommet escarpé du Calvaire.'

The Abbé then proceeds to promulgate his bull for the permission of all sorts of Parisian delights; nay, he takes a very pretty and picturesque ramble into the country, where 'les jeunes garçons et les jeunes filles s'y livrent à des danses rustiques' – and, in short gives so animated a picture of the pleasures which ought to await the Sabbath both in town and country, that it is almost impossible to read it without feeling a wish that every human being who through the six days of needful labour has been 'weary worn with care' should pass the seventh amid the bright and cheering scenes he describes. But he effectually checks this feeling of sympathy with his views by what follows. He describes habitual drunkenness with the disgust it merits; but strangely qualifies this, by adding to his condemnation of the 'homme dégradé qui, oubliant chaque jour sa dignité dans les excès d'une hideuse ivrognerie, *n'attend pas le jour que Dieu a consacré au repos, à* la distraction, aux plaisirs, pour se livrer à son ignoble passion,' these dangerous words:–

'Mais condamnerous-nous sans retour notre frère pour un jour d'intempérance passagère, et blamerons-nous celui qui, cherchant dans le vin, ce présent du Ciel, un moment d'oubli des misères humaines, n'a point su s'arrêter à cette douce ivresse, oublieuse des maux et créatrice d'heureuses illusions?'

Is not this using the spur where the rein is most wanting? I am persuaded that it is not the intention of the Abbé Auzou to advocate any species of immorality; but all the world, and particularly the French world perhaps, is so well disposed to amuse itself *coûte qui coûte*, that I confess I doubt the wisdom of enforcing the necessity of so doing from the pulpit.

The unwise, unauthorised, and most unchristian severity of the Calvanistic and Romish priesthood may, I think, lawfully and righteously be commented upon and reprobated both in the pulpit and out of it; but this reprobation should not clothe itself in license, or in any language that can be interpreted as such. There are many, I should think, in every Christian land, both clergy and laity, but neither popish nor Calvinistic, who would shrink both from the sentiment and expression of the following passage:–

'Rappelons-nous que le patriarche Noé, lui qui planta la vigne et exprima le jus de son fruit, en abusa une fois, et que

Dieu ne lui en fit point le reproche: Dieu punit, au contraire, le fils qui n'avait point caché cette faiblesse d'un père.

There is some worldly wisdom, however, in the exclamation he addresses to his intolerant brethren.

'Et vous, prêtres aveugles et impolitiques, laissez le peuple se livrer à ses plaisirs innocens; faites en sorte qu'il se contente de sa position; qu'il ne compare pas cette position pénible, douloureuse, avec l'oisiveté dans laquelle vous vivez vous-mêmes, et que vous ne devez qu'à la nouvelle dîme qui s'exprime de son front.'

He then proceeds to say, that it is not the poor only who are subjected to this severity, but the rich also . . . 'que le prêtre de la secte romaine veut arrêter, troubler dans ses plaisirs, dans ses délassemens.'. . . Un repas par lequel on célèbre l'union de deux jeunes coeurs, l'union de deux familles, et dans lequel règnent la joie, *et peut-être aussi un peu plus que de la gaîté*, est l'objet de la censure inexorable de ces prêtres rigides. . . . Ils oublient que celui qu'ils disent êtrer leur maître a consacré ces réunions par sa présence, et que le vin ayant manqué par le trop grand usage qu'on en avait fait, il n'en a pas moins changé l'eau en vin. Ils sont tous disposés à répondre comme ce Janséniste à qui l'on rappelait cet intéressant épisode de la vie de Jésus, – 'Ce n'est pas ce qu'il a fait de mieux.' – Impie! . . . tu blasphêmes contre ton maître! . . .

'Ah! mes frères, admirons, nous, dans la sincérité de notre coeur, cet exemple de bienveillance et de *sociabilité pratique*, et bénissons la bonté de Jésus.'

Then follows an earnest defence, or rather eulogy, of dancing. But though I greatly approve the exercise for young people, and believe it to be as innocent as it is natural, I would not, were I called upon to preach a sermon, address my hearers after this manner:–

'Quant aux bals, je ne chercherai point à les excuser, à les défendre, par *des exemples puisés dans l'écriture sainte*. Je ne vous représenterai point David dansant devant l'arche. . . . Je ne vous le donnerai pas non plus pour modèle, à vous, jeunes gens de notre France *si polie, si élégante*, car sans doute *il dansait mal*; puisque, suivant la Bible, Michal sa femme, voyant le roi David qui sautait et dansait, se moqua de lui et le méprisa dans son coeur.' There is about as much piety as good taste in this.

I have already given you such long extracts, that I must omit all he says, – and it is much in favour of this amusement. Such forbearance is the more necessary, as I must give you a passage or two more on other subjects. Among the general reasons which he brings forward to prove that fêtes and festivals are beneficial to the people, he very justly remarks that the occupation they afford to industry is not the least important, observing that the popish church takes no heed of such things; and then adds, addressing the manufacturers, –

'Et lorsque le besoin se fera sentir et pour vous et vos enfans, allez à l'Archevêché! . . . à l'Archevêché, . . . un jour la colère du peuple a éclaté, –

'Je n'ai fait que passer, il n'était déjà plus.' . . .

The date which this sermon bears on its title page is 1834; but the event to which this line from Racine alludes was the destruction of the archiepiscopal palace, which took place, if I mistake not in 1831. If the 'il n'était déjà plus' alludes to the palace, it is correct enough, for destruction could not have done its work better: but if it be meant to describe the fate of MONSEIGNEUR L'ARCHEVÊQUE DE PARIS, the preacher is not a prophet; for, in truth, the sacrilegious rout 'n'a fait que passer,' and MONSEIGNEUR has only risen higher from the blow. Public orators of all kinds should be very cautious, in these moveable times, how they venture to judge from today what may be tomorrow. The only oracular sentence that can be uttered at present with the least chance of success from the development of the future is, 'Who can say what may happen next?' All who have sufficient prudence to restrict their prescience to this acute form of prophecy, may have the pleasure, let come what may, of turning to their neighbours triumphantly with the question – 'Did I not tell you that something was going to happen?' – but it is dangerous to be one atom more precise. Even before this letter can reach you, my friend, M. l'Abbé's interpretation of 'il n'était déjà plus' may be more correct than mine. I say this, however, only to save my credit with you in case of the worst; for my private opinion is, that Monseigneur was never in a more prosperous condition in his life, and that, 'as no one can say what will happen next,' I should not be at all astonished if a cardinal's hat were speedily to reward him for all he has done and suffered.

I certainly intended to have given you a few specimens of the Abbé Auzou's manner of advocating theatrical exhibitions; but I fear they would lead me into too great length of citation. He is sometimes really eloquent upon the subject: nevertheless, his opinions on it, however reasonable, would have been delivered with better effect from the easy-chair of his library than from the pulpit of his church. It is not that what would be good when heard from the one could become evil when listened to from the other: but the preacher's pulpit is intended for other uses; and though the visits to a well-regulated theatre may be as lawful as eating, and as innocent too, we go to the house of God in the hope of hearing tidings more important than his minister's assurance that they are so.

LETTER XXXIII

Establishment for Insane Patients at Vanves –
Description of the arrangements – Englishman –
His religious madness

You will think perhaps that I have chosen oddly the object
which has induced me to make an excursion out of town, and
obliged me to give up nearly an entire day at Paris, when I tell
you that it was to visit an institution for the reception of the
insane. There are, however, few things which interest me
more than an establishment of this nature; especially when, as
in the present instance, my manner of introduction to it is such
as to give me the hope of hearing the phenomena of these
awful maladies discussed by those well acquainted with them.
The establishment of MM. Voisin and Fabret, at Vanves, was
mentioned to me as one in which many improvements in the
mode of treating alienation of mind have been suggested and
tried with excellent effect; and having the opportunity of
visiting it in company with a lady who was well acquainted
with the gentlemen presiding over it, I determined to take
advantage of it. My friend, too, knew how to direct my
attention to what was most interesting, from having had a
relation placed there, whom for many months she had been in
the constant habit of visiting.

Her introduction obtained for me the most attentive reception, and the fullest explanation of their admirable system,
which appears to me to combine, and on a very large and
noble scale, everything likely to assuage the sufferings, soothe
the spirits, and contribute to the health of the patients.

Vanves is situated at the distance of one league from Paris, in
a beautiful part of the country; and the establishment itself,
from almost every part of the high ground on which it is
placed, commands views so varied and extensive, as not only
to render the principal mansion a charming residence, but

really to make the walks and drives within the enclosure of the extensive premises delightful.

The grounds are exceedingly well laid out, with careful attention to the principal object for which they are arranged, but without neglecting any of the beauty of which the spot is so capable. They have shade and flowers, distant views and sheltered seats, with pleasant walks, and even drives and rides, in all directions. The enclosure contains about sixty acres, to every part of which the patients who are well enough to walk about can be admitted with perfect safety.

In this park are situated two or three distinct lodges, which are found occasionally to be of the greatest utility, in cases where the most profound quiet is necessary, and yet where too strict confinement would be injurious. Indeed, it appears to me that the object principally kept in view throughout all the arrangements, is the power of keeping patients out of sight and hearing of each other till they are sufficiently advanced towards recovery to make it a real pleasure and advantage to associate together.

As soon as they reach this favourable stage of their convalescence, they mix with the family in very handsome rooms, where books, music, and a billiard-table assist them to pass the hours without *ennui*. Every patient has a separate sleeping-apartment, in none of which are the precautions necessary for their safety permitted to be visible. What would wear the appearance of iron bars in every other place of the kind that I have seen, are here made to look like very neat *jalousies*. Not a bolt or a bar is perceptible, nor any object whatever that might shock the spirit, if at any time a gleam of recovered intellect should return to visit it.

This cautious keeping out of sight of the sufferers everything that might awaken them to a sense of their own condition, or that of the other patients, appears to me to be the most peculiar feature of the discipline, and is evidently one of the objects most sedulously kept in view. Next to this I should place the system of inducing the male patients to exercise their limbs, and amuse their spirits, by working in the garden, at any undertaking, however *bizarre* and profitless, which can induce them to keep mind and body healthily employed. I know not if this has been systematically resorted to elsewhere;

but the good sense of it is certainly very obvious, and the effect, as I was told, is found to be very generally beneficial; though it occasionally happens that some among them have fancied their dignity compromised by using a spade or a hoe, – and then some of the family join with them in the labour, to prove that it is merely a matter of amusement: in short, everything likely to cheer or soothe the spirits seems brought into use among them.

The ground close adjoining to the house is divided into many small well-enclosed gardens; the women's apartments opening to some, the men's to others of them. In several of these gardens I observed neat little tables, such as are used in the *restaurans* of Paris, with a clean cloth, and all necessary appointments, placed pleasantly and commodiously in the shade, at each of which was seated one person, who was served with a separate dinner, and with every appearance of comfort. Had I not known their condition, I should in many instances have thought the spectacle a very pleasing one.

M. Voisin walked through all parts of the establishment with us, and there appeared to exist a perfectly good understanding between him and his patients. Among many regulations, which all appeared excellent, he told me that the friends of his inmates were permitted at all times, and under all circumstances, to visit them without any restraint whatever; an arrangement which can only be productive of confidence and advantage to all parties; as it is perfectly inconceivable that any one who had felt obliged to place an unhappy friend or relative under restraint should wish to interfere with the discipline necessary for his ultimate advantage; whereas a contrary system is likely to give occasion to constant doubts and fears on one hand, and to the possibility of ill treatment or unnecessary restraint on the other. In one of the courts appropriated to the use of such male patients as were sufficiently convalescent to permit their associating together, and amusing themselves with the different games in which they are permitted to share, we saw a young Englishman, now rapidly recovering, but who had scrawled over the walls of his own sleeping-apartment, poor fellow! with a pencil, a vast quantity of writing, almost wholly on religious subjects; proving but too plainly that he was one of the many victims of fanaticism. Every thought seemed pregnant with suffering, and sometimes bursts of agony were scrawled in trembling characters, that spoke the very extremity of terror. 'Who is there can endure fire and flame for ever, for ever, and for ever?' 'Death is before us – Hell follows it!' 'The bottomless pit – groans – tortures – anguish – for ever!' . . . Such sentences as these were still legible, though much had been obliterated.

Who can wonder that a mind thus occupied should lose that fine balance with which nature has arranged our faculties, making one keep watch and ward over the other? . . . This poor fellow lost his wits under the process of conversion: Judgment being entirely overthrown, Imagination had vaulted into its seat, pregnant with visions black as night, dark – oh! far darker than the tomb! 'palled in the dunnest smoke of hell,' and armed with every image for the eternity of torture that the ingenuity of man could devise. Who can wonder at his madness? And how many crimes are there recorded in the Newgate Calendar which equal in atrocity that of so distorting a mind, that sought to raise its humble hopes towards heaven!

I felt particularly interested for this poor lunatic, both as my countryman, and the victim of by far the most fearful tyranny that man can exercise on man. Against all other injury it is not difficult to believe that a steadfast spirit can arm itself and say with Hamlet,

'I do not set my life at a pin's fee.'

But against this, it were a vain boast to add,

'And for my soul, what can it do to that,
Being a thing immortal as itself?'

For, alas! it is that very immortality which gives hope, comfort, and strength under every other persecution that paralyses the sufferer under this, and arms with such horrid strength the blasphemous wretch who teaches him to turn in terror from his God.

M. Voisin told me that this unfortunate young man had been for some time daily becoming more calm and tranquil, and that he entertained not any doubt of his ultimate recovery.

Excepting this my poor countryman, the only patient I saw whose situation it was particularly painful to contemplate was a young girl who had only arrived the preceding day. There was in her eyes a restless, anxious, agitated manner of looking about on all things, and gathering a distinct idea from none – a vague uncertainty as to where she was, not felt with sufficient strength to amount to wonder, but enough to rob her of all the feeling of repose which belongs to home. Poor girl! perhaps some faltering, unfixable thought brought at intervals the figure of her mother to her; for as I looked at her pale face, its vacant expression received more than once a sad but passing gleam of melancholy meaning. She coughed frequently; but the cough seemed affected , – or rather, it appeared to be an effort not so much required by her lungs, as by the need of some change, some relief – she knew not what, nor where nor how to seek it. She appeared very desirous of shaking off the attendance of a woman who was waiting upon her, and her whole manner indicated a sort of fretful unrest that it made one wretched to contemplate. But here again I was comforted by the assurance that there were no symptoms which forbade hope of recovery.

I remember being told, when visiting the lunatic asylum near New York, that the most frequent causes of insanity were ascertained to be religion and drunkenness. Near Paris I find that love, high play, and politics are considered as the principal causes of this calamity; and certainly nothing can be more accordant with what observation would teach one to expect than both these statements. At New York the physician told me that madness arising from excessive drinking admitted, in the great majority of cases, of a perfect cure; but that religious aberration of intellect was much more enduring.

At Paris I have heard the same; for here also it occasionally happens, though not often, that the reason becomes disturbed by repeated and frequent intoxication: but where either politics or love has taken such hold of the mind as to disturb the reasoning power, the recovery is less certain and more slow.

Dr. Voisin told me that he uniformly found the first symptoms of insanity appear in the wavering, indifferent, and altered state of the affections towards relations and friends; –

apathy, coldness, and, in some cases, dislike, and even violent antipathy, being sure to appear, wherever previous attachment had been the most remarkable. They sometimes, but not very often, take capricious fits of fondness for strangers; but never with any show of reason, and never for any length of time. The most certain symptom of approach towards recovery is when the heart appears to be re-awakened to its natural feelings and old attachments.

There was one old lady that I watched eating her dinner of vegetables and fruit at a little table in one of the gardens, who had adorned her bonnet with innumerable scraps of trumpery, and set it on her head with the most studied and coquettish air imaginable: she fed herself with the grace or grimace of a young beauty, eating grapes of a guinea a pound, from a plate of crystal, with a golden fork. I am sure she was enjoying all the happiness of feeling herself beautiful, elegant, and admired: and when I looked at the wrinkled ruin of her once handsome face, I could hardly think her madness a misfortune; for though I did not obtain any pitiful story concerning her, or any history of the cause which brought her there, I felt sure that it must in some way or other be connected with some feeling of deeply-mortified vanity: and if I am right in my conjecture, what has the world left for her equal in consolation to the wild fancies which now shed such simpering complacency over her countenance? And might we not exclaim for her in all kindness –

'Let but the cheat endure! – She asks not aught beside?'

What was passing in this poor old head, it was easy enough to guess – wild as it was, and wide from the truth. But there was another, which , though I studied it as long as I could possibly contrive to do so, wholly baffled me; and yet I would have given much to know what thoughts were flitting through that young brain.

She was a young girl, extremely pretty, with coal-black hair and eyes, and seated, quite apart from all, upon a pleasant shady bench in one of the gardens. Her face was like a fair landscape, over which passes cloud and sunshine in rapid succession: for one moment she smiled, and the next seemed preparing to weep; but before a tear could fall, her fine teeth were again displayed in an unmeaning smile. O, what could be the fleeting visions formed that worked her fancy thus? Could it be memory? Or was the fitful emotion caused by the galloping vagaries of an imagination which outstripped the power of reason to follow it? Or was it none of this, but a mere meaningless movement of the muscles, that worked in idle mockery of the intellect that used to govern them?

I have sometimes thought it very strange that people should feel such deep delight in watching on the stage the representation of the utmost extremity of human woe that the mind of man can contrive to place before them; and I have wondered more, much more, at the gathering together of thousands and tens of thousands, whenever the law has doomed that some wretched soul should be separated by the hand of man from the body in which it has sinned: but I doubt if my own intense interest in watching poor human nature when deprived of reason is not stranger still. I can in no way account for it; but so it is. I can never withdraw myself from the contemplation of a maniac without reluctance; and yet I am always conscious of painful feelings as long as it lasts, and perfectly sure that I shall be followed by more painful feelings still when it is over.

It is certain, however, that the comfort, the tenderness, the care, so evident in every part of the establishment at Vanves, render the contemplation of insanity there less painful than I ever found it elsewhere; and when I saw the air of healthy physical enjoyment (at least) with which a large number of the patients prepared to take their pastime, during their hours of exercise, each according to his taste or whim, amid the ample space and well-chosen accessories prepared for them, I could not but wish that every retreat fitted up for the reception of this unfortunate portion of the human race could be arranged on the same plan and governed by the same principles.

LETTER XXXIV

Riot at the Porte St. Martin – Prevented by a shower of Rain –
The Mob in fine weather – How to stop Emeutes –
Army of Italy – Théâtre Français –
Mademoiselle Mars in Henriette – Disappearance of Comedy

Though Paris is really as quiet at present as any great city can possibly be, still we continue to be told regularly every morning, 'qu'il y avait une émeute hier soir à la Porte St. Martin.' But I do assure you that these are very harmless little pastimes; and though it seldom happens that the mysterious hour of revolution-hatching passes by without some arrest taking place, the parties are always liberated the next morning; it having appeared clearly at every examination that the juvenile aggressors, who are seldom above twenty years of age, are as harmless as a set of croaking bullfrogs on the banks of the Wabash. The continually repeated mention, however, of these nightly meetings, induced two gentlemen of our party to go to this often-named Porte St. Martin a few nights ago, in hopes of witnessing the humours of one of these small riotings. But on arriving at the spot they found it perfectly tranquil – everything wore the proper stillness of an orderly and well-protected night. A few military were, however, hovering near the spot; and of these they made inquiry as to the cause of a repose so unlike what was usually supposed to be the state of this celebrated quarter of the town.

'Mais ne voyez-vous pas que l'eau tombe, messieurs?' said the national guard stationed there: 'c'est bien assez pour refroidir le feu de nos républicains. S'il fait beau demain soir, messieurs, nous aurons encore notre petit spectacle.'

Determined to know whether there was any truth in these histories or not, and half suspecting that the whole thing, as well as the assurance of the civil *militaire* to boot, was neither more nor less than a hoax, they last night, the weather being

203

remarkably fine, again attempted the adventure, and with very different success.

On this occasion, there was, by their description, as pretty a little riot as heart could wish. The numbers assembled were stated to be above four hundred: military, both horse and foot, were among them; pointed hats were as plenty as blackberries in September, and 'banners waved without a blast' on the tottering shoulders of little ragamuffins who had been hired for two sous apiece to carry them.

On this memorable evening, which has really made a figure this morning in some of the republican journals, a considerable number of the most noisy portion of the mob were arrested; but, on the whole, the military appear to have dealt very gently with them; and our friends heard many a crazy burst of artisan eloquence, which might have easily enough been construed into treason, answered with no rougher repartee than a laughing 'Vive le Roi!'

At one point, however, there was a vehement struggle before a young hero, equipped cap-à-pie à la Robespierre, could be secured; and while two of the civic guard were employed in taking him, a little fellow of about ten years old, who had a banner as heavy as himself on his shoulder, and who was probably squire of the body to the prisoner, stood on tiptoe before him at the distance of a few feet, roaring 'Vive la République!' as loud as he could bawl.

Another fellow, apparently of the very lowest class, was engaged, during the whole time that the tumult lasted, in haranguing a party that he had collected round him. His arms were bare to the shoulders, and his gesticulation exceedingly violent.

'Nous avons des droits!' he exclaimed with great vehemence. . . . 'Nous avons des droits! Qui est-ce qui veut les nier! . . . Nous ne démandons que la charte . . . Qu'ils nous donnent la charte!' . . .

The uproar lasted about three hours, after which the crowd quietly dispersed; and it is to be hoped that they may all employ themselves honestly in their respective callings, till the next fine evening shall again bring them together in the double capacity of actors and spectators at the 'petit spectacle.'

Porte St. Martin.

The constant repetition of this idle riot seems now to give little disturbance to any one; and were it not that the fines and imprisonments so constantly, and sometimes not very leniently inflicted, evidently show that they are thought worth some attention, (though, in fact, this system appears to produce no effect whatever towards checking the daring demonstrations of disaffection manifested by the rabble and their newspaper supporters,) one might deem this indifference the result of such sober confidence of strength in the government, as left them no anxiety whatever as to anything which this troublesome faction could achieve.

Such, I believe, is in fact the feeling of King Philippe's government: nevertheless, it would certainly conduce greatly to the well-being of the people of Paris, if such methods were resorted to as would effectually and at once put a stop to such disgraceful scenes.

'LIBERTY AND ORDER' is King Philippe's motto: he could only improve it by adding 'Repose and Quiet;' for never can he reign by any other power than that given by the hope of repose and tranquillity. The harassed nation looks to him for these blessings; and if it be disappointed, the result must be terrible.

Louis-Philippe is neither Napoleon nor Charles the Tenth. He has neither the inalienable rights of the one, nor the overpowering glory of the other; but should he be happy enough to discover a way of securing to this fine but strife-worn and weary country the tranquil prosperity that it now appears beginning to enjoy, he may well be considered by the French people as greater than either.

Bold, fearless, wise, and strong must be the hand that at the present hour can so wield the sceptre of France; and I think it may reasonably be doubted if any one could so wield it, unless its first act were to wave off to a safe distance some of the reckless spirits who are ready to lay down their lives on the scaffold – or in a gutter – or over a pan of charcoal, rather than 'live peaceably in that state of life unto which it has pleased God to call them.'

If King Louis-Philippe would undertake a crusade to restore independence to Italy, he might convert every traitor into a hero. Let him address the army raised for the purpose in the

same inspiring words that Napoleon used of yore. 'Soldats!
. . . Partons! Rétablir le capitole . . . Réveiller le peuple
romain engourdi par plusieurs siècles d'esclavage . . . Tel sera
le fruit de vos victories. Vous rentrerez alors dans vos foyers,
et vos concitoyens diront en vous montrant – Il était de
l'armée d'Italie!' And then let him institute a new order,
entitled 'L'Ordre Impérial de la Redingote grise,' or 'L'Ordre
indomptable des Bras croisés,' and accord to every man the
right of admission to it, with the honour to boot of having an
eagle embroidered on the breast of his coat if he conducted
himself gallantly and like a Frenchman in the field of battle,
and we should soon find the Porte St. Martin as quiet as the
Autocrat's dressing-room at St. Petersburg.

If such an expedient as this were resorted to, there would no
longer be any need of that indecent species of safety-valve by
which the noxious vapour generated by the ill-disposed part of
the community is now permitted to escape. It may be very
great, dignified, and high-minded for a king and his ministers
to laugh at treasonable caricatures and seditious pleasantries of
all sorts, – but I do greatly doubt the wisdom of it. Human
respect is necessary for the maintenance and support of human
authority; and that respect will be more profitably shown by a
decent degree of general external deference, than by the most
sublime kindlings of individual admiration that ever warmed
the heart of a courtier. This 'avis au lecteur' might be listened to
with advantage, perhaps, in more countries than one.

Since I last gave you any theatrical news, we have been to
see Mademoiselle Mars play the part of Henriette in Molière's
exquisite comedy of 'Les Femmes Savantes'; and I really think
it the most surprising exhibition I ever witnessed. Having seen
her in 'Tartuffe' and 'Charlotte Brown' from a box in the first
circle, at some distance from the stage, I imagined that the
distance had a good deal to do with the effect still produced by
the grace of form, movement, and toilet of this extraordinary
woman.

To ascertain, therefore, how much was delusion and how
much was truth in the beauty I still saw or fancied, I resolved
upon the desperate experiment of securing that seat in the
balcony which is nearest to the stage. It was from this place
that I saw her play Henriette; a character deriving no aid

whatever from trick or stage effect of any kind; one, too, whose charm lies wholly in simple, unaffected youthfulness: there are no flashes of wit, no startling hits either of pathos or pleasantry – nothing but youth, gentleness, modesty, and tenderness – nothing but a young girl of sixteen, rather more quiet and retiring than usual. Yet this character, which seems of necessity to require youth and beauty in the performer, though little else, was personated by this miraculous old lady in a manner that not only enchanted me – being, as I am, *rococo* – but actually drew forth from the omnipotent *jeunes gens* in the *parterre* such clamorous rapture of applause as must, I think, have completely overset any actress less used to it than herself. Is not this marvellous?

How much it is to be regretted that the art of writing comedy has passed away! They have vaudevilles here – charming things in their way; and we have farces at home that certainly cannot be thought of without enjoying the gratification of a broad grin. But for comedy, where the intellect is called upon as well as the muscles, it is dead and gone. The 'Hunchback' is perhaps the nearest approach to it, whose birth I remember in our country, and 'Bertrand and Raton' here; but in both cases the pleasurable excitement is produced more by the plot than the characters – more by the business of the scene than by the wit and elegance of the dialogue, except perhaps in the pretty wilfulness of Julia in the second act of the 'Hunchback.' But even here I suspect it was more the playful grace of the enchanting actress who first appeared in the part, than anything in the words 'set down for her,' which so delighted us.

We do now and then get a new tragedy, – witness 'Fazio' and 'Rienzi;' but Comedy – genuine, easy, graceful, flowing, talking Comedy – is dead: I think she followed Sheridan to the grave and was buried with him! But never is one so conscious of the loss, or so inclined to mourn it, as after seeing a comedy of Molière's of the first order, – for his pieces should be divided into classes, like diamonds. What a burst of new enjoyment would rush over all England, or all France, if a thing like 'The School for Scandal' or 'Les Femmes Savantes' were to appear before them!

Fancy the delight of sitting to hear wit – wit that one did not know by rote, bright, sparkling, untasted as yet by any – new and fresh from the living fountain! – not coming to one in the shape of coin, already bearing the lawful stamp of ten thousand plaudits to prove it genuine, and to refuse to accept which would be treason; but as native gold, to which the touchstone of your own intellect must be applied to test its worth! Shall we ever experience this?

It is strange that the immense mass of material for comedy which the passing scenes of this singular epoch furnish should not be worked up by some one. Molière seems not to have suffered a single passing folly to escape him. Had he lived in these days, what delicious whigs, radicals, 'penny-rint' kings, from our side of the water, – what tragic poets, republicans, and parvenus from his own, would he have cheered us withal!

'Rousseau says, that when a theatre produces pieces which represent the real manners of the people, they must greatly assist those who are present at them to see and amend what is vicious or absurd in themselves, 'comme on ôte devant un miroir les taches de son visage.' The idea is excellent; and surely there never was a time when it would be so easy or so usdul to put it in practice. Would the gods but send a Sheridan to England and a Molière to France, we might yet live to see some of our worst misfortunes turned to jest, and, like the man choking in a quinsey, laugh ourselves into health again.

LETTER XXXV

Soirée dansante – Young Ladies – Old Ladies – Anecdote –
The Consolations of Chaperones – Flirtations – Discussion
upon the variations between young Married Women in
France and in England – Making love by deputy –
Not likely to answer in England

Last night we were at a ball, – or rather, I should say, a '*soirée*
dansante;' for at this season, though people may dance from
night to morning, there are no balls. But let it be called by
what name it may, it could not have been more gay and
agreeable were this the month of January instead of May.

There were several English gentlemen present, who, to the
great amusement of some of the company, uniformly selected
their partners from among the young ladies. This may appear
very natural to you; but here it is thought the most unnatural
proceeding possible.

To a novice in French society, there is certainly no
circumstance so remarkable as the different positon which the
unmarried hold in the drawing-rooms of England and *les*
salons of France. With us, the prettiest things to look at, and
the partners first sought for the dance, are the young girls.
Brilliant in the perfection of their youthful bloom, graceful
and gay as young fawns in every movement of the most
essentially juvenile of all exercises, and eclipsing the light
elegance of their own toilet by loveliness that leaves no eyes to
study its decoration, – it is they who, in spite of diamonds and
of blonde, of wedded beauty or of titled grace, ever appear to
be the principal actors in a ballroom. But 'they manage these
matters' quite otherwise 'in France.'

Unfortunately, it may sometimes happen among us, that a
coquettish matron may be seen to lead the giddy waltz with
more sprightliness than wisdom; but she always does it at the
risk of being *mal notée* in some way or other, more or less

gravely, by almost every person present; – nay, I would by no means encourage her to be very certain that her tonish partner himself would not be better pleased to whirl round the mazy circle with one of the slight, light, sylph-like creatures he sees flying past him, than with the most fashionable married woman in London.

But in Paris all this is totally reversed; and, what is strange enough, you will find in both countries that the reason assigned for the difference between them arises from national attention to good morals.

On entering a French ballroom, instead of seeing the youngest and loveliest part of the company occupying the most conspicuous places, surrounded by the gayest men, and dressed with the most studied and becoming elegance, you must look for the young things quite in the background, soberly and quietly attired, and almost wholly eclipsed behind the more fully-blown beauties of their married friends.

It is really marvellous, considering how very much prettier a girl is at eighteen than she can possibly be some dozen years afterwards, to see how completely fashion will nevertheless have its own way, making the worse positively appear the better beauty.

All that exceeding charm and fascination which is for ever and always attributed to an elegant Frenchwoman, belongs wholly, solely, and altogether to her after she becomes a wife. A young French girl, '*parfaitement bien élevée*, looks . . . '*parfaitement bien élevée*;' but it must be confessed, also, that she looks at the same time as if her governess (and a sharp one) were looking over her shoulder. She will be dressed, of course, with the nicest precision and most exact propriety; her corsets will forbid a wrinkle to appear in her robe, and her *friseur* deny permission to any single hair that might wish to deviate from the station appointed for it by his stiff control. But if you would see that graceful perfection of the toilet, the unrivalled *agacerie* of costume which distinguishes a French woman from all others in the world, you must turn from mademoiselle to madame. The very sound of the voice, too, is different. It should seem as if the heart and soul of a French girl were asleep, or at least dozing, till the ceremony of marriage awakened them. As long as it is mademoiselle who speaks, there is something monotonous, dull, and uninteresting in the tone, or rather in the tune, of her voice; but when madame addresses you, all the charm that manner, cadence, accent can bestow, is sure to greet you.

In England, on the contrary, of all the charms peculiar to youthful loveliness, I know none so remarkable as the unconstrained, fresh, natural, sweet, and joyous sound of a young girl's voice. It is as delicious as the note of the lark, when rising in the first freshness of morning to meet the sun. It is not restrained, held in, and checked into tameness by any fear lest it should too early show its syren power.

Even in the dance itself, the very arena for the display of youthful gracefulness, the young French girl fails, when her well-taught steps are compared with the easy, careless, fascinating movements of the married woman.

In the simple kindness of manner too, which, if there were no other attraction, would ever suffice to render an unaffected, good-natured young girl charming, there must be here a cautious restraint. A *demoiselle Française* would be prevented by *bienséance* from showing it, were she the gentlest-hearted creature breathing.

A young Englishman of my acquaintance, who, though he had been a good deal in French society, was not initiated into the mysteries of female education, recounted to me the other day an adventure of his, which is germane to the matter, though not having much to do with our last night's ball. This young man had for a long time been very kindly received in a French family, had repeatedly dined with them, and, in fact, considered himself as admitted to their house on the footing of an intimate friend.

The only child of this family was a daughter, rather pretty, but cold, silent, and repulsive in manner – almost awkward, and utterly uninteresting. Every attempt to draw her into conversation had ever proved abortive; and though often in her company, the Englishman hardly thought she could consider him as an acquaintance.

The young man returned to England; but, after some months, again revisited Paris. While standing one day in earnest contemplation of a picture at the Louvre, he was startled at being suddenly addressed by an extremely beautiful woman, who in the kindest and most friendly manner imaginable asked him a multitude of questions – made a thousand inquiries after his health – invited him earnestly to come and see her, and concluded by exclaiming – 'Mais c'est un siècle depuis que je vous ai vu.'

My friend stood gazing at her with equal admiration and surprise. He began to remember that he had seen her before, but when or where he knew not. She saw his embarrassment and smiled. 'Vous m'avez oublié donc?' said she. 'Je m'appelle Eglé de P——. . . . Mais je suis mariée . . .'

But to return to our ball.

As I saw the married women taken out to dance one after the another, till at last there was not a single dancing-looking man left, I felt myself getting positively angry; for, notwithstanding the assistance given by my ignorant countrymen, there were still at least half a dozen French girls unprovided with chevaliers.

They did not, however, look by many degrees so sadly disappointed as English girls would do did the same misfortune betide them. They, like the poor eels, were used to it: and the gentlemen, too, were cruelly used to the task of torture, – making their pretty little feet beat time upon the floor, while they watched the happy wedded in pairs – not wedded pairs – swim before their eyes in mazes which they would most gladly have threaded after them.

When at length all the married ladies, young and old, were duly provided for, several staid and very respectable-looking gentlemen emerged from corners and sofas, and presenting themselves to the young expectants, were accepted with quiet, grateful smiles, and permitted to lead them to the dance.

Old ladies like myself, whose fate attaches them to the walls of a ballroom, are accustomed to find their consolation and amusement from various sources. First, they enjoy such conversation as they can catch; or, if they will sit tolerably silent, they may often hear the prettiest airs of the season exceedingly well played. Then the whole arena of twinkling feet is open to their criticism and admiration. Another consolation, and frequently a very substantial one, is found in the supper; – nay, sometimes a passing ice will be caught to cheer the weary watcher. But there is another species of amusement, the general avowal of which might lead the younger part of the civilized world to wish that old ladies wore blinkers; I allude to the quiet contemplation of half a dozen sly flirtations that may be going on around them, – some so well managed! . . . some so clumsily!

But upon all these occasions, in England, though well-behaved old ladies will always take especial care not so to see that their seeing shall be seen, they still look about them with no feeling of restraint – no consciousness that they would rather be anywhere else than spectators of what is going forward near them. They feel, at least I am sure I do, a very comfortable assurance that the fair one is engaged, not in marring, but in making her fortune. Here again I may quote the often-quoted, and say, 'They manage all these matters differently at least, if not better, in France.'

In England, if a woman is seen going through all the manoeuvres of the flirting exercise, from the first animating reception of the 'How d'ye do?' to the last soft consciousness which fixes the eyes immovably on the floor, while the head, gently inclined, seems willing to indulge the happy ear in receiving intoxicating draughts of *parfait amour*, – when this is seen in England, even should the lady be past eighteen, one feels assured that she is not married; but here, without scandal or the shadow of scandal be it spoken, one feels equally well assured that she is. She may be a widow – or she may flirt in the innocence of her heart, because it is the fashion; but she cannot do it, because she is a young lady intending to be married.

I was deeply engaged in these speculations last night, when an elderly lady – who for some reason or other, not very easy to divine, actually never waltzes – came across the room and placed herself by my side. Though she does not waltz, she is a very charming person; and as I had often conversed with her before, I now welcomed her approach with great pleasure.

'A quoi pensez-vous, Madame Trollope!' said she: 'vous avez l'air de méditer.'

I deliberated for a moment whether I should venture to tell her exactly what was passing in my mind; but as I deliberated,

I looked at her, and there was that in her countenance which assured me I should have no severity to fear if I put her wholly in my confidence: I therefore replied very frankly, –

'I am meditating; and it is on the position which unmarried women hold in France.'

'Unmarried women? . . . You will scarcely find any such in France,' said she.

'Are not those young ladies who have just finished their quadrille unmarried?'

'Ah! . . . But you cannot call them unmarried women. *Elles sont des demoiselles.*'

'Well, then, my meditations were concerning them.'

'Eh bien . . .'

'Eh bien . . . It appears to me that the ball is not given – that the music does not play – that the gentlemen are not *empressé*, for them.'

'No, certainly. It would be quite contrary to our ideas of what is right if it were so.'

'With us it is so different! . . . It is always the young ladies who are, at least, the ostensible heroines of every ballroom.'

'The ostensible heroines?' . . . She dwelt rather strongly upon the adjective, adding with a smile, – 'Our ostensible, are our real heroines upon these occasions.'

I explained. 'The real heroines,' said I, 'will, I confess, in cases of ostentation and display, be sometimes the ladies who give balls in return.'

'Well explained,' said she, laughing: 'I certainly thought you had another meaning. You think, then,' she continued, 'that our young married women are made of too much importance among us?'

'Oh no!' I replied eagerly: 'it is, in my opinion, almost impossible to make them of too much importance; for I believe that it is entirely upon their influence that the tone of society depends.'

'You are quite right. It is impossible for those who have lived as long as we have in the world to doubt it: but how can this be, if, upon the occasions which bring people together, they are to be overlooked, while young girls who have as yet no position fixed are brought forward instead?'

'But surely, being brought forward to dance in a waltz or quadrille, is not the sort of consequence which we either of us mean?'

'Perhaps not; but it is one of its necessary results. Our women marry young, – as soon, in fact, as their education is finished, and before they have been permitted to enter the world, or share in the pleasures of it. Their destiny, therefore, instead of being the brightest that any women enjoy, would be the most *triste*, were they forbidden to enter into the amusements so natural to their age and national character, because they were married.'

'But may there not be danger in the custom which throws young females, thus early and irrevocably engaged, for the first time into the society, and, as it were, upon the attentions of men whom it has already become their duty not to consider as too amiable?'

'Oh no! . . . If a young woman be well-disposed, it is not a quadrille, or a waltz either, that will lead her astray. If it could, it would surely be the duty of all the legislators of the earth to forbid the exercise for ever.'

'No, no, no!' said I earnestly; 'I mean nothing of the kind, I assure you: on the contrary, I am so convinced, from the recollections of my own feelings, and my observations on those of others, that dancing is not a fictitious, but a real, natural source of enjoyment, the inclination for which is inherent in us, that, instead of wishing it to be forbidden, I would, had I the power, make it infinitely more general and of more frequent occurrence than it is: young people should never meet each other without the power of dancing if they wished it.'

'And from this animating pleasure, for which you confess that there is a sort of *besoin* within us, you would exclude all the young women above seventeen – because they are married? . . . Poor things! . . . Instead of finding them so willing as they generally are to enter on the busy scenes of life, I think we should have great difficulty in getting their permission to *monter un ménage* for them. Marriage would be soon held in abhorrence if such were its laws.'

'I would not have them such, I assure you,' replied I, rather at a loss how to explain myself fully without saying something that might either be construed into coarseness of thinking and a cruel misdoubting of innocence, or else into a very uncivil attack upon the national manners: I was therefore silent.

My companion seemed to expect that I should proceed, but after a short interval resumed the conversation by saying, – 'Then what arrangement would you propose, to reconcile the necessity of dancing with the propriety of keeping married women out of the danger which you seem to imagine might arise from it?'

'It would be too national were I to reply, that I think our mode of proceeding in this case is exactly what it ought to be.'

'But such is your opinion?'

'To speak sincerely, I believe it is.'

'Will you then have the kindness to explain to me the difference in this respect between France and England?'

'The only difference between us which I mean to advocate is, that with us the amusement which throws young people together under circumstances the most likely, perhaps, to elicit expressions of gallantry and admiration from the men, and a gracious reception of them from the women, is considered as befitting the single rather than the married part of the community.'

'With us, indeed, it is exactly the reverse,' replied she, – 'at least as respects the young ladies. By addressing the idle, unmeaning gallantry inspired by the dance to a young girl, we should deem the cautious delicacy of restraint in which she is enshrined transgressed and broken in upon. A young girl should be given to her husband before her passions have been awakened or her imagination excited by the voice of gallantry.'

'But when she is given to him, do you think this process more desirable than before?'

'Certainly it is not desirable; but it is infinitely less dangerous. When a girl is first married, her feelings, her thoughts, her imagination are wholly occupied by her husband. Her mode of education has ensured this; and afterwards, it is at the choice of her husband whether he will secure and retain her young heart for himself. If he does this, it is not a waltz or quadrille that will rob him of it. In no country have husbands so little reason to complain of their wives as in France; for in no country does the manner in which they live with them depend so wholly on themselves. With you, if your novels, and even the strange trials made public to all the world by your newspapers, may be trusted, the very reverse is the case. Previous attachments – early affection broken off before the marriage, to be renewed after it – these are the histories we hear and read; and most assuredly they do not tempt us to adopt your system as an amendment upon our own.'

'The very notoriety of the cases to which you allude proves their rare occurrence,' replied I.

'Such sad histories would have but little interest for the public, either as tales or trials, if they did not relate circumstances marked and apart from ordinary life.'

'Assuredly. But you will allow also that, however rare they may be in England, such records of scandal and of shame are rarer still in France?'

'Occurrences of the kind do not perhaps produce so much sensation here,' said I.

'Because they are more common, you would say. Is not that your meaning?' and she smiled reproachfully.

'It certainly was not my meaning to say so,' I replied; 'and, in truth, it is neither a useful nor a gracious occupation to examine on which side the Channel the greater proportion of virtue may be found; though it is possible some good might be done on both, were the education in each country to be modified by the introduction of what is best in the other.'

'I have no doubt of it,' said she; 'and as we go on exchanging fashions so amicably, who knows but we may live to see your young ladies shut up a little more, while their mothers and fathers look out for a suitable marriage for them, instead of inflicting the awkward task upon themselves? And in return, perhaps, our young wives may lay aside their little coquetries and become *mères respectables* somewhat earlier than they do now. But, in truth, they all come to it at last.'

As she finished speaking these words, a new waltz sounded, and again a dozen couples, some ill, some well matched, swam past us. One of the pairs was composed of a very fine-looking young man, with blue-black *favoris* and *moustaches*, tall as a tower, and seeming, if air and expression may be trusted, very tolerably well pleased with himself. His *danseuse* might unquestionably have addressed her husband, who sat at no great distance from us, drawing up his gouty feet under his chair to let her pass, in these touching words:–

'Full thirty times hath Phoebus' cart gone round
Neptune's salt wash and Tellus' orbed ground,
And thirty dozen moons, with borrow'd sheen,
About the world have times twelve thirties been,
Since Love our hearts and Hymen did our hands
Unite commutual in most sacred bands.'

My neighbour and I looked up and exchanged glances as they went by. We both laughed.

'At least you will allow,' said she, 'that this is one of the cases in which a married lady may indulge her passion for the dance without danger of consequences?'

'I am not quite sure of that,' replied I. 'If she be not found guilty of sin, she will scarcely obtain a verdict that shall acquit her of folly. But what can induce that magnificent personage, who looks down upon her as if engaged in measuring the distance between them – what could induce him to request the honour of enclosing her venerable waist in his arm?'

'Nothing more easily explained. That little fair girl sitting in yonder corner, with her hair so tightly drawn off her forehead, is her daughter – her only daughter, and will have a noble *dot*. Now you understand it? . . . And tell me, in case his speculation should not succeed, is it not better that this excellent lady, who waltzes so very like a duck, should receive all the eloquence with which he will seek to render himself amiable, upon her time-steeled heart, than that the delicate little girl herself should have to listen to it?'

'And you really would recommend us to adopt this mode of love-making by deputy, letting the mamma be the substitute, till the young lady has obtained a brevet to listen to the language of love in her own person? However excellent the scheme may be, dear lady, it is vain to hope that we shall ever be able to introduce it among us. The young ladies, I suspect, would exclaim, as you do here, when explaining why you cannot permit any English innovations among you, 'Ce n'est pas dans nos moeurs.'

I assure you, my friend, that I have not composed this conversation *à loisir* for your amusement, for I have set down as nearly as possible what was said to me, though I have not quite given it all to you; but my letter is already long enough.

LETTER XXXVI

Improvements of Paris – Introduction of Carpets and Trottoirs –
Maisonnettes – Not likely to answer in Paris – The necessity of
a Porter and Porter's Lodge – Comparative Expenses of France
and England – Increasing Wealth of the Bourgeoisie

Among the many recent improvements in Paris which evidently owe their origin to England, those which strike the eye first, are the almost universal introduction of carpets within doors, and the frequent blessing of a *trottoir* without. In a few years, unless all paving-stones should be torn up in search of more immortality, there can be no doubt that it will be almost as easy to walk in Paris as in London. It is true that the old streets are not quite wide enough to admit such enormous esplanades on each side as Regent and Oxford Streets; but all that is necessary to safety and comfort may be obtained with less expense of space; and to those who knew Paris a dozen years ago, when one had to hop from stone to stone in the fond hope of escaping wet shoes in the Dogdays – tormented too during the whole of this anxious process with the terror of being run over by carts, fiacres, concous, cabs, and wheelbarrows; – whoever remembers what it was to walk in Paris then, will bless with an humble and grateful spirit the dear little pavement which, with the exception of necessary intervals to admit of an approach to the portes-cochère of the various *hôtels*, and a few short intervals beside, which appear to have been passed over and forgotten, borders most of the principal streets of Paris now.

Another English innovation, infinitely more important in all ways, has been attempted, and has failed. This was the endeavour to introduce *maisonnettes*, or small houses calculated for the occupation of one family. A few such have been built in that new part of the town which stretches away in all directions behind the Madeleine; but they are not found to answer – and that for many reasons which I should have thought it very easy to foresee, and which I suspect it would be very difficult to obviate.

In order to come at all within reach of the generality of French incomes, they must be built on too small a scale to have any good rooms; and this is a luxury, and permits a species of display, to which many are accustomed who live in unfurnished apartments, for which they give perhaps fifteen hundred or two thousand francs a year. Another accommodation which habit has made it extremely difficult for French families to dispense with, and which can be enjoyed at an easy price only by sharing it with many, is a porter and a porter's lodge. Active as is the race of domestic servants in Paris, their number must, I think, be doubled in many families, were the arrangement of the porter's lodge to be changed for our system of having a servant summoned every time a parcel, a message, a letter, or a visit arrives at the house.

Nor does the taking charge of these by any means comprise the whole duty of this servant of many masters; neither am I at all competent to say exactly what does: but it seems to me that the answer I generally receive upon desiring that anything may be done is, 'Oui, madame, le portier ou la portière fera cela;' and were we suddenly deprived of these factotums, I suspect that we should be immediately obliged to leave our apartments and take refuge in an hôtel, for I should be quite at a loss to know what or how many additional 'helps' would be necessary to enable us to exist without them.

That the whole style and manner of domestic existence throughout all the middling classes of such a city as Paris should hang upon their porters' lodges, seems tracing great effects to little causes; but I have been so repeatedly told that the failure of the *maisonnettes* has in a great degree arisen from this, that I cannot doubt it.

I know not whether anything which prevents their so completely changing their mode of life as they must do if living in separate houses, is to be considered as an evil or not. The Parisians are a very agreeable, and apparently a very happy population; and who can say what effect the quiet, steady, orderly mode of each man having a small house of his own might produce? What is admirable as a component part of one character, is often incongruous and disagreeable when met in another; and I am by no means certain if the snug little mansion which might be procured for the same rent as a handsome apartment, would not tend to circumscribe and tame down the light spirits that now send *locataires* of threescore springing to their elegant *premier* by two stairs at a time. And the prettiest and best *chaussés* little feet in the world too, which now trip *sans souci* over the common stair, would they not lag painfully perhaps in passing through a low-browed hall, whose neatness or unneatness had become a private and individual concern? And might not many a bright fancy be damped while calculating how much it would cost to have a few statues and oleanders in it? – and the head set aching by meditating how to get 'ce vilain escalier frotté' from top to bottom? Yet all these, and many other cares which they now escape, must fall upon them if they give up their apartments for *maisonnettes*.

The fact, I believe, is, that French fortunes, taken at the average at which they at present stand, could not suffice to procure the pretty elegance to which the middle classes are accustomed, unless it were done by the sacrifice of some portion of that costly fastidiousness which English people of the same rank seem to cling to as part of their prerogative.

Though I am by no means prepared to say that I should like to exchange my long-confirmed habit of living in a house of my own for the Parisian mode of inhabiting apartments, I cannot but allow that by this and sundry other arrangements a French income is made to contribute infinitely more to the enjoyment of its possessor than an English one.

Let any English person take the trouble of calculating, let their revenue be great or small, how much of it is expended in what immediately contributes to their personal comfort and luxury, and how much of it is devoted to the support of expenses which in point of fact add to neither, and the truth of this statement will become evident.

Rousseau says, that 'cela se fait,' and 'cela ne se fait pas,' are the words which regulate everything that goes on within the walls of Paris. That the same words have at least equal power in London, can hardly be denied; and, unfortunately for our individual independence, obedience to them costs infinitely more on our side of the water than it does on this. Hundreds are annually spent, out of very confined incomes, to support expenses which have nothing whatever to do with the personal enjoyment of those who so tax themselves; but it must be submitted to, because 'cela se fait,' or 'cela ne se fait pas.' In Paris, on the contrary, this imperative phrase has comparatively no influence on the expenditure of any revenue, because every one's object is not to make it appear that he is as rich as his neighbour, but to make his means, be they great or small, contribute as much as possible to the enjoyment and embellishment of his existence.

It is for this reason that a residence in Paris is found so favourable an expedient in cases of diminished or insufficient fortune. A family coming hither in the hope of obtaining the mere necessaries of life at a much cheaper rate than in England would be greatly disappointed: some articles are cheaper, but many are considerably dearer; and, in truth, I doubt if at the present moment anything that can be strictly denominated a necessary of life is to be found cheaper in Paris than in London.

It is not the necessaries, but the luxuries of life that are cheaper here. Wine, ornamental furniture, the keep of horses, the price of carriages, the entrance to theatres, wax-lights, fruit, books, the rent of handsome apartments, the wages of men-servants, are all greatly cheaper, and direct taxes greatly less. But even this is not the chief reason why a residence in Paris may be found economical to persons of any pretension to rank or style at home. The necessity for parade, so much the most costly of all the appendages to rank, may here be greatly dispensed with, and that without any degradation whatever. In short, the advantage of living in Paris as a matter of economy depends entirely upon the degree of luxury to be obtained. There are certainly many points of delicacy and refinement in the English manner of living which I should be very sorry to see given up as national peculiarities; but I think we should gain much in many ways could we learn to hang our consequence less upon the comparison of what others do. We shudder at the cruel madness of the tyrant who would force every form to reach one standard; but those are hardly less mad who insist that every one, to live *comme il faut*, must live, or appear to live, exactly as others do, though the means of doing so may vary among the silly set so prescribed to, from an income that may justify any extravagance to one that can honestly supply none.

This is a folly of incalculably rarer occurrence here than in England; and it certainly is no proof of the good sense of our 'most thinking people,' that for one private family brought to ruin by extravagance in France, there are fifty who suffer from this cause in England.

It is easy to perceive that our great wealth has been the cause of this. The general scale of expense has been set so high, that thousands who have lived in reference to that, rather than to their individual fortunes, have been ruined by the blunder; and I really know no remedy so likely to cure the evil as a residence in Paris; not, however, so much as a means of saving money, as of making a series of experiments which may teach them how to make the best and most enjoyable use of it.

I am persuaded, that if it were to become as much the fashion to imitate the French independence of mind in our style of living, as it now is to copy them in ragoûts, bonnets, moustaches, and or-molu, we should greatly increase our stock of real genuine enjoyment. If no English lady should ever again feel a pang at her heart because she saw more tall footmen in her neighbour's hall than in her own – if no sighs were breathed in secret in any club-house or at any sale, because Jack Somebody's stud was a cut above us – if no bills were run up at Gunter's, or at Howell and James's, because it was worse than death to be outdone, – we should unquestionably be a happier and a more respectable people than we are at present.

It is, I believe, pretty generally acknowledged by all parties, that the citizens of France have become a more money-getting generation since the last revolution than they ever were before it. The security and repose which the new dynasty seems to have brought with it, have already given them time and opportunity to multiply their capital; and the consequence is, that the shopkeeping propensities with which Napoleon used to reproach us have crossed the Channel, and are beginning to produce very considerable alterations here.

It is evident that the wealth of the *bourgeoisie* is rapidly increasing, and their consequence with it; so rapidly, indeed, that the republicans are taking fright at it, – they see before them a new enemy, and begin to talk of the abominations of an aristocratic *bourgeoisie*.

There is, in fact, no circumstance in the whole aspect of the country more striking or more favourable than this new and powerful impulse given to trade. It is the best ballast that the vessel of the state can have; and if they can but contrive that nothing shall happen to occasion its being thrown overboard, it may suffice to keep her steady, whatever winds may blow.

The wide-spreading effect of this increasing wealth among the *bourgeoisie* is visible in many ways, but in none more than in the rapid increase of handsome dwellings, which are springing up, as white and bright as new-born mushrooms, in the north-western division of Paris. This is quite a new world, and reminds me of the early days of Russell Square, and all the region about it. The Church of the Madeleine, instead of being, as I formerly remember it, nearly at the extremity of Paris, has now a new city behind it; and if things go on at the same rate at which they seem to be advancing at present, we shall see it, or at least our children will, occupying as central a position as St. Martin's-in-the-Fields. An excellent market, called Marché de la Madeleine, has already found its way to this new town; and I doubt not that churches, theatres, and restaurants innumerable will speedily follow.

The capital which is now going so merrily on, increasing with almost American rapidity, will soon ask to be invested; and when this happens, Paris will be seen running out of town with the same active pace that London has done before her; and twenty years hence the Bois de Boulogne may very likely be as thickly peopled as the Regent's Park is now.

This sudden accession of wealth has already become the cause of a great increase in the price of almost every article sold in Paris; and if this activity of commerce continues, it is more than probable, that the hitherto moderate fortunes of the Parisian *boursier* and merchant will grow into something resembling the colossal capitals of England, and we shall find that the same causes which have hitherto made England dear will in future prevent France from being cheap. It will then happen, that many deficiencies which are now perceptible, and which furnish the most remarkable points of difference between the two countries, will disappear; great wealth being in many instances all that is required to make a French family live very much like an English one. Whether they will not, when this time arrives, lose on the side of unostentatious enjoyment more than they will gain by increased splendour, may, I think, be very doubtful. For my own part, I am decidedly of opinion, that as soon as heavy ceremonious dinners shall systematically take place of the present easy, unexpensive style of visiting, Paris will be more than half spoiled, and the English may make up their minds to remain proudly and pompously at home, lest, instead of a light and lively contrast to their own ways, they may chance to find a heavy but successful rivalry.

LETTER XXXVII

Horrible Murder – La Morgue – Suicides – Vanity –
Anecdote – Influence of Modern Literature –
Different appearance of Poverty in
France and England

We have been made positively sick and miserable by the
details of a murder, which seems to show that we live in a
world where there are creatures ten thousand times more
savage than any beast that ranges the forest,

'Be it ounce, or cat, or bear,
Pard, or boar with bristled hair.'

This horror was perpetrated on the person of a wretched
female, who appeared, by the mangled remains which were
found in the river, to have been very young. But though thus
much was discovered, it was many days ere, among the
thousands who flocked to the Morgue to look at the severed
head and mangled limbs, any one could be found to recognise
the features. At length, however, the person with whom she
had lodged came to see if she could trace any resemblance
between her lost inmate and these wretched relics of a human
being.

   She so far succeeded as to convince herself of the identity;
though her means of judging appeared to be so little
satisfactory, that few placed any reliance upon her testimony.
Nevertheless, she at length succeeded in having a man taken
up, who had lived on intimate terms with the poor creature
whose sudden disappearance had induced this woman to visit
the Morgue when the description of this mangled body
reached her. He immediately confessed the deed, in the spirit,
though not in the words, of the poet:–

'Mourons: de tant d'horreurs qu'un trépas me délivre!
Est-ce un malheur si grand que de cesser de vivre?

*   *   *

Je ne crains pas le nom que je laisse après moi.'

The peculiarly horrid manner in which the crime was committed, and the audacious style in which the criminal appears to brave justice, will, it is thought, prevent any *extenuating circumstances* being pleaded, as is usually done, for the purpose of commuting the punishment of death into imprisonment with enforced labour. It is generally expected that this atrocious murderer will be guillotined, notwithstanding the averseness of the government to capital punishment.

The circumstances are, indeed, hideous in all ways, and the more so from being mixed up with what is miscalled the tender passion. The cannibal fury which sets a man to kill his foe that he may eat him, has fully as much tenderness in it as this species of affection.

When 'the passion is made up of nothing but the finest parts of love,' it may, perhaps, deserve the epithet of tender; but we have heard of late of so many horrible and deliberate assassinations, originating in what newspapers are pleased to call '*une grande passion*,' that the first idea which a love-story now suggests to me is, that the sequel will in all probability be murder 'most foul, strange, and unnatural!'

Is there in any language a word that can raise so many shuddering sensations as '*La Morgue*'? Hatred, revenge, murder, are each terrible; but La Morgue outdoes them all in its power of bringing together in one syllable the abstract of whatever is most appalling in crime, poverty, despair, and death.

To the ghastly Morgue are conveyed the unowned dead of every description that are discovered in or near Paris. The Seine is the great receptacle which first receives the victims of assassination or despair; but they are not long permitted to elude the vigilance of the Parisian police: a huge net, stretched across the river at St. Cloud, receives and retains whatever the stream brings down; and anything that retains a trace of human form which is found amidst the product of the fearful draught is daily conveyed to La Morgue; – DAILY; for rarely does it chance that for four-and-twenty hours its melancholy biers remain unoccupied; often do eight, ten, a dozen corpses at a time arrive by the frightful caravan from '*les filets de St. Cloud.*'

I have, in common with most people, I believe, a very strong propensity within me for seeing everything connected directly or indirectly with any subject or event which has strongly roused my curiosity, or interested my feelings; but, strange to say, I never feel its influence so irresistible as when something of shuddering horror is mixed with the spectacle. It is this propensity which has now induced me to visit this citadel of death; – this low and solitary roof, placed in the very centre of moving, living, laughing Paris.

No visit to a tomb, however solemn or however sad, can approach in thrilling horror to the sensation, caused by passing the threshold of this charnel-house.

The tomb calls us to the contemplation of the common, the inevitable lot; but this gathering place of sin and death arouses thoughts of all that most outrages nature, and most foully violates the sanctuary of life, into which God has breathed his spirit. But I was steadfast in my will to visit it, and I have done it.

The building is a low, square, carefully-whited structure, situated on the Quai de la Cité. It is open to all; and it is fearful to think how many anxious hearts have entered, how many despairing ones have quitted it.

On entering I found myself in a sort of low hall which contained no object whatever. If I mistake not, there is a chamber on each side of it: but it was to the left hand that I was led, and it was thither that about a dozen persons who entered at the same time either followed or preceded me. I do not too well remember how I reached the place where the bodies are visible; but I know that I stood before one of three large windows, through the panes of which, and very near to them, lighted also by windows in the roof, are seen a range of biers, sloping towards the spectator at an angle that gives the countenance as well as the whole figure of the persons extended on them fully to view.

In this manner I saw the bodies of four men stretched out before me; but their aspect bore no resemblance to death –

neither were they swollen or distorted in any way, but so discoloured as to give them exactly the appearance of bronze statues.

Two out of the four had evidently been murdered, for their heads and throats gave frightful evidence of the violence that had been practised upon them; the third was a mere boy, who probably met his fate by accident: but that the fourth was a suicide, it was hardly possible to doubt; even in death his features held the desperate expression that might best paint the state of mind likely to lead to such an act.

It was past midday when we entered the Morgue; but neither of the bodies had yet been claimed or recognised.

This spectacle naturally set me upon seeking information, wherever I was likely to find it, respecting the average number of bodies thus exposed within the year, the proportion of them believed to be suicides, and the causes generally supposed most influential in producing this dreadful termination.

I will not venture to repeat the result of these inquiries in figures, as I doubt if the information I received was of that strictly accurate kind which could justify my doing so; yet it was quite enough so, to excite both horror and astonishment at the extraordinary number which are calculated to perish annually at Paris by self-slaughter.

In many recent instances, the causes which have led to these desperate deeds have been ascertained by the written acknowledgment of the perpetrators themselves, left as a legacy to mankind. Such a legacy might perhaps not be wholly unprofitable to the survivors, were it not that the motives assigned, in almost every instance where they have been published, have been of so frivolous and contemptible a nature as to turn wholesome horror to most ill-placed mirth.

It can hardly be doubted, from the testimony of these singular documents, that many young Frenchmen perish yearly in this guilty and deplorable manner for no other reason in the world than the hope of being talked of afterwards.

Had some solitary instance of so perverted a vanity been found among these records, it might perhaps have been considered as no more incredible than various other proofs of the enfeebling effects of this paltry passion on the judgment, and have been set down to insanity, produced by excessive egotism: but nothing short of posthumous testimony of the persons themselves could induce any one to believe that scarcely a week passes without such an event, from such a cause, taking place in Paris.

In many instances, I am told that the good sense of surviving friends has led them to disobey the testamentary instructions left by the infatuated young men who have thus acted, requesting that the wretched reasonings which have led them to it should be published. But, in a multitude of cases, the 'Constitutionnel' and other journals of the same stamp have their columns filled with reasons why these poor reckless creatures have dared the distant justice of their Creator, in the hope that their unmeaning names should be echoed through Paris for a day.

It is not long since two young men – mere youths – entered a *restaurant*, and bespoke a dinner of unusual luxury and expense, and afterwards arrived punctually at the appointed hour to eat it. They did so, apparently with all the zest of youthful appetite and youthful glee. They called for champagne, and quaffed it hand in hand. No symptom of sadness, thought, or reflection of any kind was observed to mix with their mirth, which was loud, long, and unremitting. At last came the *café noir*, the cognac, and the bill: one of them was seen to point out the amount to the other, and then both burst out afresh into violent laughter. Having swallowed each his cup of coffee to the dregs, the *garçon* was ordered to request the company of the *restaurateur* for a few minutes. He came immediately, expecting perhaps to receive his bill, minus some extra charge which the jocund but economical youths might deem exorbitant.

Instead of this, however, the elder of the two informed him that the dinner had been excellent, which was the more fortunate as it was decidedly the last that either of them should ever eat: that for his bill, he must of necessity excuse the payment of it, as in fact they neither of them possessed a single sou: that upon no other occasion would they thus have violated the customary etiquette between guest and landlord; but that finding this world, its toils and its troubles, unworthy of them, they had determined once more to enjoy a repast of which their poverty must for ever prevent the repetition, and then – take leave of existence for ever! For the first part of this resolution, he declared that it had, thanks to his cook and his cellar, been achieved nobly; and for the last, it would soon follow – for the *café noir*, besides the little glass of his admirable cognac, had been medicated with that which would speedily settle all their accounts for them.

The *restaurateur* was enraged. He believed no part of the rhodomontade but that which declared their inability to discharge the bill, and he talked loudly, in his turn, of putting them into the hands of the police. At length, however, upon their offering to give him their address, he was persuaded to let them depart.

On the following day, either the hope of obtaining his money, or some vague fear that they might have been in earnest in the wild tale that they had told him, induced this man to go to the address they had left with him; and he there heard that the two unhappy boys had been that morning found lying together hand in hand, on a bed hired a few weeks before by one of them. When they were discovered, they were already dead and quite cold.

On a small table in the room lay many written papers, all expressing aspirations after greatness that should cost neither labour nor care, a profound contempt for those who were satisfied to live by the sweat of their brow – sundry quotations from Victor Hugo, and a request that their names and the manner of their death might be transmitted to the newspapers.

Many are the cases recorded of young men, calling themselves dear friends, who have thus encouraged each other to make their final exit from life, if not with applause, at least with effect. And more numerous still are the tales recounted of young men and women found dead, and locked in each other's arms; fulfilling literally, and with most sad seriousness, the destiny sketched so merrily in the old song:–

> Gai, gai, marions-nous –
> Mettons-nous dans la misère;
> Gai, gai, marions-nous –
> Mettons-nous la corde au cou.

I have heard it remarked by several individuals among those who are watching with no unphilosophical eyes many ominous features of the present time and the present race, or rather perhaps of that portion of the population which stand apart from the rest in dissolute idleness, that the worst of all its threatening indications is the reckless, hard indifference, and gladiator-like contempt of death, which is nurtured, taught, and lauded as at once the foundation and perfection of all human wisdom and of all human virtue.

In place of the firmness derived from hope and resignation, these unhappy sophists seek courage in desperation, and consolation in notoriety. With this key to the philosophy of the day, it is not difficult to read its influence on many a countenance that one meets among those who are lounging in listless laziness on the Boulevards or in the gardens of Paris.

The aspect of these figures is altogether unlike what we may too often see among those who linger, sunken, pale, and hopeless, on the benches of our parks, or loiter under porticos and colonnades, as if waiting for courage to beg. Hunger and intemperance often leave blended traces on such figures as these, exciting at once pity and disgust. I have encountered at Paris nothing like this: whether any such exist, I know not; but if they do, their beat is distant from the public walks and fashionable promenades. Instead of these, however, there is a race who seem to live there, less wretched perhaps in actual want of bread, but as evidently thriftless, homeless, and friendless as the other. On the faces of such, one may read a state of mind wholly different, – less degraded, but still more perverted; – a wild, bold eye, that rather seeks than turns from every passing glance – unshrinking hardihood, but founded more on indifference than endurance, and a scornful sneer for any who may suffer curiosity to conquer disgust, while they fix their eye for a moment upon a figure that looks in all ways as if got up to enact the hero of a melodrame. Were I the king, or the minister either, I should think it right to keep an eye of watchfulness upon all such picturesque individuals; for one might say most truly,

> 'Yon Cassius hath a lean and hungry look;
> He thinks too much: such men are dangerous.'

The friend to whom I addressed myself on the subject of these constantly-recurring suicides told me that there was great reason to believe that the increase of this crime, so remarkable during the last few years, might be almost wholly attributed to the 'light literature,' as it is called, of the period: – dark literature would be a fitter name for it.

The total absence of anything approaching to a virtuous principle of action in every fictitious character held up to admiration throughout all the tales and dramas of the *décousu* school, while every hint of religion is banished as if it were treason to allude to it, is in truth quite enough to account for every species of depravity in those who make such characters their study and their model. 'How oft and by how many shall they be laughed to scorn!' – yet believing all the while, poor souls! that they are producing a sensation, and that the eyes of Europe are fixed upon them, notwithstanding they once worked as a tailor or a tinker, or at some other such unpoetical handiwork; for they may all be described in the words of Ecclesiasticus, with a very slight alteration, – 'They would maintain the state of the world, and all their desire is in (forgetting) the work of their craft.'

LETTER XXXVIII

Opéra Comique – 'Cheval de Bronze' – 'La Marquise' –
Impossibility of playing Tragedy – Mrs. Siddons's Readings –
Mademoiselle Mars has equal power – Laisser aller
of the Female Performers – Decline of Theatrical
Taste among the Fashionable

The 'Cheval de Bronze' being the *spectacle par excellence* at the
Opéra Comique this season, we have considered it a matter of
sight-seeing necessity to pay it a visit; and we have all agreed
that it is as perfectly beautiful in its scenery and decorations as
the size of the theatre would permit. We gazed upon it,
indeed, with a perfection of contentment, which, in secret
committee afterwards, we confessed did not say much in
favour of our intellectual faculties.

I really know not how it is that one can sit, not only without
murmuring, but with positive satisfaction, for three hours
together, with no other occupation than looking at a collection
of gewgaw objects, with a most unmeaning crowd, made for
the most part by Nature's journeymen, incessantly undulating
among them. Yet so it is, that a skilful arrangement of blue
and white gauze, aided by the magic of many-coloured lights,
decidedly the prettiest of all modern toys, made us exclaim at
every fresh manoeuvre of the carpenter, 'Beautiful! beautiful!'
with as much delight as ever a child of five years old displayed
at a first-rate exhibition of Punch.

M. Auber's music has some pretty things in it; but he has
done much better in days of yore; and the wretched taste
exhibited by all the principal singers made me heartily wish
that the well-appointed orchestra had kept the whole
performance to themselves.

Madame Casimir has had, and indeed still has, a rich and
powerful voice: but the meanest peasant-girl in Germany,
who trims her vines to the sound of her native airs, might give

her a lesson on taste more valuable than all that science has ever taught her.

I should like, could I do so with a conscience that should not reproach me with exaggeration, to name Miss Stephens and Madame Casimir as fair national specimens of English and French singing. And in fact they are so; though I confess that the over-dressing of Madame Casimir's airs is almost as much out of the common way here, as the chaste simplicity of our native syren's strains is with us: yet the one is essentially English, and the other French.

We were told that the manager of our London theatres had been in Paris for the purpose of seeing and taking a cast from this fine Chinese butterfly. If this be so, Mr. Bunn will find great advantage from the extent of his theatre: that of the Opéra Comique is scarcely of sufficient magnitude to exhibit its gaudy but graceful *tableaux* to advantage. But, on the other hand, I doubt if he will find any actress quite so *piquante* as the pretty Madame ——, in the last act, when she relates to the enchanted princess, her mistress, the failure she had made in attempting by her *agaceries* to retain the young female who had ventured into the magic region: and if he did, I doubt still more if her performance would be received with equal applause.

A *petite comédie* called 'La Marquise' preceded this brilliant trifle. The fable must, I think, be taken, though greatly changed, from a story of George Sand. It has perhaps little in it worth talking about; but it is a fair specimen of one of that most agreeable of French nationalities, a natural, easy, playful little piece, at which you may sit and laugh in sympathy with the performers as much as with the characters, till you forget that there are such things as sorrow and sadness in the world.

The acting in this style is so very good, that the author's task really seems to be the least important part of the business. It is not at one theatre, but at all, that we have witnessed this extraordinary excellence in the performance of this species of drama; but I doubt if the chasm which seems to surround the tragic muse, keeping her apart on a pedestal sacred to recollections, be at all wider or more profound in England than in France. In truth, it is less impassible with us than it is here; for though I will allow that our tragic actresses may be no better than those of France, seeing that a woman's will in the one case, and the Atlantic Ocean in the other, have robbed us of Mrs Bartley and the Fanny – who between them might bring our stage back to all its former glory, – still they have neither Charles Kemble nor Macready to stand in the place that Talma has left vacant.

I have indeed no doubt whatever that Mademoiselle Mars could read Corneille and Racine as effectively as Mrs. Siddons read Shakespeare in the days of Argyle-street luxury, and, like our great maga, give to every part a power that it never had before. I well remember coming home from one of Mrs. Siddons's readings with a passionate desire to see her act the part of Hamlet; and from another, quite persuaded that by some means the witch-scene in Macbeth should be so arranged that she should speak every word of it.

In like manner, were I to hear Mars read Corneille, I should insist upon it that she ought to play the Cid; and if Racine, Oreste would probably be the first part I should choose for her. But as even she, with all her Garrick-like versatility, would not be able to perform every part of every play, tragedy must be permitted to repose for the present in France as well as in England.

During this interregnum, it is well for them, considering how dearly they love to amuse themselves, that they have a stock of comedians, old, young, and middle-aged, that they need not fear should fail; for the whole French nation seem gifted with a talent that might enable them to supply, at an hour's warning, any deficiencies in the company.

I seldom return from an exhibition of this sort without endeavouring in some degree to analyse the charm that has enchanted me: but in most cases this is too light, too subtle, to permit itself to be caught by so matter-of-fact a process. I protest to you, that I am often half ashamed of the pleasure I receive from . . . I know not what. A playful smile, a speaking glance, a comic tone, a pretty gesture, give effect to words that have often nothing in them more witty or more wise than may often be met with (especially here) in ordinary conversation. But the whole thing is so thoroughly understood, from the '*père noble*' to the scene-shifter – so perfect in its getting-up – the piece so admirably suited to the players, and the players to the piece, – that whatever there is to admire and enjoy, comes to you with no drawbacks from blunders or awkwardness of any kind.

That the composition of these happy trifles cannot be a work of any great labour or difficulty, may be reasonably inferred from the ceaseless succession of novelties which every theatre and every season produces. The process, for this lively and ready-witted people, must be pleasant enough – they must catch from what passes before them; no difficult task, perhaps – some *piquante* situation or ludicrous *bévue*: the slightest thread is strong enough to hold together the light materials of the plot; and then must follow the christening of a needful proportion of male and female, old and young, enchanting and ridiculous personages. The list of these once set down, and the order of scenes which are to bring forth the plot arranged, I can fancy the author perfectly enjoying himself as he puts into the mouth of each character all the saucy impertinences upon every subject that his imagination, skilful enough in such matters, can suggest. When to this is added an occasional touch of natural feeling, and a little popular high-mindedness in any line, the *petite comédie* is ready for the stage.

It is certainly a very light manufacture, and depends perhaps more upon the fearless *laisser aller* of both author and actor than upon the brilliancy of wit which it displays. That old-fashioned blushing grace too, so much in favour with King Solomon, and called in scripture phrase shamefacedness, is sacrificed rather too unmercifully by the female part of the performers, in the fear, as it should seem, of impairing the spirit and vivacity of the scene by any scruple of any kind. But I suspect these ladies miscalculate the respective value of opposing graces; Mademoiselle Mars may show them that delicacy and vivacity are not inseparable; and though I confess that it would be a little unreasonable to expect all the female vaudevillists of Paris to be like Mars, I cannot but think that, in a city where her mode of playing comedy has for so many years been declared perfect, it must be unnecessary to seek the power of attraction from what is so utterly at variance with it.

The performance of comedy is often assisted here by a freedom among the actors which I have sometimes, but not often, seen permitted in London. It requires for its success, and indeed for its endurance, that the audience should be perfectly in good-humour, and sympathise very cordially with the business of the scene. I allude to the part which the performers sometimes take not only in the acting, but in the enjoyment of it. I never in my life saw people more heartily amused, or disposed more unceremoniously to show it, than the actors in the 'Précieuses Ridicules,' which I saw played a few nights ago at the Français. On this occasion I think the spirit of the performance was certainly heightened by this license, and for this reason – the scene represents a group in which one party must of necessity be exceedingly amused by the success of the mystification which they are practising on the other. But I own that I have sometimes felt a little *English stiffness* at perceiving an air of frolic and fun upon the stage, which seemed fully as much got up for the performers as for the audience. But though the instance I have named of this occurred at the Théâtre Français, it is not there that it is likely to be carried to any offensive extent. The lesser theatres would in many instances do well to copy closely the etiquette and decorum of all kinds which the great national theatre exhibits: but perhaps it is hardly fair to expect this; and besides, we might be told, justly enough, to *look at home.*

The theatres, particularly the minor ones, appear to be still very well attended: but I constantly hear the same observations made in Paris as in London upon the decline of theatrical taste among the higher orders; and it arises, I think, from the same cause in both countries, – namely, the late dinner-hour, which renders the going to a play a matter of general family arrangement, and often of general family difficulty. The opera, which is later, is always full; and were it not that I have lived too long in the world to be surprised at anything that the power of fashion could effect, I should certainly be astonished that so lively a people as the French should throng night after night as they do to witness the exceeding dulness of this heavy spectacle.

The only people I have yet seen enjoying their theatres rationally, without abstaining from what they liked because it was unfashionable, or enduring what they did not, because it was the *mode,* are the Germans. Their genuine and universal love of music makes their delicious opera almost a necessary of life to them; and they must, I think, absolutely change their nature before they will suffer the silly conventional elegance supposed by some to attach to the act of eating their dinner late, to interfere with their enjoyment of it.

I used to think the theatre as dear to the French as music to the Germans. But what is a taste in France is, from the firmer fibre of the national character, a passion in Germany; – and it is easier to abandon a taste than to control a passion.

Perhaps, however, in England and France too, if some new-born theatrical talent of the first class were to 'flame in the forehead of the morning sky,' both Paris and London would submit to the degradation of dining at five o'clock in order to enjoy it: but late hours and indifferent performances, together, have gone far towards placing the stage among the popular rather than the fashionable amusements of either.

LETTER XXXIX

*The Abbé de Lamennais – Cobbett – O'Connell –
Napoleon – Robespierre*

I had last night the satisfaction of meeting the Abbé de
Lamennais at a *soirée*. It was at the house of Madame Benjamin
Constant; whose *salon* is as celebrated for the talent of every
kind to be met there, as for the delightful talents and amiable
qualities of its mistress.

In general appearance, this celebrated man recalls an original
drawing that I remember to have seen of Rousseau. He is
greatly below the ordinary height, and extremely small in his
proportions. His countenance is very striking, and singularly
indicative of habitual meditation; but the deep-set eye has
something very nearly approaching to wildness in its rapid
glance. His dress was black, but had certainly more of
republican negligence than priestly dignity in it; and the little,
tight, chequered cravat which encircled his slender throat,
gave him decidedly the appearance of a person who heeded
not either the fashion of the day, or the ordinary costume of
the *salon*.

He, in company with four or five other distinguished men,
had dined with Madame Constant; and we found him deep
sunk in a *bergère* that almost concealed his diminutive person,
surrounded by a knot of gentlemen, with whom he was
conversing with great eagerness and animation. On one side
of him was M. Jouy, the well-known '*Hermite*' of the
Chaussée d'Antin; and on the other a deputy well known on
the benches of the *côté gauche*.

I was placed immediately opposite to him, and have seldom
watched the play of a more animated countenance. In the
course of the evening, he was brought up and introduced to
me. His manners are extremely gentlemanlike; no stiffness or
reserve, either rustic or priestly, interfering with their easy

vivacity. He immediately drew a chair *vis-à-vis* to the sofa on which I was placed, and continued thus, with his back turned to the rest of the company, conversing very agreeably, till so many persons collected round him, many of whom were ladies, that not feeling pleased, I suppose, to sit while they stood, he bowed off, and retreated again to his *bergère*.

He told me that he must not remain long in Paris, where he was too much in society to do anything; that he should speedily retreat to the profound seclusion of his native Brittany, and there finish the work upon which he was engaged. Whether this work be the defence of the *prévenus d' Avril*, which he has threatened to fulminate in a printed form at the head of those who refused to let him plead for them in court, I know not: but this document, whenever it appears, is expected to be violent, powerful, and eloquent.

The writings of the Abbé de Lamennais remind me strongly of those of Cobbett, – not, certainly, from their matter, nor even from the manner of treating it, but from the sort of effect which they produce upon the mind. Had the pen of either of them been wholly devoted to the support of a good cause, their writings would have been invaluable to society; for they both have shown a singular power of carrying the attention, and almost the judgment, of the reader along with them, even when writing on subjects on which he and they were perfectly at issue.

Were there not circumstances in the literary history of both which contradict the notion, I should say that this species of power or charm in their writings arose from their being themselves very much in earnest in the opinions they were advocating: but as the Abbé de Lamennais and the late Mr. Cobbett have both shown that their faith in their own opinions was not strong enough to prevent them from changing them, the peculiar force of their eloquence can hardly be referred to the sincerity of it.

I remember hearing a lively young barrister declare that he would rather argue against his own judgment than according to it; and I am sure he spoke in all sincerity, – much as he would have done had he said that he preferred shooting wild game to slaughtering tame chickens: the difficulty made the pleasure. But we cannot presume to suppose that either of the two persons whose names I have so incongruously brought together have written and argued on the same principle; and even if it were so, they have not the less changed their minds, – unless we suppose that they have amused themselves and the public, by sometimes arguing for what they believed to be truth, and sometimes only to show their skill.

As to what Mr. Cobbett's principles might really have been, I think it is a question that must ever remain in uncertainty, – unless we adopt that easiest and most intelligible conclusion, that he had none at all. But it is far otherwise with M. de Lamennais: it is impossible to doubt that in his early writings he was perfectly sincere; there is a warmth of faith in them that could proceed from no fictitious fire. Nor is it easily to be imagined that he would have thrown himself from the height at which he stood in the opinion of all whom he most esteemed, had he not fancied that he saw truth at the bottom of that abyss of heresy and schism into which all good Catholics think that he has thrown himself.

The wild republicanism which M. de Lamennais has picked up in his descent is, however, what has probably injured him most in the general estimation. Some few years ago, liberal principles were advocated by many of the most able as well as the most honest men in Europe; but the unreasonable excesses into which the ultras of the party have fallen seem to have made the respectable portion of mankind draw back from it, and, whatever their speculative opinions may be, they now show themselves anxious to rally round all that bears the stamp of order and lawful authority.

It would be difficult to imagine a worse time for a man to commence republican and free-thinker than the present; – unless, indeed, he did so in the hope that the loaves and fishes were, or would be, at the disposition of that party. Putting, however, all hope of being paid for it aside, the period is singularly unpropitious for such a conversion. As long as their doctrine remained a theory only, it might easily delude many who had more imagination than judgment, or more ignorance than either: but so much deplorable mischief has arisen before our eyes every time the theory has been brought to the test of practice, that I believe the sound-minded in every land consider their speculations at present with as little respect as they would those of a joint-stock company proposing to colonize the moon.

That the Abbé de Lamennais is no longer considered in France as the pre-eminent man he has been, is most certain; and as it is easy to trace in his works a regular progression downwards, from the dignified and enthusiastic Catholic priest to the puzzled sceptic and factious demagogue, I should not be greatly surprised to hear that he, who has been spoken of at Rome as likely to become a cardinal, was carrying a scarlet flag through the streets of Paris, with a conical hat and a Robespierre waistcoat, singing '*Ça ira*' louder than he ever chanted a mass.

M. de Lamennais, in common with several other persons of republican principles with whom I have conversed since I have been in Paris, has conceived the idea that England is at this moment actually and *bona fide* under the rule, dictation, and government of Mr. Daniel O'Connell. He named him in an accent of the most profound admiration and respect, and referred to the English newspapers as evidence of the enthusiastic love and veneration in which he was held throughout Great Britain!

I waxed wroth, I confess; but I took wisdom and patience, and said very meekly, that he had probably seen only the portion of the English papers which were of Mr. Daniel's faction, and that I believed Great Britain was still under the dominion of King William the Fourth, his Lords and Commons. It is not many days since I met another politician of the same school who went farther still; for he gravely wished me joy of the prospect of emancipation which the virtue of the great O'Connell held out to my country. On this occasion, being in a gay mood, I laughed heartily, and did so with a safe conscience, having no need to set the enlightened propagandist right; this being done for me, much better than I could have done it myself, by a hard-headed doctrinaire who was with me.

'O'Connell is the Napoleon of England,' said the republican.

'Not of England, at any rate,' replied the doctrinaire. 'And if he must have a name borrowed from France, let it be Robespierre's: let him be called magnificiently the Robespierre of Ireland.'

'He has already been the redeemer of Ireland,' rejoined the republican gravely; 'and now *he has taken England under his protection.*'

'And I suspect that ere long England will take him under hers,' said my friend, laughing. 'Hitherto it appears as if the country had not thought him worth whipping; . . . mais si un chien est méchant, si même ce ne serait qu'un vilain petit hargneux, il devrait être lié, ou bien pendu.'

Having finished this oracular sentence, the doctrinaire took a long pinch of snuff, and began discoursing of other matters: and I too withdrew from the discussion, persuaded that I could not bring it to a better conclusion.

LETTER XL

Which Party is it ranks second in the estimation of all? –
No Caricatures against the Exiles – Horror of a Republic

I have been taking some pains to discover, by the aid of all the
signs and tokens of public feeling within my reach, who
among the different parties into which this country is divided
enjoys the highest degree of general consideration.

We know that if every man in a town were desired to say
who among its inhabitants he should consider as fittest to hold
an employment of honour and profit, each would probably
answer, 'Myself:' we know also, that should it happen, after
the avowal of this very natural partiality, that the name of the
second best were asked for, and that the man named as such by
one were so named by all, this second best would be accounted
by the disinterested lookers-on as decidedly the right and
proper person to fill the station. According to this rule, the
right and proper government for France is neither republican,
nor military, nor doctrinaire, but that of a legitimate and
constitutional monarchy.

When men hold office, bringing both power and wealth,
consideration will of necessity follow. That the ministers and
their friends, therefore, should be seen in pride of place, and
enjoying the dignity they have achieved, is natural, inevitable,
and quite as it should be. But if, turning from this everyday
spectacle, we endeavour to discover who it is that, possessing
neither power nor place, most uniformly receive the homage of
respect, I should say, without a shadow of doubt or misgiving,
that it was the legitimate royalists.

The triumphant doctrinaires pass no jokes at their expense;
no *bons mots* are quoted against them, nor does any shop exhibit
caricatures either of what they have been or of what they are.

The republicans are no longer heard to name them, either
with rancour or disrespect: all their wrath is now poured out

upon the present actual power of the prosperous doctrinaires. This, indeed, is in strict conformity to the principle which constitutes the foundation of their sect; namely, that whatever exists ought to be overthrown. But neither in jest nor earnest do they now show hostility to Charles the Tenth or his family: nor even do the blank walls of Paris, which for nearly half a century have been the favourite receptacle of all their wit, exhibit any pleasantries, either in the shape of hieroglyphic, caricature, or lampoon, alluding to them or their cause.

I have listened repeatedly to sprightly and to bitter jestings, to judicious and to blundering reasonings, for and against the different doctrines which divide the country; but in no instance do I remember to have heard, either in jest or earnest, any revilings against the exiled race. A sort of sacred silence seems to envelope this theme; or if it be alluded to at all, it is far from being in a hostile spirit.

'HENRI!' is a name that, without note or comment, may be read *ça et là* in every quarter of Paris, that of the Tuileries not excepted: and on a wall near the Royal College of Henri Quatre, where the younger princes of the house of Orleans will study, were inscribed not long ago these very intelligible words:–

'Pour arriver à Bordeaux, il faut passer par Orléans.'

In short, whatever feelings of irritation and anger might have existed in 1830, and produced the scenes which led to the exile of the royal family, they now seem totally to have subsided.

It does not, however, necessarily follow from this that the majority of the people are ready again to hazard their precious tranquillity in order to restore them: on the contrary, it cannot be doubted that were such a measure attempted at the present moment, it would fail – not from any dislike of their legitimate monarch, or any affection for the kinsman who has been placed upon his throne, but wholly and solely from their wish to enjoy in peace with profitable speculations at the *Bourse* – their flourishing *restaurans* – their prosperous shops – and even their tables, chairs, beds, and coffee-pots.

Very different, however, is the feeling manifested towards the republicans. Never did Napoleon in the days of his most absolute power, or the descendants of Louis le Grand in those of their proudest state, contemplate this factious, restless race with such abhorrence as do the doctrinaires of the present hour. It is not that they fear them – they have no real cause to do so; but they feel a sentiment made up of hatred and contempt, which never seems to repose, and which, if not regulated by wisdom and moderation, is very likely eventually to lead to more barricades; though to none, I imagine, that the National Guards may not easily throw down.

It is on the subject of this unpopular *clique* that by far the greater part of the ever-springing Parisian joke expends itself; though the doctrinaires get it '*pas mal*' in return, as I heard a national guardsman remark, as we were looking over some caricatures together. But, in truth, the republicans seem upon principle to offer themselves as victims and martyrs to the quizzing propensities of their countrymen. Harlequin does not more scrupulously adhere to his parti-coloured suit, than do the republicans of Paris to their burlesque costume. It is, I presume, to show their courage, that they so ostentatiously march with their colours flying; but the effect is very ludicrous. The symbolic peculiarities of their dress are classed and lithographed with infinite fun.

Drolleries, too, on the parvenus of the Empire are to be found for the seeking; and when they beset King Philippe himself, it should seem that it is done with all the enthusiasm so well expressed by Garrick in days of yore:–

"'Tis for my king, and zounds! I'll do my best!'

The only extraordinary part of all this caricaturing on walls and in print-shops, is the license taken with those who have power to prevent it. The principle of legislation on this point appears, with a little variation, to be that of the old ballad:

'Thoughts, words, and deeds, the statute blames with
     reason;
But surely *jokes* were ne'er indicted treason.'

In speaking of the parties into which France is divided, the three grand divisions of Carlists, Doctrinaires, and Republicans naturally present themselves first and foremost, and, to foreigners in general, appear to contain between them the entire nation: but a month or two passed in Paris society suffices to show one that there are many who cannot fairly be classed with either.

In the first place, the Carlist party by no means contains all those who disapprove of treating a crown like a ready-made shoe, which, if it be found to pinch the person it was intended for, may be disposed of to the first comer who is willing to take it. The Carlist party, properly so called, demand the restoration of King Charles the Tenth, the immediate descendant and representative of their long line of kings – the prince who has been crowned and anointed King of France, and who, while he remains alive, must render the crowning and anointing of any other prince an act of sacrilege. Wherefore, in effect, King Louis-Philippe has not received '*le sacre*': he is not as yet the anointed King of France, whatever he may be hereafter. Henri Quatre is said to have exclaimed under the walls of the capital, 'Paris vaut bien une messe;' and it is probable that Louis-Philippe Premier thinks so too; but hitherto he has been able to have this performed only in military style – being incapable, in fact, of going through the ceremony either civilly or religiously. The Carlists are, therefore, those only who *en rigueur* do not approve of any king but the real one.

The legitimate royalists are, I believe, a much more numerous party. As strictly attached to the throne and to the principle of regular and legitimate succession as the Carlists, they nevertheless conceive that the pressure of circumstances may not only authorise, but render it imperative upon the country to accept, or rather to permit, the abdication of a sovereign. The king's leaving the country and placing himself in exile, is one of the few causes than can justify this; and accordingly the abdication of Charles Dix is virtual death to him as a sovereign. But though this is granted, it does not follow in their creed, that any part of the nation have thereupon a right to present the hereditary crown to whom they will. The law of succession, they say, is not to be violated because the king has fled before a popular insurrection; and having permitted his abdication, the next heir becomes king. The next heir, however, choosing to follow his royal father's example, he too becomes virtually defunct, and his heir succeeds.

This heir is still an infant, and his remaining in exile cannot therefore be interpreted as his own act. Thus, according to the reasoning of those who conceive the abdication of the king and the dauphin to be acts within their own power, and beyond that of the nation to nullify, Henri, the son of the Duc de Berri, is beyond all doubt Henri Cinq, Roi de France.

Of this party, however, there are many, and I suspect their number is increasing, who, having granted the power of setting aside (by his own act) the anointed monarch, are not altogether averse to go a step farther, if so doing shall ensure the peace of the country; and considering the infancy of the rightful heir as constituting insufficiency, to confess Louis-Philippe as the next in succession to be the lawful as well as the actual King of the French.

It is this party who I always find have the most to say in support (or defence) of their opinions. Whether this proceeds from their feeling that some eloquence is necessary to make them pass current, or that the conviction of their justice is such as to make their hearts overflow on the theme, I know not; but decidedly the sect of the 'Parcequ'il est Bourbon' is that which I find most eager to discourse upon politics. And, to confess the truth, they have much to say for themselves, at least on the side of expediency.

It is often a matter of regret with me, that in addressing these letters to you I am compelled to devote so large a portion of them to politics; but in attempting to give you some idea of Paris at the present moment, it is impossible to avoid it. Were I to turn from this theme, I could only do so by labouring to forget everthing I have seen, everything I see. Go where you will, do what you will, meet whom you will, it is out of your power to escape it. But observe, that it is wholly for your sake, and not at all for my own, that I lament it; for, however flat and unprofitable my report may be, the thing itself, when you are in the midst of it, is exceedingly interesting.

When I first arrived, I was considerably annoyed by finding, that as soon as I had noted down some piece of information as an undoubted fact, the next person I conversed with assured me that it was worth considerably less than nought; inasmuch as my informer had not only failed to give me useful instruction on the point concerning which I was inquiring, but had altogether deluded, deceived, and led me astray.

These days of primitive matter-of-factness are now, however, quite passed with me; and though I receive a vast deal of entertainment from all, I give my faith in return to very few. I listen to the Carlists, the Henri-Quintists, the Philippists, with great attention and real interest, but have sometimes caught myself humming as soon as they have left me,

'They were all of them kings in their turn.'

Indeed, if you knew all that happens to me, instead of blaming me for being too political, you would be very thankful for the care and pains I bestow in endeavouring to make a digest of all I hear for your advantage, containing as few contradictions as possible. And truly this is no easy matter, not only from the contradictory nature of the information I receive, but from some varying weaknesses in my own nature, which sometimes put me in the very disagreeable predicament of doubting if what is right be right, and if what is wrong be wrong.

When I came here, I was a thorough unequivocating legitimatist, and felt quite ready and willing to buckle on armour against any who should doubt that a man once a king was always a king – that once crowned according to law, he could not be uncrowned according to mob – or that a man's eldest son was his rightful heir.

But, oh! these doctrinaires! They have such a way of proving that if they are not quite right, at least everybody else is a great deal more wrong: and then they talk so prettily of England and *our* revolution, and our glorious constitution – and the miseries of anarchy – and the advantages of letting things remain quietly as they are, till, as I said before, I begin to doubt what is right and what is wrong.

There is one point, however, on which we agree wholly and heartily; and it is this perhaps that has been the means of softening my heart thus towards them. The doctrinaires shudder at the name of a republic. This is not because their own party is regal, but is evidently the result of the experience which they and their fathers have had from the tremendous experiment which has once already been made in the country.

'You will never know the full value of your constitution till you have lost it,' said a doctrinaire to me the other evening, at the house of the beautiful Princess B——, formerly an energetic propagandiste, but now a very devoted doctrinaire, – 'you will never know how beneficial is its influene on every hour of your lives, till your Mr. O'Connell has managed to arrange a republic for you: and when you have tasted that for about three months, you will make good and faithful subjects to the next king that Heaven shall bestow upon you. You know how devoted all France was to the Emperor, though the police was somewhat tight and the conscriptions heavy; but he had saved us from a republic, and we adored him. For a few days, or rather hours, we were threatened again, five years ago, by the same terrible apparition: the result is, that four millions of armed men stand ready to protect the prince who chased it. Were it to appear a third time – which Heaven forbid! – you may depend upon it that the monarch who should next ascend the throne of France might play at *le jeu de quilles* with his subjects, and no one be found to complain.

LETTER XLI

M. Dupré – His Drawings in Greece – L'Eglise des Carmes –
M. Vinchon's Picture of the National Convention –
Léopold Robert's Fishermen – Reported cause of his Suicide –
Roman Catholic Religion – Mr. Daniel O'Connell

We went the other morning, with Miss C——, a very
agreeable countrywoman, who has however passed the
greater portion of her life in Paris, to visit the house and atelier
of M. Dupré, a young artist who seems to have devoted
himself to the study of Greece. Her princes, her peasants, her
heavy-eyed beauties, and the bright sky that glows above
them, – all the material of her domestic life, and all the
picturesque accompaniments of her classic reminiscences, are
brought home by this gentleman in a series of spirited and
highly-finished drawings, which give decidedly the most
lively idea of the country that I have seen produced.
Engravings or lithographs from them are, I believe, intended
to illustrate a splendid work on this interesting country which
is about to be published.

In our way from M. Dupré's house, in which was this
collection of Greek drawings, to his atelier – where he was
kind enough to show us a large picture recently commenced –
we entered that fatal 'Eglise des Carmes,' where the most
hideous massacre of the first revolution took place. A large
tree that stands beside it is pointed out as having been sought
as a shelter – alas! how vainly! – by the unhappy priests, who
were shot, sabred, and dragged from its branches by dozens.
A thousand terrible recollections are suggested by the interior
of the building, aided by the popular traditions attached to it,
unequalled in atrocity even in the history of that time of
horror.

Another scene relating to the same period, which, though
inferior to the massacre of the priests in multiplied barbarity,

was of sufficient horror to freeze the blood of any but a republican, has, strange to say, been made, since the revolution of 1830, the subject of an enormous picture by M. Vinchon, and at the present moment makes part of the exhibition at the Louvre.

The canvas represents a hall at the Tuileries which in 1795 was the place where the National Convention sat. The mob has broken in, and murdered Feraud, who attempted to oppose them; and the moment chosen by the painter is that in which a certain '*jeune fille nommée. Aspasie Migelli*' approaches the president's chair with the young man's head borne on a pike before her, while she triumphantly envelopes herself in some part of his dress. The whole scene is one of the most terrible revolutionary violence. This picture is stated in the catalogue to belong to the minister of the interior; but whether the present minister of the interior, or any other, I know not. The subject was given immediately after the revolution of 1830, and many artists made sketches in competition for the execution of it. One of those who tried, and failed before the superior genius of M. Vinchon, told us, that the subject was given at that time as one likely to be popular, either for love of the noble resolution with which Boissy d'Anglas keeps possession of the president's chair, which he had seized upon, or else from admiration of the energetic female who has assisted in doing the work of death. In either case, this young artist said, the popularity of such a subject was passed by, and no such order would be given now.

Finding myself again on the subject of pictures, I must mention a very admirable one which is now being exhibited at the 'Mairie du Second Arrondissement.' It is from the hand of the unfortunate Leopold Robert, who destroyed himself at Venice almost immediately after he had completed it. The subject is the departure of a party of Italian fishermen; and there are parts of the picture fully equal to anything I have ever seen from the pencil of a modern artist. I should have looked at this picture with extreme pleasure, had the painter still lived to give hope of, perhaps, still higher efforts; but the history of his death, which I had just been listening to, mixed great pain with it.

I have been told that this young man was of a very religious and meditative turn of mind, but a Protestant. His only sister, to whom he was much attached, was a Catholic, and had recently taken the veil. Her affection for him was such, that she became perfectly wretched from the danger she believed awaited him from his heresy; and she commenced a species of affectionate persecution, which, though it failed to convert him, so harassed and distracted his mind, as finally to overthrow his reason, and lead him to self-destruction. This charming picture is exhibited for the benefit of the poor, at the especial desire of the unhappy nun; who is said, however, to be so perfect a fanatic, as only to regret that the dreadful act was not delayed till she had had time to work out the salvation of her own soul by a little more persecution of his.

There is something exceedingly curious, and, perhaps, under our present lamentable circumstances, somewhat alarming, in the young and vigorous after-growth of the Roman Catholic religion, which, by the aid of a very little inquiry, may be so easily traced throughout France. Were we keeping our own national church sacred, and guarded both by love and by law, as it has hitherto been from all assaults of the Pope and . . . Mr. O'Connell, it could only be with pleasure that we should see France recovering from her long ague-fit of infidelity, – and, as far as she is concerned, we must in Christian charity rejoice, for she is unquestionably the better for it; but there is a regenerated activity among the Roman Catholic clergy, which, under existing circumstances, makes a Protestant feel rather nervous, – and I declare to you, I never pass within sight of that famous window of the Louvre, whence Charles Neuf, with his own royal and catholic hand, discharged a blunderbuss amongst the Huguenots, without thinking how well a window at Whitehall, already noted in history as a scene of horror, might serve King Daniel for the same purpose.

The great influence which the religion of Rome has of late regained over the minds of the French people has, I am told, been considerably increased by the priests having added to the strength derived from their command of pardons and indulgences, that which our Methodist preachers gain from the terrors of hell. They use the same language, too, respecting regeneration and grace; and, as one means of regaining the hold they had lost upon the human mind, they now anathematize all recreations, as if their congregations were so many aspirants to the sublime purifications of La Trappe, or so many groaning fanatics just made over to them from Lady Huntingdon's Chapel. That there is, however, a pretty strong force to stem this fresh spring-tide of moon-struck superstition, is very certain. The doctrinaires, I am told, taken as a body, are not much addicted to this species of weakness. I remember, during the prevalence of that sweeping complaint called the influenza, hearing of a 'good lady,' of the high evangelical *clique*, who said to some of the numerous pensioners who flocked to receive the crumbs of her table and the precepts of her lips, that she could make up some medicine that was very good for all POOR people that were seized with this complaint.

'What can be the difference, ma'am,' said the poor body who told me this, 'between us and Madame C—— in this illness? Is not what is good for the poor, good for the rich too?'

The same pertinent question may, I think, be asked in Paris just now respecting the medicine called religion. It is administered in large doses to the poor, to which class a great number of the fair sex of all ranks happily seem to have joined themselves, – including, at least, to rank themselves as among the poor in spirit; nay, parish doctors are regularly paid by authority; yet, if the tale be true, the authorities themselves take little of it. 'It is very good for poor people;' but, like the hot-baths which Anstie talks of,

> 'No creature e'er view'd
> Any one of the government gentry stew'd'

Whether the returning power of this pompous and aspiring faith will mount as it proceeds, and embrace within its grasp, as it was wont to do, all the great ones of the earth, is a question that it may require some years to answer; but one thing is at least certain, – that its ministers will try hard that it shall do so, whether they are likely to succeed or not; and, at the worst, they may console themselves by the reflection of Lafontaine:–

'Si de les gagner je n'emporte pas le prix,
J'aurais au moins l'honneur de l'avoir entrepris.'

One great one they have certainly already got, besides King
Charles the Tenth, – even the immortal Daniel; and however
little consequence you may be inclined to attach to this fact, it
cannot be considered as wholly unimportant, since I have
heard his religious principles and his influence in England
alluded to in the pulpit here with a tone of hope and triumph
which made me tremble.

I heartily wish that some of those who continue to vote in
his traitorous majority because they are pledged to do so,
could hear him and his power spoken of here. If they have
English hearts, it must, I think, give them a pang.

LETTER XLII

*Old Maids – Rarely to be found in France –
The reasons for this*

Several years ago, while passing a few weeks in Paris, I had a conversation with a Frenchman upon the subject of old maids, which, though so long past, I refer to now for the sake of the sequel, which has just reached me.

We were, I well remember, parading in the Gardens of the Luxembourg; and as we paced up and down its long alleys, the 'miserable fate,' as he called it, of single women in England was discussed and deplored by my companion as being one of the most melancholy results of faulty national manners that could be mentioned.

'I know nothing,' said he with much energy, 'that ever gave me more pain in society, than seeing, as I did in England, numbers of unhappy women who, however well-born, well-educated, or estimable, were without a position, without an *état,* and without a name, excepting one that they would generally give half their remaining days to get rid of.'

'I think you somewhat exaggerate the evil,' I replied: 'but even if it were as bad as you state it to be, I see not why single ladies should be better off here.'

'Here!' he exclaimed, in a tone of horror: 'do you really imagine that in France, where we pride ourselves on making the destiny of our women the happiest in the world, – do you really imagine that we suffer a set of unhappy, innocent, helpless girls to drop, as it were, out of society into the *néant* of celibacy, as you do? God keep us from such barbarity!'

'But how can you help it? It is impossible but that circumstances must arise to keep many of your men single; and if the numbers be equally balanced, it follows that there must be single women too.'

'It may seem so; but the fact is otherwise: we have no single women.'

'What, then, becomes of them?'

'I know not; but were any Frenchwoman to find herself so circumstanced, depend upon it she would drown herself.'

'I know one such, however,' said a lady who was with us: 'Mademoiselle Isabelle B—— is an old maid.'

'Est-il possible!' cried the gentleman, in a tone that made me laugh very heartily. 'And how old is she, this unhappy Mademoiselle Isabelle?'

'I do not know exactly,' replied the lady; 'but I think she must be considerably past thirty.'

'C'est une horreur!' he exclaimed again; adding, rather mysteriously, in a half-whisper, 'Trust me, she will not bear it long!'

I had certainly forgotten Mademoiselle Isabelle and all about her, when I again met the lady who had named her as the one sole existing old maid of France. While conversing with her the other day on many things which had passed when we were last together, she asked me if I remembered this conversation. I assured her that I had forgotten no part of it.

'Well, then,' said she, 'I must tell you what happened to me about three months after it took place. I was invited with my husband to pay a visit at the house of a friend in the country, – the same house where I had formerly seen the Mademoiselle Isabelle B—— whom I had named to you. While playing *écarté* with our host in the evening, I recollected our conversation in the Gardens of the Luxembourg, and inquired for the lady who had been named in it.

'"Is it possible that you have not heard what has happened to her?" he replied.

'"No, indeed; I have heard nothing. Is she married, then?'

'"Married! . . . Alas no! she had *drowned herself!*"'

Terrible as this dénouement was, it could not be heard with the solemn gravity it called for, after what had been said respecting her. Was ever coincidence more strange! My friend told me, that on her return to Paris she mentioned this catastrophe to the gentleman who had seemed to predict it;

when the information was received by an exclamation quite in character, – 'God be praised! then she is out of her misery!'

This incident, and the conversation which followed upon it, induced me to inquire in sober earnest what degree of truth there might really be in the statement made to us in this well-remembered conversation; and it certainly does appear, from all I can learn, that the meeting a single woman past thirty is a very rare occurrence in France. The arranging *un mariage convenable* is in fact as necessary and as ordinary a duty in parents towards a daughter, as the sending her to nurse or the sending her to school. The proposal for such an alliance proceeds quite as frequently from the friends of the lady as from those of the gentleman: and it is obvious that this must at once very greatly increase the chance of a suitable marriage for young women; for though we do occasionally send our daughters to India in the hope of obtaining this much-desired result, few English parents have as yet gone the length of proposing to anybody, or to anybody's son, to take their daughter off their hands.

I have not the least doubt in the world that, were the custom otherwise – were a young lady's claim to an establishment pointed out by her friends, instead of being left to be discovered or undiscovered as chance will have it, – I have no doubt in the world that in such a case many happy marriages might be the result: and where such an arrangement infringes on no feeling of propriety, but is adopted only in conformity to national custom, I can well believe that the fair lady herself may deem her having nothing to do with the business a privilege of infinite importance to her delicacy. But would our English girls like, for the satisfaction of escaping the chance of being an old maid, to give up the dear right of awaiting in maiden dignity till they are chosen – selected from out the entire world – and then of saying yes or no, as may please their fancy best?

If I do not greatly mistake the national character of Eng-lishwomen, there are very few who could be found to exchange this privilege for the most perfect assurance that could be given of obtaining a marriage in any other way. As to which is best and which is wisest, or even which is likely to produce, ultimately and generally, the most happy *ménage*, I will not pretend to say; because I have heard so much plausible, and indeed, in some respects, substantial reasoning in favour of the mode pursued here, that I feel it may be considered as doubtful; but as to which is and must be most agreeable to the parties chiefly concerned at the time the connexion is formed, herein I own I think there can be no question whatever that English men and English women have the advantage.

With all the inclination in the world to believe that France abounds with loving, constant, faithful wives, and husbands too, I cannot but think that if they are so, it is in spite of the manner in which their marriages are made, and not in consequence of it. The strongest argument in favour of their manner of proceeding undoubtedly is, that a husband who receives a young wife as totally without impressions of any kind (as a well-brought-up French girl certainly is), has a better chance – or rather, has more *power* of making her heart entirely his own, than any man can have that falls in love with a beauty of twenty, who may already have heard as tender sighs as he can utter breathed in her ear by some one who may have had no power to marry her, but who might have had a heart to love her, and a tongue to win her as well as himself.

But against this how much is to be placed! However dearly a Frenchwoman may love her husband, he can never feel that it is a love which has selected him; and though it may sometimes happen that a pretty creature is applied for because of her prettiness, yet if the application be made and answered, and no question asked as to her will or wish in the affair, she can feel but little gratification even to her vanity – and certainly nothing whatever approaching to a feeling of tenderness at her heart.

The force of habit is ever so inveterate, that it is not likely either nation can be really a fair and impartial judge of the other in a matter so entirely regulated by it. Therefore, all that I, as English, will venture to say farther on the subject is, that I should be sorry on this point to see us adopt the fashion of our neighbour France.

I have reason to believe, however, that my friend of the Luxembourg Gardens exaggerated a good deal in his statement respecting the non-existence of single women in

France. They do exist here, though certainly in less numbers than in England, – but it is not so easy to find them out. With us it is not unusual for single ladies to take what is called *brevet rank*; – that is, Miss Dorothy Tomkins becomes Mrs. Dorothy Tomkins – and sometimes *tout bonnement* Mrs. Tomkins, provided there be no collateral Mrs. Tomkins to interfere with her: but upon no occasion do I remember that any lady in this predicament called herself the widow Tomkins, or the widow anything else.

Here, however, I am assured that the case is different; and that, let the number of spinsters be great or small, no one but the near connexions and most intimate friends of the party know anything of the matter. Many a *veuve respectable* has never had a husband in her life; and I have heard it positively affirmed, that the secret is often so well kept, that the nieces and nephews of a family do not know their maiden aunts from their widowed ones.

This shows, at least, that matrimony is considered here as a more honourable state than that of celibacy; though it does not quite go the length of proving that all single women drown themselves.

But before I quit this subject, I must say a few words to you concerning the old maids of England. There are few things which chafe my spirit more than hearing single women spoken of with contempt because they are such, or seeing them treated with less consideration and attention than those who chance to be married. The cruelty and injustice of this must be obvious to every one upon a moment's thought; but to me its absurdity is more obvious still.

It is, I believe, a notorious fact, that there is scarcely a woman to be found, of any rank under that of a princess of the blood royal, who, at the age of fifty, has not at some time or in some manner had the power of marrying if she chose it. That many who have had this power have been tyrannically or unfortunately prevented from using it, is certain; but there is nothing either ridiculous or contemptible in this.

Still less does a woman merit scorn if she has had the firmness and constancy of purpose to prefer a single life because she has considered it best and fittest for her: in fact, I knew nothing more high-minded than the doing so. The sneering which follows female celibacy is so well known and so coarsely manifested, that it shows very considerable dignity of character to enable a woman to endure it, rather than act against her sense of what is right.

I by no means say this by way of running a-tilt against all the ladies in France who have submitted, *bon gré, mal gré*, to become wives at the command of their fathers, mothers, uncles, aunts, and guardians: they have done exactly what they ought, and I hope all their pretty little quiet-looking daughters will do the same; it is the custom of the country, and cannot discreetly be departed from. But being on the subject, I am led, while defending our own modes of proceeding in the important affair of marriage, to remark also on the result of them. In permitting a young woman to become acquainted with the man who proposes for her before she consents to pass her whole life with him, I certainly see some advantage; but in my estimation there is more still in the protection which our usage in these matters affords to those who, rather than marry a man who is not the object of their choice, prefer remaining single. I confess, too, that I consider the class of single women as an extremely important one. Their entire freedom from control gives them great power over their time and resources, much more than any other woman can possibly possess who is not a childless widow. That this power is often – very often – nobly used, none can deny who are really and thoroughly acquainted with English society; and if among the class there be some who love cards, and tattle, and dress, and slander, they should be treated with just the same measure of contempt as the married ladies who may also occasionally be found to love cards, and tattle, and dress, and slander, – but with no more.

It has been my chance, and I imagine that it has been the chance of most other people, to have found my dearest and most constant friends among single women. Of all the Helenas and Hermias that before marriage have sat 'upon one cushion, warbling of one song,' even for years together, how few are there who are not severed by marriage! Kind feelings may be retained, and correspondence (lazily enough) kept up; but to whom is it that the anxious mother, watching beside the sick couch of her child, turns for sympathy and consolation? – certainly not to the occupied and perhaps distant wedded confidante of her youthful days, but to her maiden sister or her maiden friend. Nor is it only in sickness that such friends are among the first blessings of life: they violate no duty by giving their time and their talents to society; and many a day through every house in England has probably owed some of its most delightful hours to the presence of those whom no duty has called

'To suckle fools or chronicle small beer,'

and whose talents, therefore, are not only at their own disposal, but in all probability much more highly cultivated than any possessed by their married friends.

Thus, spite of him of the Luxembourg, I am most decidedly of opinion, that, in England at least, there is no reason whatever that an unmarried woman should consign herself to the fate of the unfortunate Mademoiselle Isabelle.

PARIS

AND

THE PARISIANS

VOLUME II

LETTER XLIII

Peculiar Air of Frenchwomen – Impossibility that an
Englishwoman should not be known for such in Paris –
Small Shops – Beautiful Flowers, and pretty arrangement
of them – Native Grace – Disappearance of Rouge –
Grey Hair – Every article dearer than in London –
All temptations to smuggling removed

Considering that it is a woman who writes to you, I think you
will confess that you have no reason to complain of having
been overwhelmed with the fashions of Paris: perhaps, on the
contrary, you may feel rather disposed to grumble because all
I have hitherto said on the fertile subject of dress has been
almost wholly devoted to the historic and fanciful costume of
the republicans. Personal appearance, and all that concerns it,
is, however, a very important feature in the daily history of
this showy city; and although in this respect it has been made
the model of the whole world, it nevertheless contrives to
retain for itself a general look, air, and effect; which it is quite
in vain for any other people to attempt imitating. Go where
you will, you see French fashions; but you must go to Paris to
see how French people wear them.

The dome of the Invalides, the towers of Notre Dame, the
column of the Place Vendôme, the windmills of Montmartre,
do not come home to the mind as more essentially belonging
to Paris, and Paris only, than does the aspect which caps,
bonnets, frills, shawls, aprons, belts, buckles, gloves, – and
above, though below, all things else – which shoes and
stockings assume, when worn by Parisian women in the city
of Paris.

It is in vain that all the women of the earth come crowding
to this mart of elegance, each one with money in her sack
sufficient to cover her from head to foot with all that is richest
and best; – it is in vain that she calls to her aid all the *tailleuses,*

coiffeuses, modistes, couturières, cordonniers, lingères, and *friseurs* in the town: all she gets for her pains is, when she has bought, and done, and put on all and everything they have prescribed, that, in the next shop she enters, she hears one *grisette* behind the counter mutter to another, 'Voyez ce que désire cette dame anglaise;' – and that, poor dear lady! before she has spoken a single word to betray herself.

Neither is it only the natives who find us out so easily – that might perhaps be owing to some little inexplicable free-masonry among themselves; but the worst of all is, that we know one another in a moment. 'There is an Englishman,' – 'That is an Englishwoman,' is felt at a glance, more rapidly than the tongue can speak it.

That manner, gait, and carriage, – that expression of movement, and, if I may so say, of limb, should be at once so remarkable and so impossible to imitate, is very singular. It has nothing to do with the national differences in eyes and complexion, for the effect is felt perhaps more strongly in following than in meeting a person; but it pervades every plait and every pin, every attitude and every gesture.

Could I explain to you what it is which produces this effect, I should go far towards removing the impossibility of imi-tating it: but as this is now, after twenty years of trial, pretty generally allowed to be impossible, you will not expect it of me. All I can do, is to tell you of such matters appertaining to dress as are open and intelligible to all, without attempting to dive into that very occult part of the subject, the effect of it.

In milliners' phrase, the ladies dress much *less* in Paris than in London. I have no idea that any Frenchwoman, after her morning dishabille is thrown aside, would make it a practice, during 'the season,' to change her dress completely four times in the course of the day, as I have known some ladies do in London. Nor do I believe that the most *précieuses* in such matters among them would deem it an insufferable breach of good manners to her family, did she sit down to dinner in the same apparel in which they had seen her three hours before it.

The only article of female luxury more generally indulged in here than with us, is that of cashmere shawls. One, at the very least, of these dainty wrappers makes a part of every young lady's *trousseau*, and is, I believe, exactly that part of the *présent* which, as Miss Edgeworth says, often makes a bride forget the *futur*.

In other respects, what is necessary for the wardrobe of a French woman of fashion, is necessary also for that of an English one; only jewels and trinkets of all kinds are more frequently worn with us than with them. The dress that a young Englishwoman would wear at a dinner party, is very nearly the same as a Frenchwoman would wear at any ball but a fancy one; whereas the most elegant dinner costume in Paris is exactly the same as would be worn at the French Opera.

There are many extremely handsome *'magasins de nouveautés'* in every part of the town, wherein may be found all that the heart of woman can desire in the way of dress; and there are smart *coiffeuses* and *modistes* too, who know well how to fabricate and recommend every production of their fascinating art: but there is now Howell and James's wherein to assemble at a given point all the fine ladies of Paris; no reunions of tall footmen are to be seen lounging on benches outside the shops, and performing to the uninitiated the office of signs, by giving notice how many purchasers are at the moment engaged in cheapening the precious wares within. The shops in general are very much smaller than ours, – or when they stretch into great length, they have uniformly the appearance of warehouses. A much less quantity of goods of all kinds is displayed for purposes of show and decoration, – unless it be in china shops, or where or-molu ornaments, protected by glass covers, form the principal objects: here, or indeed wherever the articles sold can be exhibited without any danger of loss from injury, there is very considerable display; but, on the whole, there is much less appearance of large capital exhibited in the shops here than in London.

One great source of the gay and pretty appearance of the streets, is the number and elegant arrangement of the flowers exposed for sale. Along all the Boulevards, and in every brilliant Passage (with which latter ornamental invention Paris is now threaded in all directions), you need only shut your eyes in order to fancy yourself in a delicious flower-garden; and even on opening them again, if the delusion vanishes, you have something almost as pretty in its place.

Notwithstanding the multitudinous abominations of their streets – the prison-like locks on the doors of their *salons*, and the odious common stair which must be climbed ere one can get to them – there is an elegance of taste and love of the graceful about these people which is certainly to be found nowhere else. It is not confined to the spacious hôtels of the rich and great, but may be traced through every order and class of society, down to the very lowest.

The manner in which an old barrow-woman will tie up her sous' worth of cherries for her urchin customers might give a lesson to the most skilful decorator of the supper-table. A bunch of wild violets, sold at a price that may come within reach of the worst-paid *soubrette* in Paris, is arranged with a grace that might make a duchess covet them; and I have seen the paltry stock-in-trade of a florist, whose only pavilion was a tree and the blue heavens, set off with such felicity in the mixture of colours, and the gradations of shape and form, as made me stand to gaze longer and more delightedly than I ever did before Flora's own palace in the King's Road.

After all, indeed, I believe that the mystical peculiarity of dress of which I have been speaking wholly arises from this innate and universal instinct of good taste. There is a fitness, a propriety, a sort of harmony in the various articles which constitute female attire, which may be traced as clearly amongst the cotton *toques*, with all their variety of brilliant tints, and the 'kerchief and apron to match, or rather to accord, as amongst the most elegant bonnets at the Tuileries. Their expressive phrase of approbation for a well-dressed woman, '*faite à peindre*,' may often be applied with quite as much justice to the peasant as to the princess; for the same unconscious sensibility of taste will regulate them both.

It is this national feeling which renders their stage groups, their corps *de ballet*, and all the *tableaux* business of their theatres, so greatly superior to all others. On these occasions, a single blunder in colour, contrast, or position, destroys the whole harmony, and the whole charm with it: but you see the poor little girls hired to do angels and graces for a few sous a night, fall into the compostion of the scene with an instinct as unerring, as that which leads a flight of wild geese to cleave the air in a well-adjusted triangular phalanx, instead of scattering themselves to every point of the compass; as, *par exemple*, our *figurantes* may be often seen to do, if not kept in order by the ballet-master as carefully as a huntsman whistles in his pack.

It is quite a relief to my eyes to find how completely rouge appears to be gone out of fashion here. I will not undertake to say that no bright eyes still look brighter from having a touch of red skilfully applied beneath them: but if this be done, it is so well done as to be invisible, excepting by its favourable effect; which is a prodigious improvement upon the fashion which I well remember here, of larding cheeks both young and old to a degree that was quite frightful.

Another improvement which I very greatly admire is, that the majority of old ladies have left off wearing artificial hair, and arrange their own grey locks with all the neatness and care possible. The effect of this upon their general appearance is extremely favourable: Nature always arranges things for us much better than we can do it for ourselves; and the effect of an old face surrounded by a maze of wanton curls, black, brown, or flaxen, is infinitely less agreeable than when it is seen with its own 'sable silvered' about it.

I have heard it observed, and with great justice, that rouge was only advantageous to those who did not require it: and the same may be said with equal truth of false hair. Some of the towering pinnacles of shining jet that I have seen here, certainly have exceeded in quantity of hair the possible growth of any one head: but when this fabric surmounts a youthful face which seems to have a right to all the flowing honours that the friseur's art can contrive to arrange above it, there is nothing incongruous or disagreeable in the effect; though it is almost a pity, too, to mix anything approaching to deceptive art with the native glories of a young head. For which sentiment *messieurs les fabricans* of false hair will not thank me; – for having first interdicted the use of borrowed tresses to the old ladies, I now pronounce my disapproval of them for the young.

Au reste, all I can tell you farther respecting dress is, that our ladies must no longer expect to find bargains here in any article required for the wardrobe; on the contrary, everything of the kind is become greatly dearer than in London: and what is at least equally against making such purchases here is, that the fabrics of various kinds which we used to consider as superior to our own, particularly those of silks and gloves, are now, I think, decidedly inferior; and such as can be purchased at the same price as in England, if they can be found at all, are really too bad to use.

The only foreign bargains which I long to bring home with me are in porcelain: but this our custom-house tariff forbids, and very properly; as, without such protection, our Wedgewoods and Mortlakes would sell but few ornamental articles; for not only are their prices higher, but both their material and the fashioning of it are in my opinion extremely inferior. It is really very satisfactory to one's patriotic feelings to be able to say honestly, that excepting in these, and a few other ornamental superfluities, such as or-molu and alabaster clocks, etcetera, there is nothing that we need wish to smuggle into our own abounding land.

LETTER XLIV

Exclusive Soirées – Soirée Doctrinaire – Duc de Broglie –
Soirée Républicaine – Soirée Royaliste – Partie Impériale –
Military Greatness – Dame de l'Empire

Though the *salons* of Paris probably show at the present
moment the most mixed society that can be found mingled
together in the world, one occasionally finds oneself in the
midst of a set evidently of one stamp, and indeed proclaiming
itself to be so; for wherever this happens, the assembly is
considered as peculiarly chosen and select, and as having all the
dignity of exclusiveness.

The picture of Paris as it is, may perhaps be better caught at a
glance at a party collected together without any reference to
politics or principles of any kind; but I have been well pleased to
find myself on three different occasions admitted to *soirées* of
the exclusive kind.

At the first of these, I was told the names of most of the
company by a kind friend who sat near me, and thus became
aware that I had the honour of being in company with most of
King Philippe's present ministry. Three or four of these gentlemen were introduced to me, and I had the advantage of
seeing *de près*, during their hours of relaxation, the men who
have perhaps at this moment as heavy a weight of responsibility
upon their shoulders as any set of ministers ever sustained.

Nevertheless, nothing like gloom, preoccupation, or
uneasiness, appeared to pervade them; and yet that chiefest
subject of anxiety, the *Procès Monstre*, was by no means
banished from their discourse. Their manner of treating it,
however, was certainly not such as to make one believe that
they were at all likely to sink under their load, or that they felt in
any degree embarrassed or distressed by it.

Some of the extravagances of *les accusés* were discussed gaily
enough, and the general tone was that of men who knew

perfectly well what they were about, and who found more to laugh at than to fear in the opposition and abuse they encountered. This light spirit however, which to me seemed fair enough in the hours of recreation, had better not be displayed on graver occasions, as it naturally produces exasperation on the part of the prisoners, which, however little dangerous it may be to the state, is nevertheless a feeling which should not be unnecessarily excited. In that amusing paper or magazine – I know not which may be its title – called the 'Chronique de Paris,' I read some days ago a letter describing one of the *séances* of the Chamber of Peers on this *procès*, in which the gaiety manifested by M. de Broglie is thus censured:–

'J'ai fait moi-même partie de ce public privilégié que les accusés ne reconnaissent pas comme un vrai public, et j'ai pu assister jeudi à cette dramatique audience où la voix tonnante d'un accusé lisant une protestation, a couvert la voix du ministère public. J'étais du nombre de ceux qui ont eu la fièvre de cette scène, et je n'ai pu comprendre, au milieu de l'agitation générale, qu'un homme aussi bien élevé que M. de Broglie (je ne dis pas qu'un ministre) trouvât seul qu'il y avait là sujet de rire en lorgnant ce vrai Romain, comparable à ces tribuns qui, dans les derniers temps de la république, faisaient trembler les patriciens sur leurs chaises curules.'

'*Ce vrai Romain,*' however, rather deserved to be scourged than laughed at; for never did any criminal when brought to the bar of his country insult its laws and its rulers more grossly than the prisoner Beaune on this occasion. If indeed the accounts which reach us by the daily papers are not exaggerated, the outrageous conduct of the accused furnishes at every sitting sufficient cause for anger and indignation, however unworthy it may be of inspiring anything approaching to a feeling of alarm: and the calm, dignified, and temperate manner in which the Chamber of Peers has hitherto conducted itself may serve, I think, as an example to many other legislative assemblies.

The ministers of Louis-Philippe are very fortunate that the mode of trial decided on by them in this troublesome business is likely to be carried through by the upper house in a manner so little open to reasonable animadversion. The duty, and a most harassing one it is, has been laid upon them, as many think, illegally: but the task has been imposed by an authority which it is their duty to respect, and they have entered upon it in a spirit that does them honour.

The second exclusive party to which I was fortunate enough to be admitted, was in all respects quite the reverse of the first. The fair mistress of the mansion herself assured me that there was not a single doctrinaire present.

Here, too, the eternal subject of the *Procès Monstre* was discussed, but in a very different tone, and with feelings as completely as possible in opposition to those which dictated the lively and triumphant sort of persiflage to which I had before listened. Nevertheless, the conversation was anything but *triste*, as the party was in truth particularly agreeable; but, amidst flashes of wit, sinister sounds that foreboded future revolutions grumbled every now and then like distant thunder. Then there was shrugging of shoulders, and shaking of heads, and angry taps upon the snuff-box; and from time to time, amid the prattle of pretty women, and the well-turned *gentillesses* of those they prattled to, might be heard such phrases as, 'Tout n'est pas encore fini' . . . 'Nous verrons' . . . 'S'ils sont arbitraires!' . . . and the like.

The third set was as distinct as may be from the two former. This reunion was in the quartier St. Germain; and, if the feeling which I know many would call prejudice does not deceive me, the tone of first-rate good society was greatly more conspicuous here than at either of the others. By all the most brilliant personages who adorned the other two *soirées* which I have described, I strongly suspect that the most distinguished of this third would be classed as *rococo*; but they were composed of the real stuff that constitutes the true patrician, for all that. Many indeed were quite of the old régime, and many others their noble high-minded descendants: but whether they were old or young, – whether remarkable for having played a distinguished part in the scenes that have been, or for sustaining the chivalric principles of their race, by quietly withdrawing from the scenes that are, – in either case they had that air of inveterate superiority which I believe nothing on earth but gentle blood can give.

There is a fourth class still, consisting of the dignitaries of the Empire, which, if they ever assemble in distinct committee, I have yet to become acquainted with. But I suspect that this is not the case: one may perhaps meet them more certainly in some houses than in others; but, unless it be around the dome of the Invalides, I do not believe that they are to be found anywhere as a class apart.

Nothing, however, can be less difficult than to trace them: they are as easily discerned as a boiled lobster among a panier full of such as are newly caught.

That amusing little vaudeville called, I think, 'La Dame de l'Empire,' or some such title, contains the best portrait of a whole *clique*, under the features of an individual character, of any comedy I know.

None of the stormy billows which have rolled over France during the last forty years have thrown up a race so strongly marked as those produced by the military era of the Empire. The influence of the enormous power which was then in action has assuredly in some directions left most noble vestiges. Wherever science was at work, this power propelled it forward; and ages yet unborn may bless for this the fostering patronage of Napoleon: some midnight of devastation and barbarism must fall upon the world before what he has done of this kind can be obliterated.

But the same period, while it brought forth from obscurity talent and enterprise which without its influence would never have been greeted by the light of day, brought forward at the same time legions of men and women to whom this light and their advanced position in society are by no means advantageous in the eyes of a passing looker-on.

I have heard that it requires three generations to make a gentleman. Those created by Napoleon have not yet fairly reached a second; and, with all respect for talent, industry, and valour be it spoken, the necessity of this slow process very frequently forces itself upon one's conviction at Paris.

It is probable that the great refinement of the post-imperial aristocracy of France may be one reason why the deficiencies of those now often found mixed up with them is so remarkable. It would be difficult to imagine a contrast in manner more striking than that of a lady who would be a fair specimen of the old Bourbon *noblesse*, and a bouncing *maréchale* of Imperial creation. It seems as if every particle of the whole material of which each is formed gave evidence of the different birth of the spirit that dwells within. The sound of the voice is a contrast; the glance of the eye is a contrast; the smile is a contrast; the step is a contrast. Were every feature of a *dame de l'Empire* and a *femme noble* formed precisely in the same mould, I am quite sure that the two would look no more alike than Queen Constance and Nell Gwyn.

Nor is there at all less difference in the two races of gentlemen. I speak not of the men of science or of art; their rank is of another kind: but there are still left here and there specimens of decorated greatness which look as if they must have been dragged out of the guard-room by main force; huge moustached *militaires*, who look at every slight rebuff as if they were ready to exclaim, 'Sacré nom de D——! je suis un héros, moi! Vive l'Empereur!'

A good deal is sneeringly said respecting the parvenus fashionables of the present day: but station, and place, and court favour, must at any rate give something of reality to the importance of those whom the last movement has brought to the top; and this is vastly less offensive than the empty, vulgar, camp-like reminiscences of Imperial patronage which are occasionally brought forward by those who may thank their sabre for having cut a path for them into the salons of Paris. The really great men of the Empire – and there are certainly many of them – have taken care to have other claims to distinction attached to their names than that of having been dragged out of heaven knows what profound obscurity by Napoleon: I may say of such, in the words of the soldier in Macbeth –

> 'If I say sooth, I must report they were
> As cannon overcharged with double cracks.'

As for the elderly ladies, who, from simple little bourgeoises demoiselles, were in those belligerent days sabred and trumpeted into maréchales and duchesses, I must think that they make infinitely worse figures in a drawing-room, than those who younger in years and newer in dignity, have all their blushing honours fresh upon them. Besides, in point of fact, the having one Bourbon prince instead of another upon the throne, though greatly to be lamented from the manner in which it was accomplished, can hardly be expected to produce so violent a convulsion among the aristocracy of France, as must of necessity have ensued from the reign of a soldier of fortune, though the mightiest that ever bore arms.

Many of the noblest races of France still remain wedded to the soil that has been for ages native to their name. Towards these it is believed that King Louis-Philippe has no very repulsive feelings; and should no farther changes come upon the country – no more immortal days arise to push all men from their stools, it is probable that the number of these will not diminish in the court circles.

Meanwhile, the haut-ton born during the last revolution must of course have an undisputed *entrée* everywhere; and if by any external marks they are particularly brought forward to observation, it is only, I think, by a toilet among the ladies more costly and less simple than that of their high-born neighbours; and among the gentlemen, by a general air of prosperity and satisfaction, with an expression of eye sometimes a little triumphant, often a little patronizing, and always a little busy.

It was a duchess, and no less, who decidedly gave me the most perfect idea of an Imperial parvenue that I have ever seen off the stage. When a lady of this class attains so very elevated a rank, the perils of her false position multiply around her. A quiet bourgeoise turned into a noble lady of the third or fourth degree is likely enough to look a little awkward; but if she has the least tact in the world, she may remain tranquil and *sans ridicule* under the honourable shelter of those above her. But when she becomes a duchess, the chances are terribly against her: 'Madame la Duchesse' must be conspicuous; and if in addition to mauvais ton she should par malheur be a bel esprit, adding the pretension of literature to that of station, it is likely that she will be very remarkable indeed.

My parvenue duchess *is* very remarkable indeed. She steps out like a corporal carrying a message: her voice is the first, the last, and almost the only thing heard in the salon that she honours with her presence, – except it chance, indeed, that she

Soiree.

lower her tone occasionally to favour with a whisper some gallant *décoré*, military, scientific, or artistic, of the same standing as herself; and moreover, she promenades her eyes over the company as if she had a right to bring them all to roll-call.

Notwithstanding all this, the lady is certainly a person of talent; and had she happily remained in the station in which both herself and her husband were born, she might not perhaps have thought it necessary to speak quite so loud, and her bons mots would have produced infinitely greater effect. But she is so thoroughly out of place in the grade to which she has been unkindly elevated, that it seems as if Napoleon had decided on her fate in a humour as spiteful as that of Monsieur Jourdain, when he said –

'Votre fille sera marquise, en dépit de tout le monde: et si vous me mettez en colère, je la ferai duchesse.'

LETTER XLV

The great reputation of another preacher induced us on
Sunday to endure two hours more of tedious waiting before
the mass which preceded the sermon began. It is only thus that
a chair can be hoped for when the Abbé Lacordaire mounts the
pulpit of Notre Dame. The penalty is really heavy; but having
heard this celebrated person described as one who 'appeared
sent by Heaven to restore France to Christianity' – as 'a
hypocrite that set Tartuffe immeasurably in the background' –
as 'a man whose talent surpassed that of any preacher since
Bossuet' – and as 'a charlatan who ought to harangue from a
tub, instead of from the *chaire de Notre Dame de Paris*,' – I
determined upon at least seeing and hearing him, however
little I might be able to decide on which of the two sides of the
prodigious chasm that yawned between his friends and
enemies the truth was most likely to be found. There were,
however, several circumstances which lessened the tedium of
this long interval: I might go farther, and confess that this
period was by no means the least profitable portion of the four
hours which we passed in the church.

On entering, we found the whole of the enormous nave
railed in, as it had been on Easter Sunday for the concert (for
so in truth should that performance be called); but upon
applying at the entrance to this enclosure, we were told that no
ladies could be admitted to that part of the church – but that
the side aisles were fully furnished with chairs, and afforded
excellent places.

This arrangement astonished me in many ways: – first, as
being so perfectly un-national; for go where you will in

France, you find the best places reserved for the women, – at least, this was the first instance in which I ever found it otherwise. Next, it astonished me, because at every church I had entered, the congregations, though always crowded, had been composed of at least twelve women to one man. When, therefore, I looked over the barrier upon the close-packed, well-adjusted rows of seats prepared to receive fifteen hundred persons, I thought that unless all the priests in Paris came in person to do honour to their eloquent confrère, it was very unlikely that this uncivil arrangement should be found necessary. There was no time, however, to waste in conjecture; the crowd already came rushing in at every door, and we hastened to secure the best places that the side aisles afforded. We obtained seats between the pillars immediately opposite to the pulpit, and felt well enough contented, having little doubt that a voice which had made itself heard so well must have power to reach even to the side aisles of Notre Dame.

The first consolation which I found for my long waiting, after placing myself in that attitude of little ease which the straight-backed chair allowed, was from the recollection that the interval was to be passed within the venerable walls of Notre Dame. It is a glorious old church, and though not comparable in any way to Westminster Abbey, or to Antwerp, or Strasburg, or Cologne, or indeed to many others which I might name, has enough to occupy the eye very satisfactorily for a considerable time. The three elegant rose-windows, throwing in their coloured light from north, west, and south, are of themselves a very pretty study for half an hour or so; and besides, they brought back, notwithstanding their miniature diameter of forty feet, the remembrance of the magnificent circular western window of Strasburg – the recollection of which was almost enough to while away another long interval. Then I employed myself, not very successfully, in labouring to recollect the quaint old verses which I had fallen upon a few days before, giving the dimensions of the church, and which I will herewith transcribe for your use and amusement, in case you should ever find yourself sitting as I was, *bolt upright*, as we elegantly express ourselves when describing this ecclesiastical-Parisian attitude, while waiting the advent of the Abbé Lacordaire.

'Si tu veux savoir comme est ample
De Notre Dame le grand temple,
Il y a, dans oeuvre, pour le seur,
Dix et sept toises de hauteur,
Sur la largeur de vingt-quatre,
Et soixante-cinq, sans rebattre,
A de long; aux tours haut montées
Trente-quatre sont comptées;
Le tout fondé sur pilotis –
Aussi vrai que je te le dis.'

While repeating this poetical description, you have only to remember that *une toise* is the same as a fathom, – that is to say, six feet; and then, as you turn your head in all directions to look about you, you will have the satisfaction of knowing exactly how far you can see in each.

I had another source of amusement, and by no means a trifling one, in watching the influx of company. The whole building soon contained as many human beings as could be crammed into it; and the seats, which we thought, as we took them, were very so-so places indeed, became accommodations for which to be most heartily thankful. Not a pillar but supported the backs of as many men as could stand round it; and not a jutting ornament, the balustrade of a side altar, or any other 'point of 'vantage,' but looked as if a swarm of bees were beginning to hang upon it.

But the sight which drew my attention most was that displayed by the exclusive central aisle. When told that it was reserved for gentlemen, I imagined of course that I should see it filled by a collection of staid-looking, middle-aged, Catholic citizens, who were drawn together from all parts of the town, and perhaps the country too, for the purpose of hearing the celebrated preacher: but, to my great astonishment, instead of this I saw pouring in by dozens at a time, gay, gallant, smart-looking young men, such indeed as I had rarely seen in Paris on any other religious occasion. Amongst these was a sprinkling of older men; but the great majority were decidedly under thirty. The meaning of this phenomenon I could by no means understand; but while I was tormenting myself to discover some method of obtaining information respecting it, accident brought relief to my curiosity in the shape of a communicative neighbour.

In no place in the world is it so easy, I believe, to enter into conversation with strangers as in Paris. There is a courteous inclination to welcome every attempt at doing so which pervades all ranks, and any one who wishes it may easily find or make opportunities of hearing the opinions of all classes. The present time, too, is peculiarly favourable for this; a careless freedom in uttering opinions of all kinds being, I think, the most remarkable feature in the manners of Paris at the present day.

I have heard that it is difficult to get a tame, flat, short, matter-of-fact answer from a genuine Irishman; – from a genuine Frenchman it is impossible: let his reply to a question which seeks information contain as little of it as the dry Anglicism 'I don't know,' it is never given without a tone or a turn of phrase that not only relieves its inanity, but leaves you with the agreeable persuasion that the speaker would be more satisfactory if he could, and moreover that he would be extremely happy to reply to any further questions you may wish to ask, either on the same, or any other subject whatever.

It was in consequence of my moving my chair an inch and a half to accommodate the long limbs of a grey-headed neighbour, that he was induced to follow his 'Milles pardons, madame!' with an observation on the inconvenience endured on the present occasion by the appropriation of all the best places to the gentlemen. It was quite contrary, he added, to the usual spirit of Parisian arrangements; and yet, in fact, it was the only means of preventing the ladies suffering from the tremendous rush of *jeunes gens* who constantly came to hear the Abbé Lacordaire.

'I never saw so large a proportion of young men in any congregation,' said I, hoping he might explain the mystery to me. What I heard, however, rather startled than enlightened me.

'The Catholic religion was never so likely to be spread over the whole earth as it is at present,' he replied. 'The kingdom of Ireland will speedily become fully reconciled to the see of Rome. Le Sieur O'Connell desires to be canonized. Nothing, in truth, remains for that portion of your country to do, but to follow the example we set during our famous Three Days, and place a prince of its own choosing upon the throne.'

I am persuaded that he thought we were Irish Roman Catholics: our sitting with such exemplary patience to wait for the preaching of this new apostle was not, I suppose, to be otherwise accounted for. I said nothing to undeceive him, but wishing to bring him back to speak of the congregation before us, I replied,

'Paris at least, if we may judge from the vast crowd collected here, is more religious than she has been of late years.'

'France,' replied he with energy, 'as you may see by looking at this throng, is no longer the France of 1823, when her priests sang canticles to the tune of "*Ça ira*". France is happily become most deeply and sincerely Catholic. Her priests are once more her orators, her magnates, her highest dignitaries. She may yet give cardinals to Rome – and Rome may again give a minister to France.'

I knew not what to answer: my silence did not seem to please him, and I believe he began to suspect he had mistaken the party altogether, for after sitting for a few minutes quite silent, he rose from the place into which he had pushed himself with considerable difficulty, and making his way through the crowd behind us, disappeared; but I saw him again, before we left the church, standing on the steps of the pulpit.

The chair he left was instantly occupied by another gentleman, who had before found standing-room near it. He had probably remarked our sociable propensities, for he immediately began talking to us.

'Did you ever see anything like the fashion which this man has obtained?' said he. 'Look at those *jeunes gens*, madame! . . . might one not fancy oneself at a première représentation?'

'Those must be greatly mistaken,' I replied, 'who assert that the young men of Paris are not among her *fidèles.*'

'Do you consider their appearing here a proof that they are religious?' inquired my neighbour with a smile.

'Certainly I do, sir,' I replied: 'how can I interpret it otherwise?'

'Perhaps not – perhaps to a stranger it must have this appearance; but to a man who knows Paris . . .' He smiled again very expressively, and, after a short pause, added – 'Depend upon it, that if a man of equal talent and eloquence with this Abbé Lacordaire were to deliver a weekly discourse in favour of atheism, these very identical young men would be present to hear him.'

'Once they might,' said I, 'from curiosity: but that they should follow him, as I understand they do, month after month, if what he uttered were at variance with their opinions, seems almost inconceivable.'

'And yet it is very certainly the fact,' he replied: 'whoever can contrive to obtain the reputation of talent at Paris, let the nature of it be of what kind it may, is quite sure that *les jeunes gens* will resort to hear and see him. They believe themselves of indefeasible right the sole arbitrators of intellectual reputation; and let the direction in which it is shown be as foreign as may be to their own pursuits, they come as a matter of prescriptive right to put their seal upon the aspirant's claim, or to refuse it.'

'Then, at least, they acknowledge that the Abbé's words have power, or they would not grant their suffrage to him.'

'They assuredly acknowledge that his words have eloquence; but if by power, you mean power of conviction, or conversion, I do assure you that they acknowledge nothing like it. Not only do I believe that these young men are themselves sceptics, but I do not imagine that there is one in ten of them who has the least faith in the Abbé's own orthodoxy.'

'But what right have they to doubt it? . . . Surely he would hardly be permitted to preach at Notre Dame, where the archbishop himself sits in judgment on him, were he otherwise than orthodox?'

'I was at school with him,' he replied: 'he was a fine sharp-witted boy, and gave very early demonstrations of a mind not particularly given either to credulity, or subservience to any doctrines that he found puzzling.'

'I should say this was the greatest proof of his present sincerity. He doubted as a boy – but as a man he believes.'

'That is not the way the story goes,' said he. 'But hark! there is the bell: the mass is about to commence.'

He was right: the organ pealed, the fine chant of the voices was heard above it, and in a few minutes we saw the archbishop and his splendid train escorting the Host to its ark upon the altar.

During the interval between the conclusion of the mass and the arrival of the Abbé Lacordaire in the pulpit, my sceptical neighbour again addressed me.

'Are you prepared to be very much enchanted by what you are going to hear?' said he.

'I hardly know what to expect,' I replied: 'I think my idea of the preacher was higher when I came here, than since I have heard you speak of him.'

'You will find that he has a prodigious flow of words, much vehement gesticulation, and a very impassioned manner. This is quite sufficient to establish his reputation for eloquence among *les jeunes gens.*'

'But I presume you do not yourself subscribe to the sentence pronounced by these young critics?'

'Yes, I do, – as far, at least, as to acknowledge that this man has not attained his reputation without having displayed great ability. But though all the talent of Paris has long consented to receive its crown of laurels from the hands of her young men, it would be hardly reasonable to expect that their judgment should be as profound as their power is great.'

'Your obedience to this beardless synod is certainly very extraordinary,' said I: 'I cannot understand it.'

'I suppose not,' said he, laughing; 'it is quite a Paris fashion; but we all seem contented that it should be so. If a new play appears, its fate must be decided by *les jeunes gens*; if a picture is exhibited, its rank amidst the works of modern art can only be settled by them: does a dancer, a singer, an actor, or a preacher appear – a new member in the tribune, or a new prince upon the throne, – it is still *les jeunes gens* who must pass judgment on them all; and this judgment is quoted with a degree of deference utterly inconceivable to a stranger.'

'Chut! . . . chut!' . . . was at this moment uttered by more than one voice near us: 'le voilà!' I glanced my eye towards the pulpit, but it was still empty; and on looking round me, I perceived that all eyes were turned in the direction of a small door in the north aisle, almost immediately behind us. 'Il est entré là!' said a young woman near us, in a tone that seemed to indicate a feeling deeper than respect, and, in truth, not far removed from adoration. Her eyes were still earnestly fixed upon the door, and continued to be so, as well as those of many others, till it reopened and a slight young man in the dress of a priest prepared for the *chaire* appeared at it. A verger made way for him through the crowd, which, thick and closely wedged as it was, fell back on each side of him, as he proceeded to the pulpit, with much more docility than I ever saw produced by the clearing a passage through the intervention of a troop of horse.

Silence the most profound accompanied his progress; I never witnessed more striking demonstrations of respect: and yet it is said that three-fourths of Paris believe this man to be a hypocrite.

As soon as he had reached the pulpit, and while preparing himself by silent prayer for the duty he was about to perform, a movement became perceptible at the upper part of the choir; and presently the archbishop and his splendid retinue of clergy were seen moving in a body towards that part of the nave which is immediately in front of the preacher. On arriving at the space reserved for them, each noiselessly dropped into his allotted seat according to his place and dignity, while the whole congregation respectfully stood to watch the cer-emony, and seemed to

'Admirer un si bel ordre, et reconnaître l'église.'

It is easier to describe to you everything which preceded the sermon, than the sermon itself. This was such a rush of words, such a burst and pouring out of passionate declamation, that even before I had heard enough to judge of the matter, I felt disposed to prejudge the preacher, and to suspect that his discourse would have more of the flourish and furbelow of human rhetoric than of the simplicity of divine truth in it.

His violent action too, disgusted me exceedingly. The rapid and incessant movement of his hands, sometimes of one, sometimes of both, more resembled that of the wings of a humming-bird than anything else I can remember: but the *hum* proceeded from the admiring congregation. At every pause he made, and like the claptraps of a bad actor, they were frequent, and evidently faits exprès: a little gentle laudatory murmur ran through the crowd.

I remember reading somewhere of a priest nobly born, and so anxious to keep his flock in their proper place, that they might not come 'between the wind and his nobility,' that his constant address to them when preaching was, 'Canaille Chrétienne!' This was bad – very bad, certainly; but I protest, I doubt if the Abbé Lacordaire's manner of addressing his congregation as 'Messieurs' was much less unlike the fitting tone of a Christian pastor. This mundane apostrophe was continually repeated throughout the whole discourse, and, I dare say, had its share in producing the disagreeable effect I experienced from his eloquence. I cannot remember having ever heard a preacher I less liked, reverenced, and admired, than this new Parisian saint. He made very pointed allusions to the reviving state of the Roman Catholic Church in Ireland, and anathematized pretty cordially all such as should oppose it.

In describing the two hours' prologue to the mass, I forgot to mention that many young men – not in the reserved places of the centre aisle, but sitting near us, beguiled the tedious interval by reading. Some of the volumes they held had the appearance of novels from a circulating library, and others were evidently collections of songs, probably less spiritual than *spirituels*.

The whole exhibition certainly showed me a new page in the history of *Paris as it is*, and I therefore do not regret the four hours it cost me: but once is enough – I certainly will never go to hear the Abbé Lacordaire again.

LETTER XLVI

La Tour de Nesle

It is, I believe, nearly two years ago since the very extraordinary drama called 'La Tour de Nesle' was sent me to read, as a specimen of the outrageous school of dramatic extravagance which had taken possession of all the theatres in Paris; but I certainly did not expect that it would keep its place as a favourite spectacle with the people of this great and enlightened capital long enough for me to see it, at this distance of time, still played before a very crowded audience.

That this is a national disgrace, is most certain: but the fault is less attributable to the want of good taste, than to the lamentable blunder which permits every species of vice and abomination to be enacted before the eyes of the people, without any restraint or check whatever, under the notion that they are thereby permitted to enjoy a desirable privilege and a noble freedom. Yet in this same country it is illegal to sell a deleterious drug! There is no logic in this.

It is however an undeniable fact, as I think I have before stated, that the best class of Parisian society protest against this disgusting license, and avoid – upon principle loudly proclaimed and avowed – either reading or seeing acted these detestable compositions. Thus, though the crowded audiences contantly assembled whenever they are brought forward prove but too clearly that such persons form but a small minority, their opinion is nevertheless sufficient, or ought to be so, to save the country from the disgrace of admitting that such things are good.

We seem to pique ourselves greatly on the superiority of our taste in these matters; but let us pique ourselves rather on our theatrical censorship. Should the clamours and shoutings of misrule lead to the abolition of this salutary restraint, the consequences would, I fear, be such as very soon to rob us of our present privilege of abusing our neighbours on this point.

While things do remain as they are, however, we may, I think, smile a little at such a judgment as Monsieur de Saintfoix passes upon our theatrical compositions, when comparing them to those of France.

'Les actions de nos tragédies,' says he, 'sont pathétiques et terribles: celles des tragédies angloises sont atroces. On y met sous les yeux du spectateur les objets les plus horribles; un mari qui discourt avec sa femme, qui la caresse et l'étrangle.'

Might one not think that the writer of this passage had just arrived from witnessing the famous scene in the 'Monomane,' only he had mistaken it for English? But he goes on –

'Une fille toute sanglante . . .' (Triboulet's daughter Blanche, for instance.) – 'Après l'avoir violée . . .'

He then proceeds to reason upon the subject, and justly enough, I think – only we should read England for France, and France for England.

'Il n'est pas douteux que les arts agréables ne réussissent chez un peuple qu'autant qu'ils en prennent le génie, et qu'un auteur dramatique ne sauroit espérer de plaire si les objects et les images qu'il présente ne sont pas analogues au caractère, au naturel, et au goût de la nation: on pourroit donc conclure de la différence des deux théâtres, que l'âme d'un ANGLAIS est sombre, féroce, sanguinaire; et que celle d'un FRANÇAIS est vive, impatiente, emportée, mais généreuse même dans sa haine; idolatrant l'honneur' – (just like Buridan in this same drama of the Tour de Nesle – this popular production of *la Jeune France* – *la France régénerée*) – 'idolatrant l'honneur, et ne cessant jamais de l'apercevoir, malgré le trouble et toute la violence des passions.'

Though it is impossible to read this passage without a smile, at a time when it is so easy for the English to turn the tables against this patriotic author, one must sigh too, while reflecting on the lamentable change which has taken place in the moral feeling of revolutionised France since the period at which it was written.

What would Saintfoix say to the notion that Victor Hugo had 'heaved the ground from beneath the feet of Corneille and Racine'? The question, however, is answered by a short sentence in his 'Essais Historiques,' where he thus expresses himself:–

'Je croirois que la décadence de notre nation seroit prochaine, si les hommes de quarante ans n'y regardoient pas CORNEILLE comme le plus grand génie qui ait jamais été.'

If the spirit of the historian were to revisit the earth, and float over the heads of a party of Parisian critics while pronouncing sentence on his favourite author, he might probably return to the shades unharmed, for he would only hear 'Rococo! Rococo! Rococo,' uttered as by acclamation; and unskilled to comprehend the new-born eloquence, he would doubtless interpret it as a *refrain* to express in one pithy word all reverence, admiration, and delight.

But to return to 'La Tour de Nesle.' The story is taken from a passage in Brantôme's history 'des Femmes Galantes,' where he says, 'qu'une reine de France' – whom however he does not name, but who is said to have been Marguérite de Bourgogne, wife of Louis Dix – 'se tenoit là (à la Tour de Nesle) d'ordinaire, laquelle fesant le guet aux passans, et ceux qui lui revenoient et agréoient le plus, de quelque sorte de gens que ce fussent, les fesoit appeler et venir à soy, et après . . . les fesoit précipiter du haut de la tour en bas, en l'eau, et les fesoit noyer. Je ne veux pas,' he continues, 'assurer que cela soit vrai, mais le vulgaire, au moins la plupart de Paris, l'affirme, et n'y a si commun qu'en lui montrant la tour seulement, et en l'interrogeant, que de lui-même ne le die.'

This story one might imagine was horrible and disgusting enough; but MM. Gaillardet et —— (it is thus the authors announce themselves) thought otherwise, and accordingly they have introduced her majesty's sisters, the ladies Jeanne and Blanche of Burgundy, who were both likewise married to sons of Philippe-le-Bel, the brothers of Louis Dix, to share her nocturnal orgies. These 'imaginative and powerful' scenic historians also, according to the fashion of the day among the theatrical writers of France, add incest to increase the interest of the drama.

This is enough, and too much, as to the plot; and for the execution of it by the authors, I can only say that it is about equal in literary merit to the translations of an Italian opera handed about at the Haymarket. It is in prose – and, to my judgment, very vulgar prose; yet it is not only constantly acted, but I am assured that the sale of it has been prodigiously great, and still continues to be so.

That a fearful and even hateful story, dressed up in all the attractive charm of majestic poetry, and redeemed in some sort by the noble sentiments of the personages brought into the scenes of which it might be the foundation – that a drama so formed might captivate the imagination even while it revolted the feelings, is very possible, very natural, and nowise disgraceful either to the poet, or to those whom his talent may lead captive. The classic tragedies which long served as models to France abound in fables of this description. Alfieri, too, has made use of such, following with a poet's wing the steady onward flight of remorseless destiny, yet still sublime in pathos and in dignity, though appalling in horror. In like manner, the great French dramatists have triumphed by the power of their genius, both over the disgust inspired by these awful classic mysteries, and the unbending strictness of the laws which their antique models enforced for their composition.

If we may herein deem the taste to have been faulty, the grace, the majesty, the unswerving dignity of the tragic march throughout the whole action – the lofty sentiments, the bursts of noble passion, and the fine drapery of stately verse in which the whole was clothed, must nevertheless raise our admiration to a degree that may perhaps almost compete with what we feel for the enchanting wildness and unshackled nature of our native dramas.

But what can we think of those who, having ransacked the pages of history to discover whatever was most revolting to the human soul, should sit down to arrange it in action, detailed at full length, with every hateful circumstance exaggerated and brought out to view for the purpose of tickling the curiosity of his countrymen and countrywomen, and by that means beguiling them into the contemplation of scenes that Virtue would turn from with loathing, and before which Innocence must perish as she gazes? No gleam of goodness throughout the whole for the heart to cling to, – no thought of remorseful penitence, – no spark of noble feeling; nothing but vice, – low, grovelling, brutal vice, – from the moment the curtain rises to display the obscene spectacle, to that which sees it fall between the fictitious infamy on one side, and the real impurity left on the other!

As I looked on upon the hideous scene, and remembered the classic horrors of the Greek tragedians, and of the mighty imitators who have followed them, I could not help thinking that the performance of MM. Gaillardet et —— was exceedingly like that of a monkey mimicking the operations of a man. He gets hold of the same tools, but turns the edges the wrong way; and instead of raising a majestic fabric in honour of human genius, he rolls the materials in mud, begrimes his own paws in the slimy cement, and then claws hold of every unwary passenger who comes within his reach, and bespatters him with the rubbish he has brought together. Such monkeys should be chained, or they will do much mischief.

It is hardly possible that such dramas as the 'Tour de Nesle' can be composed with the intention of producing a great tragic effect; which is surely the only reason which can justify bringing sin and misery before the eyes of an audience. There is in almost every human heart a strange love for scenes of terror and of woe. We love to have our sympathies awakened – our deepest feelings roused; we love to study in the magic mirror of the scene what we ourselves might feel did such awful visitations come upon us; and there is an unspeakable interest inspired by looking on, and fancying that were it so with us, we might so act, so feel, so suffer, and so die. But is there in any land a wretch so lost, so vile, as to be capable of feeling sympathy with any sentiment or thought expressed throughout the whole progress of this 'Tour de Nesle'? God forbid!

I have heard of poets who have written under the inspiration of brandy and laudanum – the exhalations from which are certainly not likely to form themselves into images of distinctness or beauty; but the inspiration that dictated the 'Tour de Nesle' must have been something viler still, though not less powerful. It must, I think, have been the cruel calculation of how many dirty francs might be expressed from the pockets of the idle, by a spectacle new from its depth of atrocity, and attractive from its newness.

But, setting aside for a moment the sin and the scandal of producing on a public stage such a being as the woman to whom MM. Gaillardet et —— have chosen to give the name of Marguérite de Bourgogne, it is an object of some curiosity to examine the literary merits of a piece which, both on the stage and in the study, has been received by so many thousands – perhaps millions – of individuals belonging to '*la grande nation*' as a work deserving their patronage and support – or at least as deserving their attention and attendance for years; years, too, of hourly progressive intellect – years during which the march of mind has outdone all former marches of human intelligence – years during which Young France has been labouring to throw off her ancient coat of worn-out rococoism, and to clothe herself in new-fledged brightness. During these years she has laid on one shelf her once-venerated Corneille, – on another, her almost worshipped Racine. Molière is named but as a fine antique; and Voltaire himself, spite of his strong claims upon their revolutionary affections, can hardly be forgiven for having said of the two whom Victor Hugo is declared to have overthrown, that 'Ces hommes enseignèrent à la nation, à penser, à sentir, à s'exprimer; leurs auditeurs, instruits par eux seuls, devinrent enfin des juges sévères pour eux mêmes qui les avaient éclairés.' Let any one whose reason is not totally overthrown by the fever and delirium of innovation read the 'Tour de Nesle,' and find out if he can any single scene, speech, or phrase deserving the suffrage which Paris has accorded to it. Has the dialogue either dignity, spirit, or truth of nature to recommend it? Is there a single sentiment throughout the five acts with which an honest man can accord? Is there even an approach to grace or beauty in the *tableaux*? or skill in the arrangement of the scenes? or keeping of character among the demoniacal *dramatis personae* which MM. Gaillardet et —— have brought together? or, in short, any one merit to recommend it – except only its superlative defiance of common decency and common sense?

If there be any left among the men of France; I speak not now of her boys, the spoilt grandchildren of the old revolution; – but if there be any left among her men, as I in truth believe there are, who deprecate this eclipse of her literary glory, is it not sad that they should be forced to permit its toleration, for fear they should be sent to Ham for interfering with the liberty of the press?

It is impossible to witness the representation of one of these infamous pieces without perceiving, as you glance your eye around the house, who are its patrons and supporters. At no great distance from us, when we saw the 'Tour de Nesle,' were three young men who had all of them a most thoroughly '*jeunes gens*' and republican cast of countenance, and tournure of person and dress. They tossed their heads and snuffed the theatrical air of '*la Jeune France*,' as if they felt that they were, or ought to be, her masters: and it is a positive fact that nothing pre-eminently absurd or offensive was done or said upon the stage, which this trio did not mark with particular admiration and applause.

There was, however, such a saucy look of determination to do what they knew was absurd, that I gave them credit for being aware of the nonsense of what they applauded, from the very fact that they did applaud it.

It is easy enough sometimes to discover 'le vrai au travers du ridicule;' and these silly boys were not, I am persuaded, such utter blockheads as they endeavoured to appear. It is a bad and mischievous tone, however; and the affecting a vice where you have it not, is quite as detestable a sort of hypocrisy as any other.

Some thousand years hence perhaps, if any curious collectors of rare copies should contrive among them to preserve specimens of the French dramas of the present day, it may happen that while the times that are gone shall continue to be classed as the Iron, the Golden, the Dark, and the Augustan ages, this day of ours may become familiar in all men's mouths as the Diabolic age, – unless, indeed, some charitable critic shall step forward in our defence, and bestow upon it the gentler appellation of 'the Idiot era.'

LETTER XLVII

Palais Royal – Variety of characters – Party of English –
Restaurant – Galerie d'Orléans – Number of Loungers –
Convenient abundance of Idle Men – Théâtre du Vaudeville

Though, as a lady, you may fancy yourself quite beyond the
possibility of ever feeling any interest in the Palais Royal, its
restaurans, its trinket-shops, ribbon-shops, toy-shops &c. &c.
&c. and all the world of misery, mischief, and good cheer
which rises *étage* after *étage* above them; I must nevertheless
indulge in a little gossip respecting it, because few things in
Paris – I might, I believe, say nothing – can show an aspect so
completely un-English in all ways as this singular region. The
palace itself is stately and imposing, though not externally in
the very best taste. Corneille, however, says of it, –

> 'L'univers entier ne peut voir rien d'égal
> Au superbe dehors du Palais Cardinal,'

as it was called from having been built and inhabited by the
Cardinal de Richelieu. But it is the use made of the space
which was originally the Cardinal's garden, which gives the
place its present interest.

All the world – men, women and children, gentle and
simple, rich and poor, – in short, I suppose every living soul
that enters Paris, is taken to look at the Palais Royal. But
though many strangers linger there, alas! all too long, there are
many others who, according to my notions, do not linger
there long enough. The quickest eye cannot catch at one
glance, though that glance be in activity during a tour made
round the whole enclosure, all the national characteristic,
picturesque, and comic groups which float about there
incessantly through at least twenty hours of the twenty-four. I
know that the Palais Royal is a study which, in its higher

299

walks and profoundest depths, it would be equally difficult, dangerous, and disagreeable to pursue: but with these altitudes and profundities I have nothing to do; there are abundance of objects to be seen there, calculated and intended to meet the eyes of all men, and women too, which may furnish matter for observation, without either diving or climbing in pursuit of knowledge that, after all, would be better lost than found.

But one should have the talent of Hogarth to describe the different groups, with all their varied little episodes of peculiarity, which render the Palais Royal so amusing. These groups are, to be sure, made up only of Parisians, and of the wanderers who visit *la belle ville* in order to see and be seen in every part of it; yet it is in vain that you would seek elsewhere the same odd selection of human beings that are to be found *sans faute* in every corner of the Palais Royal.

How it happens I know not, but so it is, that almost every person you meet here furnishes food for speculation. If it be an elegant well-appointed man of fashion, the fancy instantly tracks him to a *salon de jeu*; and if you are very good-natured, your heart will ache to think how much misery he is likely to carry home with him. If it be a low, skulking, semi-genteel *moustache*, with large, dark, deep-set eyes rolling about to see whom he can devour, you are as certain that he too is making for a salon, as that a man with a rod and line on his shoulder is going to fish. That pretty *soubrette*, with her neat heels and smart silk apron, who has evidently a few francs tied up in the corner of the handkerchief which she holds in her hand – do we not know that she is peering through the window of every trinket-shop to see where she can descry the most tempting gold ear-rings, for the purchase of which a quarter's wages are about to be dis-kerchiefed?

We must not overlook, and indeed it would not be easy to do so, that well-defined domestic party of our country-folks who have just turned into the superb Galerie d'Orléans. Father, mother, and daughters – how easy to guess their thoughts, and almost their words! The portly father declares that it would make a capital Exchange: he has not yet seen La Bourse. He looks up to its noble height – then steps forward a pace or two, and measures with his eye the space on all sides – then stops, and perhaps says to the stately lady on his arm, (whose eyes meanwhile are wandering amidst shawls, gloves, Cologne bottles, and Sèvres china, first on one side and then on the other,) – 'This is not badly built; it is light and lofty – and the width is very considerable for so slight-looking a roof; but what is it compared to Waterloo-bridge!'

Two pretty girls, with bright cheeks, dove-like eyes, and 'tresses like the morn,' falling in unnumbered ringlets, so as almost to hide their curious yet timid glances, precede the parent pair; but, with pretty well-taught caution, pause when they pause, and step on when they step on. But they can hardly look at anything; for do they not know, though their downcast eyes can hardly be said to see it, that those youths with coal-black hair, favoris and imperials, are spying at them with their lorgnettes?

Here too, as at the Tuileries, are little pavilions to supply the insatiable thirst for politics; and here, too, we could distinguish the melancholy champion of the elder branch of the Bourbons, who is at least sure to find the consolation of his faithful 'Quotidienne,' and the sympathy of 'La France.' The sour republican stalks up, as usual, to seize upon the 'Réformateur;' while the comfortable doctrinaire comes forth from the Café Véry, ruminating on the 'Journal des Débats,' and the chances of his bargains at Tortoni's or La Bourse.

It was in a walk taken round three sides of the square that we marked the figures I have mentioned, and many more too numerous to record, on a day that we had fixed upon to gratify our curiosity by dining – not at Véry's, or any other far-famed artist's, but tout bonnement at a restaurant of quarante sous par tête. Having made our tour, we mounted au second at numéro – I forget what, but it was where we had been especially recommended to make this coup d'essai. The scene we entered upon, as we followed a long string of persons who preceded us, was as amusing as it was new to us all.

I will not say that I should like to dine three days in the week at the Palais Royal for quarante sous par tête; but I will say, that I should have been very sorry not to have done it once, and moreover, that I heartily hope I may do it again.

The dinner was extremely good, and as varied as our fancy chose to make it, each person having privilege to select three or four plats from a carte that it would take a day to read deliberately. But the dinner was certainly to us the least important part of the business. The novelty of the spectacle, the number of strange-looking people, and the perfect amenity and good-breeding which seemed to reign among them all, made us look about us with a degree of interest and curiosity that almost caused the whole party to forget the ostensible cause of their visit.

There were many English, chiefly gentlemen, and several Germans with their wives and daughters; but the majority of the company was French; and from sundry little circumstances respecting taking the places reserved for them, and different words of intelligence between themselves and the waiters, it was evident that many among them were not chance visitors, but in the daily habit of dining there. What a singular mode of existence is this, and how utterly inconceivable to English feelings! . . . Yet habit, and perhaps prejudice, apart, it is not difficult to perceive that it has its advantages. In the first place, there is no management in the world, not even that of Mrs. Primrose herself, which could enable a man to dine at home, for the sum of two francs, with the same degree of luxury as to what he eats, that he does at one of these restaurans. Five hundred persons are calculated upon as the daily average of company expected; and forty pounds of ready money in Paris, with the skilful aid of French cooks, will furnish forth a dinner for this number, and leave some profit besides. Add to which, the sale of wine is, I believe, considerable. Some part of the receipts, however, must be withdrawn as interest upon the capital employed. The quantity of plate is very abundant, not only in the apparently unlimited supply of forks and spoons, but in furnishing the multitude of grim-looking silver bowls in which the *potage* is served.

On the whole, however, I can better understand the possibility of five hundred dinners being furnished daily for two francs each, by one of these innumerable establishments, than I can the marvel of five hundred people being daily found by each of these to eat them. Hundreds of these houses exist in Paris, and all of them are constantly furnished with guests. But this manner of living, so unnatural to us, seems not only natural, but needful to them. They do it all so well – so pleasantly! Imagine for a moment the sort of tone and style such a dining-room would take in London. I do not mean, if limited to the same price, but set it greatly beyond the proportion: let us imagine an establishment where males and females should dine at five shillings a-head – what din, what unsocial, yet vehement chattering, would inevitably ensue! – not to mention the utter improbability that such a place, really and *bonâ fide* open to the public, should continue a reputable resort for ladies for a week after its doors were open.

But here, everything was as perfectly respectable and well-arranged as if each little table had been placed with its separate party in a private room at Mivart's. It is but fair, therefore, that while we hug ourselves, as we are all apt to do, on the refinement which renders the exclusive privacy of our own dining-rooms necessary to our feelings of comfort, we should allow that equal refinement, though of another kind, must exist among those who, when thrown thus pro-miscuously together, still retain and manifest towards each other the same deference and good-breeding which we require of those whom we admit to our private circle.

At this restaurant, as everywhere else in Paris, we found it easy enough to class our *gens*. I feel quite sure that we had around us many of the employés du gouvernement actuel – several anciens militaires of Napoleon's – some specimens of the race distinguished by Louis Dix-huit and Charles Dix – and even, if I do not greatly mistake, a few relics of the Convention, and of the unfortunate monarch who was its victim.

But during this hour of rest and enjoyment all differences seem forgotten; and however discordant may be their feelings, two Frenchmen cannot be seated near each other at table, without exchanging numberless civilities, and at last entering into conversation, so well sustained and so animated, that instead of taking them for strangers who had never met before, we, in our stately shyness, would be ready to pronounce that they must be familiar friends.

Whether it be this *causant,* social temper which makes them prefer thus living in public, or that thus living in public makes them social, I cannot determine to my own satisfaction; but the one is not more remarkable and more totally unlike our own manners than the other, and I really think that no one who has not dined thus in Paris can have any idea how very wide, in some directions, the line of demarcation is between the two countries.

I have on former occasions dined with a party at places of much higher price, where the object was to observe what a very good dinner a very good cook could produce in Paris. But this experiment offered nothing to our observation at all approaching in interest and nationality to the dinner of quarante sous.

In the first place, you are much more likely to meet English than French society at these costly repasts; and in the second, if you do encounter at them a genuine native gourmet of la Grande Nation, he will, upon this occasion, be only doing like ourselves, – that is to say, giving himself un repas exquis, instead of regaling himself at home with his family –

'Sur un lièvre flanqué de deux poulets étiques.'

But at the humble restaurant of two francs, you have again a new page of Paris existence to study, – and one which, while it will probably increase your English relish for your English home, will show you no unprofitable picture of the amiable social qualities of France. I think that if we could find a people composed in equal proportions of the two natures, they would be as near to social perfection as it is possible to imagine.

The French are almost too amiable to every one they chance to sit near. The lively smile, the kind empressement, the ready causerie, would be more flattering did we not know that it was all equally at the service of the whole world. Whereas we are more than equally wrong in the other extreme; having the air of suspecting that every human being who happens to be thrown into contact with us, before we know his birth, parentage, and education, is something very dangerous, and to be guarded against with all possible care and precaution. Query – Do not the Germans furnish something very like this juste milieu?

Having concluded our unexpensive repast with the prescribed tasse de café noir, we again sallied forth to take the tour of the Palais Royal, in order to occupy the time till the opening of the Théâtre du Vaudeville, with which, as we were so very close to it, we determined to finish the evening.

We returned, as we came, through the noble Galerie d'Orléans, which was now crowded with the assembled loungers of all the numerous restaurans. It is a gay and animated scene at any time of the day; but at this particular hour, just before the theatres open, and just after the gay people have all refreshed their animal spirits, Paris itself seems typified by the aspect of the lively, laughing, idle throng assembled there.

One reason, I believe, why Paris is so much more amusing to a looker-on than London, is, that it contains so many more people, in proportion to its population, who have nothing in the world to do but to divert themselves and others. There are so many more idle men here, who are contented to live on incomes that with us would be considered as hardly sufficient to supply a lodging; small rentiers, who prefer being masters of their own time and amusing themselves with a little, to working very hard and being very much ennuyés with a great deal of money. I am not quite sure that this plan answers well when youth is past – at least for the individuals themselves: it is probable, I think, that as the strength, and health, and spirits fade away, something of quieter and more substantial comfort must often be wished for, when perhaps it is too late to obtain it; but for others – for all those who form the circle round which the idle man of pleasure skims thus lightly, he is a never-failing resource. What would become of all the parties for amusement which take place morning, noon, and night in Paris, if this race were extinct? Whether they are married or single, they are equally eligible, equally necessary, equally welcome wherever pleasure makes the business of the hour. With us, it is only a small and highly-privileged class who can permit themselves to go wherever and whenever pleasure beckons; but in France, no lady arranging a fête, let it be of what kind it may, has need to think twice and thrice before she can answer the important but tormenting question of – 'But what men can we get?'

The Vaudeville was very full, but we contrived to get a good box au second, from whence we saw, greatly to our delectation and amusement, three pretty little pieces, – 'Les

Gants Jaunes,' 'Le Premier Amour,' and 'Elle est Folle;' which
last was of the larmoyante school, and much less to my taste
than the lively nonsense of the two former; yet it was
admirably well played too. But I always go to a vaudeville
with the intention of laughing; and if this purpose fail, I am
disappointed.

LETTER XLVIII

*Literary Conversation – Modern Novelists – Vicomte d'Arlincourt –
His Portrait – Châteaubriand – Bernardin de Saint Pierre –
Shakespeare – Sir Walter Scott – French familiarity with
English Authors – Miss Mitford – Miss Landon – Parisian
passion for Novelty – Extent of general Information*

We were last night at a small party where there was neither
dancing, music, cards, nor – (wonderful to say!) politics to
amuse or occupy us: nevertheless, it was one of the most
agreeable *soirées* at which I have been present in Paris. The
conversation was completely on literary subjects, but totally
without the pretension of a literary society. In fact, it was
purely the effect of accident; and it was just as likely that we
might have passed the evening in talking of pictures, or music,
or rocks and rivers, as of books. But Fate decreed that so it
should be; and the consequence was, that we had the pleasure
of hearing three Frenchmen and two Frenchwomen talk for
three hours of the literature of their country. I do not mean to
assert that no other person spoke – but the *frais de la*
conversation were certainly furnished by the five natives.

One of the gentlemen, and that too the oldest man in the
company, was more tolerant towards the present race of
French novel-writers than any person of his age and class that I
have yet conversed with; but nevertheless, his approval went
no farther than to declare that he thought the present mode of
following human nature with a microscope into all the recesses
to which passion, and even vice, could lead it, was calculated
to make a better novelist than the fashion which preceded it, of
looking at all things through a magnifying medium, and of
straining and striving, in consequence, to make that appear
great, which was by its nature essentially the reverse.

The Vicomte d'Arlincourt was the author he named to
establish the truth of his proposition: he would not admit him

307

to be an exaggeration of the school which has passsed away, but only the perfection of it.

'I remember,' said he, 'to have seen at the Louvre, many years ago, a full-length portrait of this gentleman, which I thought at the time was as perfect a symbol of what is called in France le style romantique, as it was well possible to conceive. He was standing erect on the rocky point of a precipice, with eye inspired, and tablets in his hand: a foaming torrent rolled its tortured waters at his feet, whilst he, calm and sublime, looked not 'comme une jeune beauté qu'on arrache au sommeil,' but very like a young incroyable snatched from a fashionable salon to meditate upon the wild majesty of nature, with all the inspiring adjuncts of tempest, wildness, and solitude. He appeared dressed in an elegant black coat and waistcoat, black silk stockings, and dancing pumps. It would be lost labour,' he continued, 'should I attempt to give you a more just idea of his style of writing than the composition of this portrait conveys. It is in vain that M. le Vicomte places himself amidst rocks and cataracts – he is still M. le Vicomte; and his silk stockings and dancing pumps will remain visible, spite of all the froth and foam he labours to raise around him.'

'It was not D'Arlincourt, however,' said M. de C——, 'who has either the honour or dishonour of having invented this *style romantique* – but a much greater man: it was Châteaubriand who first broke through all that was left of classic restraint, and permitted his imagination to run wild among everything in heaven and earth.'

'You cannot, however, accuse him of running this wild race with his imagination en habit bourgeois,' said the third gentleman: 'his style is extravagant, but never ludicrous; Châteaubriand really has, what D'Arlincourt affected to have, a poetical and abounding fancy, and a fecundity of imagery which has often betrayed him into bad taste from its very richness; but there is nothing strained, forced, and unnatural in his eloquence, – for eloquence it is, though a soberer imagination and a severer judgment might have kept it within more reasonable bounds. After all that can be said against his taste, Châteaubriand is a great man, and his name will live among the literati of France; but God forbid that any true prophet should predict the same of his imitators!'

'And God forbid that any true prophet should predict the same of the school that has succeeded them!' said Madame V—— – a delightful old woman, who wears her own grey hair, and does not waltz. 'I have sometimes laughed and sometimes yawned over the productions of the *école D'Arlincourt*,' she added; 'but I invariably turn with disgust and indignation from those of the domestic style which has succeeded to it.'

'Invariably?' . . . said the old gentleman interrogatively.

'Yes, invariably; because, if I see any symptom of talent, I lament it, and feel alarmed for the possible mischief which may ensue. I can never wish to see high mental power, which is the last and best gift of Heaven, perverted so shamelessly.'

'Come, come, dear lady,' replied the advocate of what Goethe impressively calls 'la littérature du désespoir', 'you must not overthrow the whole fabric because some portion of it is faulty. The object of our tale-writers at present is, beyond all doubt, to paint men as they are: if they succeed, their labours cannot fail of being interesting – and I should think they might be very useful too.'

'Fadaise que tout cela!' exclaimed the old lady eagerly. 'Before men can paint human nature profitably, they must see it as it really is, my good friend – and not as it appears to these *misérables* in their baraques and greniers. We have nothing to do with such scenes as they paint; and they have nothing to do (God help them!) with literary labours. Have you got Bernardin de Saint Pierre, ma chère?' said she, addressing the lady of the house. The little volume was immediately handed to her from a chiffonnière that stood behind us. 'Now this,' she continued, having found the passage she sought, – 'this is what I conceive to be the legitimate object of literature;' and she read aloud the following passage:-

'Les lettres sont un secours du Ciel. Ce sont des rayons de cette sagesse qui gouverne l'univers, que l'homme, inspiré par un art céleste, a appris à fixer sur la terre . . . Elles calment les passions; elles répriment les vices; elles excitent les vertus par les exemples augustes des gens de bien qu'elles célèbrent, et dont elles nous présentent les images toujours honorées.'

'Eh bien! a-t-il raison, ce Bernadin?' said she, laying aside her spectacles and looking round upon us. Every one admired the passage. 'Is this the use your French romancers make of letters?' she continued, looking triumphantly at their advocate.

'Not exactly,' he replied, laughing, – 'or at least not always: but I could show you passages in Michel Raymond . . .'

'Bah!' exclaimed the old lady, interrupting him; 'I will have nothing to do with his passages. I think it is Chamfort who says, that "un sot qui a un moment d'esprit, étonne et scandalise comme des chevaux de fiacre au galop." I don't like such unexpected jerks of sublimity – they startle more than they please me.'

The conversation then rambled on to Shakespeare, and to the mischief – such was the word – to the mischief his example, and the passionate admiration expressed for his writings, had done to the classic purity of French literature. This phrase, however, was not only cavilled at, but in true French style was laughed to death by the rest of the party. The word 'classic' was declared too rococo for use, and Shakespeare loudly proclaimed to be only defective as a model because too mighty to imitate.

I have, however, some faint misgivings as to the perfect sincerity of this verdict, – and this chiefly because there was but one Frenchman present who affected to know anything about him excepting through the medium of translation. Now, notwithstanding that the talent shown by M. Ducis in the translation of some passages is very considerable, we all know that Shakespeare may be very nearly as fairly judged from the Italian 'Otello' as the 'French Hamlet.' The party were however quite sincere, I am sure, in the feeling they expressed of reverence for the unequalled bard, founded upon the rank he held in the estimation of his countrymen; this being, as the clear-headed old lady observed, the only sure criterion, for foreigners, of the station which he ought to hold among the poets of the earth.

Then followed some keen enough observations – applicable to any one but Shakespeare – of the danger there might be, that in mixing tragedy and comedy together, farce might unfortunately be the result; or, if the 'fusion,' as it has been called, of tragedy and comedy into one were very skilfully performed, the sublime and prodigious monster called melodrame might be hoped for, as the happiest product that could be expected.

It being thus civilly settled that our Shakespeare might be as wild as he chose, but that it would be advisable for other people to take care how they attempted to follow him, the party next fell into a review, more individual and particular than I was well able to follow, or than I can now repeat, of many writers of verses and of novels that, I was fain to confess, I had never heard of before. One or two of the novel-writers were declared to be very successful imitators of the style and manner of Sir Walter Scott: and when this was stated, I was, to say the truth, by no means sorry to plead total and entire ignorance of their name and productions; for, having, as I fear, manifested a little national warmth on the subject of Shakespeare, I should have been sorry to start off in another tirade concerning Sir Walter Scott, which I might have found it difficult to avoid, had I known exactly what it was which they ventured to compare to him.

I do not quite understand how it happens that the Parisians are so much better acquainted with the generality of our light literature, than we are with the generality of theirs. This is the more unaccountable, from the fact so universally known, that for one French person who reads English, there are at least ten English who read French. It is, however, impossible to deny that such is the fact. I am sure I have heard the names of two or three dozen authors, since I have been here, of whose existence, or of that of their works, neither I, nor any of my literary friends, I believe, have had the least knowledge; and yet we have considered ourselves quite *au courant du jour* in such matters, having never missed any opportunity of reading every French book that came in our way, and moreover of sedulously consulting the Foreign Quarterly. In canvassing this difference between us, one of the party suggested that it might perhaps arise from the fact that no work which was popular in England ever escaped being reprinted on the Continent, – that is to say, either at Paris or Brussels. Though this is done solely as a sort of piratical speculation, for the purpose of inducing all the travelling English to purchase new books for four francs here, instead of giving thirty shillings for them at home, it is nevertheless a natural consequence of this manoeuvre, that the names of English books are familiarly known here even before they have been translated.

Many of our lady authors have the honour apparently of being almost as well known at Paris as at home. I had the pleasure of hearing Miss Mitford spoken of with enthusiasm; and one lady told me, that, judging her from her works, she would rather become acquainted with her than with any author living.

Miss Landon is also well known and much admired. Madame Tastu told me she had translated many of her compositions, and thought very highly of them. In short, English literature and English literati are at present very hospitably treated in France.

I was last night asked innumerable questions about many books, and many people, whose *renommée* I was surprised to find had crossed the Channel; and having communicated pretty nearly all the information I possessed upon the subject, I began to question in my turn, and heard abundance of anecdotes and criticisms, many of them given with all the sparkling keenness of French satire.

Many of les petits ridicules that we are accustomed to hear quizzed at home seem to exist in the same manner, and spite of the same light chastisement, here. The manner, for example, of making a very little wit and wisdom go a great way, by means of short lines and long stops, does not appear to be in any degree peculiar to our island. As a specimen of this, a quotation from a new romance by Madame Girardin (ci-devant Mademoiselle Delphine Gay) was shown me in a newspaper. I will copy it for you as it was printed, and I think you will allow that our neighbours at least equal us in this ingenious department of literary composition.

'Pensez-vous
Qu'Arthur voulût revoir Madlle de Sommery?'
    'NON:
Au lieu de l'aimer,
Il la détestait!'
    'OUI,
Il la détestait!'

I think our passion for novelty is pretty strong; but if the information which I received last night respecting the same imperious besoin here was not exaggerated by the playful spirit of the party who were amusing themselves by describing its influence, we are patient and tame in our endurance of old 'by-gones,' in comparison to the Parisians. They have, indeed, a saying which in few words paints this craving for novelty, as strongly as I could do, did I torment my memory to repeat to you every word said by my lively friends last night:

'Il nous faut du nouveau, n'en fût-il plus au monde.'

It is delightful to us to get hold of a new book or a new song – a new preacher or a new fiddler: it is delightful to us, but to the Parisians it is indispensable. To meet in society and have nothing new for the *causette*, would be worse than remaining at home.

'This fond desire, this longing after' fresh materials for the tongue to work upon, is at least as old as the days of Molière. It was this which made Madelon address herself with such energy to Mascarille, assuring him that she should be 'obligée de la dernière obligation' if he would but report to her daily 'les choses qu'il faut savoir de nécessité, et qui sont de l'essence d'un bel esprit;' for, as she truly observes, 'C'est là ce qui vous fait valoir dans les compagnies, et si l'on ignore ces choses, je ne donnerais pas un clou de tout l'esprit qu'on peut avoir;' – while her cousin Cathos gives her testimony to the same truth by this impressive declaration: 'Pour moi, j'aurais toutes les hontes du monde s'il fallait qu'on vînt à me demander si j'aurais vu quelque chose de nouveau que je n'aurais pas vu.'

I know not how it is that people who appear to pass so few hours of every day out of sight contrive to know so well everything that has been written and everything that has been done in all parts of the world. No one ever appears ignorant on any subject. Is this tact? Or is it knowledge, – real, genuine, substantial information respecting all things? I suspect that it is not wholly either the one or the other; and that many circumstances contribute both to the general diffusion of information, as well as to the rapid manner of receiving and the brilliant style of displaying it.

This at least is certain, that whatever they do know is made the very most of; and though some may suspect that so great display of general information indicates rather extent than depth of knowledge, none, I think, can refuse to acknowledge that the manner in which a Frenchman communicates what he has acquired is particularly amiable, graceful and unpedantic.

LETTER XLIX

Trial by Jury – Power of the Jury in France –
Comparative insignificance of that vested in the Judge –
Virtual Abolition of Capital Punishments –
Flemish Anecdote

Do not be terrified, my dear friend, and fancy that I am going to exchange my idle, ambling pace, and my babil de femme, to join the march of intellect, and indite wisdom. I have no such ambition in my thoughts; and yet I must retail to you part of a conversation with which I have just been favoured by an extremely intelligent friend, on the very manly subject of . . . Not political economy; – be tranquil on that point; the same drowsy dread falls upon me when those two portentous words sound in my ears with which they seem to have inspired Coleridge; – not political economy, but *trial by jury*.

M. V——, the gentleman in question, gave me credit, I believe, for considerably more savoir than I really possess, as to the actual and precise manner in which this important constitutional right works in England. My ignorance, however, though it prevented my giving much information, did not prevent my receiving it; and I repeat our conversation for the purpose of telling you in what a very singular manner, according to his account, it appears to work in France.

I must, however, premise that my friend is a staunch Henri-Quintist; which, though I am sure that in his case it would not produce any exaggeration in the statement of facts, may nevertheless be fairly presumed to influence his feelings, and consequently his manner of stating them.

The circumstance which gave rise to this grave discussion was a recent judgment passed here upon a very atrocious case of murder. I am not particularly fond of hanging; nevertheless, I was startled at hearing that this savage and most ferocious slayer of men was condemned to imprisonment and travail forcé, instead of death.

'It is very rarely that any one now suffers the extreme penalty of the law in this country,' said M. V——. in reply to my remark on this sentence.

'Is it since your last revolution,' said I, 'that the punishment of death has been commuted for that of imprisonment and labour?'

'No such commutation has taken place as an act of the legislature,' he replied: 'it rests solely with the jury whether a murderer be guillotined, or only imprisoned.'

I fancied that I misunderstood him, and repeated his words, – 'With the jury?'

'Oui, madame – absolument.'

This statement appeared to me so singular, that I still supposed I must be blundering, and that the words *le jury* in France did not mean the same thing as the word jury in England.

In this, as it subsequently appeared, I was not much mistaken. Notwithstanding, my informer, who was not only a very intelligent person, but a lawyer to boot, continued to assure me that trial by jury was exactly the same in both countries as to principle, though not as to effect.

'But,' said I, 'our juries have nothing to do with the sentence passed on the criminal: their business is to examine into the evidence brought forward by the witnesses to prove the guilt of the prisoner, and according to the impression which this leaves on their minds, they pronounce him 'guilty,' or 'not guilty;' and here their duty ends.'

'Yes, yes – I understand that perfectly,' replied M. V——; 'and it is precisely the same thing with us; only, it is not in the nature of a Frenchman to pronounce a mere dry, short, unspeculating verdict of "guilty," or "not guilty," without exercising the powers of his intellect upon the shades of culpability which attach to the acts of each delinquent.'

This impossibility of giving a verdict without *exercising the power of intellect* reminded me of an assize story on record in Cornwall, respecting the sentence pronounced by a jury upon a case in which it was very satisfactorily proved that a man had murdered his wife, but where it also appeared from the evidence that the unhappy woman had not conducted herself remarkably well. The jury retired to consult, and upon re-entering their box the foreman addressed the court in these words: 'Guilty – but sarved her right, my lord.' It was in vain that the learned judge desired them to amend their verdict, as containing matter wholly irrelevant to the duty they had to perform; the intellect of the jurymen was, upon this occasion, in a state of too great activity to permit their returning any other answer than the identical 'Guilty – but sarved her right.' I could hardly restrain a smile as this anecdote recurred to me; but my friend was too much in earnest in his explanation for me to interrupt him by an ill-timed jest, and he continued –

'This frame of mind, which is certainly essentially French, is one cause, and perhaps the most inveterate one, which makes it impossible that the trial by jury should ever become the same safe and simple process with us that it is in England.'

'And in what manner does this activity of intellect interfere to impede the course of justice?' said I.

'Thus,' he replied. 'Let us suppose the facts of the case proved to the entire satisfaction of the jury: they make up their minds among themselves to pronounce a verdict of 'guilty;' but their business is by no means finished, – they have still to decide how this verdict shall be delivered to the judge – whether with or without the declaration that there are circumstances calculated to extenuate the crime.'

'Oh yes! I understand you now,' I replied. 'You mean, that when there are extenuating circumstances, the jury assume the privilege of recommending the criminal to mercy. Our juries do this likewise.'

'But not with the same authority,' said he, smiling. 'With us, the fate of the culprit is wholly in the power of the jury; for not only do they decide upon the question of guilty or not guilty, but, by the use of this word *extenuating,* they can remit by their sole will and pleasure the capital part of the punishment, let the crime be of what nature it may. No judge in this country dare sentence a criminal to capital punishment where the verdict against him has been qualified by this extenuating clause.'

'It should seem then,' said I, 'that the duty of judge, which is attended with such awful responsibilities with us, is here little more than the performance of an official ceremony?'

'It is very nearly such, I assure you.'

'And your jurymen, according to a phrase of contempt common among us, are in fact judge and jury both?'

'Beyond all contradiction they are so,' he replied; 'and I conceive that criminal justice is at this time more loosely administered in France than in any other civilised country in the world. In fact, our artisans have become, since the revolution of 1830, not only judge and jury, but legislators also. Different crimes have different punishments assigned to them by our penal code; but it rarely, or I might say never, occurs in our days that the punishment inflicted has any reference to that which is assigned by the law. That guilt may vary even when the deed done does not, is certain; and it is just and righteous therefore that a judge, learned in the law of the land, and chosen by high authority from among his fellows as a man of wisdom and integrity, – it is quite just and righteous that such a one should have the power – and a tremendous power it is – of modifying the extent of the penalty according to his view of the individual case. The charge too of an English judge is considered to be of immense importance to the result of every trial. All this is as it should be; but we have departed most widely from the model we have professed to follow. With us the judge has no such power – at least not practically: with us a set of chance-met artisans, ignorant alike of the law of the land and of the philosophy of punishment, have this tremendous power vested in them. It matters not how clearly the crime has been proved, and still less what penalty the law has adjudged to it; the punishment inflicted is whatever it may please the jury to decide, and none other.'

'And what is the effect which this strangely assumed power has produced on your administration of justice?' said I.

'The virtual abolition of capital punishment,' was the reply. 'When a jury,' continued M. V——, 'delivers a verdict to the judge of "Guilty, but with extenuating circumstances," the judge dare not condemn the criminal to death, though the law of the land assign that punishment to his offence, and though his own mind is convinced, by all which has come out upon the trial, that instead of *extenuating circumstances*, the commission of the crime has been attended with every possible aggravation of atrocity. Such is the practical effect of the revolution of 1830 on the administration of criminal justice.'

'Does public opinion sanction this strange abuse of the functions of jurymen?' said I.

'Public opinion cannot sanction it,' he replied, 'any more than it could sanction the committal of the crime itself. The one act is, in fact, as lawless as the other; but the populace have conceived the idea that capital punishment is an undue exercise of power, and therefore our rulers fear to exercise it.'

This is a strange statement, is it not? The gentleman who made it is, I am sure, too much a man of honour and integrity to falsify facts; but it may perhaps be necessary to allow something for the colouring of party feeling. Whatever the present government does, or permits to be done, contrary to the system established during the period of the restoration, is naturally offensive to the feelings of the legitimatists, and repugnant to their judgments; yet, in this case, the relaxation of necessary power must so inevitably lead to evil, that we must, I think, expect to see the reins gathered up, and the command resumed by the proper functionaries, as soon as the new government feels itself seated with sufficient firmness to permit the needful exertion of strength to be put forth with safety.

It is certain that M. V—— supported his statement by reciting so many strong cases in which the most fearful crimes, substantiated by the most unbroken chain of evidence, have been reported by the jury to the judge as having 'extenuating circumstances' attached to them, that it is impossible, while things remain as they are, not to feel that such a mode of administering justice must make the habit of perjury as familiar to their jurymen as that of taking their oaths.

This conversation brought to my recollection some strange stories which I had heard in Belgium apropos of the trial by jury there. If those stories were correct, they are about as far from comprehending, or at least from acting upon, our noble, equitable, and well-tried institution there, as they appear to be here – but from causes apparently exactly the reverse. There, I am told, it often happens that the jury can neither read nor write; and that when they are placed in their box, they are, as might be expected, quite ignorant of the nature of the duty they are to perform, and often so greatly embarrassed by it, that they are ready and willing – nay, thankful – to pronounce as their verdict whatever is dictated to them.

I heard an anecdote of one man – and a thorough honest Fleming he was – who having been duly empannelled, entered the jury-box, and having listened attentively to a trial that was before the court, declared, when called upon for his verdict, that he had not understood a single word from the beginning to the end of it. The court endeavoured to explain the leading points of the question; but still the worthy burgher persisted in declaring that the business was not in his line, and that he could not comprehend it sufficiently to give any opinion at all. The attempt at explanation was repeated, but in vain; and at length the conscientious Fleming paid the fine demanded for the non-performance of the duty, and was permitted to retire.

In France, on the contrary, it appears that human intellect has gone on so fast and so far, that no dozen of men can be found simple-minded enough to say 'yes' or 'no' to a question asked, without insisting that they must legislate upon it.

In this case, at least, England shows a beautiful specimen of the *juste milieu*.

LETTER L

English Pastry-cook's – French horror of English Pastry –
Unfortunate experiment upon a Muffin – The Citizen King

We have been on a regular shopping tour this morning; which
was finished by our going into an English pastry-cook's to eat
buns. While thus engaged, we amused ourselves by watching
the proceedings of a French party who entered also for the
purpose of making a morning goûter upon cakes.

They had all of them more or less the air of having fallen
upon a terra incognita, showing many indications of surprise
at sight of the ultramarine compositions which appeared
before them; – but there was a young man of the party who, it
was evident, had made up his mind to quiz without measure
all the foreign dainties that the shop afforded, evidently
considering their introduction as a very unjustifiable
interference with the native manufacture.

'Est-il possible!' said he, with an air of grave and almost
indignant astonishment, as he watched a lady of his party
preparing to eat an English bun, – 'Est-il possible that you can
prefer these strange-looking comestibles à la pâtisserie
française?'

'Mais goûtez-en,' said the lady, presenting a specimen of the
same kind as that she was herself eating: 'ils sont excellens.'

'No, no! it is enough to look at them!' said her cavalier,
almost shuddering. 'There is no lightness, no elegance, no
grace in any single gâteau here.'

'Mais goûtez quelque chose,' reiterated the lady.

'Vous le voulez absolument!' exclaimed the young man;
'quelle tyrannie! . . . and what a proof of obedience I am about
to give you! . . . Voyons donc!' he continued, approaching a
plate on which were piled some truly English muffins –
which, as you know, are of a somewhat mysterious manufacture, and about as palatable if eaten untoasted as a slice from

321

a leathern glove. To this *gâteau*, as he supposed it to be, the unfortunate connoisseur in pâtisserie approached, exclaiming with rather a theatrical air, 'Voilà donc ce que je vais faire pour vos beaux yeux!'

As he spoke, he took up one of the pale, tough things, and, to our extreme amusement, attempted to eat it. Any one might be excused for making a few grimaces on such an occasion, – and a Frenchman's privilege in this line is well known: but this hardy experimentalist outdid this privilege; – he was in a perfect agony, and his spittings and reproachings were so vehement, that friends, strangers, boutiquier, and all, even down to a little befloured urchin who entered at the moment with a tray of patties, burst into uncontrollable laughter, which the unfortunate, to do him justice, bore with extreme good humour, only making his fair countrywoman promise that she would never insist upon his eating English confectionary again.

Had this scene continued a minute longer, I should have missed seeing what I should have been sorry not to have seen, for I certainly could not have left the pastry-cook's shop while the young Frenchman's sufferings lasted. Happily, however, we reached the Boulevard des Italiens in time to see King Louis-Philippe, en simple bourgeois, passing on foot just before Les Bains Chinois, but on the opposite side of the way.

Excepting a small tri-coloured cockade in his hat, he had nothing whatever in his dress to distinguish him from any other gentleman. He is a well-looking, portly, middle-aged man, with something of dignity in his step which, notwithstanding the unpretending citizen-like style of his promenade, would have drawn attention, and betrayed him as somebody out of the common way, even without the plain-speaking *cocarde tricolore*. There were two gentlemen a few paces behind him, as he passed us, who, I think, stepped up nearer to him afterwards; but there were no other individuals near who could have been in attendance upon him. I observed that he was recognised by many, and some few hats were taken off, particularly by two or three Englishmen who met him; but his appearance excited little emotion. I was amused, however, at the nonchalant air with which a young man at some distance, in full Robespierrian costume, used his lorgnon to peruse the person of the monarch as long as he remained in sight.

Le Roi Citoyen.

The last king I saw in the streets of Paris was Charles the Tenth returning from a visit to one of his suburban palaces, escorted and accompanied in kingly state and style. The contrast in the men and in the mode was striking, and calculated to awaken lively recollections of all the events which had occurred to both of them since the last time that I turned my head to look after a sovereign of France.

My fancy flew to Prague, and to the three generations of French monarchs stationed there almost as peaceably as if they had taken up their quarters at St. Denis!

How like a series of conjurer's tricks is their history! Think of this Charles the Tenth in the flower of his youth and comeliness – the gallant, gay, and dissolute Comte d'Artois; recall the noble range of windows belonging to his apartments at Versailles, and imagine him there radiant in youth and joy – the thoughtless, thriftless cadet of his royal race – the brother and the guest of the good king who appeared to reign over a willing people, by every human right, as well as right divine! Louis Seize was king of France; but the gay Comte d'Artois reigned sovereign of all the pleasures of Versailles. What joyous fêtes! . . . what brilliant jubilees! . . . Meanwhile

'Malignant Fate sat by and smiled.'

Had he then been told that he should live to be crowned king of France, and live thus many years afterwards, would he not have thought that a most brilliant destiny was predicted to him?

Few men, perhaps, have suffered so much from the ceaseless changes of human events as Charles the Tenth of France. First, in the person of his eldest brother, dethroned and foully murdered; then in his own exile, and that of another royal brother; and again, when Fortune seemed to smile upon his race, and the crown of France was not only placed upon that brother's head, but appeared fixed in assured succession on his own princely sons, one of those sons was murdered: and lastly, having reached the throne himself, and seen this lost son reviving in his hopeful offspring, comes another stroke of Fate, unexpected, unprepared for, overwhelming, which hurls him from his throne, and drives him and his royal race once more to exile and to civil death. . . . . Has he seen the last of the political earthquakes which have so shaken his existence? or has his restless star to rise again? Those who wish most kindly to him cannot wish for this.

But when I turned my thoughts from the dethroned and banished king to him who stepped on in unguarded but fearless security before me, and thought too on the vagaries of his destiny, I really felt as if this earth and all the people on it were little better than so many children's toys, changing their style and title to serve the sport of an hour.

It seemed to me at that moment as if all men were classed in their due order only to be thrown into greater confusion – knocked down but to be set up again, and so eternally dashed from side to side, so powerless in themselves, so wholly governed by accidents, that I shrunk, humbled, from the contemplation of human helplessness, and turned from gazing on a monarch to meditate on the insignificance of man. How vain are all the efforts he can make to shape the course of his own existence! There is, in truth, nothing but trusting to surer wisdom, and to surer power, which can enable any of us, from the highest to the lowest, to pass on with tranquil nerves through a world subject to such terrible convulsions.

LETTER LI

Parisian Women – Rousseau's failure in attempting to describe them –
Their great influence in Society – Their grace in Conversation –
Difficulty of growing old – Do the ladies of France or
those of England manage it best?

There is perhaps no subject connected with Paris which might give occasion to such curious inexhaustible observation as the character, position, and influence of its women. But the theme, though copious and full of interest, is not without its difficulties; and it is no small proof of this, that Rousseau, who rarely touched on any subject without persuading his reader that he was fully master of it, has nevertheless almost wholly failed on this. In one of the letters of 'La Nouvelle Héloïse,' he sketches the characters of a few very commonplace ladies, whom he abuses unmercifully for their bad taste in dress, and concludes his abortive attempt at making us acquainted with the ladies of Paris by acknowledging that they have some goodness of heart.

This is but a meagre description of this powerful portion of the human race, and I can hardly imagine a volume that I should read with greater pleasure than one which should fully supply all its deficiencies. Do not imagine, however, that I mean to undertake the task. I am even less capable of it than the sublime misanthrope himself; for though I am of opinion that it should be an unimpassioned spectator, and not a lover, who should attempt to paint all the delicate little atoms of exquisite mosaic-work which constitute *une Parisienne*, I think it should not be a woman.

All I can do for you on this subject is to recount the observations I have been myself led to make in the passing glances I have now the opportunity of giving them, supported by what I have chanced to hear from better authority than my own: but I am aware that I can do little more than excite your wish to become better acquainted with them than it is in my power to make you.

It is impossible to be admitted into French society without immediately perceiving that the women play a very distinguished part in it. So, assuredly, do the women of England in their own: yet I cannot but think that, setting aside all cases of individual exception, the women of France have more power and more important influence than the women of England.

I am aware that this is a very bold proposition, and that you may feel inclined to call me to account for it. But be I right or wrong in this judgment, it is at least sincere, and herein lies its chief value; for I am by no means sure that I shall be able to explain very satisfactorily the grounds on which it is formed.

France has been called 'the paradise of women;' and if consideration and deference be sufficient to constitute a paradise, I think it may be called so justly. I will not, however, allow that Frenchmen make better husbands than Englishmen; but I suspect they make politer husbands –

'Je ne sais pas, pour moi, si chacun me ressemble,
Mais j'entends là-dessous un million de mots:'

and, all pleasantry apart, I am of opinion that this more observant tone or style, or whatever it may be termed, is very far from superficial – at least in its effects. I should be greatly surprised to hear from good authority that a French gentleman had ever been heard to speak rudely to his wife.

Rousseau says, when he means to be what he himself calls '*souverainement impertinent*,' that 'il est convenu qu'un homme ne refusera rien à aucune femme fût-ce même la sienne.' But it is not only in refusing her nothing that a French husband shows the superiority which I attribute to him; I know many English husbands who are equally indulgent; but, if I mistake not, the general consideration enjoyed by Frenchwomen has its origin not in the conjugal indulgence they enjoy, but in the domestic respect universally shown them. What foundation there may be for the idea which prevails amongst us, that there is less strictness of morality among married women in France than in England, I will not attempt to decide; but, judging from the testimonies of respect shown them by fathers, husbands, brothers, and sons, I cannot but believe that, spite of travellers' tales, innuendoes, and all the authority of *les contes moraux* to boot, there must be much of genuine virtue where there is so much genuine esteem.

In a recent work on France, to which I have before alluded, a comparison is instituted between the conversational powers of the sex in England and in France; and such a picture is drawn of the frivolous inanity of the author's fair countrywomen, as, were the work considered as one of much authority in France, must leave the impression with our neighbours that the ladies of England are *tant soit peu Agnès*.

Now this judgment is, I think, as little founded in truth as that of the traveller who accused us all of being brandy-drinkers. It is indeed impossible to say what effect might have been produced upon the ladies from whom this description was drawn, by the awful consciousness that they were conversing with a person of overwhelming ability. There is such a thing as being 'blasted by excess of light;' but where this unpleasant accident does not occur, I believe that those who converse with educated Englishwomen will find them capable of being as intellectual companions as any in the world.

Our countrywomen however, particularly the younger part of them, labour under a great disadvantage. The majority of them I believe to be as well, or perhaps better informed than the majority of Frenchwomen; but, unfortunately, it frequently happens that they are terrified at the idea of appearing too much so: the terror of being called learned is in general much more powerful than that of being classed as ignorant.

Happily for France, there is no *blue* badge, no stigma of any kind attached to the female possessors of talent and information. Every Frenchwoman brings forward with equal readiness and grace all she knows, all she thinks, and all she feels on every subject that may be started; whereas with us, the dread of imputed blueism weighs down many a bright spirit, and sallies of wit and fancy are withheld from the fear of betraying either the reading or the genius with which many a fair girl is endued who would rather be thought an idiot than a BLUE.

This is, however, a very idle fear; and that it is so, a slight glance upon society would show, if prejudice did not interfere to blind us. It is possible that here and there a sneer or a shrug may follow this opprobrious epithet of 'blue;' but as the sneer and the shrug always come from those whose suffrage is of the least importance in society, their coming at all can hardly be a sufficient reason for putting on a masquerade habit of ignorance and frivolity.

It is from this cause, if I mistake not, that the conversation of the Parisian women takes a higher tone than that to which English females venture to soar. Even politics, that fearful quicksand which engulfs so many of our social hours, dividing our drawing-rooms into a committee of men and a coterie of women, – even politics may be handled by them without danger; for they fearlessly mix with that untoward subject so much lively persiflage, so much acuteness, and such unerring tact, that many a knotty point which may have made puzzled legislators yawn in the Chamber, has been played with in the salon till it became as intelligible as the light of wit could make it.

No one who is familiar with that delightful portion of French literature contained in their letters and memoirs, which paint the manners and the minds of those they treat of with more truth of graphic effect than any other biography in the world, – no one acquainted with the aspect of society as it is painted there, but must be aware that the character of Frenchmen has undergone a great and important change during the last century. It has become perhaps less brilliant, but at the same time less frivolous; and if we are obliged to confess that no star remains above the horizon of the same magnitude as those which composed the constellation that blazed during the age of Louis Quatorze and his successor, we must allow also that it would be difficult to find a minister of state who should now write to his friend as the Cardinal de Retz did to Boisrobert, – 'Je me sauve à la nage dans ma chambre, au milieu des parfums.'

If, however, these same minute records can be wholly trusted, I should say that no proportionate change has taken place among the women. I often fancy I can trace the same 'genre d'esprit' amongst them with which Madame du

Deffand has made us so well acquainted. Fashions must change – and their fashions have changed, not merely in dress perhaps, but in some things which appear to go deeper into character, or at least into manners; but the essentials are all the same. A petite maîtresse is a petite maîtresse still; and female wit – female French wit – continues to be the same dazzling, playful and powerful thing that it ever was. I really do not believe that if Madame de Sévigné herself were permitted to revisit the scene of her earthly brightness, and to find herself in the midst of a Paris soirée tomorrow, that she would find any difficulty in joining the conversation of those she would find there, in the same tone and style that she enjoyed so keenly in days of yore with Madame de la Fayette, Mademoiselle Scuderie, or any other sister sparkler of that glorious *via lactea* – provided indeed that she did not talk politics, – on that subject she might not perhaps be well understood.

Ladies still write romances, and still write verses. They write memoirs too, and are moreover quite as keen critics as ever they were; and if they had not left off giving *petits soupers,* where they doomed the poets of the day to oblivion or immortality according to their will, I should say, that in no good gifts either of nature or of art had they degenerated from their admired great-grandmothers.

It can hardly, I think, be accounted a change in their character, that where they used to converse respecting a new comedy of Molière, they now discuss the project of a new law about to be passed in the Chamber. The reason for this is obvious: there is no longer a Molière, but there is a Chamber; there are no longer any new comedies greatly worth talking about, but there are abundance of new laws instead.

In short, though the subjects are changed, they are canvassed in the same spirit; and however much the marquis may be merged in the doctrinaire, the ladies at least have not left off being light, bright, witty, and gay, in order to become advocates for the 'positif,' in opposition to the 'idéal.' They still keep faithful to their vocation of charming; and I trust they may contrive so far to combat this growing passion for the 'positif' in their countrymen, as to prevent their turning every salon – as they have already turned the Boulevards before Tortoni's – into a little Bourse.

I was so much struck by the truth and elegance of 'a thought' apropos to this subject, which I found the other day in turning over the leaves of a French lady's album, that I transcribed it:–

'Proscrire les arts agréables, et ne vouloir que ceux qui sont absolument utiles, c'est blâmer la Nature, qui produit les fleurs, les roses, les jasmins, comme elle produit des fruits.'

This sentiment, however, simple and natural as it is, appears in some danger of being lost sight of while the mind is kept upon such a forced march as it is at present: but the unnatural oblivion cannot fall upon France while her women remain what they are. The graces of life will never be sacrificed by them to the pretended pursuit of science; nor will a purblind examination of political economy be ever accepted in Paris as a beautiful specimen of light reading, and a first-rate effort of female genius.

Yet nowhere are the higher efforts of the female mind more honoured than in France. The memory of Madame de Staël seems enshrined in every woman's heart, and the glory she has brought to her country appears to shed its beams upon every female in it. I have heard, too, the name of Mrs. Somerville pronounced with admiration and reverence by many who confessed themselves unable to appreciate, or at least to follow, the efforts of her extraordinary mind.

In speaking of the women of Paris, however, I must not confine myself to the higher classes only; for, as we all know but too well, 'les dames de la Halle,' or, as they are more familiarly styled, 'les poissardes,' have made themselves important personages in the history of Paris. It is not, however, to the hideous part which they took in the revolution of Ninety-three that I would allude; the doing so would be equally disagreeable and unnecessary, for the deeds of Alexander are hardly better known than their infernal acts; – it is rather to the singular sort of respect paid to them in less stormy times that I would call your attention because we have nothing analogous to it with us. Upon all great public occasions, such as the accession of a king, his restoration, or the like, these women are permitted to approach the throne by a deputation, and kings and queens have accepted their bouquets and listened to their harangues. The newspapers in

recording these ceremonious visitings never name these
poissardes by any lesser title than 'les dames de la Halle;' a
phrase which could only be rendered into English by 'the
ladies of Billingsgate.'

These ladies have, too, a literature of their own, and have
found troubadours among the beaux-esprits of France to
chronicle their bons-mots and give immortality to their
adventures in that singular species of composition known by
the name of 'Chansons Grivoises.'

When Napoleon returned from Elba, they paid their
compliments to him at the Tuileries, and sang 'La
Carmagnole' in chorus. One hundred days after, they
repeated the ceremony of a visit to the palace; but this time the
compliment was addressed to Louis Dix-huit, and the *refrain*
of the song with which they favoured him was the famous
calembourg so much in fashion at the time –

'Rendez-nous notre *pére de Grand.*'

Not only do these 'dames' put themselves forward upon all
political occasions, but, if report say true, they have, *parfois*,
spite of their revolutionary ferocity, taken upon themselves to
act as conservators of public morals. When Madame la
Comtesse de N—— and her friend Madame T—— appeared
in the garden of the Tuileries with less drapery than they
thought decency demanded, les dames de la Halle armed
themselves with whips, and repairing in a body to the
promenade, actually flogged the audacious beauties till they
reached the shelter of their homes.

The influence and authority of these women among the
men of their own rank is said to be very great; and that
through all the connexions of life, as long as his mother lives,
whatever be her rank, a Frenchman repays her early care by
affection, deference, and even by obedience. 'Consolez ma
pauvre mère!' has been reported in a thousand instances to
have been the last words of French soldiers on the field of
battle; and whenever an aged female is found seated in the
chimney-corner, it is to her footstool that all coaxing
petitions, whether for great or small matters, are always
carried.

I heard it gravely disputed the other day, whether the old ladies of England or the old ladies of France have the most *bonheur en partage* amongst them. Every one seemed to agree that it was a very difficult thing for a pretty woman to grow old in any country – that it was terrible to 'devenir chenille après avoir été papillon;' and that the only effectual way of avoiding this shocking transition was, while still a few years on the handsome side of forty, to abandon in good earnest all pretensions to beauty, and claiming fame and name by the perennial charm of wit alone, to bid defiance to time and wrinkles.

This is certainly the best parachute to which a drooping beauty can trust herself on either side of the Channel: but for one who can avail herself of it, there are a thousand who must submit to sink into eternal oblivion without it; and the question still remains, which nation best understands the art of submitting to this downfall gracefully.

There are but two ways of rationally setting about it. The one is, to jump over the Rubicon at once at sight of the first grey hair, and so establish yourself betimes on a sofa, with all the comforts of footstool and elbow-room; the other is, to make a desperate resolution never to grow old at all. Nous autres Anglaises generally understand how to do the first with a respectable degree of resignation; and the French, by means of some invaluable secret which they wisely keep to themselves, are enabled to approach very nearly to equal success in the other.

LETTER LII

La Sainte Chapelle – Palais de Justice – Traces of the
Revolution of 1830 – Unworthy use made of
La Sainte Chapelle – Boileau – Ancient Records

A week or two ago we made a vain and unprofitable
expedition into the City for the purpose of seeing 'La Sainte
Chapelle;' sainte to all good Catholics from its having been
built by Louis Neuf (St. Louis) expressly for the purpose of
receiving all the ultra-extra-super-holy relics purchased by St.
Louis from Baldwin Emperor of Constantinople, and almost
equally sainte to us heretics from having been the scene of
Boileau's poem.

Great was our disappointment at being assured, by several
flitting officials to whom we addressed ourselves in and about
Le Palais de Justice, that admission was not to be obtained –
that workmen were employed upon it, and I know not what
besides; all, however, tending to prove that a long, lingering
look at its beautiful exterior was all we had to hope for.

In proportion to this disappointment was the pleasure with
which I received an offer from a new acquaintance to conduct
us over the Palais de Justice, and into the sacred precincts of La
Sainte Chapelle, which in fact makes a part of it. My
accidental introduction to M. J——, who has not only shown
us this, but many other things which we should probably
never have seen but for his kindness, has been one of the most
agreeable circumstances which have occurred to me in Paris. I
have seldom met a man so 'rempli de toutes sortes
d'intelligences' as is this new Parisian acquaintance; and
certainly never received from any stranger so much amiable
attention, shown in so profitable a manner. I really believe he
has a passe-partout for everything that is most interesting and
least easy of access in Paris; and as he holds a high judicial
situation, the Palais de Justice was of course open to him even

to its remotest recesses: and of all the sightseeing mornings I remember to have passed, the one which showed me this interesting edifice, with the commentary of our deeply-informed and most agreeable companion, was decidedly one of the most pleasant. There is but one drawback to the pleasure of having met such a man – and this is the fear that in losing sight of Paris we may lose sight of him also.

The Palais de Justice is from its extent alone a very noble building; but its high antiquity, and its connexion with so many points and periods of history, render it one of the most interesting buildings imaginable. We entered all the courts, some of which appeared to be in full activity. They are in general large and handsome. The portrait of Napoleon was replaced in one of them during the Three Days, and there it still remains: the old chancellor d'Auguesseau hangs opposite to him, being one of the few pictures permitted to retain their places. The vacant spaces, and in some instances the traces of violence with which others have been removed, indicate plainly enough that this venerable edifice was not held very sacred by the patriots of 1830.

The capricious fury of the sovereign people during this reign of confusion, if not of terror, has left vestiges in almost every part of the building. The very interesting bas relief which I remember on the pedestal of the fine statue of Malesherbes, the intrepid defender of Louis Seize, has been torn away; and the *brute* masonry which it has left displayed, is as striking and appropriate a memento of the spoilers, as the graphic group they displaced was of the scene it represented. M. J—— told me the sculpture was not destroyed, and would probably be replaced. I heartily hope, for the honour of Frenchmen, that this may happen: but if it should not, I trust that, for the sake of historic effect, the statue its mutilated pedestal will remain as they are – both the one and the other mark an epoch in the history of France.

But it was in the obscurer parts of the building that I found the most interest. In order to take a short cut to some point to which our kind guide wished to lead us, we were twisted through one of the old – the very old towers of this venerable structure. It had been, I think they said, the kitchen of St. Louis himself; and the walls, as seen by the enormous thickness pierced for the windows, are substantial enough to endure another six hundred years at least.

In one of the numerous rooms which we entered, we saw an extremely curious old picture, seized in the time of Louis Quinze from the Jesuits, as containing proof of their treasonable disrespect for kings: and certainly there is not wanting evidence of the fact; very speaking portraits of Henry the Third and Henry the Fourth are to be found most unequivocally on their way to the infernal regions. The whole performance is one of the most interesting specimens of Jesuitical ingenuity extant.

Having fully indulged our curiosity in the palace, we proceeded to the chapel. It is exquisitely beautiful, and so perfect in its delicate proportions, that the eye is satisfied, and dwells with full contentment on the whole for many minutes before the judgment is at leisure to examine and criticise the different parts of it. But even when this first effect is over, the perfect elegance of this diminutive structure still rests upon the mind, producing a degree of admiration which seems disproportioned to its tiny dimensions.

It was built for a shrine in which to preserve relics; and Pierre de Montreuil, its able architect, appears to have sought rather to render it worthy by its richness and its grace to become the casket for those holy treasures, than to give it the dignity of a church. That beautiful miniature cathedral, St. George's Chapel at Windsor, is an enormous edifice compared to this; but less light, less lofty in its proportions – in short, less enchanting in its general effect, than the lovely bijou of St. Louis.

Of all the cruel profanations I have ever witnessed, that of turning this exquisite chef-d'oeuvre into a chest for old records is the most unpardonable: as if Paris could not furnish four walls and a roof for this purpose, without converting this precious *châsse* to it! It is indeed a pitiful economy; and were I the Archbishop of Paris, I would besiege the Tuileries with petitions that these hideous presses might be removed; and if it might not be restored to the use of the church, that we might at least say of it –

'la Sainte Chapelle
Conservait du vieux tems l'oisiveté fidelle.'

This would at least be better than seeing it converted into a cupboard of ease to the overflowing records of the Palais de Justice. The length of this pretty reliquaire exactly equals its height, which is divided by a gallery into a lower and upper church, resembling in some degree as to its arrangement the much older structure at Aix-la-Chapelle, – the high minster there being represented by the Sainte Couronne here.

As we stood in the midst of the floor of the church, M. J—— pointed to a certain spot –

'Et bientôt LE LUTRIN se fait voir à nos yeux.'

He placed me to stand where that offensive mass of timber stood of yore; and I could not help thinking that if the poor chantre hated the sight of it as much as I did that of the ignoble cases containing the old parchments, he was exceedingly right in doing his utmost to make it disappear.

Boileau lies buried here. The spot must have been chosen in consequence of the connexion he had established in the minds of all men between himself and its holy precincts. But it was surely the most lively and light-hearted connexion that ever was hallowed by so solemn a result. One might fairly steal or parody Vanburgh's epitaph for him –

'Rise graceful o'er him, roof! for he
Raised many a graceful verse to thee.'

The preservation of the beautiful painted glass of the windows through the two revolutions which (both of them) were so busy in labours of metamorphosis and destruction in the immediate neighbourhood, not to mention all the ordinary chances against the safety of so frail a treasure during so many years, is little short of miraculous; and, considering the extraordinary sanctity of the place, it is probably so interpreted by *les fidèles*.

A remarkable proof of the reverence in which this little shrine was held, in consequence, I presume, of the relics it contained, may be found in the dignified style of its establishment. Kings and popes seem to have felt a holy rivalry as to which should most distinguish it by gifts and privileges. The wealth of its functionaries appears greatly to have exceeded the bounds of Christian moderation; and their pride of place was sustained, notwithstanding the *petitesse* of their dominions, by titles and prerogatives such as no *chapelains* ever had before. The chief dignitary of the establishment had the title of archichaplain; and, in 1379, Pope Clement VII permitted him to wear a mitre, and to pronounce his benediction on the people when they were assembled during any of the processions which took place within the enclosure of the palace. Not only, indeed, did this archchaplain take the title of prelate, but in some public acts he is styled 'Le Pape de la Sainte Chapelle.' In return for all these riches and honours, four out of the seven priests attached to the establishment were obliged to pass the night in the chapel, for the purpose of watching the relics. Nevertheless, it appears that, in the year 1575, a portion of the *vraie croix* was stolen in the night between the 19th and 20th of May. The thief, however, was strongly suspected to be no less a personage than King Henry III himself; who, being sorely distressed for money, and knowing from old experience that a traffic in relics was a right royal traffic, bethought him of a means of extracting a little Venetian gold from this true cross, by leaving it in pawn with the Republic of Venice. At any rate, this much-esteemed fragment disappeared from the Sainte Chapelle, and a piece of the holy rood was left *en gage* with the Venetians by Henry III.

I have transcribed, for your satisfaction, the list I find in Dulaure of the most sacred of the articles for the reception of which this chapel was erected:–

Du sang de Notre Seigneur Jésus-Christ.
Les drapeaux dont Notre Sauveur fut enveloppé en son enfance.
Du sang qui miraculeusement a distillé d'une image de Notre Seigneur, ayant été frappé d'un infidèle.
La chaîne et lien de fer, en manière d'anneau, dont Notre Seigneur fut lié.
La sainte touaille, ou nappe, en un tableau.
Du lait de la Vièrge.
Une partie du suaire dont il fut enseveli.
La verge de Moïse.
Les chefs des Saints Blaise, Clément, et Simon.

Is it not wonderful that the Emperor of Constantinople could consent to part with such precious treasures for the lucre of gain? I should like to know what has become of them all.

As late as the year 1770, the annual ceremony of turning out devils on Good Friday, from persons pretending to be possessed, was performed in this chapel. The form prescribed was very simple, and always found to answer perfectly. As soon as it was understood that all the demoniacs were assembled, *le grand chantre* appeared, carrying a cross, which, spite of King Henry's *supercherie*, was declared to enclose in its inmost recesses a morsel of the *vraie croix*, and in an instant all the contortions and convulsions ceased, and the possessed became perfectly calm and tranquil, and relieved from every species of inconvenience.

Having seen all that this lovely chapel had to show, and particularly examined the spot where the battle of the books took place, the passe-partout of M. J—— caused a mysterious-looking little door in the Sainte Couronne to open for us; and, after a little climbing, we found ourselves just under the roof of the Palais de Justice. The enormous space on the *grande salle* below is here divided into three galleries, each having its entire length, and one-third of its width. The manner in which these galleries are constructed is extremely curious and ingenious, and well deserves a careful examination. I certainly never found myself in a spot of greater interest than this. The enormous collection of records which fill these galleries, arranged as they are in the most exquisite order, is one of the most marvellous spectacles I ever beheld.

Amidst the archives of so many centuries, any document that may be wished for, however remote or however minute, is brought forward in an instant, with as little difficulty as Dr. Dibdin would find in putting his hand upon the best-known treasure in Lord Spencer's library.

Our kind friend obtained for us the sight of the volume containing all the original documents respecting the trial of poor Joan of Arc, that most ill-used of heroines. Vice never braved danger and met death with such steady, unwavering courage as she displayed. We saw, too, the fatal warrant which legalised the savage murder of this brave and innocent fanatic.

Several other death-warrants of distinguished persons were also shown to us, some of them of great antiquity; but no royal hand had signed them. This painful duty is performed in France by one of the superior law-officers of the crown, but never by the hand of majesty.

Another curious trial that was opened for our satisfaction, was that of the wretched Marquise de Brinvilliers, the famous *empoisonneuse*, who not only destroyed father, brother, husband, at the instigation of her lover, but appears to have used her power of compounding fatal drugs upon many other occasions. The murderous atrocities of this woman seem to surpass everything on record, except those of Marguérite de Bourgogne, the inconceivable heroine of the 'Tour de Nesle.'

I was amused by an anecdote which M. J—— told me of an Englishman to whom he, some years ago, showed these same curious papers – among which is the receipt used by Madame de Brinvilliers for the composition of the poison whose effects plunged Paris in terror.

'Will you do me the favour to let my copy this receipt?' said the Englishman.

'I think that my privilege does not reach quite so far as that,' was the discreet reply; and but for this, our countryman's love for chemical science might by this time have spread the knowledge of the precious secret over the whole earth.

LETTER LIII

French ideas of England – Making love – Precipitate retreat
of a young Frenchman, – Different methods of arranging
Marriages – English Divorce – English Restaurans

It now and then happens, by a lucky chance, that one finds
oneself full gallop in a conversation the most perfectly
unreserved, without having had the slightest idea or intention,
when it began, of either giving or receiving confidence.

This occurred to me a few days ago, while making a
morning visit to a lady whom I had never seen but twice
before, and then had not exchanged a dozen words with her.
But, upon this occasion, we found ourselves very nearly
tête-à-tête, and got, I know not how, into a most unrestrained
discussion upon the peculiarities of our respective countries.

Madame B—— has never been in England, but she assured
me that her curiosity to visit our country is quite as strong as
the passion for investigation which drew Robinson Crusoe
from his home to visit the . . .'

'Savages,' said I, finishing the sentence for her.

'No! no! no! . . . To visit all that is most curious in the
world.'

This phrase, 'most curious,' seemed to me of doubtful
meaning, and so I told her; asking whether it referred to the
museums, or the natives.

She seemed doubtful for a moment whether she should be
frank or otherwise; and then, with so pretty and playful a
manner as must, I think, have disarmed the angry nationality
of the most thin-skinned patriot alive, she answered –

'Well then – the natives.'

'But we take such good care,' I replied, 'that you should not
want specimens of the race to examine and make experiments
upon, that it would hardly be worth your while to cross the
Channel for the sake of seeing the natives. We import

341

ourselves in such prodigious quantities, that I can hardly conceive you should have any curiosity left about us.'

'On the contrary,' she replied, 'my curiosity is only the more *piquée*: I have seen so many delightful English persons here, that I die to see them at home, in the midst of all those singular customs, which they cannot bring with them, and which we only know by the imperfect accounts of travellers.'

This sounded, I thought, very much as if she were talking of the good people of Mongo Creek, or Karakoo Bay; but being at least as curious to know what her notions were concerning the English in their remote homes, and in the midst of all their 'singular customs,' as she could be to become better acquainted with them, I did my best to make her tell me all she had heard about us.

'I will tell you,' she said, 'what I want to see beyond everything else: I want to see the mode of making love *tout-à-fait à l' Anglaise.* You know that you are all so polite as to put on our fashions here in every respect; but a cousin of mine, who was some years ago attached to our Embassy at London, has described the style of managing love affairs as so . . . so romantic, that it perfectly enchanted me, and I would give the world to see how it was done (*comment cela se fait*).'

'Pray tell me how he described it,' said I, 'and I promise faithfully to tell you if the picture be correct.'

'Oh, that is so kind! . . . Well then,' she continued, colouring a little, from the idea, as I suppose, that she was going to say something terribly atrocious, 'I will tell you exactly what happened to him. He had a letter of introduction to a gentleman of great estate – a member of the chamber of your parliament, who was living with his family at his chateau in one of the provinces, where my cousin forwarded the letter to him. A most polite reply was immediately returned, containing a pressing invitation to my cousin to come to the chateau without delay, and pass a month with them for the hunting season. Nothing could be more agreeable than this invitation, for it offered the best possible opportunity of studying the manners of the country. Every one can cross from Calais to Dover, and spend half their year's income in walking or driving through the long wide streets of London for six weeks; but there are very few, you know, who obtain an entrée to the chateaux of the noblesse. In short, my cousin was enchanted, and set off immediately. He arrived just in time to arrange his toilet before dinner: and when he entered the salon, he was perfectly dazzled by the exceeding beauty of the three daughters of his host, who were all *décolletées*, and full-dressed, he says, exactly as if they were going to some very elegant *bal paré*. There was no other company, and he felt a little startled at being received in such a ceremonious style.

The young ladies all performed on the pianoforte and harp, and my cousin, who is very musical, was in raptures. Had not his admiration been too equally drawn to each, he assures me that before the end of that evening he must inevitably have been the conquest of one. The next morning, the whole family met again at breakfast: the young ladies were as charming as ever, but still he felt in doubt as to which he admired most. Whilst he was exerting himself to be as agreeable as he could, and talking to them all with the timid respect with which demoiselles are always addressed by Frenchmen, the father of the family startled and certainly almost alarmed my cousin by suddenly saying, – 'We cannot hunt today, mon ami, for I have business which will keep me at home; but you shall ride into the woods with Elizabeth; she will show you my pheasants. Get ready, Elizabeth, to attend Monsieur . . .!'

Madame B—— stopped short, and looked at me as if expecting that I should make some observation.

'Well?' said I.

'Well!' she repeated, laughing; 'then you really find nothing extraordinary in this proceeding – nothing out of the common way?'

'In what respect?' said I: 'what is it that you suppose was out of the common way?'

'That question,' said she, clasping her hands in an ecstasy at having made the discovery – 'That question puts me more au fait than anything else you could say to me. It is the strongest possible proof that what happened to my cousin was in truth nothing more than what is of everyday occurrence in England.'

'What did happen to him?'

'Have I not told you? . . . The father of the young ladies whom he so greatly admired, selected one of them and desired my cousin to attend her on an excursion into the woods. My dear madame . . . national manners vary so strangely . . . I beseech you not to suppose that I imagine that everything may not be exceedingly well arranged notwithstanding. My cousin is a very distinguished young man – excellent character – good name – and will have his father's estate . . . only the manner is so different . . .'

'Did your cousin accompany the young lady?' said I.

'No, he did not – he returned to London immediately.'

This was said so gravely – so more than gravely – with an air of so much more meaning than she thought it civil to express, that my gravity and politeness gave way together, and I laughed most heartily.

My amiable companion, however, did not take it amiss – she only laughed with me; and when we had recovered our gravity, she said, 'So you find my cousin very ridiculous for throwing up the party'? – *un peu timide, peut-être?*'

'Oh no!' I replied – 'only a little hasty.'

'Hasty! . . . Mais que voulez-vous? You do not seem to comprehend his embarrassment.'

'Perhaps not fully; but I assure you his embarrassment would have ceased altogether, had he trusted himself with the young lady and her attendant groom: I doubt not that she would have led the way through one of our beautiful pheasant preserves, which are exceedingly well worth seeing; but most certainly she would have been greatly astonished, and much embarrassed in her turn, had your cousin taken it into his head to make love to her.'

'You are in earnest?' said she, looking in my face with an air of great interest.

'Indeed I am,' I replied; 'I am very seriously in earnest; and though I know not the persons of whom we have been speaking, I can venture to assure you positively, that it was only because no gentleman so well recommended as your cousin could be suspected of abusing the confidence reposed in him, that this English father permitted him to accompany the young lady in her morning ride.'

'C'est donc un trait sublime!' she exclaimed: 'what noble confidence – what confiding honour! It is enough to remind one of the *paladins* of old.'

'I suspect you are quizzing our confiding simplicity,' said I; 'but, at any rate, do not suspect me of quizzing you – for I have told you nothing more than a very simple and certain fact.'

'I doubt it not the least in the world,' she replied; 'but you are indeed, as I observed at first, superiorly romantic.' She appeared to meditate for a moment, and then added, 'Mais dites moi un peu . . . is not this a little inconsistent with the stories we read in the 'novels of fashionable life' respecting the manner in which husbands are acquired for the young ladies of England? . . . You refuse yourselves, you know, the privilege of disposing of your daughters in marriage according to the mutual interests of the parties; and therefore, as young ladies must be married, it follows that some other means must be resorted to by the parents. All Frenchmen know this, and they may perhaps for that reason be sometimes too easily induced to imagine that it is intended to lead them into marriage by captivating their senses. This is so natural an inference, that you really must forgive it.'

'I forgive it perfectly,' I replied; 'but as we have agreed not to *mystify* each other, it would not be fair to leave you in the belief that it is the custom, in order to 'acquire' husbands for the young ladies, that they should be sent on lovemaking expeditions into the woods with the premier venu. But what you have said enables me to understand a passage which I was reading the other day in a French story, and which puzzled me most exceedingly. It was on the subject of a young girl who had been forsaken by her lover; and some one, reproaching him for his conduct, uses, I think, these words: 'Après l'avoir compromise autant qu'il est possible de compromettre une jeune miss – ce qui n'est pas une chose absolument facile dans la bienheureuse Albion . . .' This puzzled me more than I can express; because the fact is, that we consider the com-promising the reputation of a young lady as so tremendous a thing, that excepting in novels, where neither national man-ners nor natural probabilites are permitted to check the necessary accumulation of misery on the head of a heroine, it NEVER occurs, and this, not because nothing can compromise her, but because nothing that can compromise her is ever permitted, or, I might almost say, ever attempted. Among the lower orders, indeed, stories of seduction are but too frequent; but our present examination of national manners refers only to the middle and higher classes of society.'

Madame B—— listened to me with the most earnest attention; and after I had ceased speaking, she remained silent, as if meditating on what she had heard. At length she said, in a tone of much more seriousness than she had yet used, – 'I am quite sure that every word you say is *parfaitement exact* – your manner persuades me that you are speaking neither with exaggeration nor in jest: *cependant* . . . I cannot conceal from you my astonishment at your statement. The received opinion among us is, that private and concealed infidelities among married women are probably less frequent in England than in France – because it seems to be essentially *dans vos moeurs de faire un grand scandale* whenever such a circumstance occurs; and this, with the penalties annexed to it, undoubtedly acts as a prevention. But, on the other hand, it is universally considered as a fact, that you are as lenient to the indiscretions of unmarried ladies, as severe to those of the married ones. Tell me – is there not some truth in this idea?'

'Not the least in the world, I do assure you. On the contrary, I am persuaded that in no country is there any race of women from whom such undeviating purity and propriety of conduct is demanded as from the unmarried women of England. Slander cannot attach to them, because it is as well known as that a Jew is not qualified to sit in parliament, that a single woman suspected of indiscretion immediately dies a civil death – she sinks out of society, and is no more heard of; and it is therefore that I have ventured to say, that a compromised reputation among the unmarried ladies of England NEVER occurs.'

'Nous nous sommes singulièrement trompés sur tout cela donc, nous autres,' said Madame B——. 'But the single ladies no longer young?' she continued; – 'forgive me . . . but is it really supposed that they pass their entire lives without any indiscretion at all?'

This question was asked in a tone of such utter incredulity as to the possibility of a reply in the affirmative, that I again lost my gravity, and laughed heartily; but, after a moment, I assured her very seriously that such was most undoubtedly the case.

The naïve manner in which she exclaimed in reply, 'Est-il possible!' might have made the fortune of a young actress. There was, however, no acting in the case; Madame B——— was most perfectly unaffected in her expression of surprise, and assured me that it would be shared by all Frenchwomen who should be so fortunate as to find occasion, like herself, to receive such information from indisputable authority. 'Quant aux hommes,' she added, laughing, 'je doute fort si vous en trouverez de si croyans.'

We pursued our conversation much farther; but were I to repeat the whole, you would only find it contained many repetitions of the same fact – namely, that a very strong persuasion exists in France, among those who are not personally well acquainted with English manners, that the mode in which marriages are arranged, rather by the young people themselves than by their relatives, produces an effect upon the conduct of our unmarried females which is not only as far as possible from the truth, but so preposterously so, as never to have entered into any English head to imagine.

So few opportunities for anything approaching to intimacy between French and English women arise, that it is not very easy for us to find out exactly what their real opinion is concerning us. Nothing in Madame B———'s manner could lead me to suspect that any feeling of reprobation or contempt mixed itself with her belief respecting the extraordinary license which she supposed was accorded to unmarried woman. Nothing could be more indulgent than her tone of commentary on our *national peculiarities*, as she called them. The only theme which elicited an expression of harshness from her was the manner in which divorces were obtained and paid for: 'Se faire payer pour une aventure semblable! . . . publier un scandale si ridicule, si offensant pour son amour-propre – si fortement contre les bonnes moeurs, pour en recevoir de l'argent, was,' she said, 'perfectly incomprehensible in a nation de si braves gens que les Anglais.'

I did my best to defend our mode of proceeding in such cases upon the principles of justice and morality; but French prejudices on this point are too inveterate to be shaken by any eloquence of mine. We parted, however, the best friends in the world, and mutually grateful for the information we had received.

This conversation only furnished one, among several instances, in which I have been astonished to discover the many popular errors which are still current in France respecting England. Can we fairly doubt that, in many cases where we consider ourselves as perfectly well-informed, we may be quite as much in the dark respecting them? It is certain that the habit so general among us of flying over to Paris for a week or two every now and then, must have made a great number of individuals acquainted with the external aspect of France between Calais and Paris, and also with all the most conspicuous objects of the capital itself – its churches and its theatres, its little river and its great coffee-houses: but it is an extremely small proportion of these flying travellers who ever enter into any society beyond what they may encounter in public; and to all such, France can be very little better known than England is to those who content themselves with pursuing the descriptions we give of ourselves in our novels and newspapers.

Of the small advance made towards obtaining information by such visits as these, I have had many opportunities of judging for myself, both among English and French, but never more satisfactorily than at a dinner-party at the house of an old widow lady, who certainly understands our language perfectly, and appears to me to read more English books, and to be more interested about their authors, than almost any one I ever met with. She has never crossed the Channel, however, and has rather an overweening degree of respect for such of her countrymen as have enjoyed the privilege of looking at us face to face on our own soil.

The day I dined with her, one of these travelled gentlemen was led up and presented to me as a person well acquainted with my country. His name was placed on the cover next to the one destined for me at table, and it was evidently intended that we should derive our principal amusement from the conversation of each other. As I never saw him before or since, as I never expect to see him again, and as I do not even remember his name, I think I am guilty of no breach of confidence by repeating to you a few of the ideas upon England which he had acquired on his travels.

His first remark after we were placed at table was, – 'You do not, I think, use table-napkins in England; – do you not find them rather embarrassing?' The next was, – 'I observed during my stay in England that it is not the custom to eat soup: I hope, however, that you do not find it disagreeable to your palate?' . . . 'You have, I think, no national cuisine?' was the third observation; and upon this *singularity in our manners* he was eloquent. 'Yet, after all,' said he consolingly, 'France is in fact the only country which has one: Spain is too oily – Italy too spicy. We have sent artists into Germany; but this cannot be said to constitute *une cuisine nationale*. Pour dire vrai, however, the rosbif of England is hardly more scientific than the sundried meat of the Tartars. A Frenchman would be starved in England did he not light upon one of the imported artists, – and, happily for travellers, this is no longer difficult.'

'Did you dine much in private society?' said I.

'No, I did not: my time was too constantly occupied to permit my doing so.'

'We have some very good hotels, however, in London.'

'But no tables d'hôte!' he replied with a shrug. 'I did very well, nevertheless; for I never permitted myself to venture anywhere for the purpose of dining excepting to your celebrated Leicester-Square. It is the most fashionable part of London, I believe; or, at least, the only fashionable restaurans are to be found there.'

I ventured very gently to hint that there were other parts of London more à-la-mode, and many hotels which had the reputation of a better cuisine than any which could be found in Leicester-Square; but the observation appeared to displease the traveller, and the belle harmonie which it was intended should subsist between us was evidently shaken thereby, for I heard him say in a half-whisper to the person who sat on the other side of him, and who had been attentively listening to our discourse, – 'Pas exact . . .'

LETTER LIV

*Mixed Society – Influence of the English Clergy and their Families –
Importance of their station in Society*

Though I am still of opinion that French society, properly so
called, – that is to say, the society of the educated ladies and
gentlemen of France, – is the most graceful, animated, and
fascinating in the world; I think, nevertheless, that it is not as
perfect as it might be, were a little more exclusiveness
permitted in the formation of it.

No one can be really well acquainted with good society in
this country without being convinced that there are both men
and women to be found in it who to the best graces add the
best virtues of social life; but it is equally impossible to deny,
that admirable as are some individuals of the circle, they all
exercise a degree of toleration to persons less estimable,
which, when some well-authenticated anecdotes are made
known to us, is, to say the least of it, very startling to the
feelings of those who are not to this easy manner either born
or bred.

To look into the hearts of all who form either a Parisian or a
London lady's visiting list, in order to discover of what stuff
each individual be made, would not perhaps be very wise, and
is luckily quite impossible. Nothing at all approaching to such
a scrutiny can be reasonably wished or expected from those
who open their doors for the reception of company; but where
society is perfectly well ordered, no one of either sex, I think,
whose outward and visible conduct has brought upon them
the eyes of all and the reprobation of the good, should be
admitted.

That such are admitted much more freely in France than in
England, cannot be denied; and though there are many who
conscientiously keep aloof from such intercourse, and more
who mark plainly enough that there is a distance in spirit even

where there is vicinity of person, still I think it is greatly to be regretted that such a leven of disunion should ever be suffered to insinuate itself into meetings which would be so infinitely more agreeable as well as more respectable without it.

One reason, I doubt not, why there is less exclusiveness and severity and selection in the forming a circle here is, that there are no individuals, or rather no class of individuals, in the wide circle which constitutes what is called *en grand* the society of Paris, who could step forward with propriety and say, '*This may not be.*'

With us, happily, the case is as yet different. The clergy of England, their matronly wives and highly-educated daughters, form a distinct caste, to which there is nothing that answers in the whole range of continental Europe. In this caste, however, are mingled a portion of every other; yet it has a dignity and aristocracy of its own: and in this aristocracy are blended the high blood of the noble, the learning which has in many instances sufficed to raise to a level with it the obscure and needy, and the piety which has given station above either to those whose unspotted lives have marked them out as pre-eminent in the holy profession they have chosen.

While such men as these mingle freely in society, as they constantly do in England, and bring with them the females who form their families, there is little danger that notorious vice should choose to obtrude itself.

It will hardly be denied, I believe, that many a frail fair one, who would boldly push her way among ermine and coronets where the mitre was not, would shrink from parading her doubtful honours where it was: and it is equally certain, that many a thoughtless, easy, careless giver of fine parties has been prevented from filling up her constellation of beauties because 'It is impossible to have Lady This, or Mrs. That, when the bishop and his family are expected.'

Nor is this wholesome influence confined to the higher ranks alone; – the rector of the parish – nay, even his young curate, with a smooth cheek and almost unrazored chin, will in humbler circles produce the same effect. In short, wherever an English clergyman or an English clergyman's family appears, there decency is in presence, and the canker of known and tolerated vice is not.

Whenever we find ourselves weary of this restraint, and anxious to mix (unshackled by the silent rebuke of such a presence) with whatever may be most attractive to the eye or amusing to the spirit, let the stamp of vice be as notorious upon it as it may, whenever we reach this state, it will be the right and proper time to pass the Irish Church Bill.

These meditations have been thrust upon me by the reply I received in answer to a question which I addressed to a lady of my acquaintance at a party the other evening.

'Who is that very elegant-looking woman?' said I.

'It is Madame de C——,' was the reply. 'Have you never met her before? She is very much in society; one sees her everywhere.'

I replied, that I had seen her once or twice before, but had never learned her name; adding, that it was not only her name I was anxious to learn, but something about her. She looked like a personage, a heroine, a sybil: in short, it was one of those heads and busts that one seems to have the same right to stare at, as at a fine picture or statue; they appear a part of the decorations, only they excite a little more interest and curiosity.

'Can you not tell me something of her character?' said I: 'I never saw so picturesque a figure; I could fancy that the spirit of Titian had presided at her toilet.'

'It was only the spirit of coquetry, I suspect,' answered my friend with a smile. 'But if you are so anxious to know her, I can give you her character and history in very few words: – she is rich, high-born, intellectual, political, and unchaste.'

I do not think I started; I should be shocked to believe myself so unfit for a salon as to testify surprise thus openly at anything; but my friend looked at me and laughed.

'You are astonished at seeing her here? But I have told you that you may expect to meet her everywhere; except, indeed, chez moi, and at a few exceedingly rococo houses besides.'

As the lady I was talking to happened to be an Englishwoman, though for many years a resident in Paris, I ventured to hint the surprise I felt that a person known to be what she described Madame de C—— should be so universally received in good society.

'It is very true,' she replied: 'it is surprising, and more so to me perhaps than to you, because I know thoroughly well the irreproachable character and genuine worth of many who receive her. I consider this,' she continued, 'as one of the most singular traits in Parisian society. If, as many travellers have most falsely insinuated, the women of Paris were generally corrupt and licentious, there would be nothing extraordinary in it: but it is not so. Where neither the husband, the relatives, the servants, nor any one else, has any wish or intention of discovering or exposing the frailty of a wife, it is certainly impossible to say that it may not often exist without being either known or suspected; but with this, general society cannot interfere; and those whose temper or habits of mind lead them to suspect evil wherever it is possible that it may be concealed, may often lose the pleasure of friendship founded on esteem, solely because it is possible that some hidden faults may render their neighbour unworthy of it. That such tempers are not often to be found in France, is certainly no proof of the depravity of national manners; but where notorious irregularity of conduct has brought a woman fairly before the bar of public opinion, it does appear to me very extraordinary that such a person as our hostess, and very many others equally irreproachable, should receive her.'

'I presume,' said I, 'that Madame de C—— is not the only person towards whom this remarkable species of tolerance is exercised?'

'Certainly not. There are many others whose *liaisons* are as well known as hers, who are also admitted into the best society. But observe – I know no instance where such are permitted to enter within the narrower circle of intimate domestic friendship. No one in Paris seems to think that they have any right to examine into the private history of all the *élégantes* who fill its salons; but I believe they take as good care to know the *friends* whom they admit to the intimacy of their private hours as we do. There, however, this species of decorum ends; and they would no more turn back from entering a room where they saw Madame de C——, than a London lady would drive away from the opera because she saw the carriage of Lady —— at the door.'

'There is no parallel, however, between the cases,' said I.

'No, certainly,' she replied; 'but it is not the less certain that the Parisians appear to think otherwise.'

Now it appears evident to me, that all this arises much less from general licentiousness of morals than from general easiness of temper. SANS SOUCI is the darling device of the whole nation: and how can this be adhered to, if they set about the very arduous task of driving out of society all those who do not deserve to be in it? But while feeling sincerely persuaded, as I really do, that this difference in the degree of moral toleration practised by the two countries does not arise from any depravity in the French character, I cannot but think that our mode of proceeding in this respect is infinitely better. It is more conducive, not only to virtue, but to agreeable and unrestrained intercourse; and for this reason, if for no other, it is deeply our interest to uphold with all possible reverence and dignity that class whose presence is of itself sufficient to guarantee at least the reputation of propriety, in every circle in which they appear.

Though not very germane to Paris and the Parisians, which I promised should make the subjects of my letters as long as I remained among them, I cannot help observing how utterly this most important influence would be destroyed in the higher circles – which will ever form the model of those below them – if the riches, rank, and worldly honours of this class are wrested from them. It is indeed very certain that a clergyman, whether bishop, priest, or deacon, may perform the duty of a minister in the desk, at the altar, or in the pulpit, though he has to walk home afterwards to an humble dwelling and an humble meal: he may perform this duty well, and to the entire satisfaction of the rich and great, though his poverty may prevent him from ever taking his place among them; but he may not – he cannot, while such is the station allotted him, produce that effect on society, and exert that influence on the morals of the people, which he would do were his temporal place and power such as to exalt him in the eyes even of the most worldly.

Amidst all the varities of cant to which it is the destiny of the present age to listen, there is none which I endure with so little patience as that which preaches the '*humility of the church.*' Were there the shadow of reason or logic in the arguments for the degradation of the clergy drawn from the Scriptures, they must go the length of showing that, in order to follow the example of the great Master, they must all belong to the class of

carpenters and fishermen. Could we imagine another revelation of the Divinity accorded to man, it would be natural
enough to conceive that the rich gift of direct inspiration should
be again given to those who had neither learning, knowledge,
pride, nor power of any kind, to combat or resist, to explain or
to weaken, the communication which it was their duty simply
to record and spread abroad. But the eternal word of God once
delivered, does it follow that those who are carefully instructed
in all the various learning which can assist in giving strength
and authority to the propagation of it should alone, of all the
sons of men, be for ever doomed to the lower walks of social life
in order to imitate the humility of the Saviour of the world?

I know not if there be more nonsense or blasphemy in this.
The taking the office of preaching his own blessed will to man
was an act of humility in God; but the taking upon themselves
to instruct their fellow-men in the law thus solemnly left us, is a
great assumption of dignity in men, – and where the offices it
imposes are well performed, it becomes one of the first duties of
the believers in the doctrine they have made it their calling to
expound, to honour them with such honour as mortals can
understand and value. If any one be found who does not
perform the duties of this high calling in the best manner which
his ability enables him to do, let him be degraded as he deserves;
but while he holds it, let him not be denied the dignity of state
and station to which all his fellow-citizens in their different
walks aspire, in order forsooth to *keep him humble!* Humble
indeed – yea, humbled to the dust, will our long-venerated
church and its insulted ministers be, if its destiny and their
fortune be left at the mercy of those who have lately undertaken
to legislate for them. I often feel a sort of vapourish, vague
uncertainty of disbelief, as I read the records of what has been
passing in the House of Commons on this subject. I cannot
realise it, as the Americans say, that the majority of the English
parliament should consent to be led blindfold upon such a point
as this, by a set of lowborn, ignorant, bullying papists. I hope,
when I return to England, I shall awake and find that it is not so.

And now forgive me for this long digression: I will write to
you tomorrow upon something as essentially French as
possible, to make up for it.

LETTER LV

Le Grand Opéra – Its enormous Expense – Its Fashion –
Its acknowledged Dulness – 'La Juive' – Its heavy Music –
Its exceeding Splendour – Beautiful management of
the Scenery – National Music

Can I better keep the promise I gave you yesterday than by
writing you a letter of and concerning le grand opéra? Is
there anything in the world so perfectly French as this?
Something like their pretty opéra comique may exist
elsewhere; we have our comic opera, and Italy has her buffa;
the opéra Italien, too, may be rather more than rivalled at the
Haymarket; but where out of Paris are we to look for
anything like the Académie Royale de Musique? . . . le grand
opéra? . . . l'opéra par excellence? – I may safely answer,
nowhere.

It is an institution of which the expenses are so enormous,
that though it is more constantly and fully attended perhaps
than any other theatre in the world, it could not be sustained
without the aid of funds supplied by the government. The
extraordinary partiality for this theatre seems to have existed
among the higher classes, without any intermission from
change of fashion, occasional inferiority of the performances,
or any other cause, from the time of Louis Quatorze to the
present. That immortal monarch, whose whim was power,
and whose word was law, granted a patent privilege to this
establishment in favour of the musical Abbé Perrin, but
speedily revoked it, to bestow one more ample still on Lulli.
In this latter act, it is ordained that *'tous gentilshommes et*
demoiselles puissent chanter aux dites pièces et représentations de
notre dite Académie Royale sans que pour ça ils soient censés déroger
au dit titre de noblesse et à leurs privilèges.'

This was a droll device to exalt this pet plaything of the
fashionable world above all others. Voltaire fell into the

mode like the rest of the fine folks, and thus expressed his sensibility to its attractions:–

'Il faut se rendre à ce palais magique,
Où les beaux vers, la danse, la musique,
L'art de charmer les yeux par les couleurs,
L'art plus heureux de séduire les coeurs,
De cent plaisirs font un plaisir unique.'

But the most incomprehensible part of the business is, that with all this enthusiasm, which certainly rather goes on increasing than diminishing, every one declares that he is *ennuyé à la mort* at le grand opéra.

I do not mean that their being ennuyés is incomprehensible – Heaven knows that I understand that perfectly: but why, when this is avowed, they should continue to persecute themselves by going there two or three times in every week, I cannot comprehend.

If attendance at the opera were here, as it is with us, a sort of criterion of the love of music and *other fine arts*, it would be much less difficult to understand: but this is far from being the case, as both the Italian and the comic operas have more perfect orchestras. The style and manner of singing, too, are what no genuine lover of music could ever be brought to tolerate. When the remembrance of a German or Italian opera comes across one while listening to the dry, heavy recitative of the Academy, it produces a feeling of impatience difficult to conceive by those who have never experienced it.

If, however, instead of being taken in by the name of opera, and expecting the musical treat which that name seems to promise, we go to this magnificent theatre for the purpose of seeing the most superb and the best-fancied decorations in the world, we shall at least not be disappointed, though before the end of the entertainment we may probably become heartily weary of gazing at and admiring the dazzling pageant. I told you just now what Voltaire said of the opera, either when he was particularly enchanted by some reigning star – the adorable Sophie Arnould perhaps –

or else when he chose to be particularly à-la-mode: but he seems more soberly in earnest, I think, when he says afterwards, 'L'opéra n'est qu'un rendezvous publique, où l'on s'assemble à certains jours, sans trop savoir pourquoi: c'est une maison où tout le monde va, quoiqu'on pense mal du maître, et qu'il soit assez ennuyeux.'

That little phrase, 'où tout le monde va,' contains, I suspect after all, the only true solution of the mystery. 'Man is a gregarious animal,' say the philosophers; and it is therefore only in conformity to this well-known law of his nature that hes and shes flock by thousands to be pent up together, in defiance of most *triste musique* and a stifling atmosphere, within the walls of this beautiful puppet-show.

That it is beautiful, I am at this moment particularly willing to avouch, as we have just been regaling ourselves, or rather our eyes, with as gorgeous a spectacle there as it ever entered into the heart of a carpenter to *étaler* on the stage of a theatre. This splendid show is known by the name of 'La Juive;' but it should rather have been called 'Le Cardinal,' for a personage of no less dignity is decidedly its hero. M. Halevy is the composer, and M. Scribe the author of the 'paroles.'

M. Scribe stands so high as a dramatic composer, that I suppose he may sport a little with his fame without running much risk of doing it an injury: but as the Académie Royal has the right of drawing upon the Treasury for its necessities, it is to be hoped that the author of 'Bertrand et Raton' is well paid for lending his name to the pegs on which ermine and velvet, feathers and flowers, cardinals' hats and emperors' mantles, are hung up to view for the amusement of all who may be curious in such matters. I suspect, however, that the composition of this piece did not cost the poet many sleepless nights: perhaps he remembered that excellent axiom of the Barbier de Seville, – 'Ce qui ne vaut pas la peine d'être dit, on le chante;' and under this sentence I think such verses as the following, which strongly remind one of the famous Lilliputian ode in the Bath Guide, may fairly enough be condemned to music.

'Fille chère,
Près d'un père
  Viens mourir;
Et pardonne
Quand il donne
La couronne
  Du martyr!
Plus de plainte –
Vaine crainte
Est éteinte
  En mon coeur;
Saint délire!
Dieu m'inspire,
Et j'expire
  Vainqueur.'

Unhappily, however, the music is at least as worthless as the rhymes. There is one passage, nevertheless, that is singularly impressive and beautiful. This is the chorus at the opening of the second act, where a party of Jews assembled to eat the passover chant a grace in these words:–

'Oh! Dieu de nos pères!
Toi qui nous éclaires,
Parmi nous descends!'
  &c. &c. &c.

This is very fine, but perhaps it approaches rather too closely to the 'Dieu d'Israël' in Méhul's opera of 'Joseph' to be greatly vaunted on the score of originality.

Yet, with all these 'points of 'vantage' at which it may be hostilely attacked, 'La Juive' draws thousands to gaze at its splendour every time it is performed. Twice we attempted to get in without having secured places, and were told on both occasions that there was not even standing-room for gentlemen.

Among its attractions are two which are alike new to me as belonging to an opera; one is the performance of the 'Te Deum laudamus,' and the other the entrance of Franconi's troop of horse.

But, after all, it was clear enough that, whatever may have been the original object of this institution, with its nursery academies of music and dancing, its royal patronage and legalised extravagance, its present glory rests almost wholly on the talents of the Taglioni family, and with the sundry MM. décorateurs who have imagined and arranged the getting up this extraordinary specimen of scenic magnificence, as well as the many others of the same kind which have preceded it.

I have seen many fine shows of the kind in London, but certainly never anything that could at all be compared with this. Individual scenes – as, for instance, that of the masqued ball in 'Gustavus' – may equal, but the effect of the first coup-d'oeil, any scene in 'La Juive'; but it is the extraordinary propriety and perfection of all the accessaries which make this part of the performance worthy of a critical study from the beginning to the end of it. I remember reading in some history of Paris, that it was the fashion to be so *précieuse* as to the correctness of the costumes of the French opera, that the manager could not venture to bring out 'Les Trois Sultanes' without sending to Constantinople to obtain the dresses. A very considerable portion of the same spirit has evidently been at work to render the appearance of a large detachment of the court of Rome and the whole court of the Emperor Sigismund *comme il faut* upon the scene.

But, with all a woman's weakness at my heart in favour of velvet, satin, gold tissue, and ermine, I cannot but confess that these things, important as they are, appear but secondary aids in the magical scenic effects of 'La Juive.' The arrangement and management of the scenery were to me perfectly new. The coulisses have vanished, side scenes are no more, – and, what is more important still, these admirable mechanists have found the way of throwing across the stage those accidental masses of shadow by aid of which Nature produces her most brilliant effects; so that, instead of the aching eyes having to gaze upon a blaze of reflected light, relieved only by an occasional dip of the foot-lights and a sudden paling of gas in order to enact night, they are now enchanted and beguiled by exactly such a mixture of light and shade as an able painter would give to a picture.

How this is effected, Heaven knows! There are, I am very sure, more things at present above, about, and underneath the opera stage, than are dreamed of in any philosophy, excepting that of a Parisian carpenter. In the first scene of the 'Juive,' a very noble-looking church rears its sombre front exactly in the centre of the stage, throwing as fine, rich, deep a shadow on one side of it as Notre Dame herself could do. In another scene, half the stage appears to be sunk below the level of the eye, and is totally lost sight of, a low parapet wall marking the boundary of the seeming river.

Our box was excellently situated, and by no means distant from the stage; yet we often found it impossible to determine at what point, in different directions, the boards ended and the scenery began. The arrangement of the groups too, not merely in combinations of grace and beauty, but in such bold, easy, and picturesque variety, that one might fancy Murillo had made the sketches for them, was another source of wonder and admiration; and had all these pretty sights been shown us in the course of two acts instead of five, I am sure we should have gone home quite delighted and in the highest possible good-humour. But five acts of raree-show is too much; and acccordingly we yawned, and talked of Grétry, Méhul, Nicolo, and I know not whom beside; – in short, became as splenetic and pedantic as possible.

We indulged ourselves occasionally in this unamiable mood by communicating our feelings to each other, in a whisper however which could not go beyond our own box, and with the less restraint because we felt sure that the one stranger gentleman who shared it with us could not understand our language. But herein we egregiously deceived ourselves: though in appearance he was *Français jusqu'aux ongles*, we soon found out that he could speak English as well as any of us; and, with much real politeness, he had the good-nature to let us know this before we had uttered anything too profoundly John Bullish to be forgiven.

Fortunately, too, it appeared that our judgments accorded as well as if we had all been born in the same parish. He lamented the decadence of music in this, which ought to be its especial theatre; but spoke with enthusiasm of the Théâtre Italien, and its great superiority in science over every other in

Paris. This theatre, to my great vexation, is now closed; but I well remember that such too was my judgment of it some seven years ago.

The English and the French are generally classed together as having neither one nor the other any really national music of their own. We have both of us, however, some sweet and perfectly original airs, which will endure as long as the modulations of sound are permitted to enchant our mortal ears. Nevertheless, I am not going to appeal against a sentence too often repeated not to be universally received as truth. But, notwithstanding this absence of any distinct school of national music, it is impossible to doubt that the people of both countries are fondly attached to the science. More sacrifices are made by both to obtain good music than the happy German and Italian people would ever dream of making. Nor would it, I think, be fair to argue, from the present style of the performances at the Académie, that the love of music is on the decline here. The unbounded expense bestowed upon decorations, and the pomp and splendour of effect which results from it, are quite enough to attract and dazzle the eyes of a more 'thinking people' than the Parisians; and the unprecedented perfection to which the mechanists have brought the delusion of still-life seems to permit a relaxation in the efforts of the manager to obtain attraction from other sources.

But this will not last. The French people really love music, and will have it. It is more than probable that the musical branch of this academic establishment will soon revive; and if in doing so it preserves its present superiority of decoration, it will again become an amusement of unrivalled attraction.

I believe the French themselves generally consider us as having less claim to the reputation of musical amateurship than themselves; but, with much respect for their judgment on such subjects, I differ from them wholly in this. When has France ever shown, either in her capital or out of it, such a glorious burst of musical enthusiasm as produced the festivals of Westminster Abbey and of York?

It was not for the sake of encouraging an English school of music, certainly, that these extraordinary efforts were made. They were not native strains which rang along the vaulted roofs; but it was English taste, and English feeling, which recently, as well as in days of yore, conceived and executed a scheme of harmony more perfect and sublime than I can remember to have heard of elsewhere.

I doubt, too, if in any country a musical institution can be pointed out in purer taste than that of our ancient music concert. The style and manner of this are wholly national, though the compositions performed there are but partially so; and I think no one who truly and deeply loves the science but must feel that there is a character in it which, considering the estimation in which it has for so many years been held, may fairly redeem the whole nation from any deficiency in musical taste.

There is one branch of the 'gay science,' if I may so call it, which I always expect to find in France, but respecting which I have hitherto been always disappointed: this is in the humble class of itinerant musicians. In Germany they abound; and it not seldom happens that their strains arrest the feet and enchant the ear of the most fastidious. But whenever, in France, I have encountered an ambulant troubadour, I confess I have felt no inclination to linger on my way to listen to him. I do not, however, mean to claim much honour for ourselves on the score of our travelling minstrels. If we fail to pause in listening to those of France, we seldom fail to run whenever our ears are overtaken by our own. Yet still we give strong proof of our love of music, in the more than ordinary strains which may be occasionally heard before every coffee-house in London, when the noise and racket of the morning has given place to the hours of enjoyment. I have heard that the bands of wind instruments which nightly parade through the streets of London receive donations which, taken on an average throughout the year, would be sufficient to support a theatre. This can only proceed from a genuine propensity to being 'moved by concord of sweet sounds;' for no fashion, as is the case at our costly operas, leads to it. On the contrary, it is most decidedly mauvais ton to be caught listening to this unexclusive harmony; yet it is encouraged in a degree that clearly indicates the popular feeling.

Have I then proved to your satisfaction, as completely as I undoubtedly have to my own, that if without a national music, at least we are not without a national taste for it?

LETTER LVI

The Abbé Deguerry – His eloquence – Excursion across the water –
Library of Ste. Geneviève – Copy-book of the Dauphin –
St. Etienne du Mont – Pantheon

The finest sermon I have heard since I have been in Paris – and,
I am almost inclined to think, the finest I ever heard anywhere
– was preached yesterday by the Abbé Deguerry at St. Roch.
It was a discourse calculated to benefit all Christian souls of
every sect and denomination whatever – had no shade of
doctrinal allusion in it of any kind, and was just such a sermon
as one could wish every soi-disant infidel might be forced to
listen to while the eyes of a Christian congregation were fixed
upon him. It would do one good to see such a being cower and
shrink, in the midst of his impotent and petulant arrogance, to
feel how a 'plain word could put him down.'

The Abbé Deguerry is a young man, apparently under
thirty; but nature seems to have put him at once in possession
of a talent which generally requires long years to bring to
perfection. He is eloquent in the very best manner; for it is an
eloquence intended rather to benefit the hearer than to do
honour to the mere human talent of the orator. Beautifully as
his periods flowed, I felt certain, as I listened to him, that their
harmonious rhythm was the result of no study, but purely the
effect, unconsciously displayed, of a fine ear and an almost
unbounded command of language. He had studied his matter,
– he had studied and deeply weighed his arguments; but, for
his style, it was the free gift of Heaven.

Extempore preaching has always appeared to me to be a
fearfully presumptuous exercise. Thoughts well digested,
expressions carefully chosen, and arguments conscientiously
examined, are no more than every congregation has a right to
expect from one who addresses them with all the authority of
place on subjects of most high importance; and rare indeed is

the talent which can produce this without cautious and deliberate study. But in listening to the Abbé Deguerry, I perceived it was possible that a great and peculiar talent, joined to early and constant practice, might enable a man to address his fellow creatures without presumption even though he had not written his sermon; – yet it is probable that I should be more correct were I to say, without reading it to his congregation, for it is hardly possible to believe that such a composition was actually and altogether extempore.

His argument, which was to show the helpless insufficiency of man without the assistance of revelation and religious faith, was never lost sight of for an instant. There was no weak wordiness, no repetition, no hackneyed ornaments of rhetoric; but it was the voice of truth, speaking in that language of universal eloquence which all nations and all creeds must feel; and it flowed on with unbroken clearness, beauty, and power, to the end.

Having recently quitted Flanders, where everything connected with the Roman Catholic worship is sustained in a style of stately magnificence which plainly speaks its Spanish origin, I am continually surprised by the comparatively simple vestments and absence of ostentatious display in the churches of Paris. At the metropolitan church of Notre Dame, indeed, nothing was wanting to render its archiepiscopal dignity conspicuous; but everywhere else, there was a great deal less of pomp and circumstance than I expected. But nowhere is the relaxation of clerical dignity in the clergy of Paris so remarkable as in the appearance of the young priests whom we occasionally meet in the streets. The flowing curls, the simple round hat, the pantaloons, and in some cases the boots also, give them the appearance of a race of men as unlike as possible to their stiff and primitive predecessors. Yet they all look flourishing, and well pleased with themselves and the world about them: but little of mortification or abstinence can be traced on their countenances; and if they do fast for some portion of every week, they may certainly say with Father Philip, that 'what they take prospers with them marvellously.'

We have this morning made an excursion to the other side of the water, which always seems like setting out upon a journey; and yet I know not why it should be so, for as the river is not very wide, the bridges are not very long; but so it is, that for some reason or other, if it were not for the magnetic Abbaye-aux-Bois, we should very rarely find ourselves on the left bank of the Seine.

On this occasion, our object was to visit the famous old library of Ste. Geneviève, on the invitation of a gentleman who is one of the librarians. Nothing can be more interesting than an expedition of this sort, with an intelligent and obliging cicisbeo, who knows everything concerning the objects displayed before you, and is kindly willing to communicate as much of his *savoir* as the time may allow, or as may be necessary to make the different objects examined come forth from that venerable but incomprehensible accumulation of treasures, which form the mass of all the libraries and museums in the world, and which, be he as innocent of curiosity as an angel, every stranger is bound over to visit, under penalty, when honestly reciting his adventures, of hearing exclamations from all the friends he left at home, of – 'What! . . . did you not see that? . . . Then you have seen nothing!'

I would certainly never expose myself to this cutting reproach, could I always secure as agreeable a companion as the one who tempted us to mount to the elevated repository which contains the hundred thousand volumes of the royal library of Ste. Geneviève. Were I a student there, I should grumble prodigiously at the long and steep ascent to this temple of all sorts of learning: but once reached, the tranquil stillness, and the perfect seclusion from the eternal hum of the great city that surrounds it, are very delightful, and might, I think, act as a sedative upon the most restive and truant imagination that ever beset a student.

I was sorry to hear that symptoms of decay in the timbers of the venerable roof make it probable that this fine old room must be given up, and the large collection it has so long sheltered be conveyed elsewhere. The apartment is in the form of a cross, with a dome at the point of intersection, painted by the elder Restout. Though low, and in fact occupying only the roof of the college, formerly the Abbaye of Sainte Geneviève, there is something singularly graceful and pleasing to the eye in this extensive chamber, its ornaments and general

Pretres de la Jeune France.

arrangement; – something monastic, yet not gloomy; with an air of learned ease, and comfortable exclusion of all annoyance, that is very enviable.

The library appears to be kept up in excellent style, and in a manner to give full effect to its liberal regulations, which permit the use of every volume in the collection to all the earth. The wandering scholar at distance from his own learned cell, and the idle reader for mere amusement, may alike indulge their bookish propensities here, with exactly the same facilities that are accorded to the students of the college. The librarians or their deputies are ready to deliver to them any work they ask for, with the light and reasonable condition annexed that the reader shall accompany the person who is to find the volume or volumes required, and assist in conveying them to the spot which he has selected for his place of study.

The long table which stretches from the centre under the dome, across the transepts of the cross, was crowded with young men when we were there, who really seemed most perfectly in earnest in their occupation – gazing on the volumes before them 'with earnest looks intent,' even while a large party swept past them to examine a curious model of Rome placed at the extremity of one of the transepts. A rigorous silence, however, is enjoined in this portion of the apartments; so that even the ladies were obliged to postpone their questions and remarks till they had passed out of it.

After looking at splendid editions, rare copies, and so forth, our friend led us to some small rooms, fitted up with cases for the especial protection under lock and key of the manuscripts of the collection. Having admired the spotless vellum of some, and the fair penmanship of others, a thin morocco–bound volume was put into my hands, which looked like a young lady's collection of manuscript waltzes. This was the copy-book of the Dauphin, father of the much-regretted Duke de Bourgogne, and grandfather of Louis Quinze.

The characters were evidently written with great care. Each page contained a moral axiom, and all of them more or less especially applicable to a royal pupil. There was one of these which I thought might be particularly useful to all such at the present day: it was entitled, in large letters –

– the superfluous U being erased by a dash of the master's pen.
Then followed, in extremely clear and firm characters, these
lines:–

> Si de vos actions la satyre réjoue,
> Feignez adroitement de ne las pas ouïr:
> Qui relève une injure, il semble qu'il l'avoue;
> Qui la scait mépriser, la fait évanouir.

L   LOUIS   LOUIS   LOUIS   LOUIS

In one of these smaller rooms hangs the portrait of a negress in
the dress of a nun. It has every appearance of being a very old
painting, and our friend M. C—— told us that a legend had
been ever attached to it, importing that it was the portrait of a
daughter of Mary Queen of Scots, born before she left France
for Scotland. What could have originated such a very disagreeable piece of scandal, it is difficult to imagine; but I can
testify that all the internal evidence connected with it is strong
against its truth, for no human countenance can well be
conceived which would show less family likeness to our
lovely and unfortunate northern queen than does that of this
grim sister.

From the library of Ste. Geneviève, we went under the same
kind escort to look at the barbaric but graceful vagaries of St.
Etienne du Mont. The galleries suspended as if by magic
between the pillars of the choir, and the spiral staircases
leading to them, out of all order as they are, must nevertheless
be acknowledged as among the lightest and most fairy-like
constructions in the world. This singular church, capricious in
its architecture both within and without, is in some parts of
great antiquity, and was originally built as a chapel of ease to
the old church of Ste. Geneviève, which stood close beside it,
and of which the lofty old tower still remains, making part of
the college buildings. As a proof of the entire dependance of
this pretty little church upon its mother edifice, it was not
permitted to have any separate door of its own, the only access
to it being through the great church. This subsidiary chapel,

now dignified into a parish church, has at different periods been enlarged and beautified, and has again and again petitioned for leave from its superior to have a door of its own; but again and again it was refused, and it was not till the beginning of the sixteenth century that this modest request was at length granted. The great Pascal lies buried in this church.

I was very anxious to give my children a sight of the interior of that beautiful but versatile building called, when I first saw it, the Pantheon – when I last saw it, Ste. Geneviève, and which is now again known to all the world, or at least to that part of it which has been fortunate enough to visit Paris since the immortal days, as the Pantheon.

We could not, however, obtain an entrance to it; and it is very likely that before we shall again find ourselves on its simple and severe, but very graceful threshold, it will have again changed its vocation, and be restored to the use of the Christian church. – Ainsi soit-il!

LETTER LVII

Little Suppers – Great Dinners – Affectation of Gourmandise –
Evil effect of 'dining out' – Evening Parties –
Dinners in private under the name of Luncheons – Late Hours

How I mourn for the departed petits soupers of Paris! . . . and
how far are her pompous dinners from being able to atone for
their loss! For those people, and I am afraid there are many of
them, who really and literally live to eat, I know that the word
'dinner' is the signal and symbol of earth's best, and, perhaps,
only bliss. For them the steaming vapour, the tedious long
array, the slow and solemn progress of a dîner de quatre
services, offers nothing but joy and gladness; but what is it to
those who only eat to live?

I know no case in which injustice and tyranny are so often
practised as at the dinner-table. Perhaps twenty people sit
down to dinner, of whom sixteen would give the world to eat
just no more than they like and have done with it: but it is
known to the Amphitryon that there are four heavy persons
present whose souls hover over his ragoûts like harpies over
the feast of Phinaeus, and they must not be disturbed, or
revilings instead of admiration will repay the outlay and the
turmoil of the banquet.

A tedious, dull play, followed by a long, noisy, and
gunpowder-scented pantomine, upon the last scene of which
your party is determined to see the curtain fall; a heavy sermon
of an hour long, your pew being exactly in front of the
preacher; a morning visit from a lady who sends her carriage
to fetch her boys from school at Wimbleton, and comes to
entertain you with friendly talk about her servants till it comes
back; – each of these is hard to bear and difficult to escape; but
which of them can compare in suffering to a full-blown, stiff,
stately dinner of three hours long, where the talk is of food,
and the only relief from this talk is to eat it? . . . How can you

get away? How is it possible to find or invent any device that
can save you from enduring to the end? With cheeks burning
from steam and vexation, can you plead a sudden faintness?
Still less can you dare to tell the real truth, and confess that you
are dying of disgust and ennui. The match is so unfair between
the different parties at such a meeting as this – the victims so
utterly helpless! . . . And, after all, there is no occasion for it.
In London there are the clubs and the Clarendon; in Paris are
Périgord's and Véry's and a score beside, any one of whom
could furnish a more perfect dinner than can be found at any
private mansion whatever, where sufferings are often inflicted
on the wretched lookers-on very nearly approaching to those
necessary for the production of the *foie gras*.

Think not, however, that I am inclined in the least degree to
affect indifference or dislike to an elegant, well-spread table:
on the contrary, I am disposed to believe that the hours when
mortals meet together, all equally disposed to enjoy themselves by refreshing the spirits, recruiting the strength and
inspiring the wit, with the cates and the cups most pleasing to
the palate of each, may be reckoned, without any degradation
to human pride, among the happiest hours of life. But this no
more resembles the endless crammings of a *repas de quatre
services*, than a work in four volumes of political economy to
an epigram in four lines upon the author of it.

In fact, to give you a valuable hint upon the subject, I am
persuaded that some of the most distinguished gourmets of
the age have plunged themselves and their disciples into a
most lamentable error in this matter. They have overdone the
thing altogether. Their object is to excite the appetite as much
as possible, in order to satisfy it as largely as possible; and this
end is utterly defeated by the means used. But I will not dwell
on this; neither you nor I are very particularly interested in the
success either of the French or English eaters by profession; we
will leave them to study their own business and manage it as
well as they can.

For the more philosophical enjoyers of the goods the gods
provide I feel more interest, and I really lament the weakness
which leads so many of them to follow a fashion which must
be so contrary to all their ideas of real enjoyment; but,
unhappily, it is daily becoming more necessary for every man

who sits down at a fashionable table to begin talking like a cook. They surely mistake the thing altogether. This is not the most effectual way of proving the keenness of their gourmandise.

In nine cases out of ten, I believe this inordinate passion for good eating is pure affectation; and I suspect that many a man, especially many a young man, both in Paris and London, would often be glad to eat a reasonably good dinner, and then change the air, instead of sitting hour after hour, while dishes are brought to his elbow till his head aches in shaking it as a negative to the offer of them, were it not that it would be so dreadfully bourgeois to confess it.

If, however, on the other hand, an incessant and pertinacious 'diner-out' should take up the business in good earnest, and console himself for the long sessions he endures by really eating on from soup to ice, what a heavy penalty does he speedily pay for it! I have lived long enough to watch more than one svelte, graceful, elegant young man, the glory of the drawing-room, the pride of the Park, the hero of Almack's, growing every year rounder and redder; the clear, well-opened eye becoming dull and leaden – the brilliant white teeth looking 'not what they were, but quite the reverse,' till the noble-looking, animated being, that one half the world was ready to love, and the other to envy, sank down into a heavy, clumsy, middle-aged gentleman, before half his youth was fairly past; and this solely for the satisfaction of continuing to eat every day for some hours after he had ceased to be hungry.

It is really a pity that every one beginning this career does not set the balance of what he will gain and what he will lose by it fairly before him. If this were done, we should probably have much fewer theoretical cooks and practical crammers, but many more lively, animated table-companions, who might oftener be witty themselves, and less often the cause of wit in others.

The fashion for assembling large parties, instead of selecting small ones, is on all occasions a grievous injury to social enjoyment. It began perhaps in vanity: fine ladies wished to show the world that they had 'a dear five hundred friends' ready to come at their call. But as everybody complains of it as a bore, from Whitechapel to Belgrave-square, and from the Faubourg St. Antoine to the Faubourg du Roule, vanity would now be likely enough to put a general stop to it, were it not that a most disagreeable species of economy prevents it. 'A large party kills such a prodigious number of birds,' as I once heard a friend of mine say, when pleading to her husband for permission to overflow her dinner-table first, and then her drawing-rooms, 'that it is the most extravagant thing in the world to have a small one.' Now this is terrible, because it is true: but, at least, those blest with wealth might enjoy the extreme luxury of having just as many people about them as they liked, and no more; and if they would but be so very obliging as to set the fashion, we all know that it would speedily be followed in some mode or other by all ranks, till it would be considered as positively mauvais ton to have twice as many people in your house as you have chairs for them to sit on.

The pleasantest evening parties remaining in Paris, now that such delightful little committees as Molière brings together after the performance of 'L'Ecole des Femmes' can meet no more, are those asssembled by an announcement made by Madame une Telle to a somewhat select circle, that she shall be at home on a certain evening in every week, fortnight, or month, throughout the season. This done, nothing farther is necessary; and on these evenings a party moderately large drop in without ceremony, and depart without restraint. No preparation is made beyond a few additional lights; and the albums and portfolios in one room, with perhaps a harp or pianoforte in another, give aid, if aid be wanted, to the conversation going on in both. Ices, eau sucrée, syrup of fruits, and gaufres are brought round, and the party rarely remain together after midnight.

This is very easy and agreeable, – incomparably better, no doubt, than more crowded and more formal assemblées. Nevertheless, I am so profoundly rococo as to regret heartily the passing away of the petits soupers, which used to be the favourite scene of enjoyment, and the chosen arena for the exhibition of wit, for all the beaux esprits, male and female, of Paris.

I was told last spring, in London, that at present it was the parvenus only who had incomes unscathed by the stormy times; and that, consequently, it was rather elegant than otherwise to *chanter misère* upon all occasions. I moreover heard a distinguished confectioner, when in conversation with a lady on the subject of a ball supper, declare that 'orders were so slack, that he had countermanded a set of new ornaments which he had bespoken from Paris.'

Such being the case, what an excellent opportunity is the present for a little remuement in the style of giving entertainments! Poverty and the clubs render fine dinners at once dangerous, difficult, and unnecessary; but does it follow that men and women are no more to meet round a banqueting table? 'Because we are virtuous, shall there be no more cakes and ale?'

I have often dreamed, that were I a great lady, with houses and lands, and money at will, I would see if I could not break through the tyrannous yoke of fashion, often so confessedly galling to the patient wearers of it, and, in the place of heavy, endless dinners, which often make bankrupt the spirit and the purse, endeavour to bring into vogue that prettiest of all inventions for social enjoyment – a real supper-table: not a long board, whereat aching limbs and languid eyes may yawningly wait to receive from the hand of Mr. Gunter what must cost the giver more, and profit the receiver less, than any imaginable entertainment of the kind I propose, and which might be spread by an establishment as simply monté as that of any gentleman in London.

Then think of the luxury of sitting down at a table neither steaming with ragoûts, nor having dyspepsia hid under every cover; where neither malignant gout stands by, nor servants swarm and listen to every idle word; where you may renew the memory of the sweet strains you have just listened to at the opera, instead of sitting upon thorns while you know that your favourite overture is in the very act of being played! All should be cool and refreshing, nectarine and ambrosial, – uncrowded, easy, intimate, and as witty as Englishmen and Englishwomen could contrive to make it!

Till this experiment has been fairly made and declared to fail, I will never allow that the conversational powers of the women of England have been fully proved and found wanting. The wit of Mercury might be weighed to earth by the endurance of three long, pompous courses; and would it not require spirits lighter and brighter than those of a Peri to sustain a woman gaily through the solemn ceremonies of a fine dinner?

In truth, the whole arrangement appears to me strangely defective and ill-contrived. Let English ladies be sworn to obey the laws of fashion as faithfully as they will, they cannot live till eight o'clock in the evening without some refreshment more substantial than the first morning meal. In honest truth and plain English, they all dine in the most unequivocal manner at two or three o'clock; nay, many of those who meet their hungry brethren at dinner-parties have taken coffee or tea before they arrive there. Then what a distasteful, tedious farce does the fine dinner become!

Now just utter a 'Passe! passe!' and, by a little imagination legerdemain, turn from this needless dinner to such a petit souper as Madame de Maintenon gave of yore. Let Fancy paint the contrast; and let her take the gayest colours she can find, she cannot make it too striking. You must, however, rouse your courage, and strengthen your nerves, that they may not quail before this fearful word – SUPPER. In truth, the sort of shudder I have seen pass over the countenances of some fashionable men when it is pronounced may have been natural and unaffected enough; for who that has been eating in despite of nature from eight to eleven can find anything *appétissant* in this word 'supper' uttered at twelve.

But if we could persuade Messieurs nos Maîtres, instead of injuring their health by the long fast which now precedes their dinner, during which they walk, talk, ride, drive, read, play billiards, yawn – nay, even sleep, to while away the time, and to accumulate, as it were, an appetite of inordinate dimensions; – if, instead of this, they would for one season try the experiment of dining at five o'clock, and condescend afterwards to permit themselves to be agreeable in the drawing-room, they would find their wit sparkle brighter than the champagne at their supper-tables, and moreover their mirrors would pay them the prettiest compliments in the world before they had tried the change for a fortnight.

But, alas! all this is very idle speculation; for I am not a great lady, and have no power whatever to turn dull dinners into gay suppers, let me wish it as much as I may.

LETTER LVIII

Hôpital des Enfans Trouvés – Its doubtful advantages –
Story of a Child left there

Like diligent sightseers, as we are, we have been to visit the hospital for Les Enfans Trouvés. I had myself gone over every part of the establishment several years before, but to the rest of my party it was new – and certainly there is enough of strangeness in the spectacle to repay a drive to the Rue d'Enfer. Our kind friend and physician, Dr. Mojon, who by the way is one of the most amiable men and most skilful physicians in Paris, was the person who introduced us; and his acquaintance with the visiting physician, who attended us round the rooms, enabled us to obtain much interesting information. But, alas! it seems as if every question asked on this subject could only elicit a painful answer. The charity itself, noble as it is in extent, and admirable for the excellent order which reigns throughout every department of it, is, I fear, but a very doubtful good. If it tend, as it doubtless must do, to prevent the unnatural crime of infanticide, it leads directly to one hardly less hateful in the perpetration, and perhaps more cruel in its result, – namely, that of abandoning the creature whom nature, unless very fearfully distorted, renders dearer than life. Nor is it the least melancholy part of the speculation to know that one fourth of the innocent creatures, who are deposited at the average rate of above twenty each day, die within the first year of their lives. But this, after all, perhaps is no very just cause of lamentation: one of the sisters of charity who attend at the hospital told me, in reply to an inquiry respecting the education of these immortal but unvalued beings, that the charity extended not its cares beyond preserving their animal life and health – that no education whatever was provided for them, and that, unless some lucky and most rare accident occurred to change their destiny, they generally grew up in very nearly the same state as the animals bred upon the farms which received them.

Peasants come on fixed days – two or three times a week, I believe – to receive the children who appear likely to live, as nurslings; and they convey them into the country, sometimes to a great distance from Paris, partly for the sake of a consideration in money which they receive, but chiefly for the value of their labour.

It is a singular fact, that during the years which immediately followed the revolution, the number of children deposited at the hospital was greatly diminished; but, among those deposited, the proportion of deaths was still more greatly increased. In 1797, for instance, 3,716 children were received, 3,108 of whom died.

I have lately heard a story, of which a child received at this hospital is in some sort the heroine; and as I thought it sufficiently interesting to insert in my notebook, I am tempted to transcribe it for you. The circumstances occurred during the period which immediately followed the first revolution; but the events were merely domestic, and took no colour from the times.

M. le Comte de G—— was a nobleman of quiet and retired habits, whom delicate health had early induced to quit the service, the court, and the town. He resided wholly at a paternal chateau in Normandy, where his forefathers had resided before him too usefully and too unostentatiously to have suffered from the devastating effects of the revolution. The neighbours, instead of violating their property, had protected it; and in the year 1799, when my story begins, the count with his wife and one little daughter were as quietly inhabiting the mansion his ancestors had inhabited before him, as if it stood on English soil.

It happened, during that year, that the wife of a peasant on his estate, who had twice before made a journey to Paris, to take a nursling from among the enfans trouvés, again lost a new-born baby, and again determined upon supplying its place from the hospital. It seemed that the poor woman was either a bad nurse or a most unlucky one; for not only had she lost three of her own, but her two foster-children also.

Of this excursion, however, she prophesied a better result; for the sister of charity, when she placed in her arms the baby now consigned to her care, assured her it was the loveliest and most promising child she had seen deposited during ten years of constant attendance among the enfans trouvés. Nor were her hopes disappointed: the little Alexa (for such was the name pinned on her dress) was at five years old so beautiful, so attractive, so touching, with her large blue eyes and dark chestnut curls, that she was known and talked of for a league round Pont St. Jacques. M. and Madame de G——, with their little girl, never passed the cottage without entering to look at and caress the lovely child.

Isabeau de G—— was just three years older than the little foundling; but a most close alliance subsisted between them. The young heiress, with all the pride of a juvenile senior, delighted in nothing so much as in extending her patronage and protection to the pretty Alexa; and the forsaken child gave her in return the *prémices* of her warm heart's fondness.

No Sunday evening ever passed throughout the summer without seeing all the village assembled under an enormous lime-tree, that grew upon a sort of platform in front of the primitive old mansion, with a pepper-box at each corner, dignified with the title of Château Tourelles.

The circular bench which surrounded this giant tree afforded a resting-place for the old folks; – the young ones danced on the green before them – and the children rolled on the grass, and made garlands of buttercups, and rosaries of daisies, to their hearts' content. On these occasions it was of custom immemorial that M. le Comte and Madame la Comtesse, with as many offspring as they were blessed withal, should walk down the strait pebbled walk which led from the chateau to the tree exactly as the clock struck four, there to remain for thirty minutes and no longer, smiling, nodding, and now and then gossiping a little, to all the poor bodies who chose to approach them.

Of late years, Mademoiselle Isabeau had established a custom which shortened the time of her personal appearance before the eyes of her future tenants to somewhat less than one-sixth of the allotted time; for five minutes never elapsed after the little lady reached the tree, before she contrived to slip her tiny hand out of her mother's and pounce upon the little Alexa, who, on her side, had long learned to turn her beautiful eyes towards the chateau the moment she reached the ground, nor removed them till they found Isabeau's bright face to rest upon instead. As soon as she had got possession of her pet, the young lady, who had not perhaps altogether escaped spoiling, ran off with her, without asking leave of any, and enjoyed, either in the aristocratic retirement of her own nursery, or her own playroom or her own garden, the love, admiration, and docile obedience of her little favourite.

But if this made a fête for Isabeau, it was something dearer still to Alexa. It was during these Sabbath hours that the poor child learned to be aware that she knew a great many more wonderful things than either Père Gautier or Mère Françoise. She learned to read – she learned to speak as good French as Isabeau or her Parisian governess; she learned to love nothing so well as the books, and the pianoforte, and the pictures, and the flowers of her pretty patroness; and, unhappily, she learned also to dislike nothing so much as the dirty cottage and cross voice of Père Gautier, who, to say truth, did little else but scold the poor forsaken thing through every meal of the week, and all day long on a Sunday.

Things went on thus without a shadow of turning till Alexa attained her tenth, and Isabeau her thirteenth year. At this time the summer Sunday evenings began to be often tarnished by the tears of the foundling as she opened her heart to her friend concerning the sufferings she endured at home. Père Gautier scolded more than ever, and Mère Françoise expected her to do the work of a woman; – in short, every day that passed made her more completely, utterly, hopelessly wretched; and at last she threw her arms round the neck of Isabeau, and told her so, adding, in a voice choked with sobs, 'that she wished . . . that she wished . . . she could die!'

They were sitting together on a small couch in the young heiress's playroom when this passionate avowal was made. The young lady disengaged herself from the arms of the weeping child, and sat for a few moments in deep meditation. 'Sit still in this place, Alexa,' she said at length, 'till I return to you;' and having thus spoken, with an air of unusual gravity she left the room.

Alexa was so accustomed to show implicit obedience to whatever her friend commanded, that she never thought of quitting the place where she was left, though she saw the sun set behind the hills through a window opposite to her, and then watched the bright horizontal beams fading into twilight, and twilight vanishing in darkness. It was strange, she thought, for her to be at the chateau at night; but Mademoiselle Isabeau had bade her sit there, and it must be right. Weary with watching, however, she first dropped her head upon the arm of the sofa, then drew her little feet up to it, and at last fell fast asleep. How long she lay there my story does not tell; but when she awoke, it was suddenly and with a violent start, for she heard the voice of Madame de G—— and felt the blaze of many lights upon her eyes. In another instant, however, they were sheltered from the painful light in the bosom of her friend.

Isabeau, her eyes sparkling with even more than their usual brightness, her colour raised, and out of breath with haste and eagerness, pressed her fondly to her heart, and covered her curls with kisses; then, having recovered the power of speaking, she exclaimed, 'Look up, my dear Alexa! You are to be my own sister for evermore: papa and mamma have said it. Cross Père Gautier has consented to give you up; and Mère Françoise is to have little Annette Morneau to live with her.'

How this had all been arranged it is needless to repeat, though the eager supplication of the daughter and the generous concessions of the parents made a very pretty scene as I heard it described; but I must not make my story too long. To avoid this, I will now slide over six years, and bring you to a fine morning in the year 1811, when Isabeau and Alexa, on returning from a ramble in the village, found Madame de G—— with an open letter in her hand, and an air of unusual excitement in her manner.

'Isabeau, my dear child,' she said, 'your father's oldest friend, the Vicomte de C——, is returned from Spain. They are come to pass a month at V——; and this letter is to beg your father and me to bring you to them immediately, for they were in the house when you were born, my child, and they love you as if you were their own. Your father is gone to give orders about horses for tomorrow. Alexa dear, what will you do without us?'

'Cannot Alexa go too, mamma?' said Isabeau.

'Not this time, my dear: they speak of having their chateau filled with guests.'

'Oh, dearest Isabeau! do not stand to talk about me; you know I do not love strangers: let me help you to get everything ready.'

The party set off the next morning, and Alexa, for the first time since she became an inhabitant of Château Tourelles, was left without Isabeau, and with no other companion than their stiff governess; but she rallied her courage, and awaited their return with all the philosophy she could muster.

Time and the hour wear through the longest fortnight, and at the end of this term the trio returned again. The meeting of the two friends was almost rapturous: Monsieur and Madame had the air of being *parfaitement contents*, and all things seemed to go on as usual. Important changes, however, had been decided on during this visit. The Vicomte de C. had one son. He is the hero of my story, so believe him at once to be a most charming personage in all ways – and in fact he was so. A marriage between him and Isabeau had been proposed by his father, and cordially agreed to by hers; but it was decided between them that the young people should see something more of each other before this arrangement was announced to them, for both parents felt that the character of their children deserved and demanded rather more deference to their inclinations that was generally thought necessary in family compacts of this nature.

The fortnight had passed amidst much gaiety: every evening brought waltzing and music; Isabeau sang *à ravir*; but as there were three married ladies at the chateau who proclaimed themselves to be unwearying waltzers, young Jules, who was constrained to do the honours of his father's house, had never found an opportunity to dance with Isabeau excepting for the last waltz, on the last evening; and then there never were seen two young people waltzing together with more awkward restraint.

Madame de G——, however, fancied that he had listened to Isabeau's songs with pleasure, and moreover observed to Monsieur son Mari that it was impossible he should not think her beautiful.

Madame was quite right – Jules did think her daughter beautiful: he thought, too, that her voice was that of a syren, and that it would be easy for him to listen to her till he forgot everything else in the world.

I would not be so abrupt had I more room; but as it is necessary to hasten over the ground, I must tell you at once that Isabeau, on her side, was much in the same situation. But as a young lady should never give her heart anywhere till she is asked, and in France not before her husband has politely expressed his wish to be loved as he leads her to her carriage from the altar, Isabeau took especial good care that nobody should find out the indiscretion her feelings had committed, and having not only a mind of considerable power, but also great confidence and some pride in her own strength, she felt little fear but that she should be able both to conceal and conquer a passion so every way unauthorised.

Now it unfortunately happened that Jules de C. was, unlike the generality of his countrymen, extremely romantic; – but he had passed seven years in Spain, which may in some degree excuse it. His education, too, had been almost wholly domestic: he knew little of life except from books, and he had learned to dread, as the most direful misfortune that could befall him, the becoming enamoured of, and perhaps marrying, a woman who loved him not.

Soon after the departure of Isabeau and her parents, the vicomte hinted to his son that he thought politeness required a return of the visit of the de G—— family; and as both himself and his lady were *un peu incommodés* by some malady, real or supposititious, he conceived that it would be right that he, Jules, should present himself at Château Tourelles to make their excuses. The heart of Jules gave a prodigious leap; but it was not wholly a sensation of pleasure: he felt afraid of Isabeau, – he was afraid of loving her, – he remembered the cold and calm expression of countenance with which she received his farewell – his trembling farewell – at the door of the carriage. Yet still he accepted the commission; and in ten days after the return of the de G—— family, Jules de C. presented himself before them. His reception by the comte and his lady was just what may be imagined, – all kindness and cordiality of welcome. That of Isabeau was constrained and cold. She turned a little pale, but then she blushed again; and the shy Jules saw nothing but the beauty of the blush – was conscious only of the ceremonious curtsy, and the cold 'Bonjour, Monsieur Jules.' As for Alexa, her only feeling was that of extreme surprise. How could it be that Isabeau had seen a person so very graceful, handsome and elegant, and yet never say one word to her about him! . . . Isabeau must be blind, insensible, unfeeling, not to appreciate better such a being as that. Such was the effect produced by the appearance of Jules on the mind of Alexa, – the beautiful, the enthusiastic, the impassioned Alexa. From that moment a most cruel game of cross purposes began to be played at Château Tourelles. Alexa commenced by reproaching Isabeau for her coldness, and ended by confessing that she heartily wished herself as cold. Jules ceased not to adore Isabeau, but every day strengthened his conviction that she could never love him; and Isabeau, while every passing hour showed more to love in Jules, only drew from thence more reasons for combating and conquering the flame that inwardly consumed her.

There could not be a greater contrast between two girls, both good, than there was both in person and mind between these two young friends. Isabeau was the prettiest little brunette in France – et c'est beaucoup dire: Alexa was, perhaps, the loveliest blonde in the world. Isabeau, with strong feelings, had a command over herself that never failed: in a good cause, she could have perished at the stake without a groan. Alexa could feel, perhaps, almost as strongly as her friend; but to combat those feelings was beyond her power: she might have died to show her love, but not to conceal it; and had some fearful doom awaited her, she would not have lived to endure it.

Such being the character and position of the parties, you will easily perceive the result. Jules soon perceived the passion with which he had inspired the young and beautiful Alexa, and his heart, wounded by the uniform reserve of Isabeau, repaid her with a warmth of gratitude, which though not love, was easily mistaken for it by both the innocent rivals. Poor Jules saw that it was, and already felt his honour engaged to ratify hopes which he had never intended to raise. Repeatedly he determined to leave the chateau, and never to see either of its lovely inmates more; but whenever he hinted at such an intention, M. and Madame de G—— opposed it in such a manner that it seemed impossible to persevere in it. They, good souls, were perfectly satisfied with the aspect of affairs: Isabeau was perhaps a little pale, but lovelier than ever; and the eyes of Jules were so often fixed upon her, that there could be no doubt as to his feelings. They were very right, – yet, alas! they were very wrong too: but the situation of Alexa put her so completely out of all question of marriage with a gentleman *d'une haute naissance,* that they never even remembered that she too was constantly with Jules.

About three weeks had passed in this mischief-working manner, when Isabeau, who clearly saw traces of suffering on the handsome face of poor Jules, believing firmly that it arose from the probable difficulty of obtaining his high-born father's consent to his marriage with a foundling, determined to put every imaginable means in requisition to assist him.

Alexa had upon her breast a mark, evidently produced by gunpowder. Her nurse, and everybody else who had seen it, declared it to be perfectly shapeless, and probably a failure from the awkwardness of some one who had intended to impress a cipher there; but Isabeau had a hundred times examined it, and as often declared it to be a coronet. Hitherto this notion had only been a source of mirth to both of them, but now it became a theme of incessant and most anxious meditation to Isabeau. She remembered to have heard that when a child is deposited at the Foundling Hospital of Paris, everything, whether clothes or token, which is left with it, is preserved and registered, with the name and the date of the reception, in order, if reclamation be made within a certain time, that all assistance possible shall be given for the identification. What space this 'certain time' included Isabeau knew not, but she fancied that it could not be less than twenty years; and with this persuasion she determined to set about an inquiry that might at least lead to the knowledge either that some particular tokens had been left with Alexa, or that there were none.

With this sort of feverish dream working in her head, Isabeau rose almost before daylight one morning, and escaping the observation of every one, let herself out by the door of a salon which opened on the terrace, and hastened to the abode of Mère Françoise. It was some time before she could make the old woman understand her object; but when she did, she declared herself ready to do all and everything Mademoiselle desired for her 'dear baby,' as she persisted to call the tall, the graceful, the beautiful Alexa.

As Isabeau had a good deal of trouble to make her plans and projects clearly understood to Mère Françoise, it will be better not to relate particularly what passed between them: suffice it to say, that by dint of much repetition and a tolerably heavy purse, Françoise at last agreed to set off for Paris on the following morning, 'without telling a living soul what for.' Such were the conditions enforced; which were the more easily adhered to, because cross Père Gautier had grumbled himself into his grave some years before.

On reaching the hospital, Françoise made her demand, 'de la part d'une grande dame,' for any token which they possessed relative to a baby taken . . . &c. &c. &c. The first answer she received was, that the time of limitation for such inquiries had long expired; and she was on the point of leaving the bureau, all hope of intelligence abandoned, when an old sister of charity who chanced to be there for some message from the superior, and who had listened to her inquiries and all the particulars thus rehearsed, stopped her by saying, that it was odd enough two great ladies should send to the hospital with inquiries for the same child. 'But, however,' she added, 'it can't much matter to either of them, for the baby died before it was a twelve-month old.'

'Died!' screamed Françoise: 'why, I saw her but four days ago, and a more beautiful creature the sun never shone upon.'

An explanation ensued, not very clear in all its parts, for there had evidently been some blunder; but it plainly appeared, that within a year after the child was sent to nurse, inquiries had been made at the hospital for a baby bearing the singular name of Alexa, and stating that various articles were left with her expressly to ensure the power of recognition. An address to a peasant in the country had been given to the persons who had made these inquiries, and application was immediately made to her: but she stated that the baby she had received from the hospital at the time named had died three months after she took it; but what name she had received with it she could not remember, as she called it Marie, after the baby she had lost. It was evident from this statement that a mistake had been made between the two women, who had each taken a female foundling into the country on the same day.

It was more easy, however, to hit the blunder than to repair it. Communication was immediately held with some of the *chefs* of the establishment; who having put in action every imaginable contrivance to discover any traces which might remain of the persons who had before inquired for the babe named Alexa, at length got hold of a man who had often acted as commissionnaire to the establishment, and who said he remembered *about that time* to have taken letters from the hospital to a fine hôtel near the Elysée Bourbon.

This man was immediately conveyed to the Elysée Bourbon, and without hesitation pointed out the mansion to which he had been sent. It was inhabited by an English gentleman blessed with a family of twelve children, and who assured the gentleman entrusted with the inquiry that he had not only never deposited any of his children at the Enfans Trouvés, but that he could not give them the slightest assistance in discovering whether any of his predecessors in that mansion had done so. Discouraged, but not chilled in the ardour of his pursuit, the worthy gentleman proceeded to the proprietor of the hôtel: he had recently purchased it; from him he repaired to the person from whom he had bought it. He was only an agent; but at last, by means of indefatigable exertion during three days, he discovered that the individual who must have inhabited the hôtel when these messages were stated to have been sent thither from the Enfans Trouvés was a Russian nobleman of high rank, who, it was believed, was now residing at St. Petersburg. His name and title, however, were both remembered; and these, with a document stating all that was known of the transaction, were delivered to Mère Françoise, who, hardly knowing if she had succeeded or failed in her mission, returned to her young employer within ten days of the time she left her.

Isabeau, generously as her noble heart beat at learning what she could not but consider as a favourable report of her embassy, did feel nevertheless something like a pang when she remembered to what this success would lead. But she mastered it, and, with all the energy of her character, instantly set to work to pursue her enterprise to the end. It was certainly a relief to her when Jules, after passing a month of utter misery in the society of the woman he adored, took his leave. The old people were still perfectly satisfied: it was not the young man's business, they said, to break through the reserve which his parents had enjoined, and a few days would doubtless bring letters from them which would finally settle the business.

Alexa saw him depart with an aching heart; but she believed that he was returning home only to ask his father's consent to their union. Isabeau fed her hopes, for she too believed that the young man's heart was given to Alexa. During this time Isabeau concealed her hope of discovering the parents of the foundling from all. Day after day wore away, and brought no tidings from Jules. The hope of Alexa gave way before this cruel silence. The circumstances of her birth, which rankled at her heart more deeply than even her friend imagined, now came before her in a more dreadful shape than ever. Sin, shame, and misery seemed to her the only *dot* she had to bring in marriage, and her mind brooded over this terrible idea till it overpowered every other; her love seemed to sink before it, and, after a sleepless night of wretched meditation, she determined never to bring disgrace upon a husband – she herocially determined never to marry.

As she was opening her heart on this sad subject to Isabeau, and repeating to her with great solemnity the resolution she had taken, a courier covered with dust galloped up to the door of the chateau. Isabeau instantly suspected the truth, but could only say as she kissed the fair forehead of the foundling, 'Look up, my Alexa! . . . You shall be happy at least.'

Before any explanation of these words could even be asked for, a splendid travelling equipage stopped at the door, and, according to the rule in all such cases, a beautiful lady descended from it, handed out by a gentleman of princely rank: in brief, for I cannot tell you one half his titles and honours, or one quarter of the circumstances which had led to the leaving their only child at the Hôpital des Enfans Trouvés, Alexa was proved to be the sole and most lawful idol and heiress of this noble pair. The wonder and joy, and all that, you must guess: but poor Isabeau! . . . O! that all this happiness could but have fallen upon them before she had seen Jules de C——!

On the following morning, while Alexa, seated between her parents, was telling them all she owed to Isabeau, the door of the apartment opened and the young Jules entered. This was the moment at which the happy girl felt the value of all she had gained with the most full and perfect consciousness of felicity. Her bitter humiliation was changed to triumph; but Jules saw it not – he heard not the pompous titles of her father as she proudly rehearsed them, but, in a voice choking with emotion, he stammered out – 'Où donc est Isabeau?'

Alexa was too happy, too gloriously happy, to heed his want of politeness, but gaily exclaiming, 'Pardon, maman!' she left the room to seek for her friend.

Jules was indeed come on no trifling errand. His father, having waited in vain for some expression of his feelings respecting the charming bride he intended for him, at last informed him of his engagement, for the purpose of discovering whether the young man were actually made of ice or no. On this point he was speedily satisfied; for the intelligence robbed the timid lover of all control over his feelings, and the father had the great pleasure of perceiving that his son was as distractedly in love as he could possibly desire. As to his doubts and his fears, the experienced vicomte laughed them to scorn. 'Only let her see you as you look now, Jules,' said the proud father, 'and she will not disobey her parents, I will answer for it. Go to her, my son, and set your heart at ease at once.'

With a courage almost as desperate as that which leads a man firm and erect to the scaffold, Jules determined to follow this advice, and arrived at Château Tourelles without having once thought of poor Alexa and her tell-tale eyes by the way; – nay, even when he saw her before him, his only sensation was that of impatient agony that the moment which was to decide upon his destiny was still delayed.

As Alexa opened the door to seek her friend, she appeared, and they returned together. At the unexpected sight of Jules, Isabeau lost her self-possession, and sank nearly fainting on a chair. In an instant he was at her feet. 'Isabeau!' he exclaimed, in a voice at once solemn and impassioned – 'Isabeau! I adore you – speak my fate in one word! – Isabeau! can you love me?'

The noble strangers had already left the room. They perceived that there was some knotty point to be explained upon which their presence could throw no light. They would have led their daughter with them, but she lingered. 'One moment . . . and I will follow you,' she said. Then turning to her almost fainting friend, she exclaimed, 'You love him, Isabeau! – and it is I who have divided you!' . . . She seized a hand of each, and joining them together, bent her head upon them and kissed them both. 'God for ever bless you, perfect friend! . . . I am still too happy! . . . Believe me, Jules, – believe me, Isabeau, – I am happy – oh! too happy!' The arms that were thrown round them both, relaxed as she uttered these words, and she fell to the ground.

Alexa never spoke again. She breathed faintly for a few hours, and then expired, – the victim of intense feelings, too long and too severely tried.

This story, almost verbally as I have repeated it to you, was told me by a lady who assured me that she knew all the leading facts to be true; though she confessed that she was obliged to pass rather slightly over some of the details, from not remembering them perfectly. If the catastrophe be indeed true, I think it may be doubted whether the poor Alexa died from sorrow or from joy.

LETTER LIX

*Procès Monstre – Dislike of the Prisoners to the ceremony of Trial –
Société des Droits de l'Homme – Names given to the Sections –
Kitchen and Nursery Literature – Anecdote of Lagrange –
Republican Law*

It is a long time since I have permitted a word to escape me
about the trial of trials; but do not therefore imagine that we
are as free from it and its daily echo as I have kindly suffered
you to be.

It really appears to me, after all, that this monster trial is
only monstrous because the prisoners do not like to be tried.
There may perhaps have been some few legal incongruities in
the manner of proceeding, arising very naturally from the
difficulty of ascertaining exactly what the law is, in a country
so often subjected to revolution as this has been. I own I have
not yet made out completely to my own satisfaction, whether
these gentry were accused in the first instance of high treason,
or whether the whole proceedings rest upon an indictment for
a breach of the peace. It is however clear enough, Heaven
knows, both from evidence and from their own avowals, that
if they were not arraigned for high treason, many of them
were unquestionably guilty of it; and as they have all
repeatedly proclaimed that it was their wish to stand or fall
together, I confess that I see nothing very monstrous in
treating them all as traitors.

It is only within these few last hours that I have been made
to understand what object these simultaneous risings in April
1834 had in view. The document which has been now put into
my hands appeared, I believe, in all the papers; but it was to
me, at least, one of the thousand things that the eye glances
over without taking the trouble of communicating to the
mind what it finds. I will not take it for granted, however, that
you are as ignorant or unobservant as myself, and therefore I

shall not recite to you the evidence I have been just reading to prove that the union calling itself 'La Société des Droits de l'Homme' was in fact the mainspring of the whole enterprise; but in case the expressive titles given by the central committee of this association to its different section should have escaped you, I will transcribe them here, – or rather a part of them, for they are numerous enough to exhaust your patience, and mine too, were I to give them all. Among them, I find as pet and endearing names for their separate bands of employés the following: Section Marat, Section Robespierre, Section Quatre-vingt-treize, Section des Jacobins; Section de Guerre aux Châteaux – Abolition de la Propriété – Mort aux Tyrans – Des Piques – Canon d'Alarme – Tocsin – Barricade St. Méri, – and one which when it was given was only prophetic – Section de l'Insurrection de Lyon. These speak pretty plainly what sort of REFORM these men were preparing for France; and the trying those belonging to them who were taken with arms in their hands in open rebellion against the existing government, as traitors, cannot very justly, I think, be stigmatised as an act of tyranny, or in any other sense as a monstrous act.

The most monstrous part of the business is their conceiving (as the most conspicuous among them declare they do) that their refusing to plead, or, as they are pleased to call it, 'refusing to take any part in the proceedings,' was, or ought to be, reason sufficient for immediately stopping all such proceedings against them. These persons have been caught, with arms in their hands, in the very fact of enticing their fellow-citizens into overt acts of rebellion; but because they do not choose to answer when they are called upon, the court ordained to try them are stigmatised as monsters and assassins for not dismissing them untried!

If this is to succeed, we shall find the fashion obtain vogue amongst us, more rapidly than any of Madame Leroy's. Where is the murderer arraigned for his life who would not choose to make essay of so easy a method of escaping from the necessity of answering for his crime?

The trick is well imagined, and the degree of grave attention with which its availability is canvassed – out of doors at least – furnishes an excellent specimen of the confusion of intellect likely to ensue from confusion of laws amidst a population greatly given to the study of politics.

Never was there a finer opportunity for revolution and anarchy to take a lesson than the present. It is, I think, impossible for a mere looker-on, unbiased by party or personal feelings of any kind, to deny that the government of Louis-Philippe is acting at this trying juncture with consummate courage, wisdom, and justice: but it is equally impossible not to perceive what revolution and revolt have done towards turning lawful power into tyranny. This is and ever must be inevitable wherever there is a hope existing that the government which follows the convulsion shall be permanent.

Fresh convulsions may arise – renewed tumult, destruction of property and risk of life may ensue; but at last it must happen that some strong hand shall seize the helm, and keep the reeling vessel to her stays, without heeding whether the grasp he has got of her be taken in conformity to received tactics or not.

Hardly a day passes that I do not hear of some proof of increased vigour on the part of the present government of France; and though I, for one, am certainly very far from approving the public acts which have given the present dynasty its power, I cannot but admire the strength and ability with which it is sustained.

The example, however, can avail but little to the legitimate monarchs who still occupy the thrones their forefathers occupied before them. No legitimate sovereign, possessing no power beyond what long-established law and precedent have given him, could dare show equal boldness. A king chosen in a rebellion is alone capable of governing rebels: and happy is it for the hot-headed jeunes gens of France that they have chanced to hit upon a prince who is neither a parvenu nor a mere soldier! The first would have had no lingering kindness at all for the still-remembered glories of the land; and the last, instead of trying them by the Chamber of Peers, would have had them up by fifties to a drum-head court martial, and probably have ordered the most troublesome among them to be picked off by their comrades, as an exercise at sharp-shooting, and as a useful example of military promptitude and decision. The present government has indeed many things in its favour. The absence of every species of weakness and pusillanimity in the advisers of the crown is one; and the outrageous conduct of its enemies is another.

It is easy to perceive in the journals, and indeed in all the periodical publications which have been hitherto considered as belonging to the opposition, a gradual giving way before the overwhelming force of expediency. Conciliatory words come dropping in to the steady centre from côté droit and from côté gauche; and the louder the factious rebels roar around them, the firmer does the phalanx in which rests all the real strength of the country knit itself together.

The people of France are fully awakened to the feeling which Sheridan so strongly expresses when he says, that 'the altar of liberty has been begrimed at once with blood and mire,' and they are disposed to look towards other altars for their protection.

All the world are sick of politics in England; and all the world are sick of politics in France. It is the same in Spain, the same in Italy, the same in Germany, the same in Russia. The quiet and peaceably-disposed are wearied, worried, tormented, and almost stunned, by the ceaseless jarring produced by the confusion into which bad men have contrived to throw all the elements of social life. Chaos seems come again – a moral chaos, far worse for the poor animal called man than any that a comet's tail could lash the earth into. I assure you I often feel the most unfeigned longing to be out of reach of every sight and sound which must perforce mix up questions of government with all my womanly meditations on lesser things; but the necessity *de parler politique* seems like an evil spirit that follows whithersoever you go.

I often think, that among all the revolutions and rumours of revolutions which have troubled the earth, there is not one so remarkable as that produced on conversation within the last thirty-years. I speak not, however, only of that important branch of it – 'the polite conversation of sensible women,' but of all the talk from garret to cellar throughout the world. Go where you will, it is the same; every living soul seems persuaded that it is his or her particular business to assist in arranging the political condition of Europe.

A friend of mine entered her nursery not long ago, and spied among her baby linen a number of the Westminster Quarterly Review.

'What is this, Betty?' said she.

'It is only a book, ma'am, that John lent me to read,' answered the maid.

'Upon my word, Betty,' replied her mistress, 'I think you would be much better employed in nursing the child than in reading books which you cannot understand.'

'It does not hinder me from nursing the child at all,' rejoined the enlightened young woman, 'for I read as the baby lies in my lap; and as for understanding it, I don't fear about that, for John says it is no more than what it is the duty of everybody to understand.'

So political we are, and political we must be – for John says so.

Wherefore I will tell you a little anecdote apropos of the Procès Monstre. An English friend of mine was in the Court of Peers the other day, when the prisoner Lagrange became so noisy and troublesome that it was found necessary to remove him. He had begun to utter in a loud voice, which was evidently intended to overpower the proceedings of the court, a pompous and inflammatory harangue, accompanied with much vehement action. His fellow prisoners listened, and gazed at him with the most unequivocal marks of wondering admiration, while the court vainly endeavoured to procure order and silence.

'Remove the prisoner Lagrange!' was at last spoken by the president – and the guards proceeded to obey. The orator struggled violently, continuing, however, all the time to pour forth his rhapsody.

'Yes!' he cried, – 'yes, my countrymen! we are here as a sacrifice. Behold our bosoms, tyrants! . . . plunge your assassin daggers in our breasts! we are your victims . . . ay, doom us all to death, we are ready – five hundred French bosoms are ready to . . .'

Here he came to a dead stop: his struggles, too, suddenly ceased . . . He had dropped his cap, – the cap which not only performed the honourable office of sheltering the exterior of his patriotic head, but of bearing within its crown the written product of that head's inspired eloquence! It was in vain that he eagerly looked for it beneath the feet of his guards; the cap had been already kicked by the crowd far beyond his reach, and the bereaved orator permitted himself to be led away as quiet as a lamb.

The gentleman who related this circumstance to me added, that he looked into several papers the following day, expecting to see it mentioned; but he could not find it, and expressed his surprise to a friend who had accompanied him into court, and who had also seen and enjoyed the jest, that so laughable a circumstance had not been noticed.

'That would not do at all, I assure you,' replied his friend, who was a Frenchman, and understood the politics of the free press perfectly; 'there is hardly one of them who would not be afraid of making a joke of anything respecting *les prévenus d'Avril.*'

Before I take my final leave of these precious prévenus, I must give you an extract from a curious volume lent me by my kind friend M. J——, containing a table of the law reports inserted in the Bulletin of the Laws of the Republic. I have found among them ordinances more tyrannical than ever despot passed for the purpose of depriving of all civil rights his fellow-men; but the one I am about to give you is certainly peculiarly applicable to the question of allowing prisoners to choose their counsel from among persons not belonging to the bar, – a question which has been setting all the hot heads of Paris in a flame.

'*Loi concernant le Tribunal Révolutionnaire du 22 Prairial, l'an deuxième de la République Française une et indivisible.*

'La loi donne pour défenseurs aux patriotes calomniés, (the word 'accused' was too harsh to use in the case of these bloody patriots) – La loi donne pour défenseurs aux patriotes calomniés des jurés patriotes. Elle n'en accorde point aux conspirateurs.'

What would the LIBERALS of Europe have said of King Louis-Philippe, had he acted upon this republican principle? If he had, he might perhaps have said fairly enough –

'Caesar does never wrong but with just cause,'

for they have chosen to take their defence into their own hands; but how the pure patriots of l'an deuxième would explain the principle on which they acted, it would require a republican to tell.

LETTER LX

Memoirs of M. de Châteaubraind – The Readings at
L'Abbaye-aux-Bois – Account of these in the French Newspapers
and Reviews – Morning at the Abbaye to hear a portion
of these Memoirs – The Visit to Prague

In several visits which we have lately made to the ever-delightful Abbaye-aux-Bois, the question has been started, as to the possibility or impossibility of my being permitted to be present there 'aux lectures des Mémoires de M. de Châteaubriand.'

The apartment of my agreeable friend and countrywoman, Miss Clarke, also in this same charming Abbaye, was the scene of more than one of these anxious consultations. Against my wishes – for I really was hardly presumptuous enough to have hopes – was the fact that these lectures, so closely private, yet so publicly talked of and envied, were for the present over – nay, even that the gentleman who had been the reader was not in Paris. But what cannot zealous kindness effect? Madame Récamier took my cause in hand, and . . . in a word, a day was appointed for me and my daughters to enjoy this greatly-desired indulgence.

Before telling you the result of this appointment, I must give you some particulars respecting these Memoirs, not so much apropos of myself and my flattering introduction to them, as from being more interesting in the way of Paris literary intelligence than anything I have met with.

The existence of these Memoirs is of course well known in England; but the circumstance of their having been read *chez Madame Récamier*, to a very select number of the noble author's friends, is perhaps not so – at least, not generally; and the extraordinary degree of sensation which this produced in the literary world of Paris was what I am quite sure you can have no idea of. This is the more remarkable from the well-known politics of M. de Châteaubriand not being those of the day. The circumstances connected with the reading of these Memoirs, and the effect produced on the public by the peep got at them through those who were present, have been brought together into a very interesting volume, containing articles from most of the literary periodicals of France, each one giving to its readers the best account it had been able to obtain of these 'lectures de l'Abbaye.' Among the articles thus brought together, are *morceaux* from the pens of every political party in France; but there is not one of them that does not render cordial – I might say, fervent homage to the high reputation, both literary and political, of the Vicomte de Châteaubriand.

There is a general preface to this volume, from the pens of M. Nisard, full of enthusiasm for the subject, and giving an animated and animating account of all the circumstances attending the readings, and of the different publications respecting them which followed.

It appears that the most earnest entreaties have been very generally addressed to M. de Châteaubriand to induce him to publish these Memoirs during his lifetime, but hitherto without effect. There is something in his reasonings on the subject equally touching and true: nevertheless, it is impossible not to lament that one cannot wish for a work so every way full of interest, without wishing at the same time that one of the most amiable men in the world should be removed out of it. All those who are admitted to his circle must, I am very sure, most heartily wish never to see any more of his Memoirs than what he may be pleased himself to show them: but he has found out a way to make the world at large look for his death as for a most agreeable event. Notwithstanding all his reasonings, I think he is wrong. Those who have seen the whole, or nearly the whole of this work, declare it to be both the most important and the most able that he has composed; and embracing as it does the most interesting epoch of the world's history, and coming from the hand of one who has played so varied and distinguished a part in it, we can hardly doubt that it is so.

Of all the different articles which compose the volume entitled 'Lectures des Mémoires de M. de Châteaubriand,' the most interesting perhaps (always excepting some fragments from the Memoirs themselves) are the preface of M. Nisard, and an extract from the Revue du Midi, from the pen of M. de Lavergne. I must indulge you with some short extracts from both. M. Nisard says –

'Depuis de longues années, M. de Châteaubriand travaille à ses Mémoires, avec le dessein de ne les laisser publier qu'après sa mort. Au plus fort des affaires, quand il était ministre, ambassadeur, il oubliait les petites et les grandes tracasseries en écrivant quelques pages de ce livre de prédilection.' . . . 'C'est le livre que M. de Châteaubriand aura le plus aimé, et, chose étrange! c'est le livre en qui M. de Châteaubriand ne veut pas être glorifié de son vivant.'

He then goes on to speak of the manner in which *the readings* commenced . . . and then says, – 'Cette lecture fut un triomphe; ceux qui avaient été de la fête nous la racontèrent, à nous qui n'en étions pas, et qui déplorions que le salon de Madame Récamier, cette femme qui s'est fait une glorie de bonté et de grâce, ne fût pas grand comme la plaine de Sunium. La presse littéraire alla demander à l'illustre écrivain quelques lignes, qu'elle encadra dans de chaudes aplogies: il y eut un moment oú toute la littérature ne fut que l'annonce et la bonne nouvelle d'un ouvrage inédit.'

M. Nisard, as he says, 'n'était pas de la fête;' but he was admitted to a privilege perhaps more desirable still – namely, that of reading some portion of this precious MS. in the deep repose of the author's own study. He gives a very animated picture of this visit.

'. . . J'osai demander à M. de Châteaubriand la grace de me recevoir quelques heures chez lui, et là, pendant qu'il écrirait ou dicterait, de m'abandonner son porte-feuille et de me laisser m'y plonger à discretion . . . il y consentit. Au jour fixe, j'allai Rue d'Enfer: le coeur me battait; je suis encore assez jeune pour sentir des mouvemens intérieurs à l'approche d'une telle joie. M. de Châteaubriand fit demander son manuscrit. Il y en a trois grands porte-feuilles: *ceux-là, nul ne les lui disputera*, ni les révolutions, ni les caprices de roi, ne les lui peuvent donner ni reprendre.

'Il eut la bonté de me lire les sommaires des chapitres – Lequel choisir, lequel préférer? . . . je ne l'arrêtais pas dans la lecture, je ne disais rien . . . enfin il en vint au voyage à Prague. Une grosse et sotte interjection me trahit; du fruit défendu c'était la partie la plus défendue. Je demandai donc le voyage à Prague. M. de Châteaubriand sourit, et me tendait le manuscrit. . . . Je mets quelque vanité à rappeler ces détails, bien que je tienne à ce qu'on sache bien que j'ai été encore plus heureux que vain d'une telle faveur; mais c'est peut-être le meilleur prix que j'ai reçu encore de quelques habitudes de dignité littéraire, et à ce titre il doit m'être pardonné de m'en enorgueillir.

'Quand j'eus le précieux manuscrit, je m'accoudai sur la table, et me mis à la lecture avec une avidité recueillie . . . Quelquefois, à la fin des chapitres, regardant par-dessus mes feuilles l'illustre écrivain appliqué à son minutieux travail de révision, effaçant, puis, après quelque incertitude, écrivant avec lenteur une phrase en surcharge, et l'effaçant à moitié écrite, je voyais l'imagination et le sens aux prises. Quand, après mes deux heures de délices, amusé, instruit, intéressé, transporté, ayant passé du rire aux larmes, et des larmes au rire, ayant vu tour à tour, dans sa plus grande naïveté de sentimens, le poète, le diplomate, le voyageur, le pélerin, le philosophe, je me suis jeté sur la main de M. de Châteaubriand, et lui ai bredouillé quelques paroles de grati-tude tendre et profonde: ni lui ni moi n'étions gênés, je vous jure; – moi, parce que je donnais cours à un sentiment vrai; lui, parce qu'à ce moment-là il voulait bien mesurer la valeur de mes louanges sur leur sincérité.'

This is, I think, very well *conté*; and as I have myself been *de la fête*, and heard read precisely this same admirable *morceau, le Voyage à Prague*, I can venture to say that the feeling expressed is in no degree exaggerated.

'Que puis-je dire maintenant de ces Mémoires?' . . . he continues. 'Sur le voyage à Prague ma plume est gênée; je ne me crois pas le droit de trahir le secret de M. de Châteaubriand – mais qui est-ce qui l'ayant suivi dans tous les actes de sa glorieuse vie, ne devine pas d'avance, sauf les détails secrets, et les milles beautés de rédaction, quelle peut être la pensée de cette partie des Mémoires! Qui ne sait à merveille qu'on y trouvera la vérité pour tout le monde, douce pour ceux qui ont beaucoup perdu et beaucoup souffert, dure pour les médiocrités importantes, qui se disputent les ministères et les ambassades auprès d'une royauté qui ne peut plus même donner de croix d'honneur? Qui est-ce qui ne s'attend à des lamentations sublimes sur des infortunes inouïes, à des attendrissemens de coeur sur toutes les misères de l'exil; sur le délabrement des palais où gîtent les royautés déchues; sur ces longs corridors éclairés par un quinquet à chaque bout, comme un corps de garde, ou un cloître; sur ces salles des gardes sans gardes; sur ces antichambres sans siéges pour s'asseoir, sur ces serviteurs rares, dont un seul fait l'étiquette qui autrefois en occupait dix; sur les malheurs toujours plus grands que les malheureux, qu'on plaint de loin poir ceux qui les souffrent, et de près pour soi-même? . . . Et puis après la politique vient la poésie; après les leçons sévères, les descriptions riantes, les observations de voyage, fines, piquantes, comme si le voyageur n'avait pas causé la veille avec un vieux roi d'un royaume perdu. . . .'

I have given you this passage because it describes better than I could do myself the admirable narrative which I had the pleasure of hearing. M. Nisard says much more about it, and with equal truth; but I will only add his concluding words – 'Voilà la voyage à Prague . . . J'y ai été remué au plus profond et au meilleur de mon coeur par les choses touchantes, et j'ai pleuré sur la légitimité tombée, quoique n'ayant jamais compris cet ordre d'idées, et y étant resté, toute ma jeunesse, nonseulement étranger, mais hostile.'

I have transcribed this last observation for the purpose of proving to you that the admiration inspired by this work of M. de Châteaubriand's is not the result of party feeling, but in complete defiance of it.

In the 'Revue de Paris' for March 1834 is an extremely interesting article from M. Janin, who was present, I presume, at the readings, and who must have been permitted, I think, now and then to peep over the shoulder of the reader, with a pencil in his hand, for he gives many short but brilliant passages from different parts of the work. This gentlemen states, upon what authority he does not say, that English speculators have already purchased the work at the enormous price of 25,000 francs for each volume. It already consists of twelve volumes, which makes the purchase amount to

£12,000 sterling, – a very large sum, even if the acquisition could be made immediately available; but as we must hope that many years may elapse before it becomes so, it appears hardly credible that this statement should be correct.

Whenever these Memoirs are published, however, there can be no doubt of the eagerness with which they will be read. M. Janin remarks, that 'M. de Châteaubriand, en ne croyant écrire que ses mémoires, aura écrit en effect l'histoire de son siècle;' and adds, 'D'où l'on peut prédire, que si jamais une époque n'a été plus inabordable pour un historien, jamais aussi une époque n'aura eu une histoire plus complète et plus admirablement écrite que la nôtre. Songez donc, que pendant que M. de Châteaubriand fait ses mémoires, M. de Talleyrand écrit aussi ses mémoires. M. de Châteaubriand et M. de Talleyrand attelés l'un et l'autre à la même époque! – l'un qui en représente le sens poétique et royaliste, l'autre qui en est l'expression politique et utilitaire: l'un l'héritier de Bossuet, le conservateur du principe religieux; l'autre l'héritier de Voltaire, et qui ne s'est jamais prosterné que devant le doute, cette grande certitude de l'histoire: l'un enthousiaste, l'autre ironique; l'un éloquent partout, l'autre éloquent dans son fauteuil, au coin de son feu: l'un homme de génie, et qui le prouve; l'autre qui a bien voulu laisser croire qu'il était un homme d'esprit: celui-ci plein de l'amour de l'humanité, celui-là moins égoïste qu'on ne le croit; celui-ci bon, celui-là moins méchant qu'il ne veut le paraître: celui-ci allant par sauts et par bonds, impétueux comme un tonnerre, ou comme une phrase de l'Ecriture; celui-là qui boite, et qui arrrive toujours le premier: celui-ci qui se montre toujours grand l'autre se cache, qui parle quand l'autre se tait; l'autre qui arrive toujours quand il faut arriver, qu'on ne voit guère, qu'on n'entend guère, qui est partout, qui voit tout, qui sait presque tout: l'un qui a des partisans, des enthousiastes, des admirateurs; l'autre qui n'a que des flatteurs, des parens, et des valets: l'un aimé, adoré, chanté; l'autre à peine redouté: l'un toujours jeune, l'autre toujours vieux; l'un toujours battu, l'autre toujours vainqueur; l'un victime des causes perdues, l'autre héros des causes gagnées; l'un qui mourra on ne sait où, l'autre qui mourra prince, et dans sa maison, avec un archevêque à son chevet; l'un grand écrivain à coup sûr, l'autre qui est un grand écrivain sans qu'on s'en doute; l'un qui a écrit ses mémoires pour les lire à ses amis, l'autre qui a écrit ses mémoires pour les cacher à ses amis; l'un qui ne les publie pas par caprice, l'autre qui ne les publie pas, parce qu'ils ne seront terminés que huit jours après sa mort; l'un qui a vu de haut et de loin, l'autre qui a vu d'en bas et de près: l'un qui a été le premier gentilhomme de l'histoire contemporaine, qui l'a vue en habit et toute parée; l'autre qui en a été le valet de chambre, et qui en sait toutes les plaies cachées; – l'un qu'on appelle Châteaubriand, l'autre qu'on appelle le Prince de Bénévent. Tels sont les deux hommes que le dix-neuvième siècle désigne à l'avance comme ses deux juges les plus redoutables, comme ses deux appréci-ateurs les plus dangéreux, comme les deux historiens opposés, sur lesquels la postérité le jugera.'

This parallel, though rather long perhaps, is very clever, and, à ce qu'on dit, very just.

Though my extracts from this very interesting but not widely-circulated volume have already run to a greater length than I intended, I cannot close it without giving you a small portion of M. de Lavergne's animated recital of the scene at the old Abbaye-aux-Bois; – an Abbaye, by the way, still partly inhabited by a society of nuns, and whose garden is sacred to them alone, though a portion of the large building which overlooks it is the property of Madame Récamier.

'A une des extrémités de Paris on trouve un monument d'une architecture simple et sévère. La cour d'entrée est fermée par une grille, et sur cette grille s'élève une croix. La paix monastique règne dans les cours, dans les escaliers, dans les corridors; mais sous les saintes voûtes de ce lieu se cachent aussi d'élégans réduits qui s'ouvrent par intervalle aux bruits du monde. Cette habitation se nomme l'Abbaye-aux-Bois, – nom pittoresque d'où s'exhale je ne sais quel parfum d'ombre et de mystère, comme si le couvent et la forêt y confondaient leurs paisibles harmonies. Or, dans un des angles de cet édifice il y a un salon que je veux décrire, moi aussi, car il reparaît bien souvant dans mes rêves. Vous connaissez le tableau de Corinne de Gérard: Corinne est assise au Cap Misène, sur un rocher, sa belle tête levée vers le ciel, son beau bras tombant vers la terre avec sa lyre détendue; le chant vient de finir, mais l'inspiration illumine encore ses regards divins . . . Ce tableau couvre tout un des murs du salon, en face la cheminée avec une glace, des girandoles, et des fleurs . . . Des deux autres murs, l'un est percé de deux fenêtres qui laissent voir les tranquilles jardins de l'Abbaye, l'autre disparaît presque tout entier sous des rayons chargés de livres. Des meubles élégans sont épars çà et là, avec un gracieux désordre. Dans un des coins, la porte qui s'entr'ouvre, et dans l'autre une harpe qui attend.

'Je vivrais des milliers d'années que je n'oublierais jamais rien de ce que j'ai vu là . . . D'autres ont rapporté des courses de leur jeunesse le souvenir d'un site grandiose, ou d'une ruine monumentale; moi, je n'ai vu ni la Grèce . . . etc . . . mais il m'a a été ouvert ce salon de l'Europe et du siècle, où l'air est en quelque sorte chargé de gloire et de génie . . . Là respire encore l'ame enthousiaste de Madame de Staël; là reparaît, à l'imagination qui l'évoque, la figure mélancolique et pâle de Benjamin Constant; là retentit la parole vibrante et libre du grand Foy. Tous ces illustres morts viennent faire cortége à celle qui fut leur amie; car cet appartement est celui d'une femme célèbre dont on a déjà deviné le nom. Malgré cette pudeur de renommée qui la fait ainsi se cacher dans le silence, Madame Récamier appartient à l'historie; c'est désormais un de ces beaux noms de femme qui brillent dans la couronne des grandes époques ainsi que des perles sur un bandeau. Révélée au monde par sa beauté, elle l'a charmé peut-être plus encore par les graces de son esprit et de son coeur. Mêlée par de hautes amitiés aux plus grands événemens de l'époque, elle en a traversé les vicissitudes sans en connaître les souillures, et, dans sa vie toute d'idéal, le malheur même et l'exil n'ont été pour elle que des charmes de plus. A la voir aujourd'hui si harmonieuse et si sereine, on dirait que les orages de la vie n'ont jamais approché de ses jours; à la voir si simple et si bienveillante, on dirait que sa célébrité n'est qu'un songe, et que les plus superbes fronts de la France moderne n'ont jamais fléchi devant elle. Aimée des poètes, des grands, et du Ciel, c'est à-la-fois Laure, Eléonore et Béatrix, dont Pétrarque, Tasse et le Dante ont immortalisé les noms.

'Un jour de Février dernier il y avait dans le salon de Madame Récamier une réunion convoquée pour une lecture. L'assemblée était bien peu nombreuse, et il n'est pas d'homme si haut placé par le rang ou par le génie qui n'eût été fier de s'y trouver. A côté d'un Montmorency, d'un Larochefoucauld, et d'un Noailles, représentans de la vielle noblesse française, s'asseyaient leurs égaux par la noblesse du talent, cet autre hasard de la naissance; Saint-Beuve et Quinet, Gerbet et Dubois, Lenormand et Ampère: vous y étiez aussi, Ballanche! . . .

'Il parut enfin celui dont le nom avait réuni un tel auditoire, et toutes les têtes s'inclinèrent. . . . Son front avait toute la dignité des cheveux gris, mais ses yeux vifs brillaient de jeunesse. Il portait à la main, comme un pélerin ou un soldat, un paquet enveloppé dans un mouchoir de soie. Cette simplicité me parut merveilleuse dans un pareil sujet; car ce noble vieillard, c'était l'auteur des Martyrs, du Génie du Christianisme, de René – ce paquet du pélerin, c'étaient les Mémoires de M. de Châteaubriand . . . Mais quelle douloureuse émotion dans les premiers mots – *'Mémoires d'Outre-tombe! . . . Préface testamentaire!'* . . .

*   *   *

'Continuez, Châteaubriand, à filer en paix votre suaire. Aussi bien, il n'y a de calme aujourd'hui que le dernier sommeil, il n'y a de stable que la mort! . . . Vieux serviteur de la vieille monarchie! vous n'avez pas visité sans tressaillir ces sombres galeries du Ibradschin, où se promènent trois larves royales, avec une ombre de couronne sur le front. Vous avez baigné de vos pleurs les mains de ce vieillard qui emporte avec lui toute une société, et la tête de cet enfant dont les graces n'ont pu fléchir l'inexorable destinée qui s'attache aux races antiques . . . Filez votre suarie de soie et d'or, Châteaubriand, et enveloppez-vous dans votre gloire; il n'est pas de progrès qui vous puisse ravir votre immortalité.'

I think that by this time you must be fully aware, my dear friend, that this intellectual fête to which we were invited at the Abbaye-aux-Bois was a grace and a favour of which we have very good reason to be proud. I certainly never remember to have been more gratified in every way than I was on this occasion. The thing itself, and the flattering kindness which permitted one to enjoy it, were equally the source of pleasure. I may say with all truth, like M. de Lavergne, 'Je vivrais des milliers d'années que je ne l'oublierais jamais.'

The choice of the *morceau*, too, touched me not a little: 'du fruit défendu, cette partie la plus défendue' was most assuredly what I should have eagerly chosen had choice been offered. M. de Châteaubriand's journey to Prague furnishes as interesting an historical scene as can well be imagined; and I do not believe that any author that ever lived, Jean-Jacques and Sir Walter not excepted, could have recounted it better – with more true feeling or more finished grace: simple and unaffected to perfection in its style, yet glowing with all the fervour of a poetical imagination, and all the tenderness of a most feeling heart. It is a gallery of living portraits that he brings before the eye as if by magic. There is no minute painting, however: the powerful, the painfully powerful effect of the groups he describes, is produced by the bold and unerring touch of a master. I fancied I saw the royal race before me, each one individual and distinct; and I could have said, as one does in seeing a clever portrait, 'That is a likeness, I'll be sworn for it.' Many passages made a profound impression on my fancy and on my memory; and I think I could give a better account of some of the scenes described than I should feel justified in doing as long as the noble author chooses to keep them from the public eye. There were touches which made us weep abundantly; and then he changed the key, and gave us the prettiest, the most gracious, the most smiling picture of the young princess and her brother, that it was possible for pen to trace. She must be a fair and glorious creature, and one that in days of yore might have been likely enough to have seen her colours floating on the helm of all the doughtiest knights in Christendom. But chivalry is not the fashion of the day; – there is nothing *positif*, as the phrase goes, to be gained by it; – and I doubt if 'its ineffectual fire' burn very brightly at the present time in any living heart, save that of M. de Châteaubriand himself.

The party assembled at Madame Récamier's on this occasion did not, I think, exceed seventeen, including Madame Récamier and M. de Châteaubriand. Most of these had been present at the former readings. The Duchesses de Larochefoucauld and Noailles, and one or two other noble ladies, were among them. I felt it was a proof that genius is of no party, when I saw a grand-daughter of General Lafayette enter among us. She is married to a gentleman who is said to be of

Lecture à l'abbaye-aux-bois.

the extreme côté gauche; but I remarked that they both listened with as much deep interest to all the touching details of this mournful visit as the rest of us. Who, indeed, could help it? – This lady sat between me and Madame Récamier on one sofa; M. Ampère the reader, and M. de Châteaubriand himself, on another, immediately at right angles with it, – so that I had the pleasure of watching one of the most expressive countenances I ever looked at, while this beautiful specimen of his head and his heart was displayed to us. On the other side of me was a gentleman whom I was extremely happy to meet – the celebrated Gérard; and before the reading commenced, I had the pleasure of conversing with him: he is one of those whose aspect and whose words do not disappoint the expectations which high reputation always gives birth to. There was no formal circle; – the ladies approached themselves a little towards THE sofa which was placed at the feet of Corinne, and the gentlemen stationed themselves in groups behind them. The sun shone *delicately* into the room through the white silk curtains – delicious flowers scented the air – the quiet gardens of the Abbaye, stretched to a sufficient distance beneath the windows to guard us from every Parisian sound – and, in short, the whole thing was perfect. Can you wonder that I was delighted? or that I have thought the occurrence worth dwelling upon with some degree of lingering fondness?

The effect this delightful morning has had on us is, I assure you, by no means singular: it would be easy to fill a volume with the testimonies of delight and gratitude which have been offered from various quarters in return for this gratification. Madame Tastu, whom I have heard called the Mrs. Hemans of France, was present at one or more of the readings, and has returned thanks in some very pretty lines, which conclude thus fervently:–

'Ma tête
S'incline pour saisir jusques aux moindres sons,
Et mon genou se ploie à demi, quand je prête,
Enchantée et muette,
L'oreille à vos leçons!'

Apropos of tributary verses on this subject, I am tempted to conclude my unmercifully long epistle by giving you some lines which have as yet, I believe, been scarcely seen by any one but the person to whom they are addressed. They are from the pen of the H.G. who so beautifully translated the twelve first cantos of the 'Frithiof Saga,' which was so favourably received in England last spring.

H.G. is an Englishwoman, but from the age of two to seventeen she resided in the United States of America. Did I not tell you this, you would be at a loss to understand her allusion to the distant dwelling of her youth.

This address, as you will perceive, is not as an acknowledgement for having been admitted to the Abbaye, but an earnest prayer that she may be so; and I heartily hope it will prove successful.

TO M. LE VICOMTE DE CHATEAUBRIAND

In that distant region, the land of the West,
   Where my childhood and youth glided rapidly by,
Ah! why was my bosom with sorrow oppress'd?
   Why trembled the tear-drop so oft in mine eye?

No! 'twas not that pleasures they told me alone
   Were found in the courts where proud monarchs reside;
My knee could not bend at the foot of a throne,
   My heart could not hallow an emperor's pride.

But, oh! 'twas the thought that bright genius there dwelt,
   And breathed on a few holy spirits its flame,
That awaken'd the grief which in childhood I felt,
   When, Europe! I mutter'd thy magical name.

And now that as pilgrim I visit thy shore,
   I ask not where kings hold their pompous array;
But I fain would behold, and all humbly adore,
   The wreath which thy brows, Châteaubriand! display.

My voice may well falter – unknown is my name,
    But say, must my accents prove therefore in vain?
Beyond the Atlantic we boast of thy fame,
    And repeat that thy footstep has traversed our plain.

Great bard! – then reject not the prayer that I speak
    With trembling emotion, and offer thee now;
In thy eloquent page, oh! permit me to seek
    Thy joys and the sorrows that genius may know.

H.G.

LETTER LXI

*Jardin des Plantes – Not equal in beauty to our Zoological Gardens –
La Salpêtrière – Anecdote – Les Invalides – Difficulty of
finding English Colours there – The Dome*

Another long morning on the other side of the water has given
us abundant amusement, and sent us home in a very good
humour with the expedition, because, after very mature and
equitable consideration, we were enabled honestly to decide
that our Zoological Gardens are in few points inferior, in
many equal, and in some greatly superior, to the long and
deservedly celebrated Jardin des Plantes.

If considered as a museum and nursery for botanists, we
certainly cannot presume to compare our comparatively new
institution to that of Paris; but, zoologically speaking, it is
every way superior. The collection of animals, both birds and
beasts, is, I think, better, and certainly in finer condition. I
confess that I envy them their beautiful giraffe; but what else
have they which we cannot equal? Then as to our superiority,
look at the comparative degree of beauty of the two
enclosures. 'O England!' as I once heard a linen-draper
exclaim in the midst of his shop, intending in his march of
mind to quote Bryon –

> 'O England! with all thy faults, I can't help loving
> thee still.'

And I am quite of the linen-draper's mind: I cannot help
loving those smooth-shaven lawns, those untrimmed flowing
shrubs, those meandering walks, now seen, now lost amidst a
cool green labyrinth of shade, which are so truly English. You
have all this at the Zoological Gardens – we have none of it in
the Jardin des Plantes; and, therefore, I like the Zoological
Gardens best.

We must not say a word, my friend, about the lectures, or the free admission to them – that is not our forte; and if the bourgeoisie go on much longer as they do at present, becoming greater and more powerful with every passing day, and learning to know, as their mercantile neighbours have long known, that it is quite necessary both governments and individuals should turn all things to profit; –

> 'Car dans le siècle où nous sommes,
> On ne donne rien pour rien;' –

if this happens, as I strongly suspect it will, then we shall have no more lectures gratis even in Paris.

From the Jardin des Plantes, we visited that very magnificent hospital, La Salpêtrière. I will spare you, however, all the fine things that might be said about it, and only give you a little anecdote which occurred while we stood looking into the open court where the imbecile and the mad are permitted to take their exercise. By the way, without at all presuming to doubt that there may be reasons which the managers of this establishment conceive to be satisfactory, why these wretched objects, in different stages of their dreadful calamity, should be thus for ever placed before each other's eyes, I cannot but observe, that the effect upon the spectator is painful beyond anything I ever witnessed.

With my usual love for the terrible, I remained immovable for above twenty minutes, watching the manner in which they appeared to notice each other. If fancy did not cheat me, those who were least wildly deranged looked with a sort of triumph and the consciousness of superiority on those who were most so: some looked on the mad movements of the others and laughed distractedly; – in short, the scene is terribly full of horror.

But to return to my anecdote. A stout girl, who looked more imbecile than mad, was playing tricks, that a woman who appeared to have some authority among them endeavoured to stop. The girl evidently understood her, but with a sort of dogged obstinacy persevered, till the nurse, or matron, or whatever she was, took hold of her arm, and endeavoured to lead her into the house. Upon this the girl resisted; and it was not without some degree of violence that she was at last conquered and led away.

'What dreadful cruelty!' exclaimed a woman who like ourselves was indulging her curiosity by watching the patients. An old crone, a very aged and decrepid pensioner of the establishment, was passing by on her crutches as she spoke. She stopped in her hobbling walk, and addressing the stranger in the gentle voice of quiet good sense, and in a tone which made me fancy she had seen better days, said – 'Dreadful cruelty, good woman? . . . She is preventing her from doing what ought not to be done. If you had the charge of her, you would think it your duty to do the same, and then it would be right. But 'dreadful cruelty!' is easily said, and sounds good-hearted; and those who know not what it is to govern, generally think it is a sin and a shame to use authority in any way.' And so saying, the old woman hobbled on, leaving me convinced that La Salpêtrière did not give its shelter to fools only.

From this hospital we took a very long drive to another, going almost from the extremest east to the extremest west of Paris. The Invalides was now our object; and its pleasant, easy, comfortable aspect offered a very agreeable contrast to the scene we had left. We had become taciturn and melancholy at la Salpêtrière; but this interesting and noble edifice revived our spirits completely. Two of the party had never been there before, and the others were eloquent in pointing out all that their former visits had shown them. No place can be better calculated to stimulate conversation; there is so much to be said about our own Greenwich and Queen Elizabeth, versus Louis le Grand and the Invalides. Then we had the statue of a greater than he – even of Napoleon – upon which to gaze and moralise. Some veteran had climbed up to it, despite a wooden leg, or a single arm perhaps, and crowned the still-honoured head with a fresh wreath of bays.

While we stood looking at this, the courteous bow and promising countenance of a fine old man arrested the whole party, and he was questioned and chatted to, till he became the hero of his own tale, and we soon knew exactly where he had received his first wound, what were his most glorious campaigns, and, above all, who was the general best deserving the blessing of an old soldier.

Those who in listening to such chronicles in France expect to hear any other name than that of Napoleon will be disappointed. We may talk of his terrible conscriptions, of poisonings at Jena or forsakings at Moscow, as we will; the simple fact which answers all is, that he was adored by his soldiers when he was with them, and that his memory is cherished with a tender enthusiasm to which history records no parallel. The mere tone of voice in which the name of 'NAPOLEON!' or the title of 'L'EMPEREUR!' is uttered by his veterans, is of itself enough to prove what he was to them. They stand taller by an inch when he is named, and throw forward the chest, and snuff the air, like an old war-horse that hears the sound of a trumpet.

But still, with all these interesting speculations to amuse us, we did not forget what must ever be the primary object of a stranger's visit to the Invalides – the interior of the dome. But this is only to be seen at particular hours; and we were too late for the early, and too early for the late, opening of the doors for this purpose. Four o'clock was the hour we had to wait for – as yet it was but three. We were invited into the hall and into the kitchen; we were admitted, too, into sundry little enclosures, appropriated to some happy individuals favoured for their skill in, garden craft, who, turning their muskets into hoes and spades, enjoy their honourable leisure ten times more than their idle brethren. In three out of four of these miniature domains we found plaister Napoleons of a foot high stuck into a box-tree or a rose-bush: one of these, too, had a wreath of newly-gathered leaves twisted round the cocked-hat, and all three were placed and displayed with as much attention to dignity and effect as the finest statues in the Tuileries.

If the spirit of Napoleon is permitted to hover about Paris, to indulge itself in gathering the scattered laurels of his posthumous fame, it is not to the lofty chambers of the Tuileries that it should betake itself; – nor would it be greatly soothed by listening to the peaceful counsels of his once warlike maréchals. No – if his ghost be well inspired, it will just glide swiftly through the gallery of the Louvre, to compare it with his earthly recollections; balance itself for a moment over the statue of the Place Vendôme, and abide, for the rest of the time allotted for this mundane visit, among his

faithful invalids. There only would he meet a welcome that
would please him. The whole nation, it is true, dearly love to
talk of his greatness; but there is little now left in common
between them and their sometime emperor.

France with a charter, and France without, differs not by
many degrees so widely as France military, and France
bourgeoise and boursière. Under Napoleon she was the type
of successful war; under Louis-Philippe, she will, I think – if
the republicans will let her alone – become that of prosperous
peace: a sword and a feather might be the emblem of the one –
a loom and a long purse of the other.

But still it was not four o'clock. We were next invited to enter
the chapel; and we did so, determined to await the appointed
hour reposing ourselves on the very comfortable benches
provided for the veterans to whose use it is appropriated.

Here, stretched and lounging at our ease, we challenged
each other to discover English colours among the multitude
of conquered banners which hung suspended above our
heads. It is hardly possible that some such should not be there;
yet it is a positive fact, that not all our familiar acquaintance
with the colours we sought could enable us to discover them.
There is indeed one torn and battered relic, that it is just
possible might have been hacked and sawed from the desper-
ately firm grasp of an Englishman; but the morsel of rag left is
so small, that it was in fact more from the lack of testimony
than the presence of it that we at length came to the
conclusion that this relic of a stick might once have made part
of an English standard.

Not in any degree out of humour at our disappointment in
this search after our national banner, we followed the guide
who summoned us at last to the dome, chatting and laughing
as cheerily and as noisily as if we had not been exhausting our
spirits for the last four hours by sight-seeing. But what fatigue
could not achieve, was the next momlt produced by wonder,
admiration, and delight. Never did muter silence fall upon a
talking group, than the sight of this matchless chapel brought
on us. Speech is certainly not the first or most natural resource
that the spirit resorts to, when thus roused, yet chastened –
enchanted, yet subdued.

I have not yet been to Rome, and know not how I shall feel if ever I find myself under the dome of St. Peter's. There, I conceive that it is a sense of vastness which seizes on the mind; here it is wholly a feeling of beauty, harmony, and grace. I know nothing like it anywhere: the Pantheon (ci-devant Ste. Geneviève), with all its nobleness and majesty, is heavy, and almost clumsy, when compared to it. Though possessing no religious solemnity whatever, and in this respect inferior beyond the reach of comparison to the choir of 'Cologne, or King's College Chapel at Cambridge, it nevertheless produces a stronger effect upon the senses than either of them. This is owing, I suspect, to the circumstance of there being no mixture of objects: the golden tabernacle seems to complete rather than destroy its unity. If I could give myself a fête, it should be, to be placed within the pure, bright, lofty loveliness of this marble sanctuary, while a full and finished orchestra performed the chefs-d'oeuvre of Handel or Mozart in the church.

LETTER LXII

Expedition to Montmorency – Rendezvous in the Passage Delorme –
St Denis – Tomb prepared for Napoleon – The Hermitage –
Dîner sur l'herbe

It is more than a fortnight ago, I think, that we engaged
ourselves with a very agreeable party of twenty persons to
take a long drive out of Paris and indulge ourselves with a very
gay 'dîner sur l'herbe.' But it is no easy matter to find a day on
which twenty people shall all be ready and willing to leave
Paris. However, a steadfast will can conquer most things. The
whole twenty were quite determined that they would go to
Montmorency, and to Montmorency at last we have been.
The day was really one of great enjoyment, but yet it did not
pass without disasters. One of these which occurred at the
moment of starting very nearly overthrew the whole scheme.
The place of general rendezvous for us and our hampers was
the Galerie Delorme, and thither one of the party who had
undertaken that branch of the business had ordered the
carriages to come. At ten o'clock precisely, the first
detachment of the party was deposited with their belongings
at the southern extremity of the gallery; another and another
followed till the muster-roll was complete. Baskets were piled
on baskets; and the passers-by read our history in these, and in
our anxious eyes, which ceased not to turn with ever-
increasing anxiety the way the carriages should come.

What a *supplice*! . . . Every minute, every second, brought
the rolling of wheels to our ears, but only to mock us: the
wheels rolled on – no carriages came for us, and we remained
in statu quo to look at each other and our baskets.

Then came forth, as always happens on great and trying
occasions, the inward character of each. The sturdy and
firm-minded set themselves down on the packages,
determined to abide the eyes of all rather than shrink from

418

their intent. The timid and more frail of purpose gently whispered proposals that we should all go home again; while others, yet listening to

> 'Hope's enchanting measure,
> Which still promised coming pleasure,'

smiled, and looked forth from the gallery, and smiled again – though still no carriage came.

It was, as I suspect, these young hopes and smiles which saved us from final disappointment: for the young men belonging to the cortège, suddenly rousing themselves from their state of listless watching, declared with one voice and one spirit, that les demoiselles should not be disappointed; and exchanging *consignes* which were to regulate the number and species of vehicles each was to seek – and find, too, on peril of his reputation, – they darted forth from the gallery, leaving us with renewed spirits and courage to bear all the curious glances bestowed upon us.

Our half-dozen aides-de-camp returned triumphantly in a few minutes, each one in his delta or his citadine; and the Galerie Delorme was soon left far behind us.

It is lucky for you that we had not to make a 'voyage par mer' and 'retour par terre,' or my story might be as long – if resembling it in no other way – as the immortal expedition to St. Cloud. I shall not make a volume of it; but I must tell you that we halted at St. Denis.

The church is beautiful – a perfect bijou of true Gothic architecture – light, lofty, elegant; and we saw it, too, in a manner peculiarly advantageous, for it had neither organ, altar, nor screen to distract the eye from the great and simple beauty of the original design. The repairs going on here are of a right royal character – on a noble scale and in excellent taste. Several monuments restored from the collection made under the Empire aux Petits Augustins are now again the glory of St. Denis; and some of them have still much remaining which may entitle them to rank as very pure and perfect specimens of highly-antiquated monumental sculpture. But the chiselled treasures of a thousand years' standing cannot be made to travel about like the scenery of strolling players, in conformity to the will and whim of the successive actors who play the part of king, without great injury. In some instances the original nooks in this venerable mausoleum of royal bones have again received the effigies originally carved to repose within them; but the regal image has rarely been replaced without showing itself in some degree way-worn. In other cases, the monumental portrait, venerable and almost hallowed by its high antiquity, is made to recline on a whitened sepulchre as bright as Parisian masonry can make it.

Having fully examined the church and its medley of old and new treasures, we called a council as to the possibility of finding time for descending to the crypts: but most of the party agreeing in opinion that we ought not to lose the opportunity of visiting what a wit amongst us happily enough designated 'le Palais Royal de la Mort,' we ordered the iron gates to be unbarred for us, and proceeded with some solemnity of feeling into the pompous tomb. And here the unfortunate result of that bold spirit of change which holds nothing sacred is still more disagreeably obvious than in the church. All the royal monuments of France that could be collected are assembled in this magnificent vault, but with such incongruity of dates belonging to different parts of the same structure, as almost wholly to destroy the imposing effect of this gorgeous grave.

But if the spectator would seek farther than his eye can carry him, and inquire where the mortal relics of each sculptured monarch lie, the answer he will receive must make him believe that the royal dust of France has been scattered to the four winds of heaven. Nothing I have heard has sounded more strangely to me than the naïveté with which our guide informed us that, among all this multitude of regal tombs, there was not one which contained a single vestige of the mortal remains of those they commemorate.

For the love of good taste and consistency, these guardians of the royal sepulchre of France should be taught a more poetical lesson. It is inconceivable how, as he spoke, the solemn memorials of the illustrious dead, near which my foot had passed cautiously and my voice been mute, seemed suddenly converted into something little more sacred than the show furnishing of a stone-mason's shop. The bathos was perfect.

I could not but remember with a feeling of national pride the contrast to this presented by Westminster Abbey and St. George's Chapel. The monuments of these two royal fanes form a series as interesting in the history of art as of our royal line, and no painful consciousness of desecration mixes itself with the solemn reverence with which we contemplate the honoured tombs.

The most interesting object in the crypts of St. Denis, and which comes upon the moral feeling with a force increased rather than diminished by the incongruities which surround it, is the door of the vault prepared by Napoleon for himself. It is inscribed,

ICI REPOSENT
LES DÉPOUILLES MORTELLES
DE

This inscription still remains, as well as the massive brazen gates with their triple locks, which were designed to close the tomb. These rich portals are not suspended on hinges, but rest against a wall of solid masonry, over which the above inscription is seen. The imperial vault thus chosen by the living despot as the sanctuary for bones which it was our fortune to dispose of elsewhere is greatly distinguished by its situation, being exactly under the high altar, and in the centre of the crypts, which follow the beautiful curve of the Lady Chapel above. It now contains the bodies of Louis Dix-huit and the Duc de Berri, and is completely bricked up.

In another vault, at one end of the circular crypts, and perfectly excluded from the light of day, but made visible by a single feeble lamp, are two coffins enclosing the remains of the two last defunct princes of the blood royal; but I forget their names. When I inquired of our conductor why these two coffins were thus exposed to view, he replied, with the air of a person giving information respecting what was as unchangeable as the laws of the Medes and Persians, 'C'est toujours ainsi;' adding, 'When another royal corpse is interred, the one of these two which was the first deposited will be removed, to be placed beneath its monument; but two must ever remain thus.'

'Always' and 'ever' are words which can seldom be used discreetly without some reservation; but respecting anything connected with the political state of France, I should think they had better never be used at all.

We returned to the carriages and pursued our pretty drive. The latter part of the route is very beautiful, and we all walked up one long steep hill, as much, or more perhaps, to enjoy the glorious view, and the fresh delicious air, as to assist the horses.

Arrived at the famous *Cheval Blanc* at Montmorency, (a sign painted, as the tradition says, by no less a hand than that of Gérard, who, in a youthful pilgrimage with his friend Isabey to this region consecrated to romance, found himself with no other means of defraying their bill than by painting a sign for his host,) we quitted our wearied and wearisome citadines, and began to seek, amidst the multitude of horses and donkeys which stood saddled and bridled around the door of the inn, for twenty well-conditioned beasts, besides a sumpter-mule or two, to carry us and our provender to the forest.

And, oh! the tumult and the din that accompanied this selection! Multitudes of old women and ragamuffin boys assailed us on all sides. – 'Tenez, madame; voilà mon âne! y a-t-il une autre bête comme la mienne? . . .' 'Non, non, non, belles dames! Ne le croyez pas; c'est la mienne qu'il vous faut . . .' 'Et vous, monsieur – c'est un cheval qui vous manque, n'est-ce pas? en voilà un superbe . . .'

The multitude of hoarse old voices, and shrill young ones, joined to our own noisy mirth, produced a din that brought out half the population of Montmorency to stare at us: but at length we were mounted – and, what was of infinitely more consequence, and infinitely more difficulty also, our hampers and baskets were mounted too.

But before we could think of the greenwood tree, and the gay repast to be spread under it, we had a pilgrimage to make to the shrine which has given the region all its fame. Hitherto we had thought only of its beauty, – who does not know the lovely scenery of Montmorency? – even without the name of Rousseau to give a fanciful interest to every path around it, there is enough in its hills and dales, its forest and its fields, to cheer the spirits and enchant the eye.

A day stolen from the dissipation, the dust, and the noise of a great city, is always delightful; but when it is enjoyed in the very fullest green perfection of the last days of May, when every new-born leaf and blossom is fully expanded to the delicious breeze, and not one yet fallen before it, the enjoyment is perfect. It is like seeing a new piece while the dresses and decorations are all fresh; and never can the mind be in a state to taste with less of pain, and more of pleasure, the thoughts suggested by such a scene as *the Hermitage*. I have, however, no intention of indulging myself in a burst of tender feeling over the melancholy memory of Rousseau, or of enthusiastic gratitude at the recollection of Grétry, though both are strongly brought before the mind's eye by the various memorials of each so carefully treasured in the little parlour in which they passed so many hours: yet it is impossible to look at the little rude table on which the first and greatest of these gifted men scribbled the 'Héloïse,' or on the broken and untuneable keys of the spinette with which the eloquent visionary so often soothed his sadness and solitude, without some feeling tant soit peu approaching to the sentimental.

Before the window of this small gloomy room, which opens upon the garden, is a rose-tree planted by the hand of Rousseau, which has furnished, as they told us, cuttings enough to produce a forest of roses. The house is as dark and dull as may be; but the garden is pretty, and there is something of fanciful in its arrangement which makes me think it must be as he left it.

The records of Grétry would have produced more effect if seen elsewhere, – at least I thought so; – yet the sweet notes of 'O Richard! O mon roi!' seemed to be sounding in my ears, too, as I looked at his old spectacles, and several other little domestic relics that were inscribed with his name. But the 'Rêveries du Promeneur Solitaire' are worth all the notes that Grétry ever wrote.

A marble column stands in a shady corner of the garden, bearing an inscription which states that her highness the Duchesse de Berri had visited the Hermitage, and taken, 'le coeur de Grétry' under her august protection, which had been unjustly claimed by the Liégeois from his native France. What this means, or where her highness found the great composer's heart, I could not learn.

We took the objects of our expedition in most judicious order, fasting and fatigue being decidedly favourable to melancholy; but, even with these aids, I cannot say that I discovered much propensity to the tender vein in the generality of our party. Sentiment is so completely out of fashion, that it would require a bold spirit to confess before twenty gay souls that you felt any touch of it. There was one young Italian, however, of the party whom I missed from the time we entered the precincts of the Hermitage; nor did I see him till some time after we were all mounted again, and in full chase for the well-known chestnut-trees which have thrown their shadow over so many alfresco repasts. When he again joined us, he had a rose in his button-hole: I felt quite certain that it was plucked from the tree the sad philosopher had planted, and that he, at least, had done homage to his shade, whoever else had failed to do so.

Whatever was felt at the Hermitage, however, was now left behind us, and a less larmoyante party never entered the Forest of Montmorency. When we reached the spot on which we had fixed by anticipation for our salle-à-manger, we descended from our various *montures,* which were immediately unsaddled and permitted to refresh themselves, tied together in very picturesque groups, while all the party set to work with that indescribable air of contented confusion and happy disorder which can only be found at a picnic. I have heard a great many very sensible remarks, and some of them really very hard to answer, upon the extreme absurdity of leaving every accommodation which is considered needful for the comfort of a Christian-like dinner, for the sole purpose of devouring this needful repast without one of them. What can be said in defence of such an act? . . . Nothing, – except perhaps that, for some unaccountable reason or other, no dinner throughout the year, however sumptuously served or delicately furnished, ever does appear to produce one half so much light-hearted enjoyment as the cold repast round which the guests crouch like so many gipsies, with the turf for their table and a tree for their canopy. It is very strange – but it is very true; and as long as men and women continue to experience this singular accession of good spirits and good humour from circumstances which might be reasonably expected to destroy both, nothing better can be done than to let them go on performing the same extraordinary feat as long as the fancy lasts.

And so we sat upon the grass, caring little for what the wise might say of us, for an hour and a half at the very least. Our attendant old women and boys, seated at convenient distance, were eating as heartily and laughing as merrily as ourselves; whilst our beasts, seen through the openings of the thicket in which they were stabled, and their whimsical housings piled up together at the foot of an old thorn at its entrance, completed the composition of our gipsy festival.

At length the signal was given to rise, and the obedient troop were on their feet in an instant. The horses and the asses were saddled forthwith; each one seized his and her own and mounted. A council was then called as to whither we should go. Sundry forest paths stretched away so invitingly in different directions, that it was difficult to decide which we should prefer. 'Let us all meet two hours hence at the Cheval Blanc,' said some one of brighter wit than all the rest: whereupon we all set off, fancy-led, by twos and by threes, to put this interval of freedom and fresh air to the best account possible.

I was strongly tempted to set off directly for Eaubonne. Though I confess that Jean-Jacques' descriptions (tant vantées!) of some of the scenes which occurred between himself and his good friend Madame d'Houdetot, in which she rewards his tender passion by constant assurances of her own tender passion for Saint-Lambert, have always appeared to me the very reverse of the sublime and beautiful; yet still the place must be redolent of the man whose 'Rêveries' have been its whole region classic ground: and go where I will, I always love to bring the genius of the place as near to me as possible. But my wishes were effectually checked by the old lady whose donkey carried me.

'Oh! dame – il ne faut pas aller par là . . . ce n'est pas là le beau point de vue; laissez-moi faire . . . et vous verrez . . .'

And then she enumerated so many charming points of forest scenery that ought to be visited by 'tout le monde,' that I and my companions decided it would be our best course to permit the *laisser faire* she asked for; and accordingly we set off in the direction she chose. We had no cause to regret it, for she knew her business well, and, in truth, led us as beautiful a circuit as it was well possible to imagine. If I did not invoke Rousseau in his bosquet d'Eaubonne, or beside the 'cascade dont,' as he says, 'je lui avais donné *l'idée*, et qu'elle avait fait *exécuter*,' – (Rousseau had never seen Niagara, or he would not have talked of his Sophie's having executed his idea of a cascade;) – though we did not seek him there, we certainly met him, at every step of our beautiful forest path, in the flowers and mosses whose study formed his best recreation at Montmorency. 'Herboriser' is a word which, I think with all possible respect for that modern strength of intellect that has fixed its stigma upon *sentiment*, Rousseau has in some sort consecrated. There is something so natural, so genuine, so delightfully true, in his expressions, when he describes the pleasure this occupation has given him, contrasted as it is with his sour and querulous philosophy, and still more perhaps with the eloquent but unrighteous bursts of ill-directed passion, that its impression on my mind is incomparably greater than any he has produced by other topics.

'Brillantes fleurs, émail des prés!' . . . is an exclamation a thousand times more touching, coming from the poor solitary J.-J. at sixty-five, than any of the most passionate exclamations which he makes St. Preux utter; and for this reason the woods of Montmorency are more interesting from their connexion with him than any spot the neighbourhood of Vévay could offer.

The view from the Rendezvous de Chasse is glorious. While pausing to enjoy it, our old woman began talking politics to us. She told us that she had lost two sons, who both died fighting beside '*notre grand Empéreur*,' who was certainly 'le plus grand homme de la terre; cependant, it was a great comfort for poor people to have bread for onze sous – and that was what King Louis-Philippe had done for them.'

After our halt, we turned our heads again towards the town, and were peacefully pursuing our deliciously cool ride under the trees, when a holla! from behind stopped us. It proceeded from one of the boys of our cortége, who, mounted upon a horse that one of the party had used, was galloping and hollaing after us with all his might. The information he brought was extremely disagreeable: one of the gentlemen had been thrown from his horse and taken up for dead; and he had been sent, as he said, to collect the party together, to know what was to be done. The gentleman who was with our detachment immediately accompanied the boy to the spot; but as the unfortunate sufferer was quite a stranger to me, and was already surrounded by many of the party, I and my companion decided upon returning to Montmorency, there to await at Le Cheval Blanc the appearance of the rest. A medical man, we found, had been already sent for. When at length the whole party, with the exception of this unfortunate young man and a friend who remained with him, were assembled, we found, upon comparing notes together, that no less than four of our party had been unhorsed or undonkeyed in the course of the day; but happily three of these were accidents followed by no alarming results. The fourth was much more serious; but the report from the Montmorency surgeon, which we received before we left the town, assured us that no ultimate danger was to be apprehended.

One circumstance attending this disagreeable contre-tems was very fortunate. The accident took place at the gates of a chateau, the owners of which, though only returned a few hours before from a tour in Italy, received the sufferer and his friend with the greatest kindness and hospitality. Thus, though only eighteen of us returned to Paris to recount the day's adventures, we had at least the consolation of having a very interesting, and luckily not fatal, episode to narrate, in which a castle and most courteous knights and dames bore a part, while the wounded cavalier on whom their generous cares were bestowed had not only given signs of life, but had been pronounced, to the great joy of all the company, quite out of danger either of life or limb.

So ended our day at Montmorency, which, spite of our manifold disasters, was declared upon the whole to have been one of very great enjoyment.

LETTER LXIII

George Sand

I have more than once mentioned to you my observations on the reception given in Paris to that terrible school of composition which derives its power from displaying, with strength that exaggerates the vices of our nature, all that is worst and vilest in the human heart. I have repeatedly dwelt upon the subject, because it is one which I have so often heard treated unfairly, or at least ignorantly, in England; and a love of truth and justice has therefore led me to assure you, with reiterated protestations, that neither these mischief-doing works nor their authors meet at all a better reception in Paris than they would in London.

It is this same love of truth and justice which prompts me to separate from the pack one whom nature never intended should belong to it. The lady who writes under the signature of George Sand cannot be set aside by the sternest guardian of public morals without a sigh. With great – perhaps, at the present moment, with unequalled power of writing, Madame de D—— perpetually gives indications of a heart and mind which seem to prove that it was intended her place should be in a very different set from that with which she has chosen to mingle.

It is impossible that she should write as she has done without possessing some of the finest qualities of human nature; but she is and has been tossed about in that whirlpool of unsettled principles, deformed taste and exaggerated feeling, in which the distempered spirits of the day delight to bathe and disport themselves, and she has been stained and bruised therein. Yet she has nothing in common with their depraved feelings and distorted strength; and there is so much of the divine spirit of real genius within her, that it seems as if she could not sink in the vortex that has engulfed her companions. She floats and rises still; and would she make one bold effort to free herself from this slough, she might yet become one of the brightest ornaments of the age.

Not her own country only, but all the world have claims on her; for genius is of no nation, but speaks in a language that can be heard and understood by all. And is it possible that such a mind as hers can be insensible to the glory of enchanting the best and purest spirits in the world? . . . Can she prefer the paltry plaudits of the obscure herd who scorn at decency, to the universal hymn of love and praise which she must hear rising from the whole earth to do honour to the holy muse of Walter Scott?

The powers of this lady are of so high an order as in fact to withdraw her totally, though seemingly against her will, from all literary companionship or competition with the multitude of little authors whose moral theories appear of the same colour as her own; and in the tribute of admiration which justice compels me to pay her, my memory dwells only on such passages as none but herself could write, and which happily all the world may read.

It is sad, indeed, to be forced to read almost by stealth volumes which contain such passages, and to turn in silence from the lecture with one's heart glowing with admiration of thoughts that one might so proudly quote and boast of as coming from the pen of a woman! But, alas! her volumes are closed to the young and innocent, and one may not dare to name her among those to whom the memory clings with gratitude as the giver of high mental enjoyment.

One strong proof that the native and genuine bent of her genius would carry her far above and quite out of sight of the whole décousu school is, that, with all her magical grace of expression, she is always less herself, less original, a thousand times less animated and inspired, when she sets herself to paint scenes of unchaste love, and of unnatural and hard indifference to decorum, than when she throws the reins upon the neck of her own Pegasus, and starts away into the bright region of unsoiled thoughts and purely intellectual meditation.

I should be sorry to quote the titles of any books which ought never to have been written, and which had better not be read, even though there should be buried in them precious gems of thought and expression which produce the effect of a ray of sunshine that has entered by a crevice into a dark chamber; but there are some morsels by George Sand which stand apart from the rest, and which may be cited without mischief. 'La Revue des Deux Mondes' has more than once done good service to the public by putting forth in its trustworthy pages some of her shorter works. Amongst these is a little story called 'André,' which if not quite *faultless*, may yet be fairly quoted to prove of what its author might be capable. The character of Geneviève, the heroine of this simple, natural little tale, is evidence enough that George Sand knows what is good. Yet even here what a strange perversity of purpose and of judgment peeps out! She makes this Geneviève, whose character is conceived in a spirit of purity and delicacy that is really angelic, – she makes this sweet and exquisitely innocent creature fall into indiscretion with her lover before she marries him, though the doing so neither affects the story nor changes the catastophe in the slightest degree. It is an impropriety *à pure perte*, and is in fact such a deplorable incongruity in the character of Geneviève – so perfectly gratuitous and unnecessary, and so utterly out of keeping with the rest of the picture, that it really looks as if Madame D—— *might not* publish a volume that was not timbré with the stamp of her clique. It would not, I suppose, pass current among them without it.

This story of 'André' is still before me; and though it is quite impossible that I should be able to give you any idea of it by extracts, I will transcribe a few lines to show you the tone of thought in which its author loves to indulge.

Speaking of the universal power or influence of poetry, which certainly, like M. Jourdain's prose, often exists in the mind sans qu'on en sache rien, she says, –

'Les idées poétiques peuvent s'ajuster à la taille de tous les hommes. L'un porte sa poésie sur son front, un autre dans son coeur; celui-ci la cherche dans une promenade lente et silencieuse au sein des plaines, celui-là la poursuit au galop de son cheval à travers les ravins; un troisième l'arrose sur sa fenêtre, dans un pot de tulipes. Au lieu de demander où elle est, ne devrait-on pas demander où n'est-elle pas? Si ce n'était qu'une langue, elle pourrait se perdre; mais c'est une essence qui se compose de deux choses, la beauté répandue dans la nature extérieure, et le sentiment départi à toute l'intelligence ordinaire.'

Again she shows the real tone of her mind when, speaking of a future state, she says, –

'Qui sait si, dans un nouveau code de morale, un nouveau catéchisme religieux, le dégoût et la tristesse ne seront pas flétris comme des vices, tandis que l'amour, l'espoir, et l'admiration seront récompensés comme des vertus?'

This is a beautiful idea of the *duties* belonging to a happier state of existence; nay, I think that if we were only as good as we easily might be here, even this life would become rather an act of thanksgiving than what it too often is – a record of sighs.

I know not where I should look in order to find thoughts more true, or fanciful ideas more beautifully expressed, than I have met with in this same story, where the occupations and reveries of its heroine are described. Geneviève is by profession a maker of artificial flowers, and the minute study necessary to enable her to imitate skilfully her lovely models has led her to an intimate acquaintance with them, the pleasures of which are described, and her love and admiration of them dwelt upon, in a strain that I am quite persuaded none other but George Sand could utter. It is evident, indeed, throughout all her writings, that the works of nature are the idols she worships. In the 'Lettres d'un Voyageur,' – which I trust are only begun, for it is here that the author is perfect, unrivalled, and irreproachable, – she gives a thousand proofs of a heart and imagination which can only be truly at home when far from 'the rank city.' In writing to a friend in Paris, whom she addresses as a person devoted to the cares and the honours of public life, she says, – 'Quand tu vois passer un pauvre oiseau, tu envies son essor, et tu regrettes les cieux.' Then she exclaims, 'Que ne puis-je t'emmener avex moi sur l'aile des vents inconstans, te faire respirer le grand air des solitudes et t'apprendre le secret des poètes et des Bohémiens!' She has learned that secret, and the use she makes of it places her, in my estimation, wondrously above most of the descriptive poets that France has ever boasted. Yet her descriptions, exquisite as they sometimes are, enchant me less perhaps than the occasional shooting, if I may so express it, of a bold new thought into the regions of philosophy and metaphysics; but it is done so lightly, so playfully, that it should seem she was only jesting when she appears to aim thus wildly at objects so much beyond a woman's ken. 'Tous les trônes de la terre ne valent pas pour moi une petite fleur au bord d'un lac des Alpes,' she says: and then starts off with this strange query: 'Une grande question serait celle de savoir si la Providence a plus d'amour et de respect pour notre charpente osseuse, que pour les pétales embaumés de ses jasmins.'

She professes herself (of course) to be a republican; but only says of it, 'De toutes les causes dont je ne me soucie pas, c'est la plus belle;' and then adds, quite in her own vein, 'Du moins, les mots de patrie et de liberté sont harmonieux – tandis que ceux de, légitimité et d'obéissance sont grossiers, malsonnans, et faits pour des oreilles de gendarmes.' . . . 'Aduler une bûche couronnée,' is, she declares, 'renoncer à sa dignité d'homme, et se faire académicien.'

However, she quizzes her political friend for being 'le martyr des nobles ambitions;' adding, 'Gouvernez-moi bien tous ces vilains idiots . . . je vais chanter au soleil sur une branche, pendant ce tems-là.'

In another place, she says that she is 'bonne à rien qu'à causer avec l'écho, à regarder lever la lune, et à composer des chants mélancoliques ou moqueurs pour les étudians poètes et les écoliers amoureux.'

As a specimen of what this writer's powers of description are, I will give you a few lines from a little story called 'Mattéa,' – a story, by the way, that is beautiful, one hardly knows why, – just to show you how she can treat a theme worn threadbare before she was born. Is there, in truth, any picture much less new than that of a gondola, with a guitar in it, gliding along the canals of Venice? But see what she makes of it.

'La guitare est un instrument qui n'a son existence véritable qu'à Venise, la ville silencieuse et sonore. Quand une gondole rase ce fleuve d'encre phosphorescente, où chaque coup de rame enforne un éclair, tandis qu'une grêle de petites notes légères, nettes, et folâtres, bondit et rebondit sur les cordes que parcourt une main invisible, ou voudrait arrêter et saisir cette mélodie foible mais distincte qui agace l'oreille des passans, et qui fuit le long des grandes ombres des palais, comme pour appeler les belles aux fenêtres, et passer en leur-disant – Ce n'est pas pour vous la sérénade; et vous ne saurez ni d'où elle vient, ni où elle va.'

Could Rousseau himself have chosen apter words? Do they not seem an echo to the sound she describes?

The private history of an author ought never to mix itself with a judgment of his works. Of that of George Sand I know but little; but divining it from the only source that the public has any right to examine, – namely, her writings, – I should be disposed to believe that her story is the old one of affection either ill requited, or in some way or other unfortunate; and there is justice in quoting the passages which seem to indicate this, because they are written in a spirit that, let the circumstances be what they will, must do her honour.

In the 'Lettres d'un Voyageur' already mentioned, the supposed writer of them is clearly identified with George Sand by this passage:– 'Meure le petit George quand Dieu voudra, le monde n'en ira pas plus mal pour avoir ignoré sa façon de penser. Que veux-tu que je te dise? Il faut que je te parle encore de moi, et rien n'est plus insipide qu'une individualité qui n'a pas encore trouvé le mot da sa destinée. Je n'ai aucun intérêt à formuler une opinion quelconque. Quelques personnes qui lisent mes livres ont le tort de croire que ma conduite est une profession de foi, et le choix des sujets de mes historiettes une sorte de plaidoyer contre certaines lois: bien loin de là, je reconnais que ma vie est pleine de fautes, et je croirais commettre une lâcheté si je me battais les flancs pour trouver un système d'idées qui en autorisât l'exemple.'

After this, it is impossible to read, without being touched by it, this sublime phrase used in speaking of one who would retire into the deep solitudes of nature from struggling with the world:–

'*Les astres éternels auront toujours raison*, et l'homme, quelque grand qu'il soit parmi les hommes, sera toujours saisi d'épouvante quand il voudra interroger ce qui est au-dessus de lui. *O silence effrayant, réponse éloquente et terrible de l'éternité!*'

In another place, speaking with less lightness of tone than is generally mixed throughout these charming letters with the gravest speculations, George Sand says:–

'J'ai mal vécu, j'ai mal usé des biens qui me sont échus, j'ai négligé les oeuvres de charité; j'ai vécu dans la mollesse, dans l'ennui, dans les larmes vaines, dans les folles amours, dans les vains plaisirs. Je me suis prosterné devant des idoles de chair et de sang, et j'ai laissé leur souffle enivrant effacer les sentences austères que la sagesse des livres avait écrites sur mon front dans ma jeunesse. . . . J'avais été honnête autrefois, sais-tu bien cela, Everard? C'est de notoriété bourgeoise dans notre pays; mais il y avait peu de mérite, – j'étais jeune, et les funestes amours n'étaient pas éclos dans mon sein. Ils ont étouffé bien des qualitiés; mais *je sais qu'il en est auxquelles je n'ai pas fait la plus légère tache au milieu des plus grands revers de ma vie, et qu'aucune des autres n'est perdu pour moi sans retour.*'

I could go on very long quoting with pleasure from these pages; but I cannot, I think, conclude better than with this passage. Who is there but must wish that all the great and good qualities of this gifted woman (for she must have both) should break forth from whatever cloud sorrow or misfortune of any kind may have thrown over her, and that the rest of her days may pass in the tranquil development of her extraordinary talents, and in such a display of them to the public as shall leave its admiration unmixed?

LETTER LXIV

*'Angelo Tyran de Padoue' – Burlesque at the Théâtre
du Vaudeville – Mademoiselle Mars –
Madame Dorval – Epigram*

We have seen and enjoyed many very pretty, very gay little pieces at most of the theatres since we have been here; but we never till our last visit to the Théâtre Français enjoyed that uncontrollable movement of merriment which, setting all lady-like nonchalance at defiance, obliged us to yield ourselves up to hearty, genuine laughter; in which, however, we had the consolation of seeing many of those around us join.

And what was the piece, can you guess, which produced this effect upon us? . . . It was 'Angelo!' It was the 'Tyran de Padoue' – *pas doux* du tout, as the wits of the parterre aver. But, in truth, I ought not to assent to this verdict, for never tyrant was so *doux* to me and mine as this, and never was a very long play so heartily laughed at to the end.

But must I write to you in sober earnest about this comic tragedy? I suppose I must; for except the Procès Monstre, nothing has been more talked of in Paris than this new birth of M. Hugo. The cause for this excitement was not that a new play from this sufficiently well-known hand was about to be put upon the scene, but a circumstance which has made me angry and all Paris curious. This tragedy, as you shall see presently, has two heroines who run neck and neck through every act, leaving it quite in doubt which ought to come in prima donna. Mademoiselle Mars was to play the part of one – but who could venture to stand thus close beside her in the other part? – nobody at the Français, as it should seem: and so, wonderful to tell, and almost impossible to believe, a lady, a certain Madame Dorval, well known as a heroine of the Porte St. Martin, I believe, was enlisted into the corps of the Français to run a tilt with – Mars.

This extraordinary arrangement was talked of, and asserted, and contradicted, and believed, and disbelieved, till the noise of it filled all Paris. You will hardly wonder, then, that the appearance of this drama has created much sensation, or that the desire to see it should extend beyond the circle of M. Hugo's young admirers.

I have been told, that as soon as this arrangement was publicly made known, the application for boxes became very numerous. The author was permitted to examine the list of all those who had applied, and no boxes were positvely promised till he had done so. Before the night for the first representation was finally fixed, a large party of friends and admirers assembled at the poet's house, and, amongst them, expunged from this list the names of all such persons as were either known or suspected to be hostile to him or his school. Whatever deficiencies this exclusive system produced in the box-book were supplied by his particular partisans. The result on this first night was a brilliant success.

'L'auteur de Cromwell,' says the Revue des Deux Mondes, 'a proclamé d'une voix dictatoriale la fusion de la comédie et de la tragédie dans le drame.' It is for this reason, perhaps, that M. Hugo has made his last tragedy so irresistibly comic. The dagger and the bowl bring on the catastrophe, – therefore, *sans contredire,* it is a tragedy: but his playful spirit has arranged the incidents and constructed the dialogue, – therefore, *sans faute,* it is a comedy.

In one of his exquisite prefaces, M. Hugo says, that he would not have any audience quit the theatre without carrying with them 'quelque moralité austère et profonde;' and I will now make it my task to point out to you how well he has redeemed this promise in the present instance. In order to shake off all the old-fashioned trammels which might encumber his genius, M. Hugo has composed his 'Angelo' in prose, – prose such as old women love – (wicked old women I mean,) – lengthy, mystical, gossiping, and mischievous. I will give you some extracts; and to save the trouble of describing the different characters, I will endeavour so to select these extracts that they shall do it for me. Angelo Tyran de Padoue thus speaks of himself:–

'Oui . . . je suis le podesta que Venise met sur Padoue . . .
Et savez-vous ce que c'est que Venise? . . . C'est le conseil des
dix. Oh! le conseil des dix! . . . Souvent la nuit je me dresse
sur mon séant, j'écoute, et j'entends des pas dans mon mur
. . . Oui, c'est ainsi, Tyran de Padoue, esclave de Venise. Je
suis bien surveillé, allez. Oh! le conseil des dix!'

This gentleman has a young, beautiful, and particularly
estimable wife, by name Catarina Bragadini, (which part is
enacted on the boards of the Théâtre Français by Madame
Dorval, from the Théâtre de la Porte St. Martin,) but
unfortunately he hates her violently. He could not, however,
as he philosophically observes himself, avoid doing so, and he
shall again speak for himself to explain this.

'ANGELO

'La haine c'est notre sang. Il faut toujours qu'un Malipieri
haïse quelqu'un. Moi, c'est cette femme qu je hais. Je ne vaux
pas mieux qu'elle, c'est possible – mais il faut qu'elle meure.
C'est une nécessité – une résolution prise.'

This necessity for hating does not, however, prevent the
Podesta from falling very violently in love with a strolling
actress called la Tisbe (personated by Mademoiselle Mars).
The Tisbe also is a very remarkably virtuous, amiable, and
high-minded woman, who listens to the addresses of the
Tyrant pas doux, but hates him as cordially as he hates his
lady-wife, bestowing all her tenderness and private caresses
upon a travelling gentleman, who is a prince in disguise, but
whom she passes off upon the Tyrant for her brother. La
Tisbe, too, shall give you her own account of herself.

'LA TISBE (addressing Angelo)

'Vous savez qui je suis? . . . rien, une fille du peuple, une
comédienne . . . Eh bien! si peu que je suis, j'ai eu une mère.
Savez-vous ce que c'est que d'avoir une mère? En avez-vous
eu une, vous? . . . Eh bien! j'avais une mère, moi.'

This appears to be a species of refinement upon the old
saying, 'It is a wise child that knows its own father.' The
charming Tisbe evidently piques herself upon her sagacity in
being quite certain that she had a mother; – but she has not yet
finished her story.

'C'était une pauvre femme sans mari qui chantait des chansons dans les places publiques.' (The '*delicate*' Esmeralda again.) 'Un jour, un sénateur passa. Il regarde, il entendit,' (she must have been singing the *Ça ira* of 1549,) 'et dit au capitaine qui le suivait – A la potence cette femme! Ma mère fut saisie sur-le-champ – elb ne dit rien . . . à quoi bon? . . . m'embrassa avec une grosse larme, prit son crucifix et se laissa garrotter. Je le vois encore ce crucifix en cuivre poli, mon nom Tisbe écrit en bas . . . Mais il y avait avec le sénateur une jeune fille . . . Elle se jeta aux pieds du sénateur et obtint la grace de ma mère. . . . Quand ma mère fut déliée, elle prit son crucifix, ma mère, et le donna à la belle enfant, en lui disant, Madame, gardez ce crucifix – il vous portera bonheur.'

Imagine Mademoiselle Mars uttering this trash! . . . Oh, it was grievous! And if I do not greatly mistake, she admired her part quite as little as I did, though she exerted all her power to make it endurable, – and there were passages, certainly, in which she succeeded in making one forget everything but herself, her voice, and her action.

But to proceed. On this crucifix de cuivre poli, inscribed with the name of Tisbe, hangs all the little plot. Catarina Bragadini, the wife of the Trvant, and the most ill-used and meritorious of ladies, is introduced to us in the third scene of the second day (new style – acts are out of fashion,) lamenting to her confidential femme de chambre the intolerable long absence of her lover. The maid listens, as in duty bound, with the most respectful sympathy, and then tells her that another of her waiting-maids for whom she had inquired was at prayers. Whereupon we have a morsel of naïveté that is *impayable*.

'CATARINA

'Laisse-la prier. – Hélas! . . . moi, cela ne me fait rien de prier!'

This, I suspect, is what is called 'the natural vein,' in which consists the peculiar merit of this new style of writing. After this charming burst of natural feeling, the Podesta's virtuous lady goes on with her lament.

'CATARINA

'Il y a cinq semaines – cinq semaines éternelles que je ne l'ai vu!
. . . Je suis enfermée, gardée, en prison. Je le voyais une heure
de tems en tems: cette heure si étroite, et si vite fermée, c'était le
seul *soupirail** par où entrait un peu d'air et de soleil dans ma vie.
Maintenant tout est muré . . . Oh Rodolpho! . . . Dafné, nous
avons passé, lui et moi, de bien douces heures! . . . Est-ce que
c'est coupable tout e que je dis là de lui? Non, n'est-ce pas?'

Now you must know, that this Signor Rodolpho plays the
part of gallant to both these ladies, and, though intended by
the author for another of his estimable personages, is certainly,
by his own showing, as great a rascal as can well be imagined.
He loves only the wife, and not the mistress of Angelo; and
though he permits her par complaisance to be his mistress too,
he addresses her upon one occasion, when she is giving way to
a fit of immoderate fondness, with great sincerity.

'RODOLPHO

'Prenez garde, Tisbe, ma famille est une famille fatale. Il y a
sur nous une prédiction, une destinée qui s'accomplit presque
inévitablement de père en fils. Nous tuons qui nous aime.'

From this passage, and one before quoted, it should seem, I
think, that notwithstanding all the innovations of M. Hugo,
he has still a lingering reverence for the immutable power of
destiny which overhangs the classic drama. How otherwise
can he explain these two mystic sentences? – 'Ma famille est
une famille fatale. Il y a sur nous une destinée qui s'accomplit
de père en fils.' And this other: 'La haine c'est dans notre sang:
il faut toujours qu'un Malipieri haïsse quelqu'un.'

The only other character of importance is a very mysterious
one called Homodei; and I think I may best describe him in the
words of the excellent burlesque which has already been
brought out upon this 'Angelo' at the Vaudeville. There they
make one of the dramatis personae, when describing this very
incomprehensible Homodei, say of him, –

'C'est le plus grand dormeur de France et de Navarre.'

* Vent-hole.

In effect, he far out-sleeps the dozing sentinels in the 'Critic;' for he goes on scene after scene sleeping apparently as sound as a top, till all on a sudden he starts up wide awake, and gives us to understand that he too is exceedingly in love with Madame la Podesta, but that he has been rejected. He therefore determines to do her as much mischief as possible, observing that 'Un Sbire (for such is his humble rank) qui aime est bien petit – un Sbire qui se venge est bien grand.'

This great but rejected Sbire, however, is not contented with avenging himself on Catarina for her scorn, but is pushed, by his destiny, I presume, to set the whole company together by the ears.

He first brings Rodolpho into the bedroom of Catarina, then brings the jealous Tisbe there to look at them, and finally contrives that the Tyrant himself should find out his wife's little innocent love affair – for innocent she declares it is.

Fortunately, during this unaccountable reunion in the chamber of Madame, la Tisbe discovers that her mother the ballad-singer's crucifix is in the possession of her rival Catarina; whereupon she not only decides upon resigning her claim upon the heart of Signor Rodolpho in her favour, but determines upon saving her life from the fury of her jealous husband, who has communicated to the Tisbe, as we have seen above, his intention of killing his wife, because 'il faut toujours qu'un Malipieri haïsse quelqu'un.'

Fortunately, again, it happens that the Tisbe has communicated to her lover the Tyrant, in a former conversation, the remarkable fact that another lover still had once upon a time made her a present of two phials – one black, the other white – one containing poison, the other a narcotic. After he has discovered Catarina's innocent weakness for Rodolpho, he informs the Tisbe that the time is come for him to kill his lady, and that he intends to do it by cutting her head off privately. The Tisbe tells him that this is a bad plan, and that poison would do much better.

'ANGELO

'Oui! le poison vaudrait mieux. Mais il faudrait un poison rapide, et, *vous ne me croirez pas,* je n'en ai pas ici.

'LA TISBE

'J'en ai, moi.

'ANGELO

'Où?

'LA TISBE

'Chez moi.

'ANGELO

'Quel poison?

'LA TISBE

'Le poison Malispine, *vous savez*: cettte boîte que m'a envoyée le primicier de Saint Marc.'

After this satisfactory explanation, Angelo accepts her offer, and she trots away home and brings him the phial containing the narcotic.

The absurdity of the scene that takes place when Angelo and the Tisbe are endeavouring to persuade Catarina to consent to be killed is such, that nothing but transcribing the whole can give you an idea of it: but it is too long for this. Believe me, we were not the only part of the audience that laughed at this scene *à gorge déployée*.

Angelo begins by asking if she is ready.

'CATARINA

'Prête à quoi?

'ANGELO

'A mourir.

'CATARINA

'. . . Mourir! Non, je ne suis pas prête. Je ne suis pas prête. Je ne suis pas prête *du tout*, monsieur!

'ANGELO

'Combien de temps vous faut-il pour vous préparer?

'CATARINA

'Oh! je ne sais pas – beaucoup de temps!'

Angelo tells her she shall have an hour, and then leaves her alone: upon which she draws aside a curtain and discovers a block and an axe. She is naturally exceedingly shocked at this spectacle; her soliloquy is sublime!

'CATARINA (*replacing the curtain*)

'Derrière moi! c'est derrière moi. Ah! vous voyez bien que ce n'est pas un rêve, et que c'est bien réel ce qui passe ici, puisque *voilà des choses là derrière le rideau!*'

Corneille! Racine! Voltaire! – This is tragedy, – tragedy played on the stage of the Théâtre Français – tragedy which it has been declared in the face of day shall 'lift the ground from under you!' Such is the march of mind!

After this glorious soliloquy, her lover Rodolpho pays Catarina a visit – again in her bedroom, in her guarded palace, surrounded by spies and sentinels. How he gets there, it is impossible to guess: but in the burlesque at the Vaudeville they make this matter much clearer; – for there these unaccountable entrées are managed at one time by the falling down of a wall; at another, by the lover's rising through the floor like a ghost; and at another, by his coming flying down on a wire from an opening in the ceiling like a Cupid.

The lovers have a long talk; but she does not tell him a word about the killing, for fear it should bring him into mischief, – though where he got in, it might be easy enough for her to get out. However, she says nothing about '*les choses*' behind the curtain, but gives him a kiss, and sends him away in high glee.

No sooner does he disappear, than Angelo and the Tisbe enter, and a conversation ensues between the three on the manner of the doomed lady's death that none but M. Victor Hugo could have written. He would represent nature, and he makes a high-born princess, pleading for her life to a sovereign who is her husband, speak thus: 'Parlons simplement. Tenez . . . vous êtes infâme . . . et puis, comme vous mentez toujours, vous ne me croirez pas. Tenez, vraiment je vous méprise: vous m'avez épousée pour mon argent. . . .'

Then she makes a speech to the Tisbe in the same exquisite tone of nature; with now and then a phrase or expression which is quite beyond even the fun of the Vauderville to travestie; as for instance – 'Je suis toujours restée honnête – vous me comprenez vous – mais je ne puis dire cela à mon mari. *Les hommes ne veulent jamais nous croire,* vous savez; cependant nous leur disons *quelquefois* des choses bien vraies. . . .'

At last the Tyrant gets out of patience.

'ANGELO

'C'en est trop! Catarina Bragadina, le crime fait, veut un châtiment; la fosse ouverte, veut un cercueil; le mari outragé, veut une femme morte. *Tu perds toutes les paroles qui sortent de ta bouche* (montrant le poison).

'Voulez vous, madame?

'CATARINA

'Non!

'ANGELO

'Non? . . . J'en reviens à ma première idée alors. Les épées! les épées! Troilo! qu'on aille me chercher . . . J'y vais!'

Now we all know that his première idée was not to stab her with one or more swords, but to cut her head off on a block – and that *les choses* are all hid ready for it behind the curtain. But this 'J'y vais' is part of the machinery of the fable; for if the Tyrant did not go away, the Tisbe could have found no opportunity of giving her rival a hint that the poison was not so dangerous as she believed. So when Angelo returns, the Tisbe tells him that 'elle se résigne au poison.'

Catarina drinks the potion, falls into a trance, and is buried. (Victor Hugo is always original, they say.) The Tisbe digs her up again, and lays her upon a bed in her own house, carefully drawing the curtains round her. Then comes the great catastrophe. The lover of the two ladies uses his privilege, and enters the Tisbe's apartment, determined to fulfil his destiny and murder her, because she loves him – as written in the book of fate – and also because she has poisoned his other and his favourite love Catarina. The Signor Rodolpho knows that she brought the phial, because one of the maids told him so: this is another instance of the ingenious and skilful machinery of the fable. Rodolpho tells the poor woman what he is come for; adding, 'Vous avez un quart d'heure pour vous préparer à la mort, madame!'

There is something in this which shows that M. Hugo, notwithstanding he has some odd décousu notions, is aware of the respect which ought to be paid to married ladies, beyond what is due to those who are not so. When the Podesta announced the same intention to his wife, he says – 'Vous avez devant vous une heure, madame.' At the Vaudeville, however, they give another turn to this variation in the time allowed under circumstances so similar: they say –

> 'Catarina eut une heure au moins de son mari:
> Le tems depuis tantôt est donc bien renchéri.'

The unfortunate Tisbe, on receiving this communication from her dear Rodolpho, exclaims – 'Ah! vous me tuez! Ah! c'est la première idée qui vous vient?'

Some further conversation takes place between them. On one occasion he says – like a prince as he is – 'Mentez un peu, voyons!' – and then he assures her that he never cared a farthing for her, repeating very often, because, as he says, it is her *supplice* to hear it, that he never loved anybody but Catarina. During the whole scene she ceases not, however, to reiterate her passionate protestations of love to him, and at last the dialogue ends by Rodolpho's stabbing her to the heart.

I never beheld anything on the stage so utterly disgusting as this scene. That Mademoiselle Mars felt weighed down by the part, I am quite certain; – it was like watching the painful efforts of a beautiful racer pushed beyond its power – distressed, yet showing its noble nature to the last. But even her exquisite acting made the matter worse; to hear the voice of Mars uttering expressions of love, while the ruffian she addresses grows more murderous as she grows more tender, produced an effect at once so hateful and so absurd, that one knows not whether to laugh or storm at it. But, what was the most terrible of all, was to see Mars exerting her matchless powers to draw forth tears, and then to look round the house and see that she was rewarded by – a smile!

After Tisbe is stabbed, Catarina of course comes to life; and the whole farce concludes by the dying Tisbe's telling the lovers that she had ordered horses for them; adding tenderly, 'Elle est déliée – (how?) – morte pour le podesta, vivante pour toi. Trouves-tu cela bien arrangé ainsi?' Then Rodolpho says to Catarina, 'Par qui as-tu été sauvée?'

'LA TISBE (*in reply*)

'Par moi, pour toi!'

M. Hugo in a note at the end of the piece, apologises for not concluding with these words – 'Par moi, pour toi,' which he seems to think particularly effective: nevertheless, for some reason which he does not very clearly explain, he concludes thus:–

'LA TISBE

'Madame, permettez-moi de lui dire encore une fois, Mon Rodolpho. Adieu, mon Rodolpho! partez vite à présent. Je meurs. Vivez. Je te bénis!'

It is impossible in this running through the piece to give you any adequate idea of the loose, weak, trumpery style in which it is written. It really seems as if the author were determined to try how low he might go before the boys and grisettes who form the chorus of his admirers shall find out that he is quizzing them. One peculiarity in the plot of 'this fine tragedy' is, that the hero Angelo never appears, nor is even alluded to, after the scene in which he commissions la Tisbe to administer the poison to Madame. His sudden disappearance is thus commented upon at the Vaudeville. The Tyrant there makes his appearance after it is all over, exclaiming –

'Je veux en être, moi . . . l'on osera peut-être
Finir un mélodrame en absence du traître?
Suis-je un hors-d'oeuvre, un inutile article,
Une cinquième roue ajoutée au tricycle?'

In the preface to this immortal performance there is this passage:–

'Dans l'état où sont aujourd'hui toutes ces questions profondes qui touchent aux racines même de la société, il semblait depuis long-tems à l'auteur de ce drame qu'il pourrait y avoir utilité et grandeur' (utilité et grandeur!) 'à développer sur le théâtre quelque chose de pareil à l'idée que voici. . . .'

And then follows what he calls his idea: but this preface must be read from beginning to end, if you wish to see what sort of stuff it is that humbug and impudence can induce the noisiest part of a population to pronounce 'fine!' But you must hear one sentence more of this precious preface, for fear 'the work' may not fall into your hands.

'Le drame, comme l'auteur de cet ouvrage le voudrait faire, doit donner à la foule une philosphie; aux idées, une formule; à la poésie, des muscles, du sang, et de la vie; à ceux qui pense, une explication désintéressée; aux âmes altérées un breuvage, aux plaies secrètes un baume – à chacun un conseil, à tous une loi.' (!!!!)

He concludes thus:–

'Au siècle où nous vivons, l'horizon de l'art est bien élargi. Autrefois le poète disait, le public; aujourd'hui le poète dit, le peuple.'

Is it possible to conceive affected sublimity and genuine nonsense carried farther than this? Let us not, however, sit down with the belief that the capital of France is quite in the condition he describes; – let us not receive it quite as gospel that the raptures, the sympathy of this 'foule sympathique et éclairée,' that he talks of, in his preface to 'Angelo,' as coming nightly to the theatre to do him honour, exists – or at least that it exists beyond the very narrow limits of his own clique. The men of France do not sympathise with Victor Hugo, whatever the boys may do. He has made himself a name, it is true, – but it is not a good one; and in forming an estimate of the present state of literature in France, we shall greatly err if we assume as a fact that Hugo is an admired writer.

I would not be unjustly severe on any one; but here is a gentleman who in early life showed considerable ability; – he produced some light pieces in verse, which are said to be written with good moral feeling, and in a perfectly pure and correct literary taste. We have therefore a right to say that M. Hugo turned his talents thus against his fellow-creatures, not from ignorance – not from simple folly – but upon calculation. For it is possible to believe that any man who has once shown by his writings a good moral feeling and a correct taste, can expose to the public eye such pieces as 'Lucrèce Borgia,' 'Le Roi s'amuse,' 'Angelo,' and the rest – in good faith, believing the doing so to be, as he says, 'une tâche sainte?' Is this possible? . . . and if it be not, what follows? . . . Why, that the author is making a job of corrupting human hearts and human intellects. He has found out that the mind of man, particularly in youth, eagerly seeks excitement of any kind: he knows that human beings will go to see their fellows hanged or guillotined by way of an amusement, and on this knowledge he speculates.

But as the question relates to France, we have not hitherto treated it fairly. I am persuaded that had our stage no censorship, and were dramas such as those of Dumas and Victor Hugo to be produced, they would fill the theatres at least as much as they do here. Their very absurdity – the horror – nay, even the disgust they inspire, is quite enough to produce this effect; but it would be unwise to argue thence that such trash had become the prevailing taste of the people.

That the speculation, as such, has been successful, I have no doubt. This play, for instance, has been very generally talked of, and many have gone to see it, not only on its own account, but in order to behold the novel spectacle of Mademoiselle Mars *en lutte* with an actress from La Porte St. Martin. As for Madame Dorval, I imagine she must be a very effective melodramatic performer when seen in her proper place; but, however it may have flattered her vanity, I do not think it can have added to her fame to bring her into this dangerous competition. As an actress, she is, I think, to Mademoiselle Mars much what Victor Hugo is to Racine, – and perhaps we shall hear that she has 'heaved the ground from under her.'

Among various stories floating about on the subject of the new play and its author, I heard one which came from a gentleman who has long been in habits of intimacy with M. Hugo. He went, as in duty bound, to see the tragedy, and had immediately afterwards to face his friend. The embarrassment of the situation required to be met by presence of mind and a *coup de main:* he showed himself, however, equal to the exigency; he spoke not a word, but rushing towards the author, threw his arms round him, and held him long in a close and silent embrace.

Another pleasantry on the same subject reached me in the shape of four verses, which are certainly droll enough; but I suspect that they must have been written in honour, not of 'Angelo,' but of some one of the tragedies in verse – 'Le Roi s'amuse,' perhaps, for they mimic the harmony of some of the lines to be found there admirably.

> 'Où, ô Hugo! huchera-t-on nom?
> Justice encor rendu, que ne t'a-t-on?
> Quand donc au corps qu'académique on nomme,
> Grimperas-tu de roc en roc, rare homme?'

And now farewell to Victor Hugo! I promise to trouble you with him no more; but the consequence which has been given to his name in England, has induced me to speak thus fully of the estimation in which I find him held in France.

'RARE HOMME!'

LETTER LXV

Boulevard des Italiens – Tortoni's – Thunder-storm –
Church of the Madeleine – Mrs. Butler's 'Journal'

All the world has been complaining of the tremendous heat of
the weather here. The thermometer stands at . . . I forget
what, for the scale is not my scale; but I know that the sun has
been shining without mercy during the last week, and that all
the world declare that they are baked. Of all the cities of the
earth to be baked in, surely Paris is the best. I have been
reading that beautiful story of George Sand's about nothing at
all, called 'Lavinia,' and chose for my study the deepest shade
of the Tuileries Garden. If we could but have sat there all day,
we should have felt no inconvenience from the sun, but, on
the contrary, only have watched him from hour to hour
caressing the flowers, and trying in vain to find entrance for
one of his beams into the delightful covert we had chosen: but
there were people to be seen, and engagements to be kept; and
so here we are at home again, looking forward to a large party
for the evening!

The Boulevard as we came along was prettier than ever; –
stands of delicious flowers tempting one at every step – a rose,
and a bud, and two bits of mignonette, and a sprig of myrtle,
for five sous; but all arranged so elegantly, that the little
bouquet was worth a dozen tied up less tastefully. I never saw
so many sitters in a morning; the people seemed as if they
were reposing from necessity – as if they sat because they
could walk no farther. As we passed Tortoni's, we were
amused by a group, consisting of a very pretty woman and a
very pretty man, who were seated on two chairs close
together, and flirting apparently very much to their own
satisfaction; while the third figure in the group, a little
Savoyard, who had probably begun by asking charity, seemed
spellbound, with his eyes fixed on the elegant pair as if

studying a scene for the *gaie science*, of which, as he carried a mandoline, I presume he was a disciple. We were equally entertained by the pertinacious staring of the little minstrel, and the utter indifference to it manifested by the objects of his admiration.

A few steps farther, our eyes were again arrested by an exquisite, who had taken off his hat, and was deliberately combing his coal-black curls as he walked. In a brother beau, I doubt not he would have condemned such a degree of *laisser-aller*; but in himself, it only served to relever the beauty of his forehead and the general grace of his movements. I was glad that no fountain or limpid lake opened beneath his feet, – the fate of Narcissus would have been inevitable.

Last night we had intended to make a farewell visit to the Feydeau, – Feydeau no longer, however, – to the Opéra Comique, I should say. But fortunately we had not secured a box, and therefore enjoyed the privilege of changing our minds, – a privilege ever dear, but in such weather as this inestimable. Instead of going to the theatre, we remained at home till it began to grow dark and cool – cooler at least by some degrees, but still most heavily sultry. We then sallied forth to eat ices at Tortoni's. All Paris seemed to be assembled upon the Boulevard to breathe: it was like a very crowded night at Vauxhall, and hundreds of chairs seemed to have sprung up from the ground to meet the exigencies of the moment, for double rows of sitters occupied each side of the pavement.

Frenchwomen are so very lovely in their evening walking-dress, and I would rather see them thus than when full-dressed at parties. A drawing-room full of elegantly-dressed women, all looking prepared for a bal paré, is no unusual sight for English eyes; but truth obliges me to confess that it would be in vain at any imaginable evening promenade in London to look for such a spectacle as the Italian Boulevard showed us last night. It is the strangest thing in the world that it should be so – for it is certain that neither the bonnets, nor the pretty faces they shelter, are in any way inferior in England to any that can be seen elsewhere; but Frenchwomen have more the habit and the *knack* of looking elegantly-dressed without being full-dressed. It is impossible to enter into detail in order to

Boulevard des Italiens.

explain this – nothing less skilful than a milliner could do this; and I think that even the most skilful of the profession would not find it easy: I can only state the fact, that the general effect of an evening promenade in Paris is more elegant than it is in London.

We were fortunate enough to secure the places of a large party that were leaving a window in the upper room at Tortoni's as we entered it: and here again is a scene as totally un-English as that of a restaurant in the Palais Royal. Both the rooms above, as well as those below, were quite full of gay company, each party sitting round their own little marble table, with the large *carafe* of ice – for so it may well be called, for it only melts as you want it – the very sight of which, even if you venture not to drain a draught from the slowly yielding mass, creates a feeling of delicious coldness. Then the incessant entrées of party-coloured pyramids, with their accompaniment of gaufres, – the brilliant light within, the humming crowd without, – the refreshing coolness of the delicate regale, and the light gaiety which all the world seem to share at this pleasant hour of perfect idleness, – all are incontestably French, and, more incontestably still, not English.

While we were still at our window, amused by all within and all without, we were started by some sharp flashes of lightning which began to break through a heavy cloud of most portentous blackness that I had been for some time admiring, as forming a beautiful contrast to the blaze of light on the Boulevard. No rain was as yet falling, and I proposed to my party a walk towards the Madeleine, which I thought would give us some fine effects of light and darkness on such a night as this. The proposal was eagerly accepted, and we wandered on till we left the crowd and the gas behind us. We walked to the end of the Rue Royale, and then turned round slowly and gradually to approach the church. The effect was infinitely finer than anything I had anticipated: the moon was only a few days past the full; and even when hid behind the heavy clouds that were gathering together as it seemed from all parts of the sky, gave light enough for us dimly, yet distinctly, to discern the vast and beautiful proportions of the magnificent portico. It looked like the pale spectre of a Grecian temple. With one accord we all paused at the point where it was most perfectly and most beautifully visible; and I assure you, that with the heavy ominous mass of black clouds above and behind it – with the faint light of the 'inconstant moon,' now for a moment brightly visible, and now wholly hid behind a driving cloud, reflected from its columns, it was the most beautiful object of art that I ever looked at.

It was some time before we could resolve to leave it, quite sure as we were that it never could be our chance to behold it in such perfection again; and while we stayed, the storm advanced rapidly towards us, adding the distant rumbling of its angry voice to enhance the effect of the spectacle. Yet still we lingered; and were rewarded for our courage by seeing the whole of the vast edifice burst upon our sight in such a blaze of sudden brightness, that when it passed away, I thought for an instant that I was struck blind. Another flash followed – another and another. The spectacle was glorious; but the danger of being drenched to the skin became every moment more imminent, and we hastily retreated to the Boulevard. As we emerged from the gloom of the Madeleine Boulevard to the glaring gas-light from the cafés which illuminated the Italian, it seemed as if we had got into another atmosphere and another world. No rain had as yet fallen; and the crowd, thicker than ever, were still sitting and lounging about, apparently unconscious of the watery danger which threatened them. So great is the force of example, that, before we got to the end of the promenade, we seemed unconscious of it too, for we turned with the rest. But we were soon punished for our folly: the dark canopy burst asunder, and let down upon us as pelting a shower as ever drove feathers and flowers, and ribbons and gauze, to every point of the compass in search of shelter.

I have sometimes wondered at the short space of time it required to clear a crowded theatre of its guests; but the vanishing of the crowd from the Boulevard was more rapid still. What became of them all, Heaven knows; but they seemed to melt and dissolve away as the rain fell upon them. We took shelter in the Passage de l'Opéra; and after a few minutes the rain ceased, and we got safely home.

In the course of our excursion we encountered an English friend, who returned home with us; and though it was eleven o'clock, he looked neither shocked nor surprised when I ordered tea, but even consented to stay and partake of it with us. Our tea-table gossip was concerning a book that all the world – all the English world at least – had been long eagerly looking for, and which we had received two days before. Our English friend had made it his travelling-companion, and having just completed the perusal of it, could talk of nothing else. This book was Mrs. Butler's 'Journal.' Happily for the tranquillity of our tea-table, we were all perfectly well agreed in opinion respecting it: for, by his account, parties for and against it have been running very strong amongst you. I confess I heard this with astonishment; for it appears to me that all that can be said against the book lies so completely on the surface, that it must be equally visible to all the world, and that nobody can fail to perceive it. But these obvious defects once acknowledged – and they must be acknowledged by all, I should have thought that there was no possibility left for much difference of opinion, – I should have thought the genius of its author would then have carried all before it, leaving no one sufficiently cold-blooded and reasonable to remember that it contained any faults at all.

It is certainly possible that my familiarity with the scenes she describes may give her spirited sketches a charm and a value in my eyes that they may not have for those who know not their truth. But this is not all their merit: the glow of feeling, the warm eloquence, the poetic fervour with which she describes all that is beautiful, and gives praise to all that is good, must make its way to every heart, and inspire every imagination with power to appreciate the graphic skill of her descriptions even though they may have no power to judge of their accuracy.

I have been one among those who have deeply regretted the loss, the bankruptcy, which the stage has sustained in the tragic branch of its business by the secession of this lady: but her book, in my opinion, demonstrates such extraordinary powers of writing, that I am willing to flatter myself that we shall have gained eventually rather than lost by her having forsaken a profession too fatiguing, too exhausting to the spirits, and necessarily occupying too much time, to have permitted her doing what now we may fairly hope she will do, – namely, devote herself to literature. There are some passages of her hastily-written, and too hastily-published journal, which evidently indicate that her mind was at work upon composition. She appears to judge herself and her own efforts so severely, that, when speaking of the scenes of an unpublished tragedy, she says 'they are not bad,' – which is, I think, the phrase she uses: I feel quite persuaded that they are admirable. Then again she says, 'Began writing a novel . . .' I would that she would finish it too! – and as I hold it to be impossible that such a mind as hers can remain inactive, I comfort myself with the belief that we shall soon again receive some token of her English recollections handed to us across the Atlantic. That her next production will be less *faulty* than her last, none can doubt, because the blemishes are exactly of a nature to be found in the journal of a heedless young traveller, who having caught, in passing, a multitude of unseemly phrases, puts them forth in jest, unmindful – much too unmindful certainly – of the risk she ran that they might be fixed upon her as her own genuine individual style of expression. But we have only to read those passages where she certainly is not jesting – where poetry, feeling, goodness, and piety glow in every line – to know what her language is *when she is in earnest.* On these occasions her power of expression is worthy of the thoughts of which it is the vehicle, – and I can give it no higher praise.

LETTER LXVI

*A pleasant Party – Discussion between an Englishman and
a Frenchman – National Peculiarities*

I told you yesterday that, notwithtanding the tremendous heat
of the weather, we were going to a large party in the evening.
We courageously kept the engagement; though, I assure you, I
did it in trembling. But, to our equal surprise and satisfaction,
the rooms of Mrs. M—— proved to be deliciously cool and
agreeable. Her receiving-apartment consists of three rooms.
The first was surrounded and decorated in all possible ways
with a profusion of the most beautiful flowers, intermixed
with so many large glass vases for gold fish, that I am sure the
air was much cooled by evaporation from the water they
contained. This room was lighted wholly by a large lamp
suspended from the ceiling, which was enclosed in a sort of
gauze globe, just sufficiently thick to prevent any painful glare
of light, but not enough so to injure the beautiful effect always
produced by the illumination of flowers. The large croisées
were thrown open, with very slight muslin curtains over
them; and the whole effect of the room – its cool atmosphere,
its delicious fragrance, and its subdued light – was so
enchanting, that it was not without difficulty we passed on to
pay our compliments to Mrs. M——, who was in a larger but
much less fascinating apartment.

There were many French persons present, but the majority
of the company was English. Having looked about us a little,
we retreated to the fishes and the myrtles; and as there was a
very handsome man singing buffa songs in one of the other
rooms, with a score of very handsome women looking at and
listening to him, the multitude assembled there; and we had
the extreme felicity of finding fresh air and a sofa *à notre
disposition,* with the additional satisfaction of accepting or
refusing ices every time the trays paraded before us. You will

believe that we were not long left without companions, in a position so every way desirable: and in truth we soon had about us a select committee of superlatively agreeable people; and there we sat till considerably past midnight, with a degree of enjoyment which rarely belongs to hours devoted to a very large party in very hot weather.

And what did we talk about? – I think it would be easier to enumerate the subjects we did not touch upon than those we did. Everybody seemed to think that it would be too fatiguing to run any theme far; and so, rather in the style of idle, pampered lap-dogs, than of spirited pointers and setters, we amused ourselves by skittishly pursuing whatever was started, just as it pleased us, and then turned round and reposed till something else darted into view. The whole circle, consisting of seven persons, were English with the exception of one; and that one was – he must excuse me, for I will not name him – that one was a most exceedingly clever and superlatively agreeable young Frenchman.

As we had snarled and snapped a little here and there in some of our gambols after the various objects which had passed before us, this young man suggested the possibility of his being *de trop* in the coterie. 'Are you not gênés,' said he, 'by my being here to listen to all that you and yours may be disposed to say of us and ours? . . . Shall I have the amiability to depart?'

A general and decided negative was put upon this proposition; but one of the party moved an amendment. 'Let us,' said he, 'agree to say everything respecting France and the French with as much unreserve as if you were on the top of Notrè Dame; and do you, who have been for three months in England, treat us exactly in the same manner; and see what we shall make of each other. We are all much too languid to suffer our patriotism to mount up to "spirit-boil," and so there is no danger whatever that we should quarrel.'

'I would accept the partie instantly,' said the Frenchman, 'were it not so unequal. But six to one! . . . is not this too hard?'

'No! . . . not the least in the world, if we take it in the quizzing vein,' replied the other; 'for it is well known that a Frenchman can out-quiz six Englishmen at any time.'

'Eh bien!' . . . said the complaisant Parisian with a sigh, 'I will do my best. Begin, ladies, if you please.'

'No! no! no!' exclaimed several female voices in a breath; 'we will have nothing to do with it; fight it out between yourselves: we will be the judges, and award the honours of the field to him who hits the hardest.'

'This is worse and worse,' cried our laughing enemy: 'if this be the arrangement of the combat, the judgment, à coup sûr, will be given against me. How can you expect such blind confidence from me?'

We protested against this attack upon our justice, promised to be as impartial as Jove, and desired the champions to enter the lists.

'So then,' said the Englishman, 'I am to enact the part of St. George . . . and God defend the right!'

'And I, that of St. Denis,' replied the Frenchman, his right hand upon his breast and his left gracefully sawing the air. 'Mon bras . . . non . . .

> 'Ma *langue* à ma patrie,
> Mon coeur à mon amie,
> Mourir gaiement pour la glorie et l'amour,
> C'est la devise d'un vaillant troubadour.'

Allons! . . . Now tell me, St. George, what say you in defence of the English mode of suffering ladies – the ladies of Britain – the most lovely ladies in the world, n'est-ce-pas? – to rise from table, and leave the room, and the gentlemen – alone – with down-cast eyes and timid step – without a single preux chevalier to offer them his protection or to bear them company on their melancholy way – banished, turned out – exiled from the banquet-board! – I protest to you that I have suffered martyrdom when this has happened, and I, for my sins, been present to witness it. Croyez-moi, I would have joyfully submitted to make my exit à quatre pattes, so I might but have followed them. Ah! you know not what it is for a Frenchman to remain still, when forced to behold such a spectacle as this! . . . Alas! I felt as if I had disgraced myself for life; but I was more than spellbound – I was promise-bound; the friend who accompanied me to the party where I witnessed this horror had previously told me what I should have to endure – I did endure it – but I have not yet forgiven myself for participating in so outrageous a barbarism.'

'The gentlemen only remain to drink the fair ladies' health,' said our St. George very coolly; 'and I doubt not all ladies would tell you, did they speak sincerely, that they were heartily glad to get rid of you for half an hour or so. You have no idea, my good fellow, what an agreeable interlude this makes for them: they drink coffee, sprinkle their fans with esprit de rose, refresh their wit, repair their smiles, and are ready to set off again upon a fresh campaign, certain of fresh conquests. But what can St. Denis say in defence of a Frenchman who makes love to three women at once – as I positively declare I saw you do last night at the Opera?'

'You mistook the matter altogether, mon cher; I did not make love – I only offered adoration: we are bound to adore the whole sex, and all the petits soins offered in public are but the ceremonies of this our national worship . . . We never make love in public, my dear friend – *ce n'est pas dans nos moeurs*. But will you explain to me un peu, why Englishmen indulge themselves in the very extraordinary habit of taking their wives to market with that vilaine corde au cou that it is so dreadful to mention, and there sell them for the mesquine somme de trois francs? . . . Ah! be very sure that were there a single Frenchman present at your terrible Smithfield when this happened, he would buy them all up, and give them their liberty at once.'

The St. George laughed – but then replied very gravely, that the custom was a very useful one, as it enabled an Englishman to get rid of a wife as soon as he found that she was not worth keeping. 'But will you tell me,' he continued, 'how it is that you can be so inhuman as to take your innocent young daughters and sisters, and dispose of them as if they were Virginian slaves born on your estates, to the best bidder, without asking the charming little creatures themselves one single word concerning their sentiments on the subject?'

'We are too careful of our young daughters and sisters,' replied the champion of France, 'not to provide them with a suitable alliance and a proper protector before they shall have run the risk of making a less prudent selection for themselves:

but, what can put it into the heads of English parents to send
out whole ship-loads of young English demoiselles – si belles
qu'elles sont! – to the other side of the earth, in order to
provide them with husbands?'

Our knight paused for a moment before he answered, and I
believe we all shook for him; but at length he replied very
sententiously –

'When nations spread their conquests to *the other side of the
earth*, and send forth their generals and their judges to take and
to hold possession for them, it is fitting that their distant
honours should be shared by their fair countrywomen. But
will you explain to me why it is that the venerable grand-
mothers of France think it necessary to figure in a contre-danse
– nay, even in a waltz, as long as they think that they have
strength left to prevent their falling on their noses?'

'"Vive la bagatelle!" is the first lesson we learn in our
nurses' arms – and Heaven forbid we should any of us live
long enough to forget it!' answered the Frenchman. 'But if the
question be not too indiscreet, will you tell me, most glorious
St. George, in what school of philosophy it was that Englishmen learned to seek satisfaction for their wounded honour
in the receipt of a sum of money from the lovers of their
wives?'

'Most puissant St. Denis.' replied the knight of England, 'I
strongly recommend you not to touch upon any theme
connected with the marriage state as it exists in England;
because I opine that it would take you a longer time to
comprehend it than you may have leisure to give. It will not
take you so long perhaps to inform me how it happens that so
gay a people as the French, whose first lesson, as you say, is
"Vive la bagatelle!" should make so frequent a practice as they
do of inviting either a friend or a mistress to enjoy a tête-à-tête
over a pan of charcoal, with doors, windows, and vent-holes
of all kinds carefully sealed, to prevent the least possible
chance that either should survive?'

'It has arisen,' replied the Frenchman, 'from our great
intimacy with England – where the month of November is
passed by one half of the population in hanging themselves,
and by the other half in cutting them down. The charcoal
system has been an attempt to improve upon your insular

mode of proceeding; and I believe it is, on the whole, considered preferable. But may I ask you in what reign the law was passed which permits every Englishman to beat his wife with a stick as large as his thumb; and also whether the law has made any provision for the case of a man's having the gout in that member to such a degree as to swell it to twice its ordinary size?'

'It has been decided by a jury of physicians,' said our able advocate, 'that in all such cases of gout, the decrease of strength is in exact proportion to the increase of size in the pattern thumb, and therefore no especial law has passed our senate concerning its possible variation. As to the law itself, there is not a woman in England who will not tell you that it is as laudable as it is venerable.'

'The women of England must be angels!' cried the champion of France, suddenly starting from his chair and clasping his hands together with energy, – 'angels! and nothing else, or' (looking round him) 'they could never smile as you do now, while tyranny so terrible was discussed before them!'

What the St. Denis thus politely called a smile, was in effect a very hearty laugh – which really and bonâ fide seemed to puzzle him, as to the feeling which gave rise to it. 'I will tell you of what you all remind me at this moment,' said he, reseating himself: 'Did you ever see or read "Le Médecin malgré Lui"?'

We answered in the affirmative.

'Eh bien! . . . do you remember a certain scene in which a certain good man enters a house whence have issued the cries of a woman grievously beaten by her husband?'

We all nodded assent.

'Eh bien! . . . and do you remember how it is that Martine, the beaten wife, receives the intercessor? – 'Et je veux qu'il me batte, moi.' Voyez-vous, mesdames, I am that pitying individual – that kind-hearted M. Robert; and you – you are every one of you most perfect Martines.'

'You are positively getting angry, Sir Champion,' said one of the ladies: 'and if that happens, we shall incontestably declare you vanquished.'

'Nay, I am vanquished – I yield – I throw up the partie – I see clearly that I know nothing about the matter. What I conceived

to be national barbarisms, you evidently cling to as national
privileges. Allons! . . . je me rends!'

'We have not given any judgment, however,' said I. 'But
perhaps you are more tired than beaten? – you only want a
little repose, and you will then be ready to start anew.'

'Non! absolument non! – but I will willingly change sides,
and tell you how greatly I admire England. . . .'

The conversation then started off in another direction, and
ceased not till the number of parties who passed us in making
their exit roused us at length to the necessity of leaving our
flowery retreat, and making ours also.

LETTER LXVII

Chamber of Deputies – Punishment of Journalists – Institute for the Encouragement of Industry – Men of Genius

Of all the ladies in the world, the English, I believe, are the most anxious to enter a representative chamber. The reason for this is sufficiently obvious, – they are the only ones who are denied this privilege in their own country: though I believe that they are in general rather disposed to consider this exclusion as a compliment, inasmuch as it evidently manifests something like a fear that their conversation might be found sufficiently attractive to draw the Solons and Lycurguses from their duty.

But however well they may be disposed to submit to the privation at home, it is a certain fact that Englishwomen dearly love to find themselves in a legislative assembly abroad. There certainly is something more than commonly exciting in the interest inspired by seeing the moral strength of a great people collected together, and in the act of exerting their judgment and their power for the well-being and safety of millions. I suspect, however, that the sublimity of the spectacle would be considerably lessened by a too great familiarity with it; and that if, instead of being occasionally hoisted outside a lantern to catch an uncertain sight and a broken sound of what was passing within the temple, we were in the constant habit of being ushered into so commodious a tribune as we occupied yesterday at the Chamber of Deputies, we might soon cease to experience the sort of reverence with which we looked down from thence upon the collected wisdom of France.

Nothing can be more agreeable than the arrangement of this chamber for spectators. The galleries command the whole of it perfectly; and the orator of the hour, if he can be heard by any one, cannot fail of being heard by those who occupy them.

Another peculiar advantage for strangers is, that the position of every member is so distinctly marked, that you have the satisfaction of knowing at a glance where to find the brawling republican, the melancholy legitimatist, and the active doctrinaire. The ministers, too, are as much distinguished by their place in the Chamber as in the Red Book, (or whatever may be the distinctive symbol of that important record here,) and by giving a franc at the entrance, for a sort of map that they call a 'Table figurative' of the Chamber, you know the name and constituency of every member present.

This greatly increases the interest felt by a stranger. It is very agreeable to hear a man speak with fervour and eloquence, let him be who he may; but it enhances the pleasure prodigiously to know at the same time who and what he is. If he be a minister, every word has either more or less weight according . . . to circumstances; and if he be in opposition, one is also more au fait as to the positive value of his sentiments from being acquainted with the fact.

The business before the house when we were there was stirring and interesting enough. It was on the subject of the fines and imprisonment to be imposed on those journalists who had outraged law and decency by their inflammatory publications respecting the trials going on at the Luxembourg. General Bugeaud made an excellent speech upon the abuse of the freedom of the press; a subject which certainly has given birth to more 'cant,' properly so called, than any other I know of. To so strange an extent has this been carried, that it really requires a considerable portion of moral courage to face the question fairly and honestly, and boldly to say, that this unrestricted power, which has for years been dwelt upon as the greatest blessing which can be accorded to the people, is in truth a most fearful evil. If this unrestricted power had been advocated only by demagogues and malcontents, the difficulties respecting the question would be slight indeed, compared to what they are at present; but so many good men have pleaded for it, that it is only with the greatest caution, and the strongest conviction from the result of experience, that the law should interfere to restrain it.

Nothing, in fact, is so plausible as the sophistry with which a young enthusiast for liberty seeks to show that the unrestrained exercise of intellect must not only be the birthright of every man, but that its exercise must also of necessity be beneficial to the whole human race. How easy is it to talk of the loss which the ever-accumulating mass of human knowledge must sustain from stopping by the strong hand of power the diffusion of speculation and experience! How very easy is it to paint in odious colours the tyranny that would check the divine efforts of the immortal mind! – And yet it is as clear as the bright light of heaven, that not all the sufferings which all the tyrants who ever cursed the earth have brought on man can compare to those which the malign influence of an unchecked press is calculated to inflict upon him.

The influence of the press in unquestionably the most awful engine that Providence has permitted the hand of man to wield. If used for good, it has the power of raising us higher in the intellectual scale than Plato ever dreamed; but if employed for evil, the Prince of Darkness may throw down his arms before its unmeasured strength – he has no weapon like it.

What are the temptations – the seductions of the world which the zealous preacher deprecates, which the watchful parent dreads, compared to the corruption that may glide like an envenomed snake into the bosom of innocence from this insidious agency? Where is the retreat that can be secured from it? Where is the shelter that can baffle its assaults? – Blasphemy, treason, and debauchery are licensed by the act of the legislature to do their worst upon the morals of every people among whom an unrestricted press is established by law.

Surely, but perhaps slowly, will this truth become visible to all men: and if society still hangs together at all, our grandchildren will probably enjoy the blessing without the curse of knowledge. The head of the serpent has been bruised, and therefore we may hope for this, – but it is not yet.

The discussions in the Chamber on this important subject, not only yesterday, but on several occasions since the question of these fines has been started, have been very animated and very interesting. Never was the right and the wrong in an argument more ably brought out than by some of the speeches on this business: and, on the other hand, never did effrontery go farther than in some of the defences which have been set up for the accused gérans of the journals in question. For instance, M. Raspail expresses a very grave astonishment that the Chamber of Peers, instead of objecting to the liberties which have been taken with them, do not rather return thanks for the useful lesson they have received. He states too in this same *defence*, as he is pleased to call it, that the conductors of the 'Réformateur' have adopted a resolution to publish without restriction or alteration every article addressed to them by the accused parties or their defenders. This *resolution*, then, is to be pleaded as an excuse for whatever their columns may contain! The concluding argument of this defence is put in the form of a declaration, purporting that whoever dooms a fellow-creature to the horrors of imprisonment ought to undergo the same punishment for the term of twenty years as an expiation of the crime. This is logical.

There is a tone of vulgar, insolent defiance in all that is recorded of the manner and language adopted by the partisans of these Lyons prisoners, which gives what must, I think, be considered as very satisfactory proof that the party is not one to be greatly feared. After the vote had passed the Chamber of Peers for bringing to account the persons who subscribed the protest against their proceedings, two individuals who were not included in this vote of reprobation sent in a written petition that they might be so. What was the official answer to this piece of bravado, or whether it received any, I know not; but I was told that some one present proposed that a reply should be returned as follows:–

'The court regrets that the request cannot be granted, inasmuch as the sentence has been already passed on those whom it concerned; – but that if the gentlemen wished it, they might perhaps contrive to get themselves included in the next indictment for treason.'

In the evening we went to the Institute for the encouragement of Industry. The meeting was held in the Salle St. Jean, at the Hôtel de Ville. It was extremely full, and was altogether a display extremely interesting to a stranger. The speeches made by several of the members were in excellently good taste and extremely to the purpose: I heard nothing at all approaching to that popular strain of eloquence which has prevailed of late so much in England upon all similar occasions, – nothing that looked like an attempt to bamboozle the respectable citizens of the metropolis into the belief that they were considered by wise men as belonging to the first class in society.

The speeches were admirably calculated to excite ingenuity, emulation, and industry; and I really believe that there was not a single word of nonsense spoken on the occasion. Several ingenious improvements and inventions were displayed, and the meeting was considerably égayé by two or three pieces exceedingly well played on a piano-forte of an improved construction.

Many prizes were bestowed, and received with that sort of genuine pleasure which it is so agreeable to witness; – but these were all for useful improvements in some branch of practical mechanics, and not, as I saw by the newspapers had recently been the case at a similar meeting in London, for essays! One of the prize compositions was, as I perceived, 'The best Essay on Education,' from the pen of a young bellhanger! Next year, perhaps, the best essay on medicine may be produced by a young tinker, or a gold medal be awarded to Betty the housemaid for a digest of the laws of the land. Our long-boasted common sense seems to have emigrated, and taken up its abode here; for, spite of their recent revolution, you hear of no such stuff on this side the water; – mechanics are mechanics still, and though they some of them make themselves exceeding busy in politics, and discuss their different kings with much energy over a bottle of small wine, I have not yet heard of any of the 'operative classes' throwing aside their files and their hammers to write essays.

This queer mixture of occupations reminds me of a conversation I listened to the other day upon the best manner in which a nation could recompense and encourage her literary men. One English gentleman, with no great enthusiasm of manner or expression, quietly observed that he thought a moderate pension, sufficient to prevent the mind from being painfully driven from speculative to practical difficulties, would be the most fitting recompense that the country could offer.

'Is it possible you can really think so, my dear sir?' replied another, who is an amateur, and a connoisseur, and a bel esprit, and an antiquary, and a fiddler, and a critic, and a poet. 'I own my ideas on the subject are very different. Good God! . . . what a reward for a man of genius! . . . Why, what would you do for an old nurse?'

'I would give her a pension too,' said the quiet gentleman.

'I thought so!' retorted the man of taste. 'And do you really feel no repugnance in placing the immortal efforts of genius on a par with rocking a few babies to sleep? – Fie on such philosophy!'

'And what is the recompense which you would propose, sir?' inquired the advocate for the pension.

'I, sir? – I would give the first offices and the first honours of the state to our men of genius: by so doing, a country ennobles itself in the face of the whole earth.'

'Yes, sir . . . But the first offices of the state are attended with a good deal of troublesome business, which might, I think, interfere with the intellectual labour you wish to encourage. I should really be very sorry to see Dr. Southey made secretary-at-war, – and yet he deserves something of his country too.'

'A man of genius, sir, deserves everything of his country . . . It is not a paltry pension can pay him. He should be put forward in parliament . . . he should be . . .'

'I think, sir, he should be put at his ease: depend upon it, this would suit him better than being returned knight of the shire for any county in England.'

'Good Heaven, sir!' . . . resumed the enthusiast; but he looked up and his opponent was gone.

LETTER LXVIII

*Walk to the Marché des Innocens – Escape of a Canary Bird – A
Street Orator – Burying-place of the Victims of July*

I must give you today an account of the adventures I have
encountered in a *course à pied* to the Marché des Innocens. You
must know that there is at one of the corners of this said
Marché a shop sacred to the ladies, which débits all those
unclassable articles that come under the comprehensive term
of haberdashery, – a term, by the way, which was once
interpreted to me by a celebrated etymologist of my
acquaintance to signify '*avoir d'acheter.*' My magasin 'à la Mère
de Famille' in the Marché des Innocens fully deserves this
description, for there are few female wants in which it fails to
'avoir d'acheter.' It was to this compendium of utilities that I
was notably proceeding when I saw before me, exactly on a
spot that I was obliged to pass, a throng of people that at the
first glance I really thought was a prodigious mob; but at the
second, I confess that they shrank and dwindled considerably.
Nevertheless, it looked ominous; and as I was alone, I felt a
much stronger inclination to turn back than to proceed. I
paused to decide which I should do; and observing, as I did so,
a very respectable-looking woman at the door of a shop very
near the tumult, I ventured to address an inquiry to her
respecting the cause of this unwonted assembling of the people
in so peaceable a part of the town; but, unfortunately, I used a
phrase in the inquiry which brought upon me more evident
quizzing than one often gets from the civil Parisians. My
words, I think, were, – 'Pourriez-vous me dire, madame, ce
que signifie tout ce monde? . . . Est-ce qu'il y a quelque
mouvement?'

This unfortunate word *mouvement* amused her infinitely; for
it is in fact the phrase used in speaking of all the *real* political
hubbubs that have taken place, and was certainly on this

occasion as ridiculous as if some one, on seeing forty or fifty people collected together around a pickpocket or a broken-down carriage in London, were to gravely inquire of his neighbour if the crowd he saw indicated a revolution.

'Mouvement!' she repeated with a very speaking smile: 'est-ce que madame est effrayée? . . . Mouvement . . . oui, madame, il y a beaucoup de mouvement; mais cependant c'est sans mouvement . . . C'est tout bonnement le petit serin de la marchande de modes là-bas qui vient de s'envoler. Je puis vous assurer la chose,' she added, laughing, 'car je l'ai vu partir.'

'Is that all?' said I. 'is it possible that the escape of a bird can have brought all these people together?'

'Oui, madame, rien autre chose . . . Mais regardez – voilà les agens de police qui s'approchent pour voir ce que c'est – ils en saisissent un, je crois. . . Ah! ils ont une manière si étonnante de reconnaître leur monde!'

This last hint quite decided my return, and I thanked the obliging bonnetière for her communications.

'Bonjour, madame,' she replied with a very mystifying sort of smile, – 'bonjour; soyez tranquille – il n'y a pas de danger d'un *mouvement*.'

I am quite sure she was the wife of a doctrinaire; for nothing affronts the whole party, from the highest to the lowest, so much as to breathe a hint that you think it possible any riot should arise to disturb their dear tranquillity. On this occasion, however, I really had no such matter in my thoughts, and sinned only by a blundering phrase.

I returned home to look for an escort; and having enlisted one, set forth again for the Marché des Innocens, which I reached this time without any other adventure than being splashed twice, and nearly run over thrice. Having made my purchases, I was setting my face towards home again, when my companion proposed that we should go across the market to look at the monuments raised over some half-dozen or half-score of revolutionary heroes who fell and were buried on a spot at no great distance from the fountain, on the 29th July 1830.

When we reached the little enclosure, we remarked a man, who looked, I thought, very much like a printer's devil, leaning against the rail, and haranguing a girl who stood near him with her eyes wide open as if she were watching for, as well as listening to, every word which should drop from his oracular lips. A little boy, almost equally attentive to his eloquence, occupied the space between them, and completed the group.

I felt a strong inclination to hear what he was saying, and stationed myself doucement, doucement at a short distance, looking, I believe, almost as respectfully attentive as the girl for whose particular advantage he was evidently holding forth. He perceived our approach, but appeared nowise annoyed by it; on the contrary, it seemed to me that he was pleased to have an increased audience, for he evidently threw more energy into his manner, waved his right hand with more dignity, and raised his voice higher.

I will not attempt to give you his discourse verbatim, for some of his phrases were so extraordinary, or at least so new to me, that I cannot recall them; but the general purport of it made an impression both on me and my companion, from its containing so completely the very soul and essence of the party to which he evidently belonged. The theme was the cruel treatment of the amiable, patriotic, and noble-minded prisoners at the Luxembourg. 'What did we fight for?' . . . said he, pointing to the tombs within the enclosure: 'was it not to make France and Frenchmen free? . . . And do they call it freedom to be locked up in a prison . . . actually locked up? . . . What! can a slave be worse than that? Slaves have got chains on . . . qu'est-ce que cela fait? . . . If a man is locked up, he cannot go farther than if he was chained – c'est clair . . . it is all one, and Frenchmen are again slaves. . . . This is what we have got by our revolution. . . .'

The girl, who continued to stand looking at him with undeviating attention, and, as I presume, with proportionate admiration, turned every now and then a glance our way, to see what effect it produced on us. My attention, at least, was quite as much riveted on the speaker as her own; and I would willingly have remained listening to his reasons, which were quite as 'plentiful as blackberries,' why no Frenchman in the world, let him do what he would, (except, I suppose, when they obey their king, like the unfortunate victims of popular tyranny at Ham,) should ever be restricted in his freedom –

'V'la les Restes de notre Revolution de Juillet'.

because freedom was what they fought for – and being in prison was not being free – and so on round and round in his logical circle. But as his vehemence increased, so did his audience; and as I did not choose to be present at a second 'mouvement' on the same day, or at any rate of running the risk of again seeing the police approaching a throng of which I made one, I walked off. The last words I heard from him, as he pointed piteously to the tombs, were – 'V'là les restes de notre révolution de Juillet!' In truth, this fellow talked treason so glibly, that I felt very glad to get quietly away; but I was also glad to have fallen in with such an admirable display of popular eloquence, with so little trouble or inconvenience.

We lingered long enough within reach of the tombs, while listening to this man, for me to read and note the inscription on one of them. The name and description of the 'victime de Juillet' who lay beneath it was, 'Hapel, du département de la Sarthe, tué le 29 Juillet 1830.'

Nothing can be more trumpery than the appearance of this burying-place of 'the immortals,' with its flags and its foppery of spears and halberds. There is another similar to it in the most eastern court of the Louvre, and, I believe, in several other places. If it be deemed advisable to leave memorials upon these unconsecrated graves, it would be in better taste to make them of such dignity as might excuse their erection in these conspicuous situations; but at present the effect is decidedly ludicrous. If the bodies of those who fell are really deposited within these fantastical enclosures, it would show much more reverence for them and their cause if they were all to receive Christian burial at Père Lachaise, with all such honours, due or undue, as might suit the feelings of the time; and over them it would be well to record, as a matter of historical interest, the time and manner of their death. This would look like the result of national feeling, and have something respectable in it; which certainly cannot be said of the faded flaunting flags and tassels which now wave over them, so much in the style of decorations in the barn of a strolling company of comedians.

As we left the spot, my attention was directed to the Rue de la Féronnerie, which is close to the Marché des Innocens, and in which street Henri Quatre lost his life by the assassin hand of Ravaillac. It struck me as we talked of this event, and of the many others to which the streets of this beautiful but turbulent capital have been witness, that a most interesting – and, if accompanied by good architectural engravings, a most beautiful – work might be compiled on the same plan, or at least following the same idea as Mr. Leigh Hunt has taken in his work on the interesting localities of London. A history of the streets of Paris might contain a mixture of tragedy, comedy, and poetry – of history, biography, and romance, that might furnish volumes of 'entertaining knowledge,' which being the favourite *genre* amidst the swelling mass of modern literature, could hardly fail of meeting with success.

How pleasantly might an easy writer go on anecdotizing through century after century, as widely and wildly as he pleased, and yet sufficiently tied together to come legitimately under one common title; and how wide a grasp of history might one little spot sometimes contain! Where some scattered traces of the stones may still be seen that were to have been reared into a palace for the King of Rome, once stood the convent of the 'Visitation de Sainte Marie,' founded by Henriette the beautiful and the good, after the death of her martyred husband, our first Charles; within whose church were enshrined her heart, and those of her daughter, and of James the Second of England. Where English nuns took refuge from English protestantism, is now – most truly English still – a manufactory for spinning cotton. Where stood the most holy altar of Le Verbe Incarné, now stands a caserne. In short, it is almost impossible to take a single step in Paris without discovering, if one does but take the trouble of inquiring a little, some tradition attached to it that might contribute information to such a work.

I have often thought that a history of the convents of Paris during that year of barbarous profanation 1790, would make, if the materials were well collected, one of the most interesting books in the world. The number of nuns returned upon the world from the convents of that city alone amounted to many thousands; and when one thinks of all the varieties of feeling which this act must have occasioned, differing probably from the brightest joy for recovered hope and life, to the deepest desolation of wretched helplessness, it seems extraordinary that so little of its history has reached us.

Paris is delightful enough, as every one knows, to all who look at it, even with the superficial glance that seeks no farther than its external aspect at the present moment; but it would, I imagine, be interesting beyond all other cities of the modern world if carefully travelled through with a consummate antiquarian who had given enough learned attention to the subject to enable him to do justice to it. There is something so piquant in the contrasts offered by some localities between their present and their past conditions, – such records furnished at every corner, of the enormous greatness of the human animal, and his most *chétif* want of all stability – traces of such wit and such weakness, such piety and profanation, such bland and soft politeness, and such ferocious barbarism, – that I do not believe any other page of human nature could furnish the like.

I am sure, at least, that no British records could furnish pictures of native manners and native acts so dissimilar at different times from each other as may be found to have existed here. The most striking contrast that we can show is between the effects of Oliver Cromwell's rule and that of Charles the Second; but this was unity and concord compared to the changes in character which have repeatedly taken place in France. That this contrast with us was, speaking of the general mass of the population, little more than the mannerism arising from adopting the style of 'the court' for the time being, is proved by the wondrously easy transition from one tone to the other which followed the restoration. This was chiefly the affair of courtiers, or of public men, who as necessarily put on the manners of their master as a domestic servant does a livery; but Englishmen were still in all essentials the same. Not so the French when they threw themselves headlong, from one extremity of the country to the other, into all the desperate religious wildness which marks the history of the Ligue; not so the French when from the worship of their monarchs they suddenly turned as at one accord and flew at their throats like bloodhounds. Were they then the same people! – did they testify any single trait of moral affinity to what the world thought to be their national character one short year before? Then again look at them under Napoleon, and look at them under Louis-Philippe. It is a great, a powerful, a magnificent people, let them put on what outward seeming they will; but I doubt if there be any nation in the world that would so completely throw out a theorist who wished to establish the doctrine of distinct races as the French.

You will think that I have made a very circuitous ramble from the Marché des Innocens; but I have only given you the results of the family speculation we fell into after returning thence, which arose, I believe, from my narrating how I had passed from the tombeaux of the *victimes de Juillet* to the place where Henri Quatre received his death. This set us to meditate on the different political objects of the slain; and we all agreed that it was a much easier task to define those of the king than those of the subject. There is every reason in the world to believe that the royal Henri wished the happiness and prosperity of France; but the guessing with any appearance of correctness what might be the especial wish and desire of the Sieur Hapel du département de la Sarthe, is a matter infinitely more difficult to decide.

LETTER LXIX

A Philosophical Spectator – Collection of Baron Sylvestre –
Hôtel des Monnaies – Musée d'Artillerie

We have been indebted to M. J——, the same obliging and
amiable friend of whom I have before spoken, for one or two
more very delightful mornings. We saw many things, and we
talked of many more.

M. J—— is inexhaustible in piquant and original observation, and possesses such extensive knowledge on all those
subjects which are the most intimately connected with the
internal history of France during the last eventful forty years,
as to make every word he utters not only interesting, but
really precious. When I converse with him, I feel that I have
opened a rich vein of information, which if I had but time and
opportunity to derive from it all it could give, would positively leave me ignorant of nothing I wish to know respecting
the country.

The Memoirs of such a man as M. J—— would be a work of
no common value. The military history of the period is as
familiar to all the world as the marches of Alexander or the
conquests of Caesar; the political history of the country during
the same interval is equally well known; its literary history
speaks for itself: but such Memoirs as I am sure M. J——
could write, would furnish a picture that is yet wanting.

We are not without full and minute details of all the great
events which have made France the principal object for all
Europe to stare at for the last half-century; but these details
have uniformly proceeded from individuals who have either
been personally engaged in or nearly connected with these
stirring events; and they are accordingly all tinctured more or
less with such strong party feeling, as to give no very impartial
colouring to every circumstance they recount. The inevitable
consequence of this is, that, with all our extensive reading on

the subject, we are still far from having a correct impression of the internal amd domestic state of the country throughout this period.

We know a great deal about old nobles who have laid down their titles and become men of the people, and about new nobles who have laid down their muskets to become men of the court, – of ministers, ambassadors, and princes who have dropped out of sight, and of parvenus of all sorts who have started into it; but, meanwhile, what do we know of the mass – not of the people – of them also we know quite enough, – but of the gentlemen, who, as each successive change came round, felt called upon by no especial duty to quit their honourable and peaceable professions in order to resist or advance them? Yet of these it is certain there must be hundreds who, on the old principle that 'lookers-on see most of the game,' are more capable of telling us what effect these momentous changes really produced than any of those who helped to cause them.

M. J—— is one of these; and I could not but remark, while listening to him, how completely the tone in which he spoke of all the public events he had witnessed was that of a philosophical spectator. He seemed disposed, beyond any Frenchman I have yet conversed with, to give to each epoch its just character, and to each individual his just value: I never before had the good fortune to hear any citizen of the Great Nation converse freely, calmly, reasonably, without prejudice or partiality, of that most marvellous individual Napoleon.

It is not necessary to attempt recalling the precise expressions used respecting him; for the general impression left on my mind is much more deeply engraven than the language which conveyed it: besides, it is possible that my inferences may have been more conclusive and distinct than I had any right to make them, and yet so sincerely the result of the casual observations scattered here and there in a conversation that was anything but *suivie*, that were I to attempt to repeat the words which conveyed them, I might be betrayed into involuntary and unconscious exaggeration.

The impression, then, which I received is, that he was a most magnificent tyrant. His projects seem to have been conceived with the vastness and energy of a moral giant, even when they related to the internal regulation only of the vast empire he had seized upon; but the mode in which he brought them into action was uniformly marked by barefaced, unshrinking, uncompromising tyranny. The famous Ordonnances of Charles Dix were no more to be compared, as an act of arbitrary power, to the daily deeds of Napoleon, than the action of a dainty pair of golden sugar-tongs to that of the firmest vice that ever Vulcan forged. But this enormous, this tremendous power, was never wantonly employed; and the country when under his dominion had more frequent cause to exclaim in triumph –

     ''Tis excellent to have a giant's strength,'

than to add in suffering,

     'But tyrannous to use it like a giant.'

It was the conviction of this – the firm belief that the GLORY of France was the object of her autocrat, which consecrated and confirmed his power while she bent her proud neck to his yoke, and which has since and will for ever make his name sound in the ears of her children like a paean to their own glory. What is there which men, and most especially Frenchmen, will not suffer and endure to hear that note? Had Napoleon been granted to them in all his splendour as their emperor for ever, they would for ever have remained his willing slaves.

When, however, he was lost to them, there is every reason to believe that France would gladly have knit together the severed thread of her ancient glory with her hopes of future greatness, had the act by which it was to be achieved been her own: but it was the hand of an enemy that did it – the hand of a triumphant enemy; and though a host of powerful, valiant, noble, and loyal-hearted Frenchmen welcomed the son of St. Louis to his lawful throne with as deep and sincere fidelity as ever warmed the heart of man, there was still a national feeling of wounded pride which gnawed the hearts of the multitude, and even in the brightest days of the Restoration prevented their rightful king from being in their eyes what he would have been had they purchased his return by the act of drawing their swords, instead of laying them down. It was a greatness that was thrust upon them – and for that reason, and I truly believe for that reason only, it was distasteful.

In days of old, if it happened by accident that a king was unpopular, it mattered very little to the general prosperity of his country, and still less to the general peace of Europe. Even if hatred went so far as to raise the hand of an assassin against him, the tranquillity of the rest of the human race was but little affected thereby. But in these times the effect is very different: disaffection has been taught to display itself in acts that may at one stroke overthrow the prosperity of millions at home, and endanger the precious blessings of peace abroad; and it becomes therefore a matter of importance to the whole of Europe that every throne established within her limits should be sustained not only by its own subjects, but by a system of mutual support that may insure peace and security to all. To do this where a king is rejected by the majority of the people, is, to say the least of it, a very difficult task; and it will probably be found that to support power firmly and legally established, will contribute more to the success of this system of mutual support for the preservation of universal tranquillity, than any crusade that could be undertaken in any part of the world for the purpose of substituting an exiled dynasty for a reigning one.

This is the *doctrine* to which I have now listened so long and so often, that I have ceased all attempts to refute it. I have, however, while stating it, been led to wander a little from those reminiscences respecting fair France which I found so interesting, coming forth as they did, as if by accident, from the rich storehouse of my agreeable friend's memory: but I believe it would be quite in vain were I to go back to the point at which I deviated, for I could do justice neither to the matter nor the manner of the conversations which afforded me so much pleasure; – I believe therefore that I had better spare you any more politics just at present, and tell you something of several things which we had the pleasure of seeing with him.

One of these was Baron Gros' magnificent sketch, if I must so call a very finished painting, of his fine picture of the Plague of Jaffa. A week or two before I had seen the picture itself at the Luxembourg, and felt persuaded then that it was by far the finest work of the master; but this first development of his idea is certainly finer still. It is a beautiful composition, and there are groups in it that would not have lowered the reputation of Michael Angelo. The severe simplicity of the Emperor's figure and position is in the very purest taste.

This very admirable work was, when we saw it, in the possession of the Baron de Sylvestre, whose collection, without having the dignity of a gallery, has some beautiful things in it. Our visit to it and its owner was one of great interest to me. I have seldom seen any one with a more genuine and enthusiastic love of art. He has one cabinet, – it is, I believe, his own bedroom, – which almost from floor to ceiling is hung with little gems, so closely set together as to produce at first sight the effect of almost inextricable confusion; – portraits, landscapes, and historic sketches – pencil crayon, water-colour and oil – with frames and without frames, all blended together in utter defiance of all symmetry or order whatever. But it was a rich confusion, and many a collector would have rejoiced at receiving permission to seize upon a chance handful of the heterogeneous mass of which it was composed.

Curious, well-authenticated, original drawings of the great masters, though reduced to a mere rag, have always great interest in my eyes, – and the Baron de Sylvestre has many such: but it was his own air of comfortable domestic intimacy with every scrap, however small, on the lofty and thickly-studded walls of this room, which delighted me; – it reminded me of Denon, who many years ago showed me his large and very miscellaneous collection with equal enthusiasm. I dearly love to meet with people who are really and truly in earnest.

On the same morning that we made this agreeable acquaintance, we passed an hour or two at the Hôtel des Monnaies, which is situated on the Quai Conti, and, I believe, on the exact spot where the old Hôtel de Conti formerly stood. The building, like all the public establishments in France, is very magnificent, and we amused ourselves very agreeably with our intelligent and amiable cicisbeo in examining an immense collection of coins and medals. This collection was formerly placed at the Louvre, but transferred to this hôtel as soon as its erection was completed. The medals, as usual in all such examinations, occupied the greater part of our time and attention. It is quite a gallery of portraits, and many of them of the highest historical interest: but perhaps our amusement was as much derived from observing how many ignoble heads, who had no more business there than so many turnips, had found place nevertheless, by the outrageous vanity either of themselves or their friends, amidst kings, heroes, poets, and philosophers. It is perfectly astonishing to see how many such as these have sought a bronze or brazen immortality at the Hôtel des Monnaies: every medal struck in France has an impression preserved here, and it is probably the knowledge of this fact which has tempted these little people so preposterously to distinguish themselves.

On another occasion we went with the same agreeable escort to visit the national museum of ancient armour. This Musée d'Artillerie is not quite so splendid a spectacle as the same species of exhibition at the Tower; but there are a great many beautiful things there too. Some exquisitely-finished muskets and arquebuses of considerable antiquity, and splendid with a profusion of inlaid ivory, mother-of-pearl, and precious stones, are well arranged for exhibition, as are likewise some complete suits of armour of various dates; – among them is one worn in battle by the unfortunate Maid of Orleans.

But this is not only a curious antiquarian exhibition, – it is in truth a national institution wherein military men may study the art of war from almost its first barbarous simplicity up to its present terrible perfection. The models of all manner of slaughtering instruments are beautifully executed, and must be of great interest to all who wish to study the theory of that science which may be proved 'par raison démonstrative,' as Molière observes, to consist wholly 'dans l'art de donner et ne pas recevoir.' But I believe the object which most amused me in the exhibition, was a written notice, repeated at intervals along all the racks on which were placed the more modern and ordinary muskets, to this effect:–

'Manquant, au second-rang de ce ratelier d'armes, environ quatre-vingt carabines à rouet, *ornées d'incrustation d'ivoire et de nacre, dans le genre de celles du premier rang.* Toutes celles qu'on voit ici ont servi dans les journées de Juillet, et ont été rendues après. Les personnes qui auraient encore celles qui manquent sont priées de les rapporter.'

There is such a superlative degree of *bonhomie* in the belief that because all the ordinary muskets which were seized upon by the July patriots were returned, those also adorned with 'incrustations d'ivoire et de nacre' would be returned too, that it was quite impossible to restrain a smile at it. Such unwearied confidence and hope deserve a better reward than, I fear, they will meet: the 'incrustations d'ivoire et de nacre' are, I doubt not, in very safe keeping, and have been converted, by the patriot hands that seized them, to other purposes, as dear to the hearts they belonged to as that of firing at the Royal Guard over a barricade. Our doctrinaire friend himself confessed that he thought it was time these naïve notices should be removed.

It was, I think, in the course of this excursion that our friend gave me an anecdote which I think is curious and characteristic. Upon some occasion which led to a private interview between Charles Dix and himself, some desultory conversation followed the discussion of the business which led to the audience. The name of Malesherbes, the intrepid defender of Louis Seize, was mentioned by our friend. The monarch frowned.

'Sire!' – was uttered almost involuntarily.

'Il nous a fait beaucoup de mal,'– said the king in reply to the exclamation – adding with emphasis, 'Mais il l'a payé par sa tête!'

LETTER LXX

Concert in the Champs Elysées – Horticultural Exhibition –
Forced Flowers – Republican Hats – Carlist Hats –
Juste-Milieu Hats – Popular Funeral

The advancing season begins to render the atmosphere of the
theatres insupportable, and even a crowded soirée is not so
agreeable as it has been; so last night we sought our
amusement in listening to the concert 'en plein air' in the
Champs Elysées. I hear that you too have been enjoying this
new delight of al-fresco music in London. France and England
are exceedingly like the interlocutors of an eclogue, where first
one puts forth all his power and poetry to enchant the world,
and then the other 'takes up the wondrous tale,' and does his
utmost to exceed and excel, and so go on, each straining
every nerve to outdo the other.

Thus it is with the two great rivals who perform their
various feats à l'envi l'un de l'autre on the opposite sides of the
Channel. No sooner does one burst out with some new and
bright idea which like a newly-kindled torch makes for awhile
all other lights look dim, than the other catches it, finds out
some ingenious way of making it his own, and then grows as
proud and as fond of it as if it had been truly the offspring of
his own brain. But in this strife and this stealing neither party
has any right to reproach the other, for the exchange is very
nearly at par between them.

A very few years ago, half a dozen scraping fiddlers, and
now and then a screaming 'sirène ambulante,' furnished all the
music of the Champs Elysées; but now there is the prettiest
'salon de concert en plein air' imaginable.

By the way, I confess that this phrase 'salon de concert en
plein air' has something rather paradoxical in it: nevertheless,
it is perfectly correct; the concerts of the Champs Elysées are
decidedly *en plein air*, and yet they are enclosed within what

may very fairly be called a salon. The effect of this fanciful arrangement is really very pretty; and if you have managed your echo of this agreeable fantasia as skilfully, an idle London summer evening has gained much. Shall I tell you how it has been done in Paris?

In the lower part of the Champs Elysées, a round space is enclosed by a low rail. Within this, to the extent of about fifteen or twenty feet, are ranged sundry circular rows of chairs that are sheltered by a light awning. Within these, a troop of graceful nymphs, formed of white plaster, but which a spectator if he be amiably disposed may take for white marble, stand each one with a lamp upon her head, forming altogether a delicate halo, which, as daylight fades, throws a faint but sufficient degree of illumination upon the company. In the centre of the enclosure rises a stage, covered by a tent-like canopy and brilliant as lamps can make it. Here the band is stationed, which is sufficiently good and sufficiently full to produce a very delightful effect: it must indeed be very villanous music which, listened to while the cool breeze of a summer's evening refreshes the spirit, should not be agreeable. The whole space between the exterior awning and the centre pavilion appropriated to the band is filled with chairs, which, though so very literally en plein air, were all filled with company, and the effect of the whole thing was quite delightful.

The price of entrance to all this prettiness is one franc! This, by the bye, is a part of the arrangement which I suspect is not rivalled in England. Neither will you, I believe, soon learn the easy sort of unpremeditated tone in which it is resorted to. It is ten to one, I think, that no one – no ladies at least – will ever go to your al-fresco concert without arranging a party beforehand; and there will be a question of whether it shall be before tea or after tea, in a carriage or on foot, &c. &c. But here it is enjoyed in the very spirit of sans souci: – you take your evening ramble – the lamps sparkle in the distance, or the sound of the instruments reaches your ears, and this is all the preparation required. And then, as you may always be perfectly sure that everybody you know in Paris is occupied as well as yourself in seeking amusement, the chances are greatly in your favour that you will not reach the little bureau at the gate without encountering some friend or friends whom you may induce to *promener* their idleness the same way.

I often marvel, as I look around me in our walks and drives, where all the sorrow and suffering which we know to be the lot of man contrives to hide itself at Paris. Everywhere else you see people looking anxious and busy at least, if not quite woe-begone and utterly miserable: but here the glance of every eye is a gay one; and even though this may perhaps be only worn in the sunshine and put on just as other people put on their hats and bonnets, the effect is delightfully cheering to the spirits of a wandering stranger.

It was we, I think, who set the example of an annual public exhibition by an horticultural society. It has been followed here, but not as yet upon the same splendid scale as in London and its neighbourhood. The Orangery of the Louvre is the scene of this display, which is employed for the purpose as soon as the royal trees that pass their winters in it are taken out to the Gardens of the Tuileries. I never on any occasion remember having been exposed to so oppressive a degree of heat as on the morning that we visited this exhibition. The sun shone with intolerable splendour upon the long range of windows, and the place was so full of company, that it was with the greatest difficulty we crept on an inch at a time from one extremity of the hall to the other. Some of the African plants were very fine; but in general the show was certainly not very magnificent. I suspect that the extreme heat of the apartment had considerably destroyed the beauty of some of the more delicate flowering plants, for there were scarcely any of the frail blossoms of our hothouse treasures in perfection. The collecton of geraniums was, compared to those I have seen in England, very poor, and so little either of novelty or splendour about them, that I suspect the cultivation of this lovely race, and the production of a new variety in it, is not a matter of so great interest in France as in England.

The climate of France is perhaps more congenial to delicate flowers than our own; and yet it appears to me that, with some few exceptions, such as oranges and the laurier-rose, I have seen nothing in Paris this year equal to the specimens found at the first-rate florists' round London. Even in the decoration of rooms, though flowers are often abundant here, they are certainly less choice than with us; and, excepting in one or two instances, I have observed no plants whatever forced into premature bloom to gratify the pampered taste of the town amateur. I do not, however, mention this as a defect; on the contrary, I perfectly agree in the truth of Rousseau's observation, that such impatient science by no means increases the sum of the year's enjoyment. 'Ce n'est pas parer l'hiver,' he says, – 'c'est déparer le printemps:' and the truth of this is obvious, not only in the indifference with which those who are accustomed to receive this unnatural and precocious produce welcome the abounding treasurers of that real spring-time which comes when it pleases Heaven to send it, but also in the worthless weakness of the untimely product itself. I certainly know many who appear to gaze with ecstasy on the pale hectic-looking bloom of a frail rose-tree in the month of February, who can walk unmoved in the spicy evenings of June amidst thousands of rich blossoms all opening their bright bosoms to the breeze in the sweet healthy freshness of unforced nature: yet I will not assert that this proceeds from affectation – indeed, I verily believe that fine ladies do in all sincerity think that roses at Christmas are really much prettier and sweeter things than roses in June; but, at least, I may confess that I think otherwise.

Among the numerous company assembled to look at this display of exotics, was a figure perhaps the most remarkably absurd that we have yet seen in the grotesque extremity of his republican costume. We watched him for some time with considerable interest, – and the more so, as we perceived that he was an object of curiosity to many besides ourselves. In truth, his pointed hat and enormous lapels out-Heroded Herod; and I presume the attention he excited was occasioned more by the extravagant excess than the unusual style of his costume. A gentleman who was with us at the Orangery told me an anecdote respecting a part of this sort of symbolic attire, which had become, he said, the foundation of a vaudeville, but which nevertheless was the record of a circumstance which actually occurred at Paris.

A young provincial happened to arrive in the capital just at the time that these hieroglyphic habiliments were first brought into use, and having occasion for a new hat, repaired to the magasin of a noted chapelier, where everything of the newest invention was sure to be found. The young man, alike innocent of politics and ignorant of its symbols, selected a hat as high and as pointed as that of the toughest roundhead at the court of Cromwell, and sallied forth, proud of being one of the first in a new fashion, to visit a young relative who was en pension at an establishment rather celebrated for its freely-proclaimed Carlist propensities. His young cousin, he was told, was enjoying the hour of recreation with his schoolfellows in the playground behind the mansion. He desired to be led to him; and was accordingly shown the way to the spot, where about fifty young legitimatists were assembled. No sooner, however, had he and his hat obtained the entrée to this enclosure, than the most violent and hideous yell was heard to issue from every part of it.

At first the simple-minded provincial smiled, from believing that this uproar, wild as it was, might be intended to express a juvenile welcome; and having descried his young kinsman on the opposite side of the enclosure, he walked boldly forward to reach him. But, before he had proceeded half a dozen steps, he was assailed on all sides by pebbles, tops, flying hoops, and well-directed handfuls of mud. Startled, astounded, and totally unable to comprehend the motives for so violent an assault, he paused for a moment uncertain whether to advance boldly, or shelter himself by flight from an attack which seemed every moment to increase in violence. Ere he had well decided what course to pursue, his bold-hearted little relative rushed up to him, screaming, as loud as his young voice would allow, – 'Sauve-toi, mon cousin! sauve-toi! Ote ton vilain chapeau! . . . C'est le chapeau! le méchant chapeau!'

The young man again stopped short, in the hope of being able to comprehend the vociferations of his little friend; but the hostile missives rang about his ears with such effect, that he suddenly came to the decision at which Falstaff arrived before him, and feeling that, at least on the present occasion, discretion was the better part of valour, he turned round, and made his escape as speedily as possible, muttering, however, as he went, 'Qu'est-ce que c'est donc qu'un chapeau à-la-mode pour en faire ce vacarme de diable?'

Having made good his retreat, he repaired without delay to the hatter of whom he had purchased this offensive article, described the scene he had passed through, and requested an explanation of it.

'Mais, monsieur,' replied the unoffending tradesman, 'c'est tout bonnement un chapeau républicain;' adding, that if he had known monsieur's principles were not in accordance with a high crown, he would most certainly have pointed out the posssible inconvenience of wearing one. As he spoke, he uncovered and displayed to view one of those delicate light-coloured hats which are known at Paris to speak the loyal principles of the wearer.

'This hat,' said he, gracefully presenting it, 'may be safely worn by monsieur even if he chose to take his seat in the extremest corner of the côté droit.'

Once more the inexperienced youth walked forth: and this time he directed his steps towards the stupendous plaster elephant on the Place de la Bastile, now and ever the favourite object of country curiosity. He had taken correct instructions for his route, and proceeded securely by the gay succession of Boulevards towards the spot he sought. For some time he pursued his pleasant walk without any adventure or interruption whatever; but as he approached the region of the Porte St. Martin sundry little *sifflemens* became audible, and ere he had half traversed the Boulevard du Temple he became fully convinced that whatever fate might have awaited his new, new hat at the pensionnat of his little cousin, both he and it ran great risk of being rolled in the mud which stagnated in sullen darkness near the spot where once stood the awful Temple.

No sooner did he discover that the covering of his unlucky head was again obnoxious, than he hastened once more to the treacherous hatter, as he now fully believed him to be, and in no measured tone expressed his indignation of a line of conduct which had thus twice exposed the tranquillity – nay, perhaps the life of an unoffending individual to the fury of the mob. The worthy hatter with all possible respect and civility repelled the charge, declaring that his only wish and intention was to accommodate every gentleman who did him the honour to enter his magasin with exactly that species of hat which might best accord with his taste and principles. 'If, however,' he added with a modest bow, 'monsieur really intended to condescend so far as to ask his advice as to which species of hat it was best and safest to wear at the present time in Paris, he should beyond the slightest shadow of doubt respectfully recommend the *juste milieu*.' The young provincial followed his advice; and the moral of the story is, that he walked in peace and quietness through the streets of Paris as long as he stayed.

On our way home this morning we met a most magnificent funeral array: I reckoned twenty carriages, but the *piétons* were beyond counting. I forget the name of the individual, but it was some one who had made himself very popular among the people. There was not, however, the least appearance of riot or confusion; nor were there any military to *protect the procession*, – a dignity which is always accorded by this thoughtful government to every person whose funeral is likely to be honoured by too great a demonstration of popular affection. Every man as it passed took off his hat; but this they would have done had no cortége accompanied the hearse, for no one ever meets a funeral in France without it.

But though everything had so peaceful an air, we still felt disposed to avoid the crowd, and to effect this, turned from the quay down a street that led to the Palais Royal. Here there was no pavement; and the improved cleanliness of Paris, which I had admitted an hour before to a *native* who had remarked upon it, now appeared so questionable to some of my party, that I was challenged to describe what it had been before this improvement took place. But notwithstanding this want of faith, which was perhaps natural enough in the Rue des Bons Enfans, into which we had blundered, it is nevertheless a positive fact that Paris is greatly improved in this respect; and if the next seven years do as much towards its purification as the last have done, we may reasonably hope that in process of time it will be possible to drive – nay, even walk through its crowded streets without the aid either of aromatic vinegar or eau de Cologne. Much, however, still remains to be done; and done it undoubtedly will be, from one end of the '*belle ville*' to the other, if no barricades arise to interfere with the purifying process. But English noses must still have a little patience.

LETTER LXXI

Minor French Novelists

It is not long since, in writing to you of modern French works of imagination, I avowed my great and irresistible admiration for the high talent manifested in some of the writings published under the signature of George Sand; and I remember that the observations I ventured to make respecting them swelled into such length as to prevent my then uttering the protest which all Christian souls are called upon to make against the ordinary productions of the minor French story-tellers of the day. I must therefore now make this amende to the cause of morality and truth, and declare to you with all sincerity, that I believe nothing can be more contemptible, yet at the same time more deeply dangerous to the cause of virtue, than the productions of this unprincipled class of writers.

While conversing a short time ago on the subject of these noxious ephemera with a gentleman whose professional occupations of necessity bring him into occasional contact with them, he struck off for my edification a sketch which he assured me might stand as a portrait, with wonderfully little variation, for any individual of the fraternity. It may lose something of its raciness by the processes of recollecting and translating; but I flatter myself that I shall be able to preserve enough of the likeness to justify my giving it to you.

'These authors,' said their lively historian, 'swarm *au sixième* in every quarter of Paris. For the most part, they are either idle scholars who, having taken an aversion to the vulgar drudgery of education, determine upon finding a short cut to the temple of Fame; or else they are young artisans – journeymen workers at some craft or other, which brings them in just francs enough to sustain an honest decent existence, but wholly insufficient to minister to the sublime necessities of revolutionary ambition. As perfect a sympathy

492

appears to exist in the politics of all these gentry as in their doctrine of morals: they all hold themselves ready for rebellion at the first convenient opportunity – be it against Louis, Charles, Henri, or Philippe, it is all one; rebellion against constituted and recognised authority being, according to their high-minded code, their first duty, as well as their dearest recreation.

They must wait, however, till the fitting moment comes; and, meanwhile, how may they better the condition in which the tyranny of kings and law-makers has placed them? Shall they listen to the inward whisperings which tell them, that, being utterly unfitted to do their duty in that state of life to which it has pleased God to call them, they must of necessity and by the inevitable nature of things be fitted for some other? . . . What may it be? . . . Treason and rapine, of course, if time be ripe for it – but *en attendant*?

To trace on an immortal page the burning thoughts that mar their handicraft . . . to teach the world what fools the sages who have lived, and spoken, and gone to rest, would make of them . . . to cause the voice of passion to be heard high above that of law or of gospel . . . Yes . . . it is thus they will at once beguile the tedious hours that must precede another revolution, and earn by the noble labours of genius the luxuries denied to grovelling industry.

This sublime occupation once decided on, it follows as a necessary result that they must begin by awakening all those tender sympathies of nature, which are to the imagination what oil is to the lamp. A favourite grisette is fixed upon, and invited to share the glory, the cabbage, the inspiration, and the garret of the exalted journeyman or truant scholar. It is said that the whole of this class of authors are supposed to place particular faith in that tinsel sentiment, so prettily and poetically untrue, –

'Love, light as air, at sight of human ties,
    Spreads his bright wings, and in a moment flies;'

and the inspired young man gently insinuates his unfettered ideas on the subject to the chosen fair one, who, if her acquaintance has lain much among these 'fully-developed intelligences,' is not unfrequently found to be as sublime in her notions of such subjects as himself; so the interesting little ménage is monté on the immortal basis of freedom.

Then comes the literary labour, and its monstrous birth – a volume of tales, glowing with love and murder, blasphemy and treason, or downright obscenity, affecting to clothe itself in the playful drapery of wit. It is not difficult to find a publisher who knows where to meet with young customers ever ready to barter their last sous for such commodities, and the bargain is made.

At the actual sight and at the actual touch of the unhoped-for sum of three hundred francs, the flood of inspiration rises higher still. More hideous love and bloodier murders, more phrensied blasphemy and deadlier treason, follow; and thus the fair metropolis of France is furnished with intellectual food for the craving appetites of the most useful and productive part of its population.

Can we wonder that the Morgue is seldom untenanted? . . . or that the tender hand of affection is so often seen to pillow its loved victim where the fumes of charcoal shall soon extinguish a life too precious to be prolonged in a world where laws still exist, and where man must live, and woman too, by the sweat of their brows?

It was some time after the conversation in which I received this sketch, that I fell into company with an Englishman who enjoys the reputation of high cultivation and considerable talent, and who certainly is not without that species of power in conversation which is produced by the belief that hyperbole is the soul of eloquence, and the stout defence of a paradox the highest proof of intellectual strength.

To say I *conversed* with this gifted individual would hardly be correct; but I listened to him, and gained thereby additional confirmation of a fact which I had repeatedly heard insisted on in Paris, that admiration for the present French school of décousu writing is manifested by critics of a higher class in England than could be found to tolerate it in France

'Have you read the works of the *young men* of France?' was the comprehensive question by which this gentleman opened the flood-gates of the eloquence which was intended to prove, that without having studied well the bold and sublime compositions which have been put forth by this class, no one had a right to form a judgment of the existing state of human intelligence.

For myself, I confess that my reading in this line, though greatly beyond what was agreeable to my taste, has never approached anything that deserved the name of study; and, indeed, I should as soon have thought of forming an estimate of the 'existing state of human intelligence' from the height to which the boys of Paris made their kites mount from the top of Montmartre, as from the compositions to which he alluded: but, nevertheless, I listened to him very attentively; and I only wish that my memory would serve me, that I might repeat to you all the fine things he said in praise of a multitude of authors, of whom, however, it is more than probable you never heard, and of works that it is hardly possible you should have ever seen.

It would be difficult to give you any just idea of the energy and enthusiasm which he manifested on this subject. His eyes almost started from his head, and the blood rushed over his face and temples, when one of the party hinted that the taste in which most of these works were composed was not of the most classic elegance, nor their apparent object any very high degree of moral utility.

It is a well-known fact that people are seldom angry when they are quite in the right; and I believe it is equally rare to see such an extremity of vehemence as this individual displayed in asserting the high intellectual claims of his favourites exhibited on any question where reason and truth are on the side espoused by the speaker. I never saw the veins of the forehead swell in an attempt to prove that 'Hamlet' was a fine tragedy, or that 'Ivanhoe' was a fine romance; but on this occasion most of the company shrank into silence before the impassioned pleadings of this advocate for . . . modern French historiettes.

In the course of the discussion many *young* names were cited; and when a few very palpable hits were made to tell on the literary reputations of some among them, the critic seemed suddenly determined to shake off all slighter skirmishing, and to defend the broad battle-field of the cause under the distinguished banner of M. Balzac himself. And here, I confess, he had most decidedly the advantage of me; for my acquaintance with the writings of this gentleman was exceedingly slight and superficial, – whereas he appeared to have studied every line he has ever written, with a feeling of reverence that seemed almost to bear a character of religious devotion. Among many of his works whose names he cited with enthusiasm, that entitled 'La Peau de Chagrin' was the one which evidently raised his spirit to the most exalted pitch. It is difficult to imagine admiration and delight expressed more forcibly; and as I had never read a single line of this 'Peau de Chagrin,' my preconceived notions of the merit of M. Balzac's compositions really gave way before his enthusiasm; and I not only made a silent resolution to peruse this incomparable work with as little delay as possible, but I do assure you that I really and truly expected to find in it some very striking traits of genius, and a perfection of natural feeling and deep pathos which could not fail to give me pleasure, whatever I might think of the tone of its principles or the correctness of its moral tendency.

Early then on the following morning I sent for 'La Peau de Chagrin.' . . . I have not the slightest wish or intention of entering into a critical examination of its merits; it would be hardly possible, I think, to occupy time more unprofitably: but as every author makes use of his preface to speak in his own person, whatever one finds written there assuming the form of a literary dictum may be quoted with propriety as furnishing the best and fairest testimony of his opinions, and I will therefore take the liberty of transcribing a few short sentences from the preface of M. Balzac, for the purpose of directing your attention to the theory upon which it is his intention to raise his literary reputation.

The preface to 'La Peau de Chagrin' appears to be written chiefly for the purpose of excusing the licentiousness of a former work entitled 'La Physiologie du Mariage.' In speaking of this work he says, frankly enough certainly, that it was written as 'une tentative faite pour retourner à la littérature fine, vive, railleuse et gaie du dix-huitième siècle, où les auteurs ne se tenaient pas toujours droits et raides . . . L'auteur de ce livre cherche à favoriser la réaction littéraire que préparent certains bons esprits . . . Il ne comprend pas la pruderie, l'hypocrisie de nos moeurs, et refuse, du reste, aux gens blasés le droit d'être difficiles.'

This is telling his readers fairly enough what they have to expect; and if after this they will persist in plunging headlong into the mud which nearly a century of constantly-increasing refinement has gone far to drag us out of . . . why they must.

As another reason why his pen has done . . . what it has done, M. Balzac tells us that it is absolutely necessary to have something in a *genre* unlike anything that the public has lately been familiar with. He says that the reading world (which is in fact all the world) 'est las aujourd'hui' . . . of a great many different styles of composition which he enumerates, summing up all with . . . 'et l'Histoire de France, Walter-Scottée . . . Que nous reste-t-il donc?' he continues. 'Si le public condamne les efforts des écrivains qui essaient de remettre en honneur la littérature *franche* de nos ancêtres. . . .'

As another specimen of the theories of these new immortals, let me also quote the following sentence:– 'Si Polyeucte n'existait pas, plus d'un poète moderne est capable de *refaire* Corneille.'

Again, as a reason for going back to the tone of literature which he has chosen, he says, – 'Les auteurs ont souvent raison dans leurs impertinences contre le tems présent. Le monde nous demande de belles peintures – où en seraient les types? Vos habits mesquins – vos révolutions manquées – vos bourgeois discoureurs – votre réligion morte – vos pouvoirs éteints – vos rois en demi-solde – sont-ils donc si poétiques qu'il faille vous les transfigurer? . . . Nous ne pouvons aujourd'hui que nous moquer – la raillerie est toute la littérature des sociétés expirantes.'

M. Balzac concludes this curious eassay on modern literature thus:– 'Enfin, le tems présent marche si vite – la vie intellectuelle déborde partout avec tant de force, que plusieurs idées ont vieilli pendant que l'auteur imprimait son ouvrage.'

This last phrase is admirable, and gives the best and clearest idea of the notions of the school on the subject of composition that I have anywhere met with. Imagine Shakespeare and Spenser, Swift and Pope, Voltaire and Rousseau, publishing a work with a similar prefatory apology! . . . But M. Balzac is quite right. The ideas that are generated today will be old tomorrow, and dead and buried the day after. I should indeed be truly sorry to differ from him on this point; for herein lies the only consolation that the wisdom of man can suggest for the heavy calamity of witnessing the unprecedented perversion of the human understanding which marks the present hour. IT WILL NOT LAST: Common Sense will reclaim her rights, and our children will learn to laugh at these spasmodic efforts to be great and original as cordially as Cervantes did at the chronicles of knight-errantry which turned his hero's brain.

LETTER LXXII

*Breaking-up of the Paris season – Soirée at Madame Récamier's –
Recitation – Storm – Disappointment – Atonement – Farewell*

My letters from Paris, my dear friend, must now be brought
to a close – and perhaps you will say that it is high time it
should be so. The summer sun has in truth got so high into the
heavens, that its perpendicular beams are beginning to make
all the gay folks in Paris fret – or, at any rate, run away.
Everybody we see is preparing to be off in some direction or
other, – some to the sea, some to philosophise under the
shadow of their own vines, and some, happier than all the rest,
to visit the enchanting watering-places of lovely Germany.

We too have at length fixed the day for our departure, and
this is positively the last letter you will receive from me dated
from the beauteous capital of the Grand Nation. It is lucky for
our sensibilities, or for our love of pleasure, or for any other
feeling that goes to make up the disagreeable emotion usually
produced by saying farewell to scenes where we have been
very happy, that the majority of those whose society made
them delightful are going to say farewell to them likewise:
leaving Paris a month ago would have been a much more
dismal business to us than leaving it now.

Our last soirée has been passed at the Abbaye-aux-Bois; and
often as I have taken you there already, I must describe this last
evening, because the manner in which we passed it was more
essentially un-English than any other.

About ten days before this our farewell visit, we met, at one
of Madame Récamier's delightful reception-nights, a M.
Lafond, a tragic actor of such distinguished merit, that even in
the days of Talma he contrived, as I understand, to obtain a
high reputation in Paris, though I do not believe his name is
much known to us; – in fact, the fame of Talma so completely
overshadowed every other in his own walk, that few actors of

his day were remembered in England when the subject of the French drama was on the tapis.

On the evening we met this gentleman at the Abbaye-aux-Bois, he was prevailed upon by our charming hostess (to whom I suspect that nobody can be found tough enough to pronounce a refusal of anything she asks) to recite a very spirited address from the pen of Casimir Delavigne to the people of Rouen, which M. Lafond has publicly spoken in the theatre of that city when the statue of Racine, who was native to it, was erected there.

The verses are good, full of fervour, spirit and true poetical feeling, and the manner in which they were spoken by M. Lafond gave them their full effect. The whole scene was, indeed, striking and beautiful. A circle of elegant women, – among whom, by the way, was a niece of Napoleon's – surrounded the performer: the gentlemen were stationed in groups behind them; while the inspired figure of Gérard's Corinne, strongly brought forward from the rest of the picture by a very skilful arrangement of lamps concealed from the eye of the spectator, really looked like the Genius of Poetry standing apart in her own proper atmosphere of golden light to listen to the honours rendered to one of her favourite sons.

I was greatly delighted; and Madame Récamier, who perceived the pleasure which this recitation gave me, proposed to me that I should come to her on a future evening to hear M. Lafond read a play of Racine's.

No proposition could have been more agreeable to us all. The party was immediately arranged; M. Lafond promised to be punctually there at the hour named, and we returned home well pleased to think that the last soirée we should pass in Paris would be occupied so delightfully.

Last night was the time fixed for this engagement. The morning was fair, but there was no movement in the air, and the heat was intense. As the day advanced, thick clouds came to shelter us from the sun while we set forth to make some of our last farewell calls; but they brought no coolness with them, and their gloomy shade afforded little relief from the heavy heat that oppressed us: on the contrary, the sultry weight of the atmosphere seemed to increase every moment, and we were soon driven home by the ominous blackness which appeared to rest on every object, giving very intelligible notice of a violent summer-storm.

It was not, however, till late in the evening that the full fury of this threatened deluge fell upon Paris; but about nine o'clock it really seemed as if an ocean had broken through the dark canopy above us, so violent were the torrents of rain which then fell in one vast waterspout upon her roofs.

We listened to the rushing sound with very considerable uneasiness, for our anxious thoughts were fixed upon our promised visit to the Abbaye-aux-Bois; and we immediately gave orders that the porter's scout – a sturdy little personage well known to be good at need – should be despatched without a moment's delay for a fiacre; and you never, I am sure, saw a more blank set of faces than those exhibited in our drawing-room when the tidings reached us that not a single voiture could be found!

After a moment's consultation, it was decided that the experienced porter himself should be humbly requested to run the risk of being drowned in one direction, while his attendant satellite again dared the same fate in another. This prompt and spirited decision produced at length the desired effect; and after another feverish half-hour of expectation, we had the inexpressible delight of finding ourselves safely enveloped in cloaks, which rendered it highly probable we might be able to step from the vehicle without getting wet to the skin, and deposited in the corners of one of those curiously-contrived swinging machines, whose motion is such that nothing but long practice or the most vigilant care can enable you to endure without losing your balance, and running a very dangerous tilt against the head of your opposite neighbour with your own.

I never quitted the shelter of a roof in so unmerciful a night. The rain battered the top of our vehicle as if enraged at the opposition it presented to its impetuous descent upon the earth. The thunder roared loud above the rattling and creaking of all the crazy wheels we met, as well as the ceaseless grinding of those which carried us; and the lightning flashed with such rapidity and brightness, that the very mud we dashed through seemed illuminated.

The effect of this storm as we passed the Pont Neuf was really beautiful. One instant our eyes looked out upon the

thickset darkness; and the next, the old towers of Notre
Dame, the pointed roofs of the Palais de Justice, and the fine
bold elevation of St. Jacques, were 'instant seen and instant
gone.' One bright blue flash fell full, as we dashed by it, on the
noble figure of Henri Quatre, and the statua gentilissima,
horse and all, looked as ghastly and as spectre-like as heart
could wish.

At length we reached the lofty iron grille of the venerable
Abbaye. The ample court was filled with carriages: we felt
that we were late, and hastening up the spacious stairs, in a
moment found ourselves in a region as different as possible
from that we had left. Instead of darkness, we were
surrounded by a flood of light; rain and the howling blast were
exchanged for smiles and gentle greetings; and the growling
thunder of the storm, for the sweet voice of Madame
Récamier, which told us however that M. Lafond was not yet
arrived.

As the party expected was a large one, it was Miss C——'s
noble saloon that received us. It was already nearly full, but its
stately monastic doors still continued to open from time to
time for the reception of new arrivals – yet still M. Lafond
came not.

At length, when disappointment was beginning to take
place of expectation, a note arrived from the tragedian to
Madame Récamier, stating that the deluge of rain which had
fallen rendered the streets of Paris utterly impassable without a
carriage, and the same cause made it absolutely impossible to
procure one; ergo, we could have no M. Lafond – no Racine.

Such a contre-tems as this, however, is by no means very
difficult to bear at the Abbaye-aux-Bois. But Madame
Récamier appeared very sorry for it, though nobody else did;
and admirable as M. Lafond's reading is known to be, I am
persuaded that the idea of her being vexed by his failing to
appear caused infinitely more regret to every one present than
the loss of a dozen tragedies could have done. And then it was
that the spirit of genuine French *amabilité* shone forth; and in
order to chase whatever was disagreeable in this change in the
destination of our evening's occupations, one of the gentlemen
present most good-humouredly consented to recite some
verses of his own, which, both from their own merit, and

from the graceful and amiable manner in which they were given, were well calculated to remove every shadow of dissatisfaction from all who heard them.

This example was immediately followed in the same delightful spirit by another, who in like manner gave us more than one proof of his own poetic power, as well as that charming national amenity of manner which knows so well how to round and polish every rough and jutting corner which untoward accidents may and must occasionally throw across the path of life.

One of the pieces thus recited was an extremely pretty legend, called if I mistake not, 'Les Soeurs Grises,' in which there is a sweet and touching description of a female character made up of softness, goodness, and grace. As this description fell trait by trait from the lips of the poet, many an eye turned involuntarily towards Madame Récamier; and the Duchesse d'Abrantes, near whom I was sitting, making a slight movement of the hand in the same direction, said in a half-whisper, –

'C'est bien elle!'

On the whole, therefore, our disappointment was but lightly felt; and when we rose to quit this delightful Abbaye-aux-Bois for the last time, all the regret of which we were conscious arose from recollecting how doubtful it was whether we should ever find ourselves within its venerable walls again.

POSTSCRIPT

The letters which are herewith presented to the public contain nothing beyond passing notices of such objects as chiefly attracted my attention during nine very agreeable weeks passed amidst the care-killing amusements of Paris. I hardly know what they contain; for though I have certainly been desirous of giving my correspondent, as far as I was able, some idea of Paris at the present day, I have been at least equally anxious to avoid everything approaching to so presumptuous an attempt as it would have been to give a detailed history of all that was going on there during the period of our stay.

These letters, therefore, have been designedly as unconnected as possible: I have in this been *décousu* upon principle, and would rather have given a regular journal, after the manner of Lloyd's List, noting all the diligences which have come in and gone out of 'la belle ville' during my stay there, than have attempted to analyse and define the many unintelligible incongruities which appeared to me to mark the race and mark the time.

But though I felt quite incapable of philosophically examining this copious subject, or, in fact, of going one inch beneath the surface while describing the outward aspect of all around me, I cannot but confess that the very incongruity which I dared not pretend to analyse appeared to me by far the most remarkable feature in the present state of the country.

There has, I know, always been something of this kind attributed to the French character. Splendour and poverty – grace and grimace – delicacy and filth – learning and folly – science and frivolity, have often been observed among them in a closeness of juxta-position quite unexampled elsewhere; but of late it has become infinitely more conspicuous, – or rather, perhaps, this want of consistency has seemed to embrace objects of more importance than formerly. Heretofore, though it was often suspected in graver matters, it was openly demonstrated only on points which concerned the externals of society rather than the vital interests of the country; but from the removal of that restraint which old laws, old customs, and old authority imposed upon the public acts of the people, the unsettled temper of mind which in time past showed itself only in what might, comparatively speaking, be called trifles, may in these latter days be traced without much difficulty in affairs of much graver moment.

No one of any party will now deny, I believe, that many things which by their very nature appear to be incompatible have been lately seen to exist in Paris, side by side, in a manner which certainly resembled nothing that could be found elsewhere.

As instances of this kind pressed upon me, I have sometimes felt as if I had got behind the scenes of a theatre, and that all sorts of materials, for all sorts of performances, were jumbled together around me, that they might be ready at a moment's notice if called for. Here a crown – there a cap of liberty. On this peg, a mantle embroidered with fleurs-de-lis; on that, a tri-coloured flag. In one corner, all the paraphernalia necessary to deck out the pomp and pageantry of the Catholic church; and in another, all the symbols that can be found which might enable them to show respect and honour to Jews, Turks, infidels and heretics. In this department might be seen very noble preparations to support a grand military spectacle; and in that, all the prettiest pageants in the world, to typify eternal peace.

I saw all these things, for it was impossible not to see them; but as to the scene-shifters who were to prepare the different tableaux, I in truth knew nothing about them. Their trap-doors, wires, and other machinery were very wisely kept out of sight of such eyes as mine; for had I known anything of the matter, I should most assuredly have told it all, which would greatly tend to mar the effect of the next change of decorations.

It was with this feeling, and in this spirit of purely superficial observation, that the foregoing letters were written; but, ere I commit them to the press, I wish to add a few graver thoughts which rest upon my mind as the result of all that I saw and heard while at Paris, connected as they now are with the eventful changes which have occurred in the short interval that has elapsed since I left it.

'*The country is in a state of transition,*' is a phrase which I have often listened to, and often been disposed to laugh at, as a sort of oracular interpretation of paradoxes which, in truth, no one could understand: but the phrase may now be used without any Delphic obscurity. France was indeed in a state of transition exactly at the period of which I have been writing; but this uncertain state is past, nearly all the puzzling anomalies which so completely defied interpretation have disappeared, and it may now be fairly permitted, to simple-minded travellers who pretend not to any conjuring skill, to guess a little what she is about.

I revisited France with that animating sensation of pleasure which arises from the hope of reviving old and agreeable impressions; but this pleasure was nevertheless dashed with such feeling of regret as an *English conservative* may be supposed to feel for the popular violence which had banished from her throne its legitimate sovereign.

As an abstract question of right and wrong, my opinion of this act cannot change; but the deed is done, – France has chosen to set aside the claim of the prince who by the law of hereditary succession has a right to the crown, in favour of another prince of the same royal line, whom in her policy she deems more capable of insuring the prosperity of the country. The deed is done; and the welfare of tens of millions who had, perhaps, no active share in bringing it about now hangs upon the continuance of the tranquillity which has followed the change.

However deep therefore may be the respect felt for those who, having sworn fealty to Charles the Tenth, continue steadfastly undeviating in their declaraton of his right, and firm in their refusal to recognise that of any other, still a stranger and sojourner in the land may honestly acknowledge the belief that the prosperity of France at the present hour depends upon her allegiance to the king she has chosen, without being accused of advocating the cause of revolution.

To judge fairly of France as she actually exists, it is absolutely necessary to throw aside all memory of the purer course she might have pursued five years ago, by the temperate pleading of her chartered rights, to obtain redress of such evils as really existed. The popular clamour which rose and did the work of revolution, though it originated with factious demagogues and idle boys, left the new power it had set in action in the hands of men capable of redeeming the noble country they were called to govern from the state of disjointed weakness in which they found it. The task has been one of almost unequalled difficulty and peril; but every day gives greater confidence to the hope, that after forty years of blundering, blustering policy, and changes so multiplied as to render the very name of revolution ridiculous, this superb kingdom, so long our rival, and now, as we firmly trust, our most assured ally, will establish her government on a basis firm enough to strengthen the cause of social order and happiness throughout all Europe.

The days, thank Heaven! are past when Englishmen believed it patriotic to deny their Gallic neighbours every faculty except those of making a bow and of eating a frog, while they were repaid by all the weighty satire comprised in the two impressive words JOHN BULL. We now know each other better – we have had a long fight, and we shake hands across the water with all the mutual good-will and respect which is generated by a hard struggle, bravely sustained on both sides, and finally terminated by a hearty reconciliation.

The position, the prospects, the prosperity of France are become a subject of the deepest interest to the English nation; and it is therefore that the observations of any one who has been a recent looker-on there may have some value, even though they are professedly drawn from the surface only. But when did ever the surface of human affairs present an aspect so full of interest? Now that so many of the circumstances which have been alluded to above as puzzling and incongruous have been interpreted by the unexpected events which have lately crowded upon each other, I feel aware that I have indeed been looking on upon the dénouement of one of the most interesting political dramas that ever was enacted. The movements of King Philippe remind one of those by which a bold rider settles himself in the saddle, when he has made up his mind for a rough ride, and is quite determined not to be thrown. When he first mounted, indeed, he took his seat less firmly; one groom held the stirrup, another the reins: he felt doubtful how far he should be likely to go – the weather looked cloudy – he might dismount directly . . . But soon the sun burst from behind the cloud and that threatened him: Now for it, then! neck or nothing! He orders his girths to be tightened, his curb to be well set, and the reins fairly and horsemanly put into his hands . . . Now he is off! and may his ride be prosperous! – for should he fall, it is impossible to guess how the dust which such a catastrophe might raise would settle itself.

The interest which his situation excites is sufficiently awakening, and produces a species of romantic feeling, that may be compared to what the spectators experienced in the tournaments of old, when they sat quietly by to watch the result of a combat *à outrance*. But greater, far greater is the interest produced by getting a near view of the wishes and hopes of the great people who have placed their destinies in his hands.

Nothing that is going on in Paris – in the Chamber of Deputies, in the Chamber of Peers, or even in the Cabinet of the King – could touch me so much, or give me half so much pleasure to listen to, as the tone in which I have heard some of the most distinguished men in France speak of the repeated changes and revolutions in her government.

It is not in one or two instances only that I have remarked this tone, – in fact, I might say that I have met it whenever I was in the society of those whose opinions especially deserved attention. I hardly know, however, how to describe it, for it cannot be done by repeating isolated phrases and observations. I should say, that it marks distinctly a consciousness that such frequent changes are not creditable to any nation – that they feel half ashamed to talk of them gravely, yet more than half vexed to speak of the land they love with anything approaching to lightness or contempt. That the men of whom I speak do love their country with a true, devoted, Roman-like attachment, I am quite sure; and I never remember to have felt the conviction that I was listening to real patriots so strongly as when I have heard them reason on the causes, deplore the effects, and deprecate the recurrence of these direful and devastating convulsions.

It is, if I mistake not, this noble feeling of wishing to preserve their country from the disgrace of any farther demonstrations of such frail inconstancy, which will tend to keep Louis-Philippe on his throne as much, or even more perhaps, than that newly-awakened energy in favour of the *boutique* and the *bourse* of which we hear so much.

It is nowise surprising that this proud but virtuous sentiment should yet exist, notwithstanding all that has happened to check and to chill it. Frenchmen have still much of which they may justly boast. After a greater continuance of external war and internal commotion than perhaps any country was ever exposed to within the same space of time, France is in no degree behind the most favoured nations of Europe in any one of the advantages which have ever been considered as among the especial blessings of peace. Tremendous as have been her efforts and her struggles, the march of science has never faltered: the fine arts have been cherished with unremitting zeal and a most constant care, even while every citizen was a soldier; and now, in this breathing-time that Heaven has granted her, she presents a spectacle of hopeful industry, active improvement, and prosperous energy, which is unequalled, I believe, in any European country except our own.

Can we wonder, then, that the nation is disposed to rally round a prince whom Fate seems to have given expressly as an anchor to keep her firm and steady through the heavy swell that the late storms have left? Can we wonder that feelings, and even principles, are found to bend before an influence so salutary and so strong?

However irregular the manner in which he ascended the throne, Louis-Philippe had himself little more to do with it than yielding to the voice of the triumphant party who called upon him to mount its troublesome pre-eminence; and at the moment he did so, he might very fairly have exclaimed –

'If chance will have me king, why chance may crown me Without my stir.'

Never certainly did any event brought on by tumult and confusion give such fair promise of producing eventually the reverse, as the accession of King Louis-Philippe to the throne of France.

The manner of this unexpected change itself, the scenes which led to it, and even the state of parties and of feelings which came afterwards, all bore a character of unsettled confusion which threatened every species of misery to the country.

When we look back upon this period, all the events which occurred during the course of it appear like the rough and ill-assorted fragments of worsted on the reverse of a piece of tapestry. No one could guess, not even the agents in them, what the final result would be. But they were at work upon a design drawn by the all-powerful and unerring hand of Providence; and strange as the medley has appeared to us during the process, the whole when completed seems likely to produce an excellent effect.

The incongruous elements, however, of which the chaos was composed from whence this new order of things was to arise, though daily and by slow degrees assuming shape and form, were still in a state of 'most admired disorder' during our abode in Paris. It was impossible to guess whereunto all those things tended which were evidently in movement around us; and the signs of the times were in many instances so contrary to each other, that nothing was left for those who came to view the land, but to gaze – to wonder, and pass on, without attempting to reconcile contradictions so totally unintelligible.

But, during the few weeks that have elapsed since I left the capital of France, this obscurity has been dispersed like a mist. It was the explosion of an infernal machine that scattered it; but it is the light of heaven that now shines upon the land, making visible to the whole world on what foundation rest its hopes, and by what means they shall be brought to fruition.

Never, perhaps, did even a successful attempt upon the life of an individual produce results so important as those likely to ensue from the failure of the atrocious plot against the King of the French and his sons. It has roused the whole nation as a sleeping army is roused by the sound of a trumpet. The indifferent, the doubting – nay, even the adverse, are now bound together by one common feeling: an assassin has raised his daring arm against France, and France in an instant assumes an attitude so firm, so bold, so steady, and so powerful, that all her enemies must quail before it.

As for the wretched faction who sent forth this bloody agent to do their work, they stand now before the face of all men in the broad light of truth. High and noble natures may sometimes reason amiss, and may mistake the worse cause for the better; but however deeply this may involve them in error, it will not lead them one inch towards crime. Such men have nothing in common with the republicans of 1835.

From their earliest existence as a party, these republicans have avowed themselves the unrelenting enemies of all the powers that be; social order, and all that sustains it, is their abhorrence; and neither honour, conscience, nor humanity has force sufficient to restrain them from the most hideous crimes when its destruction is the object proposed. Honest men of all shades of political opinion must agree in considering this unbridled faction as the common enemies of the human race. In every struggle to sustain the laws which bind society together, their hand is against every man; and the inevitable consequence must and will be, that every man's hand shall be against them.

Deplorable therefore as were the consequences of the Fieschi plot in its partial murderous success, it is likely to prove in its ultimate result of the most important and lasting benefit to France. It has given union and strength to her councils, energy and boldness to her acts; and if it be the will of Heaven that anything shall stay the plague of insurrection and revolt which, with infection more fearful than that of the Asiatic pest, has tainted the air of Europe with its poisonous breath, it is from France, where the evil first arose, that the antidote to it is most likely to come.

It will be in vain that any republican clamour shall attempt to stigmatise the acts of the French legislature with the odium of an undue and tyrannical use of the power which it has been compelled to assume. The system upon which this legislature has bound itself to act is in its very nature incompatible with individual power and individual ambition: its acts may be absolute and high time is it that they should be so, – but the absolutism will not be that of an autocrat.

The theory of the doctrinaire government is not so well, or at least so generally, understood as it will be; but every day is making it better known to Europe, – and whether the new principles on which it is founded be approved or not, its power will be seen to rest upon them, and not upon the tyrannical will of any man or body of men whatever.

It is not uncommon to hear persons declare that they understand no difference between the juste-milieu party and that of the doctrinaires; but they cannot have listened very attentively to the reasonings of either party.

The juste-milieu party, if I understand them aright, consists of politicians whose principles are in exact conformity to the expressive title they have chosen. They approve neither of a pure despotism nor of a pure democracy, but plead for a justly-balanced constitutional government with a monarch at its head.

The doctrinaires are much less definite in their specification of the form of government which they believe the circumstances of France to require. It might be thought indeed, from some of their speculations, that they were almost indifferent as to what form the government should assume, or by what name it should be known to the world, provided always that it have within itself power and efficacy sufficient to adopt and carry into vigorous effect such measures as its chiefs shall deem most beneficial to the country for the time being. A government formed on these principles can pledge itself by no guarantee to any particular line of politics, and the country must rest contented in the belief that its interests shall be cared for by those who are placed in a situation to control them.

Upon these principles, it is evident that the circumstances in which the country is placed, internally and externally, must regulate the policy of her cabinet, and not any abstract theory connected with the name assumed by her government. Thus despotism may be the offspring of a republic; and liberty, the gift of a dynasty which has reigned for ages by right divine.

M. de Carné, a political writer of much ability, in his essay on parties and 'le mouvement actuel,' ridicules in a spirit of keen satire the idea that any order of men in France at the present day should be supposed to interest themselves seriously for any abstract political opinion.

'Croit-on bien sérieusement encore,' he says, 'au mécanisme constitutionnel – à la multiplicité de ses poids et contre-poids – à l'inviolabilité sacrée de la pensée dirigeante, combinée avec la responsabilité d'argent?' . . .

And again he says, – 'Est-il beaucoup d'esprits graves qui attachent aujourd'hui une importance de premier ordre pour le bien-être moral et matériel de la race humaine à la substitution d'une présidence américaine, à la royauté de 1830?'

It is evident from the tone sustained through the whole of this ingenious essay, that it is the object of M. Carné to convince his readers of the equal and total futility of every political creed founded on any fixed and abstract principle. Who is it, he asks, 'qui a établi en France un despotisme dont on ne trouve d'example qu'en remontant aux monarchies de l'Asie? – Napoléon – lequel régnait comme les Césars Romains, en vertu de la souveraineté du peuple. Qui a fondé, après tant d'impuissantes tentatives, une liberté sérieuse, et l'a fait entrer dans nos moeurs au point de ne pouvoir plus lui résister? – La maison de Bourbon, qui régnait par le droit divin.'

In advocating this system of intrusting the right as well as the power of governing a country to the hands of its rulers, without exacting from them a pledge that their measures shall be guided by a theoretical instead of practical wisdom, M. Carné naturally refers to his own – that is to say, the doctrinaire party, and expresses himself thus: – 'Cette disposition à chercher dans les circonstances et dans la morale privée la seule règle d'action politique, a donné naissance à un parti qui s'est trop hâté de se produire, mais chez lequel il y a assez d'avenir pour résister à ses propres fautes. Il serait difficile d'en formuler le programme, si vaporeux encore, autrement qu'en disant qu'il s'attache à substituer l'étude des lois de la richesse publique aux spéculations constitutionnelles, dont le principal résultat est d'équilibrer sur le papier des forces qui se déplacent inévitablement dans leur action.'

It is certainly possible that this distaste for pledging themselves to any form or system of government, and the apparent readiness to accommodate their principles to the exigences of the hour, may be as much the result of weariness arising from all the restless experiments they have made, as from conviction that this loose mode of wearing a political colour, ready to drop it, or change it according to circumstances, is in reality the best condition in which a great nation can place itself.

It can hardly be doubted that the French people have become as weary of changes and experiments as their neighbours are of watching them. They have tried revolutions of every size and form till they are satiated, and their spirits are worn out and exhausted by the labour of making new projects of laws, new charters, and new kings. It is, in truth, contrary to their nature to be kept so long at work. No people in the world, perhaps, have equal energy in springing forward to answer some sudden call, whether it be to pull down a Bastile with Lafayette, to overturn a throne with Robespierre, to overrun Europe with Napoleon, or to reorganise a monarchy with Louis-Philippe. All these deeds could be done with enthusiasm, and therefore they were natural to Frenchmen. But that the mass of the people should for long years together check their gay spirits, and submit themselves, without the recompense of any striking stage effect, to prose over the thorny theories of untried governments, is quite impossible, – for such a state would be utterly hostile to the strongest propensities of the people. 'Chassez le naturel, il revient au galop.' It is for this reason that 'la loi bourgeoise' has been proclaimed; which being interpreted, certainly means the law of being contented to remain as they are, making themselves as rich and as comfortable as they possibly can, under the shelter of a king who has the will and the power to protect them.

M. Carné truly says, – 'Le plus puissant argument que puisse employer la royauté pour tenir en respect la bourgeoisie, est celui dont usait l'astrologue de Louis Onze pour avoir raison des capricieuses velléités de son maître, – 'Je mourrai juste trois jours avant votre majesté.'

This quotation, though it sound not very courtier-like, may be uttered before Louis-Philippe without offence; for it is impossible, let one's previous political bias have been what it will, not to perceive in every act of his government a firm determination to support and sustain in honour and in safety the order of things which it has established, or to perish; and the consequence of this straightforward policy is, that thousands and tens of thousands who at first acknowledged his rule only to escape from anarchy, now cling to it, not only as a present shelter, but as a powerful and sure defence against the return of the miserable vicissitudes to which they have been so long exposed.

Among many obvious advantages which the comprehensive principles of the 'doctrine' offered to France under the peculiar circumstances in which she was placed at the time it was first propagated, was, that it offered a common resting-place to all who were weary of revolutions, let them be of what party they would. This is well expressed by M. Carné when he says, – 'Ce parti semble appelé, par ce qu'il a de vague en lui, à devenir le sympathique lien de ces nombreuses intelligences dévoyées qui ont pénétré le vide de l'idée politique.'

There cannot, I think be a happier phrase to describe the host who have bewildered themselves in the interminable mazes of a science so little understood by the multitude, than this of '*intelligences dévoyées qui ont pénétré le vide de l'idée politique.*' For these, it is indeed a blessing to have found one common name (vague though it be) under which they may all shelter themselves, and, without the slightest reproach to the consistency of their patriotism, joint heart and hand in support of a government which has so ably contrived to 'draw golden opinions from all sorts of men.'

In turning over the pages of Hume's History in pursuit of a particular passage, I accidentally came upon his short and pithy sketch of the character and position of our Henry the Seventh. In many points it approaches very nearly to what might be said of Louis-Philippe.

'The personal character of the man was full of vigour, industry, and severity; deliberate in all his projects, steady in every purpose, and attended with caution, as well as good fortune, in each enterprise. He came to the throne after long and bloody civil wars. The nation was tired with discord and intestine convulsions, and willing to submit to usurpations and even injuries rather than plunge themselves anew into like miseries. The fruitless efforts made against him served always, as is usual, to confirm his authority.'

Such a passage as this, and some others with which I occasionally indulge myself from the records of the days that are gone, have in them a most consoling tendency. We are apt to believe that the scenes we are painfully witnessing contain, amidst the materials of which they are formed, elements of mischief more terrible than ever before threatened the tranquillity of mankind; yet a little recollection, and a little confidence in the Providence so visible in every page of the world's history, may suffice to inspire us with better hopes for the future than some of our doubting spirits have courage to anticipate.

'The fruitless efforts made against' King Philippe 'have served to confirm his authority,' and have done the same good office to him that similar outrages did to our 'princely Tudor' in the fifteenth century. The people were sick of 'discord and intestine convulsions' in his days: so are they at the present time in France; so will they be again, at no very distant period, in England.

While congratulating the country I have so recently left, as I do most heartily, on the very essential improvements which have taken place since my departure, I feel as if I ought to apologise for some statements to be found in the preceding pages of these volumes which if made now might fairly be challenged as untrue. But during the last few months, letters from France should have been both written and read post-haste, or the news they contained would not be of much worth. We left Paris towards the end of June, and before the end of July the whole moral condition of France had received a shock, and undergone a change which, though it does not falsify any of my statements, renders it necessary at least that the tense of many of them should be altered.

Thus, when I say that an unbounded license in caricaturing prevails, and that the walls of the capital are scrawled over with grotesque representations of the sovereign, the errata should have – 'for *prevails*, read *did prevail*; for *are*, read *were*;' and the like in may other instances.

The task of declaring that such statements are no longer correct is, however, infinitely more agreeable than that of making them. The daring profligacy of all kinds which was exposed to the eyes and the understanding at Paris before the establishment of the laws, which have now taken the morals of the people under their protection, was fast sinking the country into the worst and coarsest species of barbarism; and there is a sort of patriotism, not belonging to the kingdom, but to the planet that gave one birth, which must be gratified by seeing a check given to what tended to lower human nature itself.

As a matter of hope, and consolation too, under similar evils which beset us at home, there is much satisfaction to be derived from perceiving that, however inveterate the taint may appear which unchecked licentiousness has brought upon a land, there is power enough in the hands of a vigorous and efficient magistracy to stay its progress and wipe out the stain. A 'Te Deum' for this cleansing law should be performed in every church in Christendom.

There is something assuredly of more than common political interest in the present position of France, interesting to all Europe, but most especially interesting to us. The wildest democracy has been advocated by her press, and even in her senate. The highest court of justice in the kingdom has not been held sufficiently sacred to prevent the utterance of opinions within it which, if acted upon, would have taken the sceptre from the hands of the king and placed it in those of the mob. Her journals have poured forth the most unbridled abuse, the most unmitigated execrations against the acts of the government, and almost against the persons of its agents. And what has been the result of all this? Steadily, tranquilly, firmly, and without a shadow of vacillation, has that government proceeded in performing the duties intrusted to it by the country. It has done nothing hastily, nothing rashly, nothing weakly. On first receiving the perilous deposit of a nation's welfare, – at a moment too when a thousand dangers from within and without were threatening, – the most cautious and consummate wisdom was manifested, not only in what it did, but in what it did not do. Like a skilful general standing on the defensive, it remained still a while, till the first headlong rush which was intended to dislodge it from its new position had passed by; and when this was over, it contemplated well the ground, the force, and the resources placed under its command, before it stirred one step towards improving them.

When I recollect all the nonsense I listened to in Paris previous to the trial of the Lyons prisoners; the prophecies that the king would not DARE to persevere in it; the assurances from some that the populace would rise to rescue them, – from others, that the peers would refuse to sit in judgment, – and from more still, that if nothing of all this occurred in Paris, a counter-revolution would assuredly break out in the South; – when I remember all this, and compare it to the steady march of daily-increasing power which has marked every act of this singularly vigorous government from that period to the present, I feel it difficult to lament that, at this eventful epoch of the world's history, power should have fallen into hands so capable of using it wisely.

Yet, with all this courage and boldness of decision, there has been nothing reckless, nothing like indifference to public opinion, in the acts of the French government. The ministers have uniformly appeared willing to hear and to render reason respecting all the measures they have pursued; and the king himself has never ceased to manifest the same temper of mind which, through all the vicissitudes of his remarkable life, have rendered him so universally popular. But it is quite clear that, whatever were the circumstances which led to his being placed on the throne of France, Louis-Philippe can never become the tool of a faction: I can well conceive him replying, to any accusation brought against him, in the gentle but dignified words of Athalie –

'Ce que j'ai fait, Abner, j'ai cru le devoir faire –
Je ne prends point pour juge un peuple téméraire.'

And who is there, of all those whom nature, fortune, and education have placed, as it were, in inevitable opposition to him, but must be forced to acknowledge that he is right? None, I truly believe, – save only that unfortunate, bewildered, puzzle-headed set of politicians, the republicans, who seem still to hang together chiefly because no other party will have anything to say to them, and because they alone, of all the host of would-be lawgivers, dare not to seek for standing-room under the ample shelter of *the doctrine,* inasmuch as its motto is 'Public Order,' and the well-known gathering word of their tribe is 'Confusion and Misrule.'

There are still many persons, I believe, who, though nowise desirous themselves of seeing any farther change in the government of France, yet still anticipate that change must come, because they consider it impossible that this restless party can long remain quiet. I have heard several who wish heartily well to the government of Louis-Philippe express very gloomy forebodings on this subject. They say, that however beneficial the present order of things has been found for France, it is vain to hope it should long endure, contrary to the wish and will of so numerous a faction; especially as the present government is formed on the doctrine, that the protection of arts and industry, and the fostering of all the objects connected with that wealth and prosperity to which the restoration of peace has led, should be its first object: whereas the republicans are ever ready to be up and doing in any cause that promises change and tumult, and will therefore be found, whenever a struggle shall arise, infinitely better prepared to fight it out than the peaceable and well-contented majority, of whom they are the declared enemies.

I think, however, that such reasoners are altogether wrong: they leave out of their consideration one broad and palpable fact, which is, however, infinitely more important than any other, – namely, that a republic is a form of government completely at variance with the spirit of the French people. That it has been already tried and found to fail, is only one among many proofs that might easily be brought forward to show this. That love of glory which all the world seems to agree in attributing to France as one of her most remarkable national characteristics, must ever prevent her placing the care of her dignity and her renown in the hands of a mob. It was in a moment of 'drunken enthusiasm' that her first degrading revolution was brought about; and deep as was the disgrace of it, no one can fairly say that the nation should be judged by the wild acts then perpetrated. Everything that has since followed goes to establish the conviction, that France cannot exist as a republic.

There is a love of public splendour in their nature that seems as much born with them as their black eyes; and they must have, as a centre to that splendour, a king and a court, round which they may move, and to which they may do homage in the face of Europe without fearing that their honour or their dignity can be compromised thereby. It has been said (by an Englishman) that the present is the government of the bourgeoisie, and that Louis-Philippe is 'un roi bourgeois.' His Bourbon blood, however, saves him from this jest; and if by 'the government of the bourgeoisie' is meant a cabinet composed of and sustained by the wealth of the country, as well as its talent and its nobility, there is nothing in the statement to shock either patrician pride or regal dignity.

The splendid military pageant in which the French people followed the imperial knight-errant who led them as conquerors over half Europe, might well have sufficient charm to make so warlike a nation forget for a while all the blessings of peace, as well as the more enduring glory which advancing science and well-instructed industry might bring. But even had Napoleon not fallen, the delirium of this military fever could not have been much longer mistaken for national prosperity by such a country as France; and, happily for her, it was not permitted to go on long enough to exhaust her strength so entirely as to prevent her repairing its effects, and starting with fresh vigour in a far nobler course.

But even now, with objects and ambition so new and so widely different before their eyes, what is the period to which the memory of the people turns with the greatest complacency? . . . Is it to the Convention, or to the Directory? – Is it to their mimicry of Roman Consulships? Alas! for the classic young-headed republicans of France! . . . they may not hope that their cherished vision can ever endure within the realm of St. Louis long enough to have its lictors' and its tribunes' robes definitively decided on.

No! it is not to this sort of schoolboy mummery that Gallic fancies best love to return, – but to that portentous interval when the bright blaze of a magnificent meteor shone upon their iron chains, and made them look like gold. If this be true – if it cannot be denied that the affections of the French people cling with more gratitude to the splendid despotism of

Napoleon than to any other period of their history, is it to be greatly feared that they should turn from the substantial power and fame that now

'Flames in the forehead of the morning sky'

before their eyes, accompanied as they are by the brightest promise of individual prosperity and well-being, in order to plunge themselves again into the mingled 'blood and mire' with which their republic begrimed its altars?

Were there even no other assurance against such a deplorable effort at national self-destruction than that which is furnished by the cutting ridicule so freely and so generally bestowed upon it, this alone, in a country where a laugh is so omnipotent, might suffice to reassure the spirits of the timid and the doubting. It has been said sturdily by a French interpreter of French feelings, that 'si le diable sortait de l'enfer pour se battre, il se présenterait un Français pour accepter le défi.' I dare say this may be very true, provided said diable does not come to the combat equipped from the armoury of Ridicule, – in which case the French champion would, I think, be as likely to run away as not: and for this reason, if for no other, I truly believe it to be impossible that any support should now be given in France to a party which has not only made itself supremely detestable by its atrocities, but supremely ridiculous by its absurdities.

It is needless to recapitulate here observations already made. They have been recorded lightly, however, and their effect upon the reader may not be so serious as that produced upon my own mind by the circumstances which drew them forth; but it is certain that had not the terrible and most ferocious plot against the King's life given a character of horror to the acts of the republican party in France, I should be tempted to conclude my statement of all I have seen and heard of them by saying, that they had mixed too much of weakness and of folly in their literature, in their political acts, and in their general bearing and demeanour, to be ever again considered as a formidable enemy by the government.

I was amused the other day by reading in an English newspaper, or rather in an extract from an Irish one, (The

Dublin Journal,) a passage in a speech of Mr. Daniel O'Connell's to the 'Dublin Trades' Union,' the logic of which, allowing perhaps a little for the well-known peculiarities in the eloquence of the 'Emerald Isle,' reminded me strongly of some of the republican reasonings to which I have lately listened in Paris.

'The House of Commons,' says Mr. Daniel O'Connell, 'will always be a pure and *independent* body, BECAUSE we are under the lash of our masters, and we will be kicked out if we do not perform the duties imposed on us by the people.'

Trifling as are the foregoing pages, and little as they may seem obnoxious to any very grave criticism, I am quite aware that they expose me to the reproach of having permitted myself to be wrought upon by the '*wind of doctrine*.' I will not deny the charge; but I will say in defence of this 'shadow of turning,' (for it is in truth no more,) that I return with the same steadfast belief which I carried forth, in the necessity of a government for every country which should possess power and courage to resist at all times the voice of a wavering populace, while its cares were steadily directed to the promotion of the general welfare.

As well might every voice on board a seventy four be lifted to advise the captain how to manage her, as the judgment of all the working classes in a state be offered on questions concerning her government.

A self-regulating populace is a chimera, and a dire one. The French have discovered this already; the Americans are beginning, as I hear, to feel some glimmerings of this important truth breaking in upon them; and for our England, spite of all the trash upon this point that she has been pleased to speak and to hear, she is not a country likely to submit, if the struggle should come, to be torn to pieces by her own mob.

Admirably, however, as this jury-mast of 'the doctrine' appears to answer in France, where the whirlwind and the storm had nearly made the brave vessel a wreck, it would be a heavy day for England were she to find herself compelled to have recourse to the same experiment for safety – for the need of it can never arise without being accompanied by a necessity for such increased severity of discipline as would be very distasteful to her. It is true, indeed, that her spars do creak and crack rather ominously just at present: nevertheless, it will require a tougher gale than any she has yet had to encounter, before she will be tempted to throw overboard such a noble piece of heart of oak as her constitution, which does in truth tower above every other, and, 'like the tall mast of some proud admiral,' looks down upon those around, whether old or new, well-seasoned and durable, or only skilfully erected for the nonce, with a feeling of conscious superiority that she would be very sorry to give up.

But whatever the actual position of England may be, it must be advantageous to her, as well as to every other country in Europe, that France should assume the attitude she has now taken. The cause of social order is a common cause throughout the civilised world, and whatever tends to promote it is a common blessing. Obvious as is the truth, its importance is not yet fully understood; but the time must come when it will be, – and then all the nations of the earth will be heard to proclaim in chorus, that

'Le pire des états, c'est l'état populaire.'

FANNY TROLLOPE

DOMESTIC MANNERS OF THE AMERICANS

Pursued by debt, Fanny Trollope, mother of the famous novelist, emigrated to Ohio. Here she was assisted by her husband – a poor provider – in a fancy goods bazaar, a venture which failed as surely as others before. But when, on her return to England, she published *Domestic Manners of the Americans* in 1832, she achieved profit and fame overnight, and was able to support her family ever after by her pen.

Her candid and sometimes critical observations were bitterly resented in the United States. Throughout Europe, however, the book was quickly admired as an authentic account of a novel society where momentous change and expansion had already begun. The New World, with its contrasts powerfully described, already seemed foreign to the Old. . . .

JONATHAN SWIFT
JOURNAL TO STELLA

The *Journal to Stella* was addressed to Esther Johnson, whom Swift met as a girl when she was staying in Surrey. She afterwards settled in Ireland at his suggestion. The *Journal* was dispatched in fortnightly packets to Ireland and is a day by day record of Swift's life in London. The entries provide a close observation of London events and society in the early eighteenth century and, as such, are a valuable biographical and historical record. At the same time, in their expression, they show a tenderness and affection not found elsewhere in Swift's writings, revealing him at his most personal and intimate.

DANIEL DEFOE

CAPTAIN SINGLETON

Defoe had that power to create the illusion of truth which is the very life force of fiction, and nowhere is this more evident than in his portrait of the piratical Captain Singleton.

Taken by a gypsy child-stealer, Singleton soon finds himself cast ashore on the island of Madagascar; how he crosses Africa with a party of marooned sailors from Mozambique to the Gold Coast is a book in itself. His years of piracy are still to come. The story moves to the West Indies where he falls in with William the Quaker, an unusual pirate with whom Singleton becomes a lifelong friend, sharing adventures from the Spanish Main to the Indian Ocean before, filled with remorse, he decides to end it all. . . .

THOMAS HARDY
A CHANGED MAN

This collection contains, as well as the title story, *The Waiting Supper; Alicia's Diary; The Grave by the Handpost; Enter a Dragoon; A Tryst at an Ancient Earthwork; What the Shepherd Saw; A Committee-Man of 'The Terror'; Master John Horseleigh, Knight; The Duke's Reappearance;* and *The Romantic Adventures of a Milkmaid.*

Hardy's love of the eerie and the supernatural are brought out in full measure here. His skill at depicting topographical detail is also apparent, particularly in *A Changed Man* – set in Casterbridge and instantly recognisable to readers familiar with that town. The story is that of a young hussar captain who resigns his commission to preach in a poor parish and, by so doing, causes his wife to leave him for another soldier. It is a fine portrait in a vivid set of stories guaranteed to delight all Hardy devotees.

R.S. SURTEES
MR FACEY ROMFORD'S HOUNDS

'Our friend was called Charley at school, but his real name was Francis – hence, perhaps "Facey".' Thus is Mr Romford introduced to the reader and from the first page on, we are transported into the zany, comic, full-blooded world of the Victorian hunting scene as created by Surtees. Soapey Sponge crops up again as do many of the best and memorable characters from that previous novel, *Mr Sponge's Sporting Tour* (also available in this series) including Lucy Glitters who triumphs at last.

His inventions are absurd but marvellously sustained, his creations are comic and often silly but they are so real and their adventures, whilst larger than life, are nevertheless rooted in fact and real knowledge. The whole is perfectly complimented by the illustrations of John Leech.

EDMUND GOSSE

FATHER AND SON

Lord David Cecil considered this book to be one of the half-dozen English prose masterpieces of the twentieth century; a classic among autobiographies.

After a difficult birth, Edmund Gosse was left for dead, while all anxiety and attention were concentrated on his mother. An old woman turned her attention to the abandoned infant and succeeded in reviving him and so Gosse lived to write: 'For all the rapture of life, for all its turmoils, its anxious desires, its manifold pleasures, and even for its sorrow and suffering, I bless and praise that anonymous old lady from the bottom of my heart'.

Father and Son mingles merriment and humour with a discussion of the most solemn subjects . . . 'Most funny books try to be funny throughout while theology is scandalised if it awakens a single smile. But life is not constituted thus . . .' and if the proof lies anywhere, it lies here.

W.N.P. BARBELLION

THE JOURNAL OF A DISAPPOINTED MAN

While millions of young men were being slaughtered on the battlefields of Europe a young Englishman was dying of an incurable disease. He was Bruce Frederick Cummings ('W.N.P. Barbellion'), born in 1889, struck down with multiple sclerosis in early manhood and dead at thirty. Yet into those few short years he crammed a lifetime of passionate intensity. He breathed life into every sentence of the journal which he created to analyse his emotions and painful existence. His courage was boundless – he was in love with life and far from being a catalogue of misfortune, the journal is infused with a rage to live.

Started at the age of thirteen, the journal documents the rest of his life, including his remarkable studies in natural history. The result is an inspired and expressive masterpiece by a 'scientist with an artist's sensitivity'. There never was a half-dead man more alive.

ARTHUR CONAN DOYLE

THE LOST WORLD

The Lost World is the story of an expedition by four men to a remote plateau in South America, a region out of time, cut off from the outside world by unscaleable, vertical cliffs. In an area the size of an English county, pterodactyls, iguanodons, ape men and other dinosaurs still exist.

Into this nightmare world come Professor Challenger, Summerbee, Lord John Roxton and the reporter Malone. After many adventures they return at last to London with proof of their incredible discovery.

Conan Doyle tried in vain to kill off his more famous creation, Sherlock Holmes, but in the character of Challenger, he was content.